Design and Usability of Digital Libraries:
Case Studies in the Asia Pacific

Yin-Leng Theng
Nanyang Technological University, Singapore

Schubert Foo
Nanyang Technological University, Singapore

 Information Science Publishing

Hershey • London • Melbourne • Singapore

Acquisition Editor:	Mehdi Khosrow-Pour
Senior Managing Editor:	Jan Travers
Managing Editor:	Amanda Appicello
Development Editor:	Michele Rossi
Copy Editor:	Alana Bunis
Typesetter:	Marko Primorac
Cover Design:	Lisa Tosheff
Printed at:	Yurchak Printing Inc.

Published in the United States of America by
Information Science Publishing (an imprint of Idea Group Inc.)
701 E. Chocolate Avenue, Suite 200
Hershey PA 17033
Tel: 717-533-8845
Fax: 717-533-8661
E-mail: cust@idea-group.com
Web site: http://www.idea-group.com

and in the United Kingdom by
Information Science Publishing (an imprint of Idea Group Inc.)
3 Henrietta Street
Covent Garden
London WC2E 8LU
Tel: 44 20 7240 0856
Fax: 44 20 7379 3313
Web site: http://www.eurospan.co.uk

Library of Congress Cataloging-in-Publication Data

Design and usability of digital libraries : case studies in the Asia-Pacific / Yin-Leng Theng and Schubert Foo, editors.
    p. cm.
  Includes bibliographical references and index.
  ISBN 1-59140-441-X (h/c) -- ISBN 1-59140-442-8 (s/c) -- ISBN 1-59140-443-6 (ebook)
  1. Digital libraries--Case studies. 2. Information storage and retrieval systems--Case studies. 3. Digital libraries--Asia--Case studies. 4. Digital libraries--Pacific Area--Case studies. I. Theng, Yin-Leng, 1961- II. Foo, Schubert.
  ZA4080.D47 2004
  025'.00285--dc22
                                                                    2004022145

British Cataloguing in Publication Data
A Cataloguing in Publication record for this book is available from the British Library.

All work contributed to this book is new, previously-unpublished material. The views expressed in this book are those of the authors, but not necessarily of the publisher.

Design and Usability of Digital Libraries:
Case Studies in the
Asia Pacific

Table of Contents

Section IV: Use and Impact

SectionV: Users and Usability

Preface

Digital libraries are part of the global infrastructure being envisioned to inter-connect many computer networks and various forms of information technolo-gies around the world, a partial fulfillment of Bush's 1945 dream "memex" of a personal microfiche-based system to tackle the problem of information over-load. Digital libraries, more organized and structured than the Web, an over-whelming example of a shared worldwide collection of information. Educa-tional institutions, governments and corporations are spending millions of dol-lars on researching, developing and implementing digital libraries around the world.

Research done on the Web has shown that many Web sites are plagued with problems of usability and effectiveness. We can expect a similar situation in digital libraries since they are much more than just Web sites. In fact, they are complex and advanced forms of information systems that can be endowed with a multiplicity of functions and features. These can include collaboration sup-port, distributed database management, hypertext, multimedia information ser-vices, information retrieval, information filtering, selective dissemination of in-formation, intellectual property rights management, question answering and ref-erence services, and resource discovery, among many others. Digital libraries can serve very large user populations that are composed of different stake-holder groups with different information needs. Improvements in design, devel-opment and evaluation can have a major organizational, national and interna-tional impact.

We need better theories, tools and techniques to support designers in designing, developing and evaluating digital libraries in ways that will improve usability and effectiveness to enhance users' experience of digital library collections and services.

This book was inspired by the very successful gathering and exchange of ideas among international and local participants of the Fourth International Conference on Asian Digital Libraries at Singapore (2002), where the need to highlight and share the best practices on digital library research and development in the Asia Pacific region emerged. The Asia Pacific focus is opportune to the increasing global effort to encourage and promote the sharing of research and development around the world that are largely limited, at the moment, to America and Europe.

To provide a global perspective, this book contains invited chapters from major key players and eminent researchers in digital library research and development to draw parallels of issues and challenges faced not only in the Asia Pacific region, but across the world. Special emphasis is placed on the design, use and usability of digital libraries, which include work surrounding digital libraries and related technologies, the management of knowledge in digital libraries, and the associated usability and social issues.

Organization

The book is written for academics, practitioners and undergraduate/postgraduate students interested in digital library design and development, with particular focus in the Asia Pacific region. It is organised around six sections into chapters with the following major themes:

(1) Digital Library Development History and Landscape

(2) Design Architecture and Systems

(3) Implementation Issues and Challenges

(4) Use and Impact

(5) Users and Usability

(6) Future Trends of Digital Libraries

Although all these areas are likely to be covered as part of the design, development and use of digital libraries at varying levels of detail, the chapter authors were requested to focus more on the specific area of the respective section in which their chapters were featured, thereby providing a more congruent approach for the reader to follow. References in each chapter, as well as an Appendix containing further sources of information at the end of the book, provide additional resources to the reader to pursue a more detailed study of a particular aspect of digital library research and development.

Overview

Section I is concerned with **Digital Library Development History and Landscape** in the Asia Pacific region. Through a meta-analysis of the publications and content within the International Conference on Asian Digital Libraries (ICADL) conference series and other major regional digital library conferences over the past few years, Hsinchun Chen and Yilu Zhou, in Chapter I, *"Survey and History of Digital Library Development in the Asia Pacific,"* noted an increase in the level of activity in Asian digital library research over the past decade. They posit that Asia Pacific is uniquely positioned to contribute significantly in the areas of cultural heritage and indigenous knowledge, and hence advance cross-cultural and cross-lingual digital library research.

Section II focuses on **Design Architecture and Systems**, encompassing the overall structure of a digital library system and the way in which the structure provides conceptual integrity for the whole system, examining input processing, process and control function, output processing, process and control functions, and user interface processing. Section II consists of four chapters.

Chapter II, *"Design Architecture: An Introduction and Overview"* by Edward Fox, Hussein Suleman, Ramesh Gaur & Devika Madalli, looks at current research and emerging best practices adopted in designing digital libraries, and discusses various interoperability standards and practices providing users with seamless access to highly distributed information sources in distributed/networked digital libraries. It also provides an overview of the rest of the chapters in Section II.

In Chapter III, Ismail Fahmi discusses the *"Development of Indonesia's National Digital Library Network (IndonesiaDLN),"* shares technical and social issues, and challenges communities to develop their own digital library networks for integration into IndonesiaDLN.

Chapter IV, by Shien-chiang Yu, Hsueh-hua Chen & Chao-chen Chen on *"Dynamic Metadata Management System for Digital Archives: Design and Construction,"* describes Metalogy, an XML/metadata framework that can handle several different metadata formats. Metalogy was developed under the Digital Museum Project funded by the National Science Council of Taiwan.

Chapter V, *"Information Filtering and Personalization Services"* by Chunxiao Xing, Chun Zeng, Zhiqiang Zhang & Lizhu Zhou, analyzes several key technologies and the related works in information filtering and personalized services, and then presents their research in building a prototype TH-PASS to provide personalized searching and recommending services.

Section III examines **Implementation Issues and Challenges** focusing on the "how" aspects of digital libraries with regard to algorithms, techniques, and/ or methods. Discussions on pertinent implementation issues and results for comparisons serve as useful lessons learnt and provide a gauge of the efficiency and effectiveness of the implementation. Section III consists of three chapters.

Chapter VI, *"Implementation of Next Generation Digital Libraries"* by Ee-Peng Lim & San-Yih Hwang, outlines major implementation issues of next generation digital libraries and reviews existing standards, tools and related research topics. The authors discuss advanced digital library services and highlight new challenges in metadata harvesting, search and retrieval that require standardized protocols to be adopted across different digital libraries. It also provides an overview of the remaining chapters in Section III.

Chapter VII, *"Using Multi-Document Summarization to Facilitate Semi-Structured Literature Retrieval: A Case Study in Consumer Healthcare"* by Min-Yen Kan, describes a framework used in a consumer healthcare digital library that incorporates techniques used by librarians to discover common and unique topics among its input from a combination of structural and lexical cues. The framework brings together commonalities between documents and highlights their salient differences to target the needs of users when using the browsing and searching modes of information seeking.

Chapter VIII, *"KEA: Practical Automatic Keyphrase Extraction"* by Ian Witten, Gordon Paynter, Eibe Frank, Carl Gutwin & Craig Nevill-Manning, describes KEA, an algorithm for automatically extracting keyphrases from text. KEA identifies candidate keyphrases using lexical methods, calculates feature values for each candidate, and uses a machine-learning algorithm to predict which candidates are good keyphrases. KEA is available under the GNU General Public License and this chapter provides instructions for use of KEA.

Chapter IX, *"Cross-Lingual Information Retrieval: The Challenge in Multi-lingual Libraries"* by Christopher Yang & Kar Wing Li, reviews challenges in addressing structural and semantic interoperability, searching and retrieving objects across variations in protocols, formats, disciplines and languages. In particular, the chapter focuses on cross-lingual semantic interoperability to build the bridge between the representations of user queries and documents when they are based on different languages.

Chapter X, *"Evolving Tool Support for Digital Librarians"* by David Nichols, David Bainbridge, Gary Marsden, Dynal Patel, Sally Jo Cunningham, John Thompson, Stefan Boddie & Ian Witten, describes usability issues that face the digital librarian in creating and maintaining a digital library. The Greenstone digital library software suite is used as an example to examine how to support digital librarians in their work.

Section IV examines **Use and Impact**, delving on the applicability, use and impact on the targeted users of the digital library systems. The importance of these various forms of digital libraries, and their roles, key success factors, problems, issues, and contribution to the society at large, are important aspects that are typically expounded on in this section. Section IV consists of four chapters.

Ian Witten in Chapter XI, *"Digital Libraries and Society: New Perspectives on Information and Dissemination,"* reviews trends in today's information environment, introduces digital library technology and explores the use of digital libraries for disseminating humanitarian information in developing countries, a context that is both innovative and socially motivated. The author demonstrates how currently available technology empowers users to build and publish information collections, but similar to conventional public libraries, the author highlights that open access in digital libraries presents a challenge to interface design. It also provides an overview of the rest of the chapters in Section IV.

In Chapter XII, *"Sharing Digital Knowledge with End-Users: Case Study of the International Rice Research Institute Library and Documentation Service in the Philippines,"* Mila Ramos portrays how resources of the International Rice Research Institute Library and Documentation Service are harnessed to develop its collection of technical rice literature and other information sources by searching, selecting and organizing print and electronic resources for inclusion in its Web page or online catalog. The author also highlights problems and recommends possible ways of dealing with them.

Chapter XIII, *"Multimedia Digital Library as Intellectual Property"* by Hideyasu Sasaki & Yasushi Kiyoki, discusses issues in intellectual property rights and copyrights regarding multimedia digital libraries with content-based retrieval mechanisms. Recognising the importance of protecting intellectual property rights in digital libraries, the authors present schemes for protecting multimedia digital libraries with keyword-based retrieval and content-based image retrieval mechanisms.

Chapter XIV, *"Digital Libraries as Learning Environments for Youth"* by Natalie Lee-San Pang, looks specifically at the process of learning between peers in a group and how digital libraries can lend themselves as a learning environment towards this purpose. Using a participatory process involving two groups of youths, a pilot study was conducted in which observations were made to suggest design features for digital libraries used for electronic learning.

Section V examines **Users and Usability**, focusing on usability evaluation techniques employed in the design and development of digital library systems, addressing users, requirements and context of use. Section V consists of five chapters.

In Chapter XV, *"Usability of Digital Libraries in a Multicultural Environment,"* Christine Borgman & Edie Rasmussen explain that besides understanding users in terms of their knowledge and expertise, they advocate that usability is further complicated by multicultural issues, as digital library users may come from many cultures and nations. Hence, it may be necessary to orient a digital library toward the needs of users from one or more specific localities or cultures. The chapter provides an overview of the remaining chapters in Section V and their projects employing different forms of evaluation – formative, summative, iterative – to improve usability of their systems.

Chapter XVI, *"Cross-Cultural Design and Usability of a Digital Library Supporting Access to Maori Cultural Heritage Resources"* by Chern Li Liew, looks specifically at issues supporting access to Maori heritage materials available in New Zealand through digital library technologies. This chapter examines the Mâori culture, nature and forms of Mâori heritage resources and their specific requirements for representation, organisation and retrieval. It concludes with identifying a set of critical research issues that need to be addressed for the success of such DLs.

Chapter XVII, *"From GeogDL to PAPER: The Evolution of an Educational Digital Library"* by Dion Hoe-Lian Goh, Yin-Leng Theng & Ee-Peng Lim, traces the evolution of GeogDL, a geospatial digital library of geography examination resources into PAPER (**P**ersonalized **A**daptive **P**athways for Examination **R**esources) that provides mock examinations and personalized recommendations of examination questions. This chapter describes two initial studies involving student and teacher design partners, and discusses implications for the future development of PAPER.

In Chapter XVIII, *"Designing a Music Digital Library: Discovering What People Really Want,"* David Bainbridge, Sally Jo Cunningham, John McPherson, Stephen Downie & Nina Reeves review a set of techniques that have been successfully employed in eliciting user needs for a music digital library. This chapter concentrates on studying authentic music information needs in terms of the information seeking behavior of real people engaged in attempting to satisfy real music-related questions, outside of a lab, and discusses the lessons learned in designing contents, interface, and search interactions for a music digital library.

In Chapter XIX, *"Quantitative and Qualitative Evaluations of the Singapore National Library Board's Digital Library"* by Yin-Leng Theng, Mei-Yee Chan, Ai-Ling Khoo & Raju Buddharaju, reports on two empirical studies – a quantitative and a qualitative study – conducted on the *eLibraryHub*, the Singapore National Library Board's Digital Library. Findings from the two studies show users' satisfaction of the effectiveness of the *eLibraryHub*, and that most usability problems occurred during the interpretation and evaluation stages of navigational actions. The chapter illustrates the rich interplay of quantitative and qualitative data crucial in helping designers/developers to better understand users, uses and usability of deployed systems like the *eLibraryHub*, to address the dilemma of Carroll's task-artifact cycle of changing user needs and design possibilities.

Section VI examines **Future Trends of Digital Libraries**. In Chapter XX, *"A Snapshot of Digital Library Development: The Way Forward in the Asia Pacific,"* Schubert Foo & Yin-Leng Theng highlight various key issues and assess the current situation of digital library development in the Asia Pacific. Although emphasis on cross-cultural and cross-lingual research would especially be beneficial to address the diversity and richness of the heritage, cultures and languages of this region, a fundamental digital divide problem poses the greatest challenge that needs to be resolved. This final chapter proposes that a concerted international collaborative effort is needed not only to push ahead the various aspects of the digital library research agenda, but to derive novel solutions to eliminate or close the gap of digital divide across various parts of the world, if the vision of a global digital library is to be realized in the near future.

Acknowledgments

The editors would like to thank all the authors who have submitted chapter proposals, and all authors and reviewers for their excellent contributions and insights, without which this book would not have been possible. Special thanks go to Hsinchun Chen, Edward Fox, Ee-Peng Lim, Ian Witten, Christine Borgman and Edie Rasmussen. We are also grateful to Idea Group Publishing for the opportunity to publish this book focusing on the Asia Pacific region, which we hope will be the first of many more books to come in the future.

Yin-Leng Theng and Schubert Foo
29 May 2004

Section I

Digital Library Development History and Landscape

Chapter I

Survey and History of Digital Library Development in the Asia Pacific

Hsinchun Chen
University of Arizona, USA

Yilu Zhou
University of Arizona, USA

Abstract

Over the past decade the development of digital library activities within Asia Pacific has been steadily increasing. Through a meta-analysis of the publications and content within ICADL and other major regional digital library conferences over the past few years, we see an increase in the level of activity in Asian digital library research. This reflects high continuous interest among digital library researchers and practitioners internationally. Digital library research in the Asia Pacific is uniquely positioned to help develop digital libraries of significant cultural heritage and indigenous knowledge and advance cross-cultural and cross-lingual digital library research.

Introduction

The location and provision of information services have dramatically changed over the last 10 years. There is no need to leave the home or office to locate and access information now readily available online via digital gateways furnished by a wide variety of information providers, for example, libraries, electronic publishers, businesses, organizations, and individuals. Information access is no longer restricted to what is physically available in the nearest library. It is electronically accessible from a wide variety of globally distributed information repositories.

Digital libraries represent a form of information technology in which social impact matters as much as technological advancement. It is hard to evaluate a new technology in the absence of real users and large collections. The best way to develop effective new technology is in multi-year large-scale research and development projects that use real-world electronic test-beds for actual users and aim at developing new, comprehensive, and user-friendly technologies for

Table 1. Major (Asian) digital library research and development milestones

1994	• NSF Digital Library Initiative Phase 1 (DLI-1)
	• The First Annual Conference on the Theory and Practice of Digital Libraries, College Station, Texas
1995	• First IEEE Advances in Digital Libraries Conference, McClean, Virginia
1996	• First ACM Conference on Digital Libraries, Bethesda, Maryland
1997	• First European Conference on Research and Advanced Technology for Digital Libraries (ECDL), Pisa, Italy
1998	• The First International Conference on Asian Digital Libraries (ICADL 1998), Hong Kong, China
1999	• President's Information Technology Advisory Committee (PITAC) Report
	• NSF Digital Library Initiative Phase 2 (DLI-2)
	• Institute of Museum and Library Services (IMLS) Program
	• NSF National Science, Mathematics, Engineering, and Technology Digital Library (NSDL) Program
	• ICADL 1999, Taipei, Taiwan
2000	• ICADL 2000, Seoul, Korea
2001	• ICADL 2001, Bangalore, India
	• First ACM/IEEE-CS Joint Conference on Digital Libraries (JCDL 2001), Roanoke, Virginia
2002	• ICADL 2002, Singapore
2003	• ICADL 2003, Kuala Lumpur, Malaysia
2004	• JCDL 2004, Tucson, Arizona

digital libraries. Typically, these test-bed projects also examine the broad social, economic, legal, ethical, and cross-cultural contexts and impacts of digital library research.

The NSF DLI-1, DLI-2 and NSDL Programs DLI-1, 1994-1998

The original Digital Library Initiative (DLI or DLI-1), sponsored by the NSF, DARPA, and NASA, was started in 1994. The original program announcement stated:

> "The Initiative's focus is to dramatically advance the means to collect, store, and make it available for searching, retrieval, and processing via communication networks – all in user-friendly ways. Digital libraries basically store materials in electronic format and manipulate large collections of those materials effectively. Research into digital libraries is research into network information systems, concentrating on how to develop the necessary infrastructure to effectively mass-manipulate the information on the Net. The key technical issues are how to search and display desired selections from and across large collections."

After a competitive proposal solicitation and review process, six large-scale projects ($4 million per project on average) were selected. Most projects were more technical in nature and led by reputable computer scientists. Each project consisted of a strong team of computer, information and library science researchers, sociologists, and content specialists (*http://www.dli2.nsf.gov/dlione/*). The DLI projects were extremely successfully and had helped build an international digital library community.

DLI-2, ITR, IMLS, and NSDL, 1999-Present

The excitement of Internet-enabled IT developments and e-commerce opportunities in the 1990s prompted the U.S. Government to examine the role of IT research for long-term U.S. interest. A President's Information Technology Advisory Committee (PITAC) was formed, which included many leading U.S. IT researchers and practitioners. Digital library research was identified as one of the successful federal research programs and a target research area.

The success of the original DLI program and the continued IT research interest as stated in the PITAC report allowed the NSF to continue to spearhead the development of the DLI Phase 2 (DLI-2) research program:

(http://www.dli2.nsf.gov/).

DLI-2 funded 29 research projects, with an additional nine projects with an undergraduate emphasis:

(http://www.dli2/nsf/gov/projects.html).

An additional 15 projects have been funded since 1999 under the Information Technology Research (ITR) program *(http://www.dli2.nsf.gov/ itrprojects.html)*. Some address language (e.g., CMU's AVENUE project for adaptive voice translation for minority languages) and 3D modeling topics (e.g., Columbia's project for modeling, visualizing, and analyzing historical and archaeological sites), others research topics in law enforcement information sharing and knowledge management (e.g., University of Arizona's COPLINK agent project) and multilingual access to large spoken archives (e.g., Survivors of the Shoah Visual History Foundation, a $7.5 million project, 2001-2006).

In addition to the core DLI-2 and related ITR projects, DLI-2 also sponsors 12 international digital library projects *(http://www.dli2.nsf.gov/intl.html)* involving partners from the U.K. (University of Liverpool, Southampton University, King's College London), Germany (University Library of Gottingen, University of Trier), China (Tsinghua University, National Taiwan University), Japan (National Institute for Informatics), and Africa (West African Research Center). Most international projects face unique logistics and collaboration challenges.

Several U.S. agencies also began to develop digital library projects that are uniquely tailored to their institution's function. For example, the Institute of Museum and Library Services *(IMLS, http://www.imls.gov/about/index.htm)*, which is an independent federal agency that fosters leadership, innovation, and lifetime learning, supports a series of 130+ smaller-scale digital project grants to libraries and museums for research, digitization, and management of digital resources *(http://www.imls.gov/closer/cls_po.asp)*, from the Brooklyn's Children's Museum to the Chicago Academy of Sciences, and from Duke University's Library to the Georgia Department of Archives and History.

Another significant digital library research program was developed concurrently under the NSF National Science, Mathematics, Engineering, and Technology Digital Library Program (NSDL, *http://www.nsdl.nsf.gov/indexx.html*). The NSDL will offer, via the Internet, high-quality materials for science, mathematics, engineering, and technology education. It will strongly affect education at all levels, including preK-12, undergraduate, graduate, and life-long learning, by providing anytime, anywhere access to a rich array of authoritative and reliable interactive materials and learning environments. More than 60 projects have been funded since 1998 in three areas: the collection track for offering contents (e.g., National Biology Digital Library, Digital Mathematics Library; Experimental Economics Digital Library); the service track for providing technologies and services (e.g., University of Arizona's GetSmart e-learning concept map system); and the core integration track for linking all contents and services under a unified framework.

JCDL, ECDL, and ICADL: Building an International Digital Library Community JCDL, ECDL, and ICADL, 1995-Present

Digital libraries have become far more important nationally and internationally in 2003 than they were in 1996. Many new and significant national digital library initiatives have emerged. In addition, international conferences in digital library have proliferated from their roots of ACM and IEEE Digital Conferences (and then the Joint Conference on Digital Libraries, JCDL) to the European version of ECDL (European Conference on Digital Libraries) and the Asian version of ICADL (International Conference of Asian Digital Libraries).

The ICADL has evolved from its modest inception of about 80 participants in Hong Kong in 1998, to 150+ participants in Taipei, Taiwan in 1999, 300+ participants in Seoul, Korea in 2000, 600+ participants from 12 countries in Bangalore, India in 2001, 400+ participants from 20 countries in Singapore in 2002, and 350+ participants from 16 countries in Malaysia in 2003. Even regional digital library conferences, such as the recent First China Digital Library Conference, hosted by the National Library of China and held in Beijing on July 9-11, 2002, drew 450 participants from 18 countries and 125 exhibitors. Such a high level of activity is due to the continuous interest among digital library researchers and practitioners internationally. This is also partially due to the exponential growth of information content on the Web around the globe, which

Web searchers are rapidly failing to handle successfully. The next ICADL 2004 is scheduled to be held in Shanghai, China in December 2004.

Digital Library Development in Asia Pacific: Analysis through ICADL

Over the past decade the development of digital library activities within Asia Pacific has been steadily increasing. Through a meta-analysis of the publications and content within ICADL over the past six years, the countries that have contributed and participated in digital library research can be determined. In addition, the various disciplines involved and the research focus of each region can be ascertained. Other major regional digital library conferences held in the past few years are also discussed, following the ICADL analysis.

Country and Institution Analysis

In August of 1998 the first ICADL was held at the University of Hong Kong. The theme of the conference, "East Meets West," emphasized to the participants the ongoing exchange of ideas between researchers located in the Western and Eastern parts of the globe. Researchers in seven countries/regions of the world presented 23 papers. Of those papers, 18 were from Asian Pacific countries such as mainland China, Hong Kong, Taiwan, Singapore, Korea, and New Zealand.

The following year the National Taiwan University in Taipei, Taiwan, hosted ICADL 1999. Eighteen papers were from five Asian and two Western countries, 14 being directly from Asia. In 2000, ICADL was held in Seoul, Korea, where 37 papers from 14 countries were presented at the conference. This conference saw an increase in interest by countries that were not originally associated with the conference. The number of Asian countries involved in this conference increased from five to seven. The fourth ICADL in 2001, held in Bangalore, India, hosted 14 countries: nine from Asia Pacific; four from Europe; and 1 from North America; and a total of 35 papers. Two newcomers from Asia, India and Thailand, were present at the conference. The fifth ICADL conference was held in Singapore in 2002. ICADL 2002 saw a dramatic increase in paper presentations, from 35 in the previous year to 54. In addition to the papers, 16 poster presentations were added to the conference's schedule. The number of countries being represented also increased from 14 to 20: 12 from Asia Pacific, seven from Europe, and one from North America; Malaysia and Nepal were two of the new Asian Pacific country additions. The most recent ICADL conference was held in Malaysia in 2003. Despite the fact that the Iraq war and SARS affected world travel, ICADL 2003 still recorded six invited talks, 68 research paper presentations, and 15 poster presentations from 16 countries: 11 from Asia Pacific, four from Europe, and one from North America. Iran was the newest country that attended the conference.

Table 2 summarizes the previous six ICADL conferences: the number of papers accepted and the number of participating countries; institutions; and departments. *Figures 1-3* illustrate the increased number of papers presented at the conferences, as well as the number of countries and institutions attending the conferences.

Table 2. Participation summary of ICADL conferences

	ICADL 1998	ICADL 1999	ICADL 2000	ICADL 2001	ICADL 2002
# of Papers	23	18	37	34	54
# of Papers from Asia	18	14	26	25+	31+
# of Countries	7	7	12	12	20
# of Countries from Asia	6	5	7	9	12
# of Institutions	17+	14+	31+	33+	55+
# of Institutions from Asia	12+	10+	21+	22+	23+
# of Academic Departments/Disciplines	6+	6+	8+	8+	11+

Figure 1. Number of papers accepted in ICADL

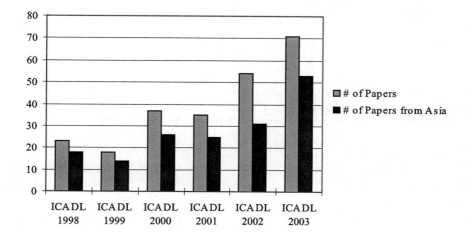

Figure 2. Number of countries represented in ICADL

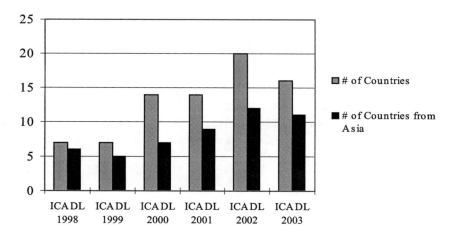

Figure 3: Number of institutions represented in ICADL

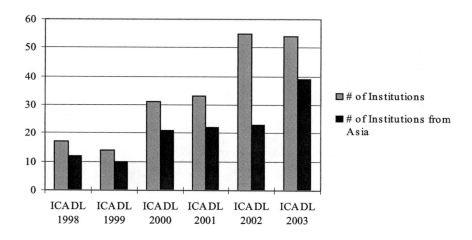

Academic Department (Discipline) Analysis

The digital library research and development being conducted within Asian Pacific countries spans many different academic departments and disciplines. Over the past six ICADL conferences, there was an increase from 6+ academic departments to over 17 academic departments being accounted for in technical sciences, such as computer science and engineering, as well as within the social

Figure 4. Number of departments (disciplines) in ICADL

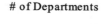

# of Departments

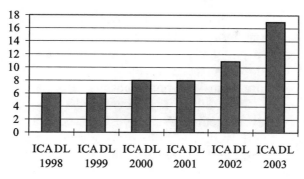

science domains. The overwhelming majority of participants came from disciplines such as Information Science (Studies), Library Science, Management Information Systems, Computer Science, Information Engineering, System Engineering, Electrical Engineering, Communication and Information, Education, Anthropology, Geography, Mathematics, Linguistics, and Medical Informatics.

Figure 4 shows the growth in the number of departments (disciplines) that have participated in ICADL.

Aside from popular belief, digital library research is not restricted to those researchers involved in the technical aspects and components of the system; research within digital libraries involves social aspects as well. From a technological standpoint, digital libraries are a set of electronic resources that are built to help create, search, and use information. From a sociological perspective, digital libraries are constructed by a community of users who use the system to better support their informational needs and applications (Borgman, 1998). In the following sections we analyze the research presented at the ICADL conferences according to these two aspects.

Topical Analysis: Technical Aspect

Several major technical research areas, including content building and management, text indexing and retrieval, document summarization and categorization, personalization and visualization, interoperability, and multimedia information retrieval, have been reported in the ICADL proceedings over the past six years.

- **Content Building and Management**: Digital libraries consist of the collections of digitized resources as well as the links or pointers to other digital sources. Oftentimes they are based on library collections that have been selected by existing library collections or development/archival criteria (Smith, 1998). The Internet has also been classified as a (somewhat chaotic) digital library by some, where spidering or crawling techniques are needed in order to navigate and create unique content. For example, HelpfulMed, developed at the University of Arizona, provides medical information not only from Web pages but also from a variety of online medical databases (Chen, 2001). A medical spider was designed specifically to collect relevant medical Web pages. As a collection building tool, the Greenstone Digital Library Software produced by the New Zealand Digital Library Project has been used to build many digital library collections all over the world (Witten, 2002).

- **Text Indexing and Retrieval**: Indexing is another rapidly growing topic of interest in digital libraries. Indexing is an important task for retrieval. However, while indexing research is on the rise, the ability to correctly index Asian languages such as Chinese and Japanese becomes challenging due to the lack of explicit word boundaries inherent in the language (Yang et al., 1998). New research techniques involving the use of n-gram indexing and phrase-extraction algorithms within the Asian digital library community have been used in many research works in order to transcend the word boundary problem. Yang et al. (1998) compared n-gram and mutual information-based indexing approaches for the Chinese language and found that a mutual information algorithm could extract more correct Chinese phrases for indexing and retrieval. Ong & Chen (1999) presented a Chinese phrase extraction algorithm using an updateable PAT-tree and obtained a precision level of 70%.

- **Document Summarization and Categorization**: Summarization offers a concise representation of a document and reduces its overall size and complexity. In order to automate the summarization of documents, text extraction research has found ways to take sentences from the original document and use them to form coherent summaries (McDonald and Chen, 2002). In ICADL, summarization techniques have been developed for Asian languages such as Chinese (Yeh et al., 2002; Tang et al., 2000). Additionally, in order to help users identify relevant documents from databases containing thousands of pieces of information, categorization and clustering are often used. Text categorization is the process of assigning documents to one or more predefined categories based on their content (Chan et al., 2001). Various categorization techniques have been presented in previous ICADL conferences. Heß & Drobnik (1999) proposed a clustering algorithm, which analyzed hyperlinks of Web pages;

Jones & Mahoui (2000) described a key phrase-based hierarchical categorization approach; Chan et al. (2001) applied a Support Vector Machine algorithm to document categorization.

- **Personalization and Visualization**: End users of a system want to be able to organize the information space according to their own subjective perspectives (Renda & Straccia, 2002). Personalization provides the ability for users to create their own profiles based on their interests, behaviors, and activities. Chan et al. (2001) described a personalized categorization system in which a user could define his/her own category names and refine the categories by providing feedback to the system. Renda & Straccia (2002) presented a personalized collaborative digital library system where users could organize the information according to their own interests as well as exchange information with each other. Information visualization is also necessary when designing a human-computer interface to effectively explore information (Yang & Kao, 1999). Several visualization techniques have been studied in ICADL conferences to visualize queries or documents. Yang & Kao (1999) considered a 2D presentation of hierarchical information structure called Core Trees. Anderson et al. (2000) designed a system, which visualizes the frequency of query terms within a document using pie charts, and found the pie charts view was preferred by users over a normal text view.

- **Interoperability**: Interoperability in digital library concerns the need for and benefits of integrating distributed collections and systems (Paepcke et al., 1998). Research in this area includes Metadata Encoding and Transmission Standard (METS), Open Archival Information System (OAIS), and Open Archives Initiative (OAI) (Borgman, 2002).

  Digital libraries typically include content and associated metadata. These metadata provide a description of content, format, ownership, and security as well as links to other versions, source codes, viewers, and related materials (Borgman, 1998). Many different metadata proposals have been presented in ICADL conferences. Existing common metadata schemas such as Dublin Core and Resource Discovery Framework (RDF) were widely adopted in Asian digital library projects (Yang et al., 1998; Lo & Chen, 1999; Chen et al., 2001). The Open Archives Initiative (OAI) and Open Archival Information System (OAIS) are designed to provide a low barrier for interoperability and are beneficial to collaboration between communities and service providers. Several prototype systems based on OAI protocol were presented in past ICADL conferences (Boone & Pennington, 2001; Chen & Chen, 2002). Multimedia data descriptions based on the MPEG-7 standard and other XML-based representations have also been described in various projects (Joung et al., 2000; Yen, 2000).

- **Multimedia Digital Libraries**: The contents of a digital library can contain text files, images, audio, and video representations. Because digital libraries are capable of containing multimedia collections, research areas involving the searching and browsing techniques of these content collections have increased. In the ICADL proceedings, Cha & Chung (2000) introduced a system for lecture (audio) databases; whereas Rowe et al. (2001) described a 3D retrieval system for American ceramic vessels. Ying & Heng (2002) introduced the Digital Media Gallery (DMG), a Web-based system that was designed for audio, video, image, and clipart retrieval. It is worth mentioning that digital music libraries have attracted significant interest recently. Bainbridge et al. (2002) evaluated different symbolic music matching strategies and explored the effectiveness and efficiency of those strategies under different conditions.

Topical Analysis: Social Aspect

The social aspect of digital libraries emphasizes the activities people engage in when they create, seek, and use information resources. Research within this area focuses on user studies, usage log analysis, multicultural issues, and language-specific issues (Borgman, 1998).

- **User Studies**: How end users use and respond to digital libraries is always an important concern of system designers and researchers. User studies provide a glimpse into understanding the users' behavioral patterns when seeking information. Liew et al. (2000) conducted an empirical evaluation to study the design of e-journals and how users interacted with them. Their findings showed valuable insights for the designing of e-journals, such as the need for advanced interactivity as compared with their print antecedents.

- **Usage Log Analysis**: Usage log analysis is one of the latest additions to digital library research. This technique analyzes the use of terms, operators, and number of queries per search from usage logs in order to provide a better understanding of digital library usage, user information needs, and system effectiveness (Cunningham & Mahoui, 2000). Wolfram & Xie (2001) reported on their experience analyzing usage logs and Web-based surveys for end users of the BadgerLink system and drew some conclusions about the behavioral differences between searching and browsing. Cunningham & Mahoui (2000) collected usage logs for two digital library systems and compared different searching behaviors in terms of query length, query refinement, and so on when using the two systems. Fu et al. (2003) investigated a hybrid method to cluster user queries by utilizing both the query terms and the results returned to queries. By determining and clustering similar queries in query logs, their system could augment the information seeking process by recommending related queries to users.

- **Multicultural Issues**: Digital libraries can help ensure the preservation of collective history and cultural memorabilia (Witten, 2001). In Asian digital library applications, there are countless scenarios that involve creating and distributing locally produced information collections. ICADL publications have included local digital libraries ranging from teachers preparing educational material to medicinal knowledge based on local plants and herbs. For example, the INFLIBNT project aimed at creating a digital library of theses and dissertations from India (Vijayakumar & Murthy, 2001). SNDT Women's University Library in India developed content for a digital library on Women and Health in South Asia (Parekh, 2001). The Tsinghua University Architecture Digital Library developed a prototype system to provide rich, valuable resources for traditional Chinese architecture research and education (Xing et al., 2002). Vaidya & Shrestha (2002) produced a study on rural digital library development in Nepal and provided suggestions on technical aspects and cost-effective solutions for digital library development in rural Nepal.

- **Asian Languages and Cross-lingual Issues**: A crucial feature of Asian digital libraries is the ability to work in various local languages (Witten, 2001). The Chinese language has been widely studied for information retrieval and extraction techniques. In ICADL 1998, Wong & Li (1998) and Yang et al. (1998) both studied Chinese information retrieval and discussed issues related to Chinese language indexing techniques. In ICADL 1999, Wong et al. (1999) presented their method for Chinese news event detection and tracking, where Chinese segmentation was discussed. Ong & Chen (1999) studied an updateable PAT-Tree approach to Chinese key phrase extraction. Other Asian languages studied include Japanese, Korean, and Thai. A dictionary-based morphological analysis approach for the Japanese language was proposed by Ando et al. (2000). Theeramunkong et al. (2002) investigated using n-gram and HMM approaches for Thai OCR application.

Cross-lingual information retrieval between English and Asian languages has been more widely studied in ICADL conferences than in other Western digital library conferences. Choi et al. (2000) proposed a dictionary-based method of Korean-English query translation. Yang & Luk (2000) constructed a Chinese-English cross-lingual concept space by utilizing a Hopfield network. In ICADL 2001, Sugimoto (2001) presented a multilingual document browsing tool and its metadata creation carried out at ULIS. The application was designed for Japanese, Chinese, Korean, and Arabic languages. Although no query translation was involved in the project, it was the first project of its kind to address the multilingual applications of digital libraries. Recently, in ICADL 2003, Qin et al. (2003) presented an English-Chinese cross-lingual Web retrieval system in the business domain. Their system adopted a dictionary-based approach that combines phrasal translation, co-occurrence analysis, and pre- and post-translation query expansion. Sembok et al. (2003) implemented a Malay-English scientific terms retrieving software. Several stemming algorithms for the Malay language were discussed and evaluated.

Many papers have focused on language specific applications in digital libraries. In addition to the ones discussed, several projects and papers were dedicated to looking at collections contained within local languages. For example, Adachi (2000) presented NACSIS-ELS, a digital library system of Japanese academic journals. Although the language issue was not the focus in those projects, the experiences were valuable for applying digital library technologies in a multilingual world. Zhou et al. (2003) developed a Chinese medical portal, CMedPort, which integrates various techniques such as meta-search, cross-regional search, summarization, and categorization. Their experience provides a good example of adopting information retrieval techniques to non-English languages.

Other Related Conferences in Asia Pacific

Several other conferences have been gaining worldwide attention for their efforts within the digital library research domain. Chaired by Ching-chih Chen, the 12th International Conference on New Information Technology was held at Tsinghua University, Beijing, in May 2001 (Chen, 2001). She organized twelve International Conferences on New Information Technology (NIT) in various places, including Asian countries such as Thailand, Singapore, Hong Kong, Vietnam, and Taiwan. This series of conferences has helped to encourage international collaboration among information and library professionals.

The International Conference of Digital Library—Opportunities and Challenges in the New Millennium, hosted by the National Library of China, was held in Beijing in July 2002 (Sun, 2002). The gathering promoted the development of digital libraries in China as well as other countries. More than 100 papers were published in the proceedings with participants from more than 140 digital libraries and information institutions. The meeting also featured 125 exhibitors ranging from provincial libraries and museums to digital library hardware and software vendors. In addition, the International Symposium on Digital Libraries (ISDL) was held in Japan in 1995, 1997, and 1999 (Tabata & Sugimoto, 1995, 1997, 1999). The symposium was hosted by the University of Library and Information Science (ULIS) in Japan and attracted significant Asian and international participation.

Conclusion

Digital library researchers in Asia Pacific are facing some challenges in common with researchers in the U.S., Europe, and other parts of the world. However, they are also uniquely positioned to help develop digital libraries of significant cultural heritage and indigenous knowledge and advance cross-cultural and cross-lingual digital library research.

Digital library collections have the widest range of content and media types, ranging from 3D chemical structures to tornado simulation models, from the statue of David to paintings by Van Gogh. A mix of text, audio, and video is common among digital library applications. Collection, organization, indexing, searching, and analysis of such diverse information content continue to create unique technical challenges.

Unlike digital government or e-commerce applications that often generate their own content, digital libraries provide content management and retrieval services to many other content owners. The intellectual property issues (rights and fee collection) surrounding such diverse collections need to be carefully addressed.

Many patrons often would like library services to be "free" or at least extremely affordable. Compounding the issue further is the notion of "free" Internet content. However, for high-quality, credible content to be accessible through digital libraries, cost and sustainability problems needed to be resolved. Different digital library pricing models would need to be developed for different contents and services.

The long history and diversity of the different cultures and peoples in the Asian Pacific region has created a fertile environment for developing digital libraries of cultural heritage and indigenous knowledge. Such content and knowledge could help promote global understanding and collaboration.

Digital library content is often of interest to people all over the world, not just in one region. Many content creation and development processes also require collaboration among researchers and librarians in different parts of the world. Digital library researchers are facing the unique challenge of creating a global service to bridge cultural and language barriers. Researchers in Asia Pacific could significantly contribute to research advancement in cultural and language issues of relevance to the region and to the digital library community as well.

Acknowledgments

This research is supported by: NSF Digital Library Initiative-2, "High-Performance Digital Library Systems: From Information Retrieval to Knowledge Management," IIS-9817473, April 1999-March 2002.

References

Adachi, J. (2000). NACSIS-ELS: Digital library of Japanese academic journals. In *Proceedings of the Third International Conference on Asian Digital Library* (pp. 15-22). Seoul, Korea.

Anderson, T., Hussam, A., Plummer, B., & Jacobs, N. (2002). Pie charts for visualizing query term frequency in search results. In *Proceedings of the Fifth International Conference on Asian Digital Library* (pp. 440-451). Singapore.

Ando, K., Lee, T., Shishibori, M., & Aoe, J. (2000). Dictionary structure for agglutinative languages. In *The Proceedings of the Third International Conference on Asian Digital Library* (pp. 255-260). Seoul, Korea.

Bainbridge, D., Dewsnip, M., & Witten, I. (2002). Searching digital music libraries. In *Proceedings of the Fifth International Conference on Asian Digital Library* (pp. 129-140). Singapore.

Boone, D., & Pennington, S. (2001). Adapting the open archival information system reference model for consumer initiated ingestion: A multi-media resource delivery architecture for the National Gallery of the Spoken Word. In *Proceedings of the Fourth International Conference on Asian Digital Library* (pp. 258-273). Bangalore, India.

Borgman, C. L. (1998). Social Aspects of Digital Libraries: Making Information Technology Usable and Useful. In the *Proceedings of the First Asian Digital Library Workshop,* Hong Kong (pp. 6-12).

Borgman, C. L. (2002). Challenges in building digital libraries for the 21st century. In *Proceedings of the Fifth International Conference on Asian Digital Library* (pp. 1-13). Singapore.

Cha, G. H., & Chung, C. W. (2000). Modeling and summarizing lecture databases. In *Proceedings of the Third International Conference on Asian Digital Library* (pp. 261-266). Seoul, Korea.

Chan, C. H., Sun, A., & Lim, E. P. (2001). Automated online news classification with personalization. In *Proceedings of the Fourth International Conference on Asian Digital Library* (pp. 320-329). Bangalore, India.

Chen, C. C. (ed.) (2001). *Proceedings of global digital library development in the new millennium: Fertile ground for distributed cross-disciplinary collaboration*. Tsinghua University Press.

Chen, C. C., & Chen, H. H. (2002). Building an OAI-based union catalog for the National Digital Archives Program in Taiwan. In *Proceedings of the Fifth International Conference on Asian Digital Library* (pp. 425-426). Singapore.

Chen, H. (2001). Medical text mining: A DLI-2 status report. In *Proceedings of the Fourth International Conference on Asian Digital Library* (pp. 41-61). Bangalore, India.

Chen, I. X., Chen, C. M., & Yang, C. Z. (2001). Design of a search engine for cross-library search based on metalogy metadata. In *Proceedings of the Fourth International Conference on Asian Digital Library* (pp. 274-282). Bangalore, India.

Choi, Y. S., Chun, J., & Choi, K. S. (2000). A study on dynamic threshold for Korean English query translation. In *Proceedings of the Third International Conference on Asian Digital Library* (pp. 201-208). Seoul, Korea.

Cunningham, S. J., & Mahoui, M. (2000). Search behavior in two digital libraries: A comparative transaction log analysis. In *Proceedings of the Third International Conference on Asian Digital Library* (pp. 193-200). Seoul, Korea.

Fu, L., Goh, D. H., Foo, S. S., & Na, J. (2003). Collaborative querying through a hybrid query clustering approach. In *Proceedings of the Sixth International Conference on Asian Digital Library* (pp. 111-122). Kuala Lumpur, Malaysia.

Heß, M., & Drobnik, O. (1999). Clustering specialized Web-databases by exploiting hyperlinks. In *Proceedings of the Second Asian Digital Library Workshop* (pp. 19-29). Taipei, Taiwan.

Jones, S., & Mahoui, M. (2000). Hierarchical document clustering using automatically extracted key phrases. In *Proceedings of the Third International Conference on Asian Digital Library* (113-120). Seoul, Korea.

Joung, Y. S., Hyun, S. J., & Kim, H. B. (2000). A metadata repository system for efficient description of multimedia documents in digital libraries. In

Proceedings of the Third International Conference on Asian Digital Library. Seoul, Korea.

Liew, C. L., Foo, S., & Chennupati, K. R. (2000). Enhancing user interaction with electronic journals via interactivity and value-adding features. In *Proceedings of the Third International Conference on Asian Digital Library* (pp. 289-294). Seoul, Korea.

Lo, S. C., & Chen, H. H. (1999). Resources organization and searching specification: The "Butterflies of Taiwan" project. In *Proceedings of the Second Asian Digital Library Workshop* (pp. 182-201). Taipei, Taiwan.

McDonald, D., & Chen, H. (2002). Using sentence selection heuristics to rank text segments in TXTRACTOR. In *Proceedings of JCDL'02* (pp. 28-35). Portland, Oregon. ACM/IEEE-CS.

Ong, T. H., & Chen, H. (1999). Updateable PAT-Tree approach to Chinese key phrase extraction using mutual information: A linguistic foundation for knowledge management. In *Proceedings of the Second Asian Digital Library Workshop* (pp. 63-84). Taipei, Taiwan.

Parekh, H. (2001). Library on women and health in South Asia: Report of an international collaboration. In *Proceedings of the Fourth International Conference on Asian Digital Library* (367-375). Bangalore, India.

Qin, J., Zhou, Y., Chau, M., & Chen, H. (2003). Supporting multilingual information retrieval in Web applications: An English-Chinese Web portal experiment. In *Proceedings of the Sixth International Conference on Asian Digital Library* (pp. 149-152). Kuala Lumpur, Malaysia.

Renda, M. E., & Straccia, U. (2002). A personalized collaborative digital library environment. In *Proceedings of the Fifth International Conference on Asian Digital Library* (pp. 262-274). Singapore.

Rowe, J., Razdan, A., Collins, D., & Panchanahan, S. (2001). A 3D digital library system: capture, analysis, query, and display. In *Proceedings of the Fourth International Conference on Asian Digital Library* (pp. 149-159). Bangalore, India.

Sembok, T. M. T., Ali, K. P. N. M., Aidanismah, Y., & Wook, T. S. M. T. (2003). ISTILAH SAINS: A Malay-English terminology retrieval system experiment using stemming and n-gram approach on Malay words. In *Proceedings of the Sixth International Conference on Asian Digital Library* (pp. 173-177). Kuala Lumpur, Malaysia.

Smith, A. G. (1998). Criteria for evaluation of Internet resources in a digital library environment. In *Proceedings of the First Asian Digital Library Workshop* (pp. 81-87). Hong Kong.

Sugimoto, S. (2001). Helping information access across languages using simple tools: Multilingual projects at ULIS and lessons learned. In *Proceedings of the Fourth International Conference on Asian Digital Library* (pp. 16-29). Bangalore, India.

Sun, J. (ed.). (2002). *Proceedings of IT Opportunities and Challenges in the New Millennium*, Beijing, China.

Tabata, K., & Sugimoto, S. (ed.). (1995). *Proceedings of the Third International Symposium on Digital Libraries 1995*. Tsukuba, Japan.

Tabata, K., & Sugimoto, S. (ed.). (1997). *Proceedings of the International Symposium on Research, Development and Practice in Digital Libraries 1997*. Tsukuba, Japan.

Tabata, K., & Sugimoto, S. (ed.). (1999). *Proceedings of the International Symposium on Digital Libraries 1999*. Tsukuba, Japan.

Tang, S., Law, C., & Yen, J. (2000). Summarization for multi-document using concept space approach. In *Proceedings of the Third International Conference on Asian Digital Library* (pp. 121-130). Seoul, Korea.

Theeramunkong, T., Wongtapan, C., & Sinthupinyo, S. (2002). Offline isolated handwritten Thai OCR using island-based projection with n-gram models and hidden Markov Models. In *Proceedings of the Fifth International Conference on Asian Digital Library* (pp. 340-351). Singapore.

Vaidya, B., & Shrestha, J. N. (2002). Rural digital library: Connecting rural communities in Nepal. In *Proceedings of the Fifth International Conference on Asian Digital Library* (pp. 354-365). Singapore.

Vijayakumar, J. K., & Murthy, T. A. V. (2001). Need of a digital library of Indian theses and dissertations: A model on par with the ETD initiatives at international level. In *Proceedings of the Fourth International Conference on Asian Digital Library* (pp. 384-390). Bangalore, India.

Walfram, D., & Xie, H. (2001). State digital libraries: Developing systems for general audiences. In *Proceedings of the Fourth International Conference on Asian Digital Library* (pp. 62-74). Bangalore, India.

Witten, I. H. (2001). Visions of the digital libraries. In *Proceedings of the Fourth International Conference on Asian Digital Library* (pp. 3-15). Bangalore, India.

Witten, I. H. (2002). Examples of practical digital libraries: Collections built internationally using Greenstone. In *Proceedings of the Fifth International Conference on Asian Digital Library* (67-74). Singapore.

Wong, K. F., & Li, W. (1998). Intelligent Chinese information retrieval: Why is it so difficult? In *Proceedings of the First Asian Digital Library Workshop* (pp 47-56). Hong Kong.

Wong, K. L., Lam, W., & Yen, J. (1999). Interactive Chinese news event detection and tracking. In *Proceedings of the Second Asian Digital Library Workshop* (pp. 30-46). Taipei, Taiwan.

Xing, C., Zhou, L. Zhang, Z., Zeng, C., & Zhou, X. (2002). Developing Tsinghua University architecture digital library for Chinese architecture study and university education. In *Proceedings of the Fifth International Conference on Asian Digital Library* (pp. 206-217). Singapore.

Yang, C. C., & Luk, J. (2000). Constructing Chinese-English concept space. In *Proceedings of the Third International Conference on Asian Digital Library* (139-146). Seoul, Korea.

Yang, C. C., Yen, J., Yung, S. K., & Chung, A. K. L. (1998). Chinese indexing using mutual information. In *Proceedings of the First Asian Digital Library Workshop* (57-64). Hong Kong.

Yang, C. Z., & Kao, C. H. (1999). Visualizing large hierarchical information structures in digital libraries. In *Proceedings of the Second Asian Digital Library Workshop* (pp. 243-254). Taipei, Taiwan.

Yang, Y. J., Lee, S. D., & Choi, H. S. (1998). A metadata framework for multimedia resource discovery systems in digital library. In *Proceedings of the First Asian Digital Library Workshop* (pp. 216-226). Hong Kong.

Yeh, J. Y., Ke, H. R., & Yang, W. P. (2002). Chinese text summarization using a trainable summarizer and latent semantic analysis. In *Proceedings of the Fifth International Conference on Asian Digital Library* (pp. 76-87). Singapore.

Yen, J. (2000). From unstructured HTML to structured XML: How XML supports financial knowledge management. In *Proceedings of the Third International Conference on Asian Digital Library* (pp. 71-80). Seoul, Korea.

Ying, P. M., & Heng, J. S. H. (2002). The NUS digital media gallery: A dynamic architecture for audio, image, clipart, and video repository accessible via the campus learning management system and the digital library. In *Proceedings of the Fifth International Conference on Asian Digital Library* (pp. 141-152). Singapore.

Zhou, Y., Qin, J., & Chen, H. (2003). CMedPort: Intelligent searching for Chinese medical information. In *Proceedings of the Sixth International Conference on Asian Digital Library* (pp. 34-45). Kuala Lumpur, Malaysia.

Section II

Design Architecture and Systems

Chapter II

Design Architecture:
An Introduction and Overview

Edward A. Fox
Virginia Tech, USA

Hussein Suleman
University of Cape Town, South Africa

Ramesh C. Gaur
Tata Institute of Fundamental Research, India

Devika P. Madalli
Indian Statistical Institute, India

Abstract

Digital libraries evolved in response to the need to manage the vast quantities of electronic information that we produce, collect, and consume. Architects of such systems have adopted a variety of design approaches, which are summarized and illustrated in this chapter. We also introduce the following three chapters, and provide suitable background. From a historical perspective, we note that early systems were designed independently to afford services to specific communities. Since then, systems that store and mediate access to information have become commonplace and are scattered all over the Internet. Consequently, information retrieval also has to contend with distributed/networked systems in a transparent and scalable fashion. In this context, digital library architects have adopted various interoperability standards and practices to provide users with seamless access to highly distributed information sources. This chapter looks at current research and emerging best practices adopted in designing digital libraries, whether individual or distributed.

Introduction

Every digital library (DL) is constructed according to some design and architecture. These DLs are built upon suitable technology, and must support operations, as well as function as integrated systems, to support a target user community. While there are generic needs common for most DLs, such as searching and browsing, specific communities often require specialized services and prefer particular types of user interfaces and display formats. In accordance with one of S.R. Ranganathan's Five Laws of Library Science, that is, "Every Reader His/Her Book," DLs should be designed so that user information needs are met.

Individual systems must address conformance to standards, digital preservation, indexing styles, logging, security, and tuning. In the case of distributed DLs, there also are requirements for data federation, interoperability, scalability, service federation, and Web services.

This chapter presents an overview of DL design architecture. While this chapter provides an introduction and overview, the remaining chapters focus on particular issues in design and architecture, presenting focused results from the research and development arena.

Chapter III describes the Indonesian Digital Library Network (IndonesiaDLN), a nation-wide DL initiative, from inception to its current status. The basic objective of IndonesiaDLN is to collect, manage, share, and reuse the nation's intellectual capital towards the development of a knowledge-based society. Early work was guided in part by the evolution of the Networked Digital Library of Theses and Dissertations (NDLTD). The overall initiative is explained using the 5S (Societies, Scenarios, Spaces, Structures, Streams) Framework and the Ganesha Digital Library (GDL) open source software is introduced.

Chapter IV describes dynamic metadata management for digital archives. It discusses the development, features, structure, functions, and use of Metalogy - an XML metadata framework system developed in the context of the Digital Museum Project in Taiwan. Beginning with the basic design concept of a metadata system with the requirement of supporting various metadata formats, a solution based on multi-XML schema is presented in terms of information organization, schema construction, and metadata management.

Chapter V addresses information filtering and personalized services. Content-based filtering addresses the difficult task of delivering relevant information resources to diverse users, through tracking, studying, and representing users' interests. Theoretical and experimental results of the advantages of a probabilistic model over the vector space model are presented. Results are given regarding training set size and improving performance and prediction. The architecture and services of the TH-PASS system are discussed as a practical example.

The sections that follow provide an introduction and overview to DL design and architecture, helping prepare the reader for subsequent chapters in this part of the book.

Individual Systems

Before any single DL can address the questions of scalability and interoperability with other systems, it has to meet the needs of its local users. These needs may include submission workflows, peer review, subscription-based "push" services, or a myriad of other popular DL services. The most obvious, however, is the ability to search through a local collection. Thus, much of this section is devoted to recent ideas in information retrieval, largely from the perspective of a single DL system.

DL systems are usually complex, with many components, handling authentication and authorization, user interaction, searching and browsing, retrieval and presentation, analysis and indexing, multimedia management, logging, preservation, link management, and other functions. To reinforce the need for modularity in the system as a whole, we argue next for modularity with regard to a specific operation: query expansion.

Provision of a simple and efficient DL retrieval interface is imperative, though the content may be complex and varied. General purpose search engines incorporating merely technical mechanisms for information search and access cannot guarantee precision. Providing retrieval tools for a collection is more complex, involving mapping user needs and collection concepts in the proper context and order. Accordingly, facet analysis is regarded as a powerful methodology for the creation of structures appropriate to specific retrieval requirements in a range of contexts (Broughton, 2001). The emphasis is on the problems of complex subject description and representation of multi-dimensionality in the domain to aid retrieval. While in the traditional environment information organizing tools such as library classification systems have proven to be indispensable, the potential of such facet analytical knowledge structures for the management of digital materials has been demonstrated in several systems (Egan et al., 1989). The Subject Based Domain Search System (SBDSS, see *Figure 1*) (Madalli et al., 2003), a system for supporting query modification and reformulation using knowledge structures, demonstrates the significance of the subject approach to digital library retrieval. SBDSS accepts a user query and retrieves thesaurus entries that contain at least one of the query keywords at every level of the hierarchy. It ranks and displays the retrieved entries. The input module accepts a natural language query. Stop words are identified and removed. After the standard stemming procedure, a set of keywords remains; these are sent to the lookup module.

The lookup module, augmented with a thesaurus database, searches for the keywords; each resulting context specifies the hierarchies for a term occurrence. The user may interactively choose the term in the context best suited and issue the final search query. The system design (*Figure 1*) is modular; thus, the thesaurus may be replaced by other formal knowledge structures such as classification schemes.

Shifting to another aspect of the user interface, we note that the structured display and visualization of result sets is a long-standing topic for retrieval systems (Tudhope & Cunliffe, 2001). Result set displays should carry sufficient semantic information about the retrieved resources; this can be enhanced through the use of metadata, when available. Thus, a display with bibliographic element descriptions, using widely used standards such as Dublin Core (DC), can add semantic value to retrieval.

Many types of stand-alone DLs have been built. Some are derived from information retrieval systems. Several evolved from library catalog systems. Other origins include: computer-supported cooperative work systems, database management systems, directory systems, educational technology systems, geographic information systems, multimedia information systems, and text processing systems. Because of strong current interest, we first focus on institutional repositories in the next subsection.

Institutional Archives

The information revolution is leading to a "flood of publications" or "information glut." Users have more journals to read but prices have increased faster than library budgets, so it is difficult for libraries even to maintain their current subscriptions. To balance budgets, libraries have been forced to cancel some journal subscriptions. Yet, scholarly communications are a must for any institution. In part to help cope with this situation, "institutional repositories" or "institutional archives" have emerged - representing one of the potentially major

Figure 1. Architecture of SBDSS

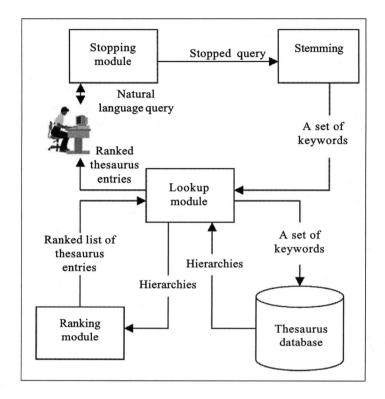

components in the evolution of scholarly communications towards digital collections.

Institutional archives may contain a wide range of intellectual assets such as preprints, articles, handouts, theses and dissertations, monographs, meeting proceedings, and notes. Data formats include text documents, research data, and multimedia. In addition to typical DL services, advanced services such as registration, (self-) archiving, certification, preservation, and awareness are needed to support this wide range of assets.

Institutional archives are beneficial to all researchers, scholarly institutions, and the entire research community. Major benefits include cost saving, avoiding duplication of effort, broadening of the communication process, reduction in time in announcing findings, expansion of audience, and, above all, preserving information assets for the use of future generations. Since local electronic storage is employed, many large multimedia works may be included, eliminating the page limit constraints of traditional journals. Institutional archives may help an institution to improve its prestige, as well as visibility, worldwide. Thus, it may lead indirectly to additional revenues. Institutional archives are especially beneficial in the developing world, which is little represented in the journal literature. Institutions may immediately become visible if their works are indexed by popular search engines. Institutional archives can help in bridging the digital divide and also may help in enriching education, by sharing learning resources among rich and poor nations.

Case Study: EPrints (http://www.eprints.org/) and DSpace (http://www.dspace.org/)

EPrints, developed by the University of Southampton, and DSpace, developed by Hewlett-Packard for MIT, are both open source software systems that support the submission, archiving, and dissemination of documents. EPrints is motivated by a need to open access to the refereed research literature online through author/institution self-archiving. DSpace is more concerned with communities and preservation. Both packages are widely used in a variety of settings, some of which are mentioned below.

Case Study: India (DRTC and other DLs)

A specialist Digital Library for Library and Information Science is hosted by the Documentation Research and Training Center, Indian Statistical Institute, (*https://drtc.isibang.ac.in/*). The DRTC DL is open to worldwide participation for both access and submission. The collection is structured into seminars and conference proceedings, student theses and dissertations, multilingual resources, and pre-prints. The DRTC DL is powered by DSpace and is compliant with OAI-PMH v2.0. It uses CNRI's Handle server to generate unique URIs for independent access to each resource. As a Unicode implementation, DRTC DL offers multilingual support and hosts resources (and accepts submissions) in Indian and other languages.

There are a variety of other systems of interest in India, including the following:

- Indian Academy of Sciences (IAS) Journals (*http://www.ias.ac.in/*): 11 journals available online at no charge, covering key scientific results from India and beyond.

- IndMed Database (http://indmed.delhi.nic.in/): It is the first Web-based Indian biomedical database, covering 75 Indian Journals. Lead responsibility is with the Indian MEDLARS Centre, New Delhi.

- The Digital Library of India Site (*http://www.dli.gov.in/*): The Indian Institute of Science developed this collection in distributed scanning centres around India.

- Indian Institute of Information Technology, Bangalore, (*http://www.iiitb.ac.in/digital_library.htm*), Hyderabad (*http://www.iiit.net/infrastructure.htm*), and Indian Institute of Technology, Delhi (*http://www.iitd.ernet.in/acad/library/ project.html*): These initiatives provide access to existing international collections (such as those of ACM and IEEE) as well as local collections of books, articles, courseware, etc. Indian National Science Academy (INSA): INSA, with membership of leading Indian scientists, makes available to scientific organizations and institutions access to its key DL projects: records of its fellows and online journals of the academy.

- NCSI, Indian Institute of Science: NCSI has designed, developed and is hosting the SciGate Science Journal Gateway. Among other activities, it is beta testing the Greenstone DL software for UNESCO and providing local institutional archiving, using EPrints software for papers, book chapters, technical reports, etc. (*http://www.eprints.iisc.ernet.in/*).

- University of Hyderabad Central Library: The Indira Gandhi Memorial Library (IGML), recognized by Sun Microsystems as a "Centre of Excellence for Digital Libraries," provides access to key databases like EBSCO and ScienceDirect, a pioneering effort in bringing these services to the Indian academic world.

Distributed Digital Libraries

Federation and Harvesting

While the provision of discovery and management services has largely driven the design of digital libraries, an increasingly important requirement is the need for interoperability with peer systems. Most of the early attempts have focused on the sharing of data among systems, as this replication improved system reliability, reduced latency, and made more effective use of precious network bandwidth by bringing resources closer to users.

More recently, designers of digital library systems have had to contend with a shift in emphasis of Internet use from file-based systems such as FTP to service-based systems such as the WWW. Early projects such as RePEc (Krichel, 2000) are based on a strong foundation of FTP-able data collections. Modern online information systems, however, exploit the increased capabilities of the WWW to provide advanced services that mediate between users and data. In this context, interoperability can be viewed as a service provided by a system. Early interoperability experiments (Payette, Blanchi, Lagoze, & Overly, 1999) showed that it is feasible but not simple to implement, manage, and maintain such configurations over time.

In searching for a simple interoperability solution, the Open Archives Initiative (OAI) was launched to develop a low cost interoperability solution (Lagoze & Van de Sompel, 2001). Initially, the process was driven by the need to exchange metadata about electronic pre-prints, but a number of initial discussions and workshops expanded the scope of this mandate well beyond e-prints, ultimately resulting in the design of the OAI Protocol for Metadata Harvesting (PMH) (Lagoze, Van de Sompel, Nelson & Warner, 2002), a simple high-level network protocol to incrementally transfer metadata from one system to another.

The OAI-PMH is an almost stateless client-server network protocol that facilitates the transfer of metadata from a provider of data to a provider of services. A data provider is defined as that network-accessible entity that owns a collection of metadata, which is to be made available to others. A service provider is defined as the entity that obtains metadata from the data provider, usually with the intention of providing user-directed services. This functional split was largely motivated by the realization that data providers do not often have the best suite of services available and, conversely, that service providers do not often make available the best data sets. A data provider is a Web application that listens for and processes requests for data. A service provider runs an application, known as a harvester, which periodically obtains new and updated metadata from a data provider. The data thus obtained then either is merged into the local metadata collection or passed on to a service provider component, such as a search engine, for further processing.

The OAI-PMH has proven to be popular because of its unobtrusive nature and loosely connected mode of operation. For greater control, data providers can moderate the flow of data by sending back truncated lists of data along with resumption tokens that service providers may return in order to resume transferring the list (of metadata records, identifiers, etc.). In addition, data providers may utilize HTTP headers to deny, delay, or postpone requests. In practice, these mechanisms contribute to avoiding denial-of-service attacks and ensure that providers of data are always in full control of the process of metadata harvesting, albeit that it is initiated by service providers.

Ultimately, the simplicity, adherence to standards, clean separation of responsibilities and preservation of autonomy of individual systems rank high on the list of reasons why existing digital libraries are comfortable using OAI-PMH in order to interoperate. Also, new systems that are designed to be highly distributed can readily adopt OAI-PMH, because of the user community and toolsets that have already been and are being developed.

Integration of Services

Besides data transfer, a large-scale digital library could conceivably include multiple user interfaces or multiple variants of the same service. Additionally, these interfaces and services could be provided at different physical locations, connected only by a network. In order to present users with a coherent view of the collection of data and a sensible set of services, there is a need for remote access mechanisms for digital library services. The simplest of these is the concept of remote searching, where the machine interface to a search engine can be accessed remotely in addition to, or in place of the human interface, thus allowing integration of remote search engines into local user interfaces and workflows.

The Z39.50 protocol was specifically designed for such remote retrieval operations and is popular in library systems. However, it uses older technology (pre-XML) and is not popular among designers of smaller individual systems because of a high degree of complexity. Given that large-scale digital libraries are frequently aggregations of small projects, the added complexity can be problematic. In addition, as the scale of a digital library network increases, remote searching becomes less viable as a basic interoperability mechanism because of the increase in points of failure and an increased possibility of network latency effects. A solution that builds on the best of both worlds is to use data harvesting to create one or more central collections of data, and then provide one or more remote search interfaces on these data collections. This is the approach adopted in NDLTD, as illustrated in *Figure 2*. A single service provider at OCLC harvests data from many remote sites and then exposes an OAI-PMH interface as well as a remote search interface. A second service provider mirrors the metadata and provides yet another remote search interface as well as a user interface that makes use of it.

The figure makes reference to SRU, which is part of the "Z39.50 International: Next Generation" (ZING) project (Library of Congress, 2003) to upgrade Z39.50 so that it is simpler and more accessible as a Web-based service. ODL-Union and ODL-Search are experimental protocols that were developed as part of the Open Digital Library (ODL) project (Suleman & Fox, 2001), where popular services were cast as extensions of the OAI-PMH. Although ZING and ODL have been motivated by different needs, they are both based on the concept of location-independence or federation of digital library services.

DLs and Web Services

The basic idea behind federated services is, however, not at all specific to digital libraries and is more widely known as the "service-oriented computing" paradigm (Papazoglou & Georgakopoulos, 2003). In this model, the components of a system are analogous to service providers with well-defined machine interfaces. One realization of this model is the Web services project of the World Wide Web Consortium (*W3C, http://www.w3.org/*), which is defining a framework whereby service-oriented components can interact over the WWW.

At the core of this framework is the SOAP protocol that defines how to encapsulate an XML-formatted message for delivery between components of a distributed system. The SOAP specification concentrates on genericity so that the payloads, sequence of data transfer, and transport protocols has as much flexibility as possible. For example, SOAP messages may be sent and received by e-mail communication, thus enabling the use of e-mail for directly requesting services from a system.

However, SOAP defines only the encoding and transportation parameters for messages. The syntax and semantics are specified and enforced using different mechanisms. The Web Services Description Language (WSDL), as the next logical step, defines syntactic elements such as the interfaces and parameters associated with specific services. The Universal Description, Discovery and Integration of Web Services (UDDI) registries then provide public access to these descriptions of interfaces. A popular example is the Google search engine's free Web service, a WSDL definition of which can be discovered through the UDDI registries. This allows any software developer to incorporate machine access to Google using SOAP messages sent over the WWW. Based on this SOAP, WSDL, and UDDI foundation, newer standards such as the Web Services Flow Language (WSFL) (Leymann, 2001) are being developed to coordinate workflows and enable aggregation and composition of service components.

The SRU service, introduced in the previous section, adheres to the Web service standards and is a prime example of how Web service technology pervades the networked digital library community. Newer digital library standards for highly connected systems may build on the Web services initiative – a prototype SOAP-based version of the OAI-PMH has already been developed and tested (Merchant, Gaylord & Congia, 2003) to illustrate the effectiveness and efficiency of Web services applied to digital library standards. Other standards will likely follow suit as more Web Services specifications are standardized.

Figure 2. Architecture of NDLTD digital library network

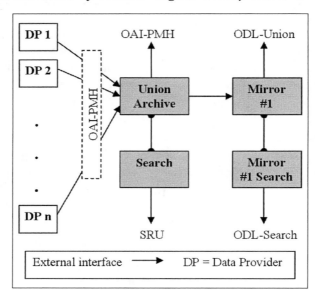

DLs and Internet Technology

The explicit adoption of Web services standards by projects such as ZING and implicit adoption of the service-oriented computing architecture by initiatives such as OAI point to an impending convergence between the fields of digital libraries and Internet-based information systems. Just as the Web is becoming a highly connected system of semantically rich services, so too are DLs becoming a network of service-based components and systems.

The boundaries between DLs and other Web-based systems are no longer well defined. In the domain of content management systems, the popular RSS standard (Winer, 2002) allows for syndication of content such as "newsfeeds" among dynamically generated websites. The principles and operation of RSS are very similar to OAI-PMH, except that there are fewer parameters in the former protocol. In contrast, the IMS Digital Repositories specification (IMS Global Learning Consortium, 2003) explicitly avoids overlapping standards and recommends different externally defined protocols for different scenarios, including the OAI-PMH for metadata harvesting.

From a security perspective, DL projects may opt to use existing standards defined for rights management and authentication/authorization. The RoMEO project (Gadd, Oppenheim, & Probets, 2003) studied issues in rights management and recommended use of the existing Open Digital Rights Language (ODRL) and Creative Commons licences for rights specification in an interoperable environment. The Shibboleth project defines a trust relationship framework for authentication and authorisation in a distributed system, and is a prime technology enabler for remote data access and service invocation for DLs (Gourley, 2003).

As we move towards larger-scale service-oriented networked information systems, the projects discussed above indicate an increasing degree to which DLs rely on emerging Internet standards and vice versa. In the context of this convergence of technologies, it is crucial to design modern distributed DLs taking into account current best practices in DLs as well as Internet standards to enable the broadest possible spectrum of use cases.

Case Study: NDLTD (http://www.ndltd.org/)

The Networked Digital Library of Theses and Dissertations (Fox, 1998) is a collaborative effort of universities around the world to promote creating, archiving, distributing, and accessing Electronic Theses and Dissertations (ETDs), as well as to encourage local advancement and adoption of DL technologies. Initially, when numbers were small, a federated search approach was adopted. As membership expanded, NDLTD shifted to maintain a union catalog that provides a means to search and retrieve ETDs from the combined collections of NDLTD member institutions. To gather metadata in the ETD metadata standard (ETDMS) format and then to make it accessible at a central portal, the system uses the OAI-PMH. NDLTD has more than 200 international members from over twenty countries sharing ETDs, with a growing number contributing to the union catalog.

Case Study: NSDL (http://www.nsdl.org/)

The National Science, Technology, Engineering, and Mathematics (STEM) Education Digital Library is an effort initiated by the U.S. National Science Foundation to organize and make easily accessible electronic resources for teaching and learning in the STEM areas. There are over 100 projects that have made up this initiative, engaged in targeted research, services development and deployment, and in supporting varied communities with specialized collections. NSDL offers interoperability at three levels: federation, harvesting, and gathering (Arms et al., 2002). Federation enables interaction with collections that are compliant with standards such as Z39.50. However, since the limitations and challenges of federated searching are widely known, NSDL provides the facility of harvesting from OAI-compliant repositories and building a central searchable database. Over and above these, crawlers and community-based activities are deployed to gather resources, similar to the method used by general-purpose Web search engines. NSDL uses the latest technology and best practices outlined in this document in supporting both a broad base of remote sites and a varied and configurable set of user services at central locations. NSDL and NDLTD are both featured in a UNESCO report that advocates a digital library for education in every nation (Kalinichenko, 2003).

Case Study: Universal Digital Library (http://disc.iisc.ernet.in/unidiglib.html)

The aim of this project is to digitize around a million books in the next three years. This joint initiative is planned to synergistically capitalise on the availability of state-of-the-art hardware and software in the US for digitizing, storing, and accessing information, and the high quality manpower available in India. This would act as a forerunner for many such initiatives with other countries, particularly in China and Korea, and would culminate in the grand vision of digitizing all formal knowledge and making it available in a location- and time-independent way for the benefit of mankind.

Summary and Future Directions

DLs have been under development since the early 1990s. There have been centralized and distributed architectures, wherein content and/or services have been in one place, or distributed according to a variety of design principles. Some DLs serve an individual, and use lightweight methods (Maly, Zubair, & Liu, 2001). Many DLs serve an institution, including its various communities. Larger DLs serve a regional or national or worldwide community, typically in a particular disciplinary area (e.g., economics) or with regard to a particular genre (e.g., theses).

Distributed systems, early on, supported federated search. Later systems shifted to OAI-PMH. Newer systems are moving toward a Web services paradigm. Continuing research is needed to ensure interoperability, efficiency, robustness, and reliability across the global Internet.

As these systems become more widely used, including commercial activities, further work is needed with regard to authentication, digital rights management, and security. In addition, as a DL industry emerges, the separation of data from services promulgated in OAI is likely to be extended, with rapid growth not only of specialized collections, but also of integrated services. In academic settings these already are called for with regard to learning management systems. More broadly, they fit into the move towards a Semantic Web.

This introduction should help readers explore other design and architectural issues in the DL context, such as those discussed in the next three chapters. More broadly, it is hoped that it will provide some foundation for considering the spread of DLs throughout Asia and beyond.

References

Arms, W. et al. (2002, January). A spectrum of interoperability: The site for science prototype for the NSDL. *D-Lib Magazine, 8*(1). Retrieved July 11, 2003, from the World Wide Web: *http://www.dlib.org/dlib/january02/arms/01arms.html*

Broughton, V. (2001). Faceted classification as a basis for knowledge organisation in a digital environment: The Bliss Bibliographic Classification as a model for vocabulary management and the creation of multidimensional knowledge structures. *The New Review of Hypermedia and Multimedia, 7*, 67-102.

Egan, D., Remde, J.R., Gomez, L.M., Landauer, T.K., Eberhardt, J., & Lochbaum, C.C. (1989). Formative design and evaluation of *SuperBook. ACM Transactions on Information Systems, 7*, 30-57.

Fox, E.A. (1999, August). Networked Digital Library of Theses and Dissertations (NDLTD). *Nature Web Matters.* Retrieved February 28, 2003, from the World Wide Web: *http://www.nature.com/nature/webmatters/library/library.html*

Gadd, E., Oppenheim, C., & Probets, S. (2003). The intellectual property rights issues facing self-archiving: Key findings of the RoMEO Project. *D-Lib Magazine, 9*(9). Retrieved November 5, 2003, from the World Wide Web: *http://www.dlib.org/dlib/september03/gadd/09gadd.html*

Ginsparg, P. (2003). *Can peer review be better focused?* Cornell University. Retrieved March 4, 2003, from the World Wide Web: *http://arxiv.org/blurb/pg02pr.html*

Google. (2003). *Google Web APIs.* Retrieved November 7, 2003, from the World Wide Web: *http://www.google.com/apis/*

Gourley, D. (2003). *Library portal roles in a Shibboleth framework.* Shibboleth Project. Retrieved November 5, 2003, from the World Wide Web:

http://shibboleth.internet2.edu/docs/gourley-shibboleth-library-por-tals-200310.html

IMS Global Learning Consortium, Inc. (2003). *IMS digital repositories interoperability: Core functions information model.* Retrieved November 5, 2003, from the World Wide Web: *http://www.imsglobal.org/digitalrepositories/driv1p0/imsdri_infov1p0.html*

Kalinichenko, L. (coordinating author). (2003). *Digital libraries in education: Analytical survey.* Moscow: UNESCO Institute for Information Technologies in Education.

Krichel, T. (2000). Working towards an open library for economics: The RePEc project. In *Proceedings of The Economics and Usage of Digital Library Collections,* Ann Arbor, Michigan, USA, November 23-24. Retrieved November 7, 2003, from the World Wide Web: *http://openlib.org/home/krichel/myers.html*

Lagoze, C., & Van de Sompel, H. (2001). The Open Archives Initiative: Building a low-barrier interoperability framework. In *Proceedings of the ACM-IEEE Joint Conference on Digital Libraries* (pp. 54-62). Roanoke, Virginia, June 24-28.

Lagoze, C., Van de Sompel, H., Nelson, M., & Warner, S. (2002, June). *The Open Archives Initiative protocol for metadata harvesting – Version 2.0.* Open Archives Initiative. Retrieved November 5, 2003, from the World Wide Web: *http://www.openarchives.org/OAI/2.0/open archivesprotocol.htm*

Leymann, F. (2001, May). *Web services flow language (WSFL 1.0).* IBM.

Library of Congress. (2003). *ZING Z39.50 International: Next generation.* Retrieved November 7, 2003, from the World Wide Web: *http://www.loc.gov/z3950/agency/zing/zing-home.html*

Liu, X., Maly, K., Zubair, M., & Nelson, M. L. (2001). Arc: An OAI service provider for cross-archive searching. *Proceedings of First ACM/IEEE-CS Joint Conference on Digital Libraries* (pp. 65-66). Roanoke, Virginia, USA, June 24-28.

Madalli, D. P. et al. (2003). *Subject based domain search system.* Paper based on internal project report of CS department, Virginia Tech, Blacksburg, Virginia (unpublished).

Maly, K., Zubair, M., & Liu, X. (2001, April). Kepler: An OAI data/service provider for the individual. *D-Lib Magazine, 7*(4). Retrieved March 4, 2004, from the World Wide Web: *http://www.dlib.org/dlib/april01/maly/04maly.html*

Merchant, B., Gaylord, M., & Congia, S. (2003). *SOAPifying the Open Archives*. Technical Report CS03-13-00. Cape Town: Department of Computer Science, University of Cape Town.

Papazoglou, M. P., & Georgakopoulos, D. (2003). Service-oriented computing. *Communications of the ACM, 46*(10), 25-28.

Payette, S., Blanchi, C., Lagoze, C., & Overly, E. A. (1999, May). Interoperability for digital objects and repositories: The Cornell/CNRI experiments. *D-Lib Magazine, 5*(5). Retrieved November 7, 2003, from the World Wide Web: *http://www.dlib.org/dlib/may99/payette/05payette.html*

Suleman, H., & Fox, E. A. (2001, December). A framework for building open digital libraries. *D-Lib Magazine, 7*(12). Retrieved November 5, 2003, from the World Wide Web: *http://www.dlib.org/dlib/december01/suleman/12suleman.html*

Tudhope, D., & Cunliffe, D. (2001). Editorial: Introduction to theme on digital libraries. *The New Review of Hypermedia and Multimedia, 7*. Retrieved June 11, 2003, from the World Wide Web: *http://www.comp.glam.ac.uk/~NRHM/volume7/e-2001.htm*

Winer, D. (2002). *RSS 2.0 Specification*. Retrieved November 5, 2003, from the World Wide Web: *http://blogs.law.harvard.edu/tech/rss*

Chapter III

Development of Indonesia's National Digital Library Network

Ismail Fahmi
Institut Teknologi Bandung, Indonesia

Abstract

This chapter describes various technical and social issues in the development of the Indonesia's National Digital Library Network (IndonesiaDLN). The success of the network was attributed to the use of the Protocol for Metadata Posting (PMP) to allow member institutions without a permanent Internet connection to join the digital library (DL) network, the use and distribution of open source software, and the application of the Network of Networks concept that motivated and permitted communities to develop their own DL networks that are integrated to the IndonesiaDLN. Such a network model and lessons learned should prove invaluable when shared with third-world or developing countries on similar journeys to develop national DLs.

Introduction

Budgets for libraries in Indonesia are very small and this influences their ability to provide information for users. According to the Indonesian University Libraries Forum (FPPTI), every university in Indonesia should allocate 5% of its budget for the library. A survey by this forum in 2003 showed that only five of 125 universities had managed to follow such a recommendation while 40% of them allocated less than 2%. With this condition it is very difficult for the libraries to achieve a standard set by the Ministry of National Education to provide minimum of two book titles for every course and to cover 10% of their students (Media Indonesia, 2003).

Apparently, electronic journal subscriptions are also very limited at most university libraries in Indonesia. In 2001, the Indonesian Cyber-library Society (ICS) submitted a proposal to several big universities to subscribe the electronic journals as a consortium (Liawatimena, 2002). Nonetheless, the limitation of budgets and the lack of wide availability of the Internet access were reasons why these institutions did not consider such a consortium.

Realizing this limitation, a librarian and IT professionals' meeting was convened to discuss the development of a national digital library network in Bandung in October 2000 (Fahmi et al., 2000). The main goal was to develop an innovative and collaborative strategy to acquire, maintain, and share local resources. As the ultimate result, they initiated the development of a digital library (DL) network

Figure 1. Map of the Indonesia's islands that denotes the location of the IndonesiaDLN members

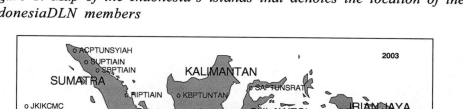

known as the Indonesia Digital Library Network (IndonesiaDLN). This was developed using an open source software known as the Genasha Digital Library (GDL, *http://gdl.itb.ac.id*). It was expected that by sharing local resources, students from one institution would be able to improve their information literacy by utilizing resources from other institutions. IndonesiaDLN can therefore be seen as a network that integrates DLs of many institutions in Indonesia by collecting and sharing their local resources. Through every DL server, a user can browse, search, and download any resources shared by the IndonesiaDLN members.

The growth of this DL network was significantly fast. Within three years of its launch in 2001, the number of new DLs that were developed and joined the network has reached more than 90. As shown in *Figure 1*, these are distributed over all big islands of Indonesia (i.e., Java, Sumatra, Kalimantan, Sulawesi, and Irian Jaya). Every member in the map is denoted by a PublisherID following a standard convention. The majority members of IndonesiaDLN are from universities while others comprise both government and non-government organizations and individuals.

This earlier initiative was followed by other initiatives such as the development of regional and community based DL networks. For example, the Environmental Digital Library Network (JPLH, *http://lco.jplh.or.id*) and Muhammadiyah Digital Library Network (MDLN) are both community-based DL networks established in 2003, while the Public University Link System of East Java (PULSE, *http://www.pulse.web.id*) is a regional-based initiative of eight universities in East Java.

This chapter describes our proposed solution to integrate the Indonesian library resources under the situation where budgets and Internet access for libraries are still very limited. We start this discussion by describing related DL initiatives at the international, regional, and national level. The challenges that will be addressed are explained, which then lead to the concept and design of the network. We emphasize our focus on the technical aspect of the IndonesiaDLN, including the network model, metadata standards, metadata exchange protocol and implementation. The statistics of its usage, problems, future works, and conclusion is also addressed in this chapter.

Related Works

In 1996, the National Digital Library of Theses and Dissertations (NDLTD) was launched by the Virginia Tech project team to improve graduate education in the U.S. Due to wider international interests, the NDLTD was renamed in 1997 as the Networked Digital Library of Theses and Dissertations (Fox, 1999). When the IndonesiaDLN was established in 2000, NDLTD already had more than 70 members across different countries. They published and shared their collections within the network. This shows that developing a DL is not merely about developing an independent system but part of a global information infrastructure.

Many discussions and efforts have been made to develop a DL framework that can lead to the specification of protocols when various components are involved and many DL servers are integrated (Fox, 1999b). For example, Powell (1998) developed a scalable system for searching heterogeneous multilingual collections on the World Wide Web and the first production was actually the NDLTD Federated Search. Another initiative that produced a protocol for metadata harvesting over various repository configurations is the Open Archive Initiative (OAI). The OAI Protocol for Metadata Harvesting (OAI-PMH) provides an application-independent interoperability framework based on a metadata harvesting mechanism (OAI, 2003). The protocol has been developed since 1999 and the latest version, Protocol version 2, was released in February 2003. The number of institutions that have adopted this protocol is increasing rapidly.

One country in the South East Asia region that has been involved with the NDLTD since its inception is Singapore. In 1997, it signed a collaborative research on DL with the U.S., especially in building a distributed content management system that will handle bibliographic, multilingual, full-text, image, and video information and to provide for search and distribution of such information easily across thousands of universities. This DL network uses the very high-speed Internet connection between SINGAREN (Singapore Internet Next Generation Advanced Research and Education Network) and vBNS (very high-performance Broadband Network Service) (Virginia Tech News and Information, 1997).

Unfortunately, such initiatives are not immediately suitable for Indonesia. They require DL members to have dedicated Internet connection for 24 hours a day for seven days of the week (24/7). This requirement is difficult for Indonesia to achieve because more than 50% of the IndonesiaDLN members are connected to the Internet using dial-up connections (64 Kbps). As such, there was a need to find another alternative solution for libraries in Indonesia.

The Gyandoot Digital Library, a rural DL government initiative in India, is a good example on how to develop a DL network in a place with very low Internet density, such as in a rural area. The Indian government is making efforts for the establishment of regional rural cybercafes (144 Kbps) to provide services to people in the region. A local village DL in the cybercafe keeps the village people updated about water tanker schedule, workforce database, and other public information. Since the cost of Gyandoot operation for most villagers is high, Gyandoot is seen as an important development for basic service (e.g., e-mail, government database) rather than as a high-end application (Sharma & Yurcik, 2000).

The Indonesian government also initiated a similar effort in 2001, with the development of Warintek (Warung Informasi Teknologi "The Information Technology Kiosk"). The government provided grants to the universities, research institutions, and private sector to develop the Internet kiosks. The program aimed to act as an integrated information service to draw scientific information nearer to all facets of society, both in rural and urban places, thereby supporting the information needs of SMEs and cooperatives (Minister of State for Research and Technology, 2001).

One year before IndonesiaDLN was established in 2000, there had been a virtual library network initiative known as the Indonesian Christian University Virtual Library (InCU-VL, *http://incuvl.petra.ac.id*). Pioneered by the Petra Christian University in Surabaya, the network was originally intended to serve the Christian universities community. It later became known as the SPEKTRA Virtual Library (SVL, *http://svl.petra.ac.id*) after it broadened the scope of its members. Institutions can join the SVL by acquiring and using the SPEKTRA proprietary software. Currently, there is no automatic mechanism for the institution's SVL server to share its metadata to other SVL servers. The process of creating a union database was to upload database records manually to a SVL central server through an online Web interface.

The solution that we proposed and selected for the DL network in Indonesia is unique. It adopts the latest DL network solution (i.e., OAI protocol) but still accommodates libraries with very limited resources to join the network. It can make use of existing DL infrastructure such as the Warintek, and at same time, is still able to communicate with existing DL networks such as the SVL.

Concept and Design

Societies or communities that became target members of the IndonesiaDLN include individuals and institutions that want to share and get information through the network. They are not limited to academic and research communities so that any party that wants to join the knowledge sharing initiative can become members. Currently, communities that have expressed their interests to join the network include schools, universities, research institutions, government and non-government organizations, small and medium enterprises, and others.

Their knowledge domains are heterogeneous including children's education, heritage, agriculture, health, theses and dissertations, and etcetera. Thus, the type and format of digital resources also vary. These include text, audio, video, image, source codes, and so on. As long as the resources were created and owned by the members, or the copyright allows these resources to be disseminated publicly, IndonesiaDLN members will share and have access to them.

The Network Model

The IndonesiaDLN network model is designed to solve challenges related to the technical and social issues. The first challenge is related to the condition of the information technology infrastructure of the majority of libraries in Indonesia. Due to very limited budgets, few libraries from big universities and institutions have good Internet access. Thus, the network model should be able to accommodate those having only dial-up connectivity and access.

The social challenge is not easy to solve since it is related to the willingness of communities to share their information resources. To motivate and enforce them to join the knowledge sharing initiative, the concept is developed based on a sociological aspect of their communication nature. Usually, people from the same community will have frequent interaction among themselves rather than with people from other communities. Instead of inviting them into one big network, we propose the development of sub-networks that consist of various community members. They can be grouped together into a cluster network

Figure 2. IndonesiaDLN bridges the networks of digital libraries through a network of networks

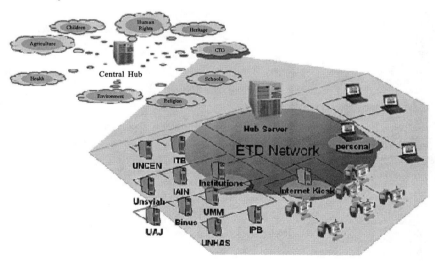

according to their knowledge domains or regions. For example, there can be networks of agriculture, health, children, East Java universities, and so on.

Each cluster will manage its own activities, including registration of new nodes, managing users, maintaining cluster hub server, socialization of the knowledge sharing initiative, and provide services to its users. By bringing such administration requirements to the cluster level, it will decrease the workload at the central network of the IndonesiaDLN, and give more flexibility and room for each group's initiatives and activities. In this instance, IndonesiaDLN will act as a

Figure 3. Metadata in XML format provides short description about a digital resource and links to its related files

```xml
<dc>
  <title>Zebra bermimpi tentang kebun binatang</title>
  <creator>Ainun Sabila Hamdillah</creator>
  <creator>
     <orgname>Ismail_Family</orgname>
  </creator>
  <publisher>JBKLISMAIL</publisher>
  <subject>
     <keywords>zebra, kebun binatang, gambar anak</keywords>
  </subject>
  <description>Lala menggambar zebra yang sedang bermimpi tentang kebun
     binatang. Ada bonbin berbentuk rectangle dan circle. Ada rumah zebra,
     yang di dalamnya ada rumput berbentuk triangle.</description>
  <contributor>
     <modifiedby>i.fahmi@let.rug.nl</modifiedby>
  </contributor>
  <date>2003-04-10</date>
  <date>
     <modified>2003-08-07 18:06:01</modified>
  </date>
  <type>image</type>
  <type>
     <schema>dc_image</schema>
  </type>
  <identifier>jbklismail-gdl-image-2003-ainunsabil-2</identifier>
  <identifier>
     <hierarchy>/Activities/Ainun_Sabila_Hamdillah_Ismail/2003/4-April/</hierarchy>
  </identifier>
  <source></source>
  <language>Bahasa Indonesia</language>
  <relation>
     <count>2</count>
  </relation>
  <relation>
     <no>1</no>
     <datemodified>2003-08-07 16:55:08</datemodified>
     <haspart>jbklismail-gdl-image-2003-ainunsabil-2-bonbin.jpg</haspart>
     <haspath>files/disk1/1/jbklismail-gdl-image-2003-ainunsabil-2-bonbin.jpg</haspath>
     <hasfilename>bonbin.jpg</hasfilename>
     <hasformat>image/pjpeg</hasformat>
     <hassize>159440</hassize>
     <hasuri>/download.php?id=jbklismail-gdl-image-2003-ainunsabil-2&amp;no=1</hasuri>
     <hasnote>Zebra sedang bermimpi tentang berbagai bentuk kebun binatang.</hasnote>
  </relation>
  <relation>
     <no>2</no>
     [related file #2]
  </relation>
  <rights></rights>
</dc>
```

bridge for these sub-networks and finally will consist of networks of DLs, or become a network of networks (NeONs), as shown by *Figure 2* (Fahmi, 2003). In this example, it consists of a central hub server and nine clusters. The figure also shows an example of the ETD (Electronic Theses and Dissertation) cluster network. This cluster consists of nine university nodes, four individual nodes, and an Internet kiosk. It has one cluster hub server that bridges their resource exchanges.

How Does the IndonesiaDLN Work?

Metadata and Resources

A DL system manages various digital resources such as documents, images, audios, videos, or source codes. Every resource consists of one or more files that are represented by one metadata. In practice, metadata is defined as a structured set of descriptive elements to describe an information resource or any definable entity.

We use the Dublin Core metadata specification to describe digital resources. This specification contains 15 element terms that include the title, creator,

Figure 4. IndonesiaDLN uses both protocols for metadata posting and harvesting to disseminate the metadata

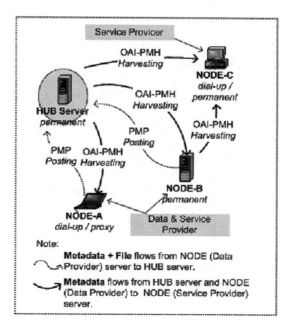

subject, description, publisher, contributor, date, type, format, identifier, source, language, relation, coverage, and rights (DCMI, 2003). In our implementation, we added several sub-elements to accommodate more detailed information about a resource.

The XML format is used to encode the metadata as shown by *Figure 3*. This metadata describes a children's drawing (*image*) entitled *Zebra bermimpi tentang kebun binatang* "A zebra is dreaming about a zoo" (*title*) that contains two image files (*relation*). The metadata also provides other information, such as creator, publisher's identifier, subject, description, contributor's e-mail, date, metadata's identifier, source, language, and rights.

Identifier

The metadata in *Figure 3* describes important information about identifiers. There are two important identifiers in the form of the publisher's identifier (e.g., *JBKLISMAIL*) and metadata's identifier (e.g., jbklismail-gdl-image-2003-ainunsabil-2).

Every node (publisher) in IndonesiaDLN should have a unique identifier, which is required when it exchanges metadata with other nodes. We follow the existing library code convention that was suggested by the National Library of Indonesia to identify every library using a unique code. The code contains information about library's location, type of its institution, and institution name. For example *JBPTITB* is code for ITB Central Library, where JB stands for *Jawa Barat* "West Java" (*location*), PT for *Perguruan Tinggi* "University" (*type*), and ITB for Institute of Technology Bandung (*name*). Thus, JBKLISMAIL in the example means JB for *Jawa Barat* (*location*), KL for *Keluarga* "Family" (*type*), and ISMAIL for individual name.

The construction of a metadata identifier, for example, *jbklismail-gdl-image-2003-ainunsabil-2*, uses the publisher's identifier. It contains information about the publisher (e.g., *jbklismail*), DL software name (e.g., *gdl* "Ganesha Digital Library"), type of the resource (e.g., *image*), year of creation (e.g., *2003*), creator's name (e.g., *ainunsabil*), and record sequence number (e.g., *2*). With this naming model, it would be fast and easy to extract important information about a metadata only by just reading and parsing its identifier.

Implementation of OAI Requests and Responses Protocol

We only disseminate the metadata which size is normally smaller than the described file. The resource file itself will remain in its original server. If the

Figure 5. An example of a request and response strings for the PutListRecords verb

```
HTTP POST Header
POST http://agri/web/OAI-v2-script.php?verb=PutListRecords&
PHPSESSID=fa19ac4cba0ef1edbe43c3a1fa5d4eaa&countRecords=30&resumptionToken=0
HTTP/1.0 Content-type: application/x-www-form-urlencoded Content-length: 42181

HTTP POST Data
<?xml version="1.0" encoding="UTF-8"?>
<OAI-PMP xmlns="http://www.indonesiadln.org/OAI/1.0/"
      xmlns:xsi="http://www.w3.org/2001/XMLSchema-instance"
      xsi:schemaLocation="http://www.indonesiadln.org/OAI/1.0/
      http://www.indonesiadln.org/OAI/1.0/OAI-PMP.xsd">
  <requestDate>2004-03-20T08:38:30Z</requestDate>
  <PutListRecords>
   <record>
      <header>
         <identifier>jbklismail-gdl-image-2003-ainunsabil-2</identifier>
         <status></status>
         <datestamp>2003-08-07 11:49:00</datestamp>
      </header>
      <metadata>
         [metadata...]
      </metadata>
   </record>

   <record>
      [next records...]
   </record>

  </PutListRecords>
</OAI-PMP>
```

server is not connected to the Internet in 24/7, its administrator can mirror the files into its hub server.

Figure 4 shows how the metadata and files are stored and exchanged. It illustrates the example of a cluster network in IndonesiaDLN that consists of a hub server and three node servers (A, B, and C). The nodes may use a permanent (B) or a temporary (A and C) connection to the Internet.

The metadata exchange process is started when a data provider (A or B) stores digital resources containing a metadata and file(s). It posts the metadata into a hub server, using the Protocol for Metadata Posting (OAI-PMP). This protocol is developed specifically for the IndonesiaDLN by adapting the OAI protocol for Metadata Harvesting (OAI-PMH) (Fahmi et al., 2002).

OAI is an international effort to develop a standard for metadata harvesting protocol among DL servers (OAI, 2003). The protocol is very simple, which is based on requests and responses services on top of the HTTP protocol. When we developed the IndonesiaDLN, the metadata posting services were not supported by the OAI-PMH. For this reason, we had to develop the metadata posting services (OAI-PMP) for our implementation.

All nodes are allowed to make mirrors of the union collection into their local repositories, using the Protocol for Metadata Harvesting (OAI-PMH). They can provide searching and browsing services over all metadata collection for their users. Whenever users need to download related files, they will be redirected to the original location of the files.

The OAI-PMH provides five request verbs, namely, *GetRecord, Identify, ListIdentifiers, ListMetadataFormats, ListRecords,* and *ListSets* (OAI, 2003). For our implementation, we added six request verbs that include *Connect, Disconnect, PutRecord, PutListRecords, PutFileFragment,* and *MergeFileFragments.* These verbs are referred to as OAI-PMP services (Fahmi, 2002).

The first two verbs of the OAI-PMP, Connect and Disconnect, are intended for a server authentication before it is allowed to post and harvest metadata from other servers. The server uses PutRecord and PutListRecords verbs for posting one or more metadata at a time. The last two verbs, PutFileFragment and MergeFileFragments are used for the file posting purpose.

Figure 6. Screenshot of the GDL shows the list of the DL nodes and the number of the shared metadata

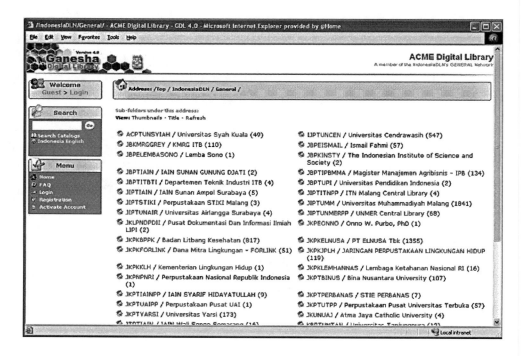

The HTTP POST method is implemented for the PutRecord and PutListRecords verb by using the content-type "application/x-www-form-urlencoded" argument.

Figure 5 shows a detailed request and response of the PutListRecords verb. This verb requires three arguments, that is, PHPSESSID, countRecords, and resumptionToken. In this example, a node is sending maximally 30 metadata records to the "agri" hub server. Each record contains information about metadata header including the identifier, status, datestamp, and metadata content (refer to the example of this metadata in *Figure 3*).

For the PutFileFragment verb, the HTTP POST method is implemented with content-type "multipart/form-data." The file is sent fragment-by-fragment to a hub server whose size can be adjusted according to the Internet bandwidth of the node, such as 10KBytes, 20KBytes, 50 Kbytes, and so on.

Implementation

To provide an idea of the usage of IndonesiaDLN, some statistics of the implementation are presented in this section. These were processed from the access data of the central hub server *(http://gdlhub.indonesiadln.org)* and ITB node server *(http://digilib.itb.ac.id)*, which were collected since the beginning of the IndonesiaDLN operation from May 17, 2001 to June 13, 2003.

The Open Source Software

The first software developed for the IndonesiaDLN is the Ganesha Digital Library (GDL). It is distributed as an open source software and can be downloaded for free from *http://gdl.itb.ac.id* (GDL, 2003). It is written using the PHP scripting language *(www.php.net)* and uses the MySQL (www.mysql.com) database and the Simple Web Indexing for Humans – Enhanced (SWISH-E, *www.swish-e.org*), the software for indexing and searching the metadata.

Figure 6 shows a screenshot of the GDL interface, which was installed by ACME Digital Library (an anonymous institution). It displays a list of DL nodes in the IndonesiaDLN from which their metadata has been harvested by this institution. Each item contains a Publisher ID, institution name, number of the shared metadata and links to its deeper sub-categories.

The user can read the detailed metadata and download the related files. The download links will guide the user to the source server that stores the files. The administrators can activate or disable the authentication module if they want to restrict or provide access to the files.

Profiles and Activities

In this reporting period, there are 94 nodes registered at the central hub. Based on their Internet connection, 50 nodes utilize permanent connections while 44 nodes use dial-up connections. This data confirm the technical challenge faced by the IndonesiaDLN as previously described in this chapter.

There are five nodes that share more than 500 metadata records, 12 nodes share more than 100 metadata records, and 22 nodes share more than 30 metadata records. The top five nodes are University of Muhammadiyah Malang (JIPTUMM), Institut of Technology Bandung (JBPTITBPP), Elnusa (JKPKELNUSA), Indonesian Health Research (JKPKBPPK), and University of Cendrawasih (UNCEN). The last node is located at the eastern most of the Indonesia's archipelago and used a dial-up connection (which has now been improved by using a satellite connection).

Most of our users are from Indonesia (98%). Other countries that contribute 10 to 20 users are from Malaysia, Japan, Australia, Singapore, Germany, U.S., U.K., Canada, and India.

There are ten universities that have contributed more than 50 users. The biggest three universities are ITB, UMM, and IPB (Agricultural Institute of Bogor). Other users are from hundreds of education institutions, private companies, organizations, and individuals. Most of the current users are undergraduate students. An interesting observation is that users from private companies are ranked second. They could be tapping into these resources for learning purposes to support their work needs. This information should become a strong motivation for members to provide more resources in their DLs and, more importantly, to provide services to their users.

There are more than 100 teachers and 90 students from schools that have become users. The actual number is likely to be higher since the data reported so far was collected only from central hub and not all members would actively send their users' data to the central hub. This data shows that the school community is also interested to reap benefits from the DL networks, and thus provide more impetus to continue developing and making resources accessible for children and schools.

Figure 7. Cumulative and anonymous accesses to the hub server and node server

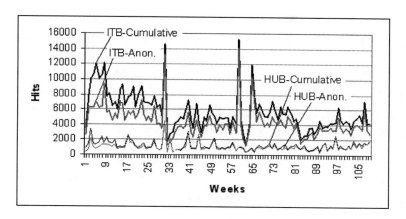

Utilization and Behavior

The utilization of the collection at the central hub and at the nodes is compared in *Figure 7*. The highest line indicates access to the node server (ITB), while the lowest line indicates accesses to the hub server by anonymous users and all users (cumulative). The accesses to the node server are higher compared with the accesses to the hub server. This information signifies that services for users will be highly concentrated at the nodes level. They will experience faster and better accesses from their closer nodes.

The fluctuation of the accesses is closer to the anonymous accesses. This means that users prefer to access the collections anonymously. Searching, browsing, and viewing metadata that do not need an authentication seem to be the most frequent activities.

There are two peaks in the figure that relate to the socialization and advertisement of the IndonesiaDLN during its second (Week 33) and third (Week 60) annual meeting. The lowest access after the meetings was around the New Year holiday period. During other weeks, average accesses were similar. This trend implies the need to promote the network more intensively in order to increase the utilization and pervasiveness of the DL.

Conclusion and Future Work

Although the IndonesiaDLN is just three years old since its inception in 2001, it has garnered much interest from many institutions that have now become members. Many problems, especially technical ones, have been encountered and resolved. Non-technical issues continue to dominate and pose a challenge as IndonesiaDLN strives to achieve an open and sustainable consortium in future.

We have developed a Network of Networks (NeONs) concept, where every different community can develop its own DL network, manage its knowledge process and sharing, and provide services to its nodes and users. We are in progress of implementing this concept and the GDL software has been improved to accommodate it. It is interesting to note that the sustainability of the network is mainly due to the distribution of the code as open source (Purbo, 2004).

The networking model using the OAI protocol has shown its ability to integrate DLs with very limited Internet access into a big network, where nearly 50% of our members are using dial-up connection. This situation is common in most developing countries. We expect our experience in developing a nation-wide DL network to be invaluable when shared with third-world or developing countries on similar journeys.

The next important stage of work is to define a national framework of DL network systems, which is more open, robust, and accommodative. While most of the institutions in IndonesiaDLN opted to choose the easier way by adopting the existing GDL software, some big institutions preferred to develop their own systems. An integrating national framework of DL network systems is thus an important activity to bring these efforts together into a collaborative and constructive manner to realize better DLs and, ultimately, information sharing in the future.

Acknowledgments

The work described in this chapter was sponsored by the International Development Research Center (IDRC), Canada under the CCOHS Project Number: 001.1.2, and by the Indonesian Foundation for Telecommunication and Information Research (YLTI), Indonesia, under the grant number: YLTI.04/HK/PRG-Lbry/2000.

References

DCMI. (2003, November 19). Dublin Core Metadata Initiative (DCMI) Metadata Terms. Retrieved March 20, 2004, from the World Wide Web: *http://dublincore.org/documents/dcmi-terms/*

Fahmi, I. (2003). The network of networks (NeONs). In *The Fourth IndonesiaDLN Meeting*, Institut Teknologi Surabaya, Surabaya.

Fahmi, I., Muharto, R., & Ibrahim, I.K. (2002). Extending the OAI protocol as the data integration framework for the digital library network in the third world. In *Proceeding iiWAS 4ᵗʰ Conference*, Bandung, Indonesia, September 12, 2002.

Fahmi, I., Utama, M.C., & Dwiyanto, A.R. (2000, October 3-4). IndonesiaDLN Meeting Report. In meeting report, IndonesiaDLN, Bandung, Indonesia, October 2000.

Fox, E. A. (1999). *FIPSE final report: Improving graduate education with the National Digital Library of Theses and Dissertations*. Retrieved October 10, 2003, from the World Wide Web: *http://www.ndltd.org/pubs/FIPSEfr.pdf*

Fox, E. A. (1999b). Digital libraries. In R.B. Yates & B. R. Neto (Eds.), *Modern information retrieval* (pp. 415-432). New York: Addison Wesley.

Liawatimena, S. (2002). Inisiatif berlangganan database secara konsorsium level nasional "An initiative to subscribe the electronic journal as a consortium." In *The Third IndonesiaDLN Meeting*, Bandung, Indonesia, April 2002.

OAI. (2003, February). The Open Archives Initiative Protocol for Metadata Harvesting. Retrieved October 16, 2003, from the World Wide Web: *http://www.openarchives.org/OAI/openarchivesprotocol.html*

Perpustakaan Perguruan Tinggi belum Maksimal "University libraries is not yet maximum." (2003, September 24). *Media Indonesia*. Retrieved March 16, 2004, from the World Wide Web: *http://www.mediaindo.co.id/cetak/berita.asp?id=20030924035233393*

Purbo, O. W. (2004). When east meet west: In ICT4D. IDRC Sabbatical paper. Retrieved March 25, 2004, from the World Wide Web: *http://sandbox.bellanet.org/~onno/ict4d-roadmap/when-east-meet-west-in-ict4d.doc*

Speech of the Minister of State for Research and Technology, RI. (2001, February 27). Retrieved March 24, 2004, from the World Wide Web: *http://www.warintek.net/spe_menristek.htm*

Virginia Tech signs digital library research agreement with Singapore. (1997, November 13). *Virginia Tech News and Information*. Retrieved March 24, 2004, from the World Wide Web: *http://www.technews.vt.edu/Archives/1997/Nov/97463.html*

Chapter IV

Dynamic Metadata Management System for Digital Archives:
Design and Construction

Shien-chiang Yu
Shih Hsin University, Taiwan

Hsueh-hua Chen
National Taiwan University, Taiwan

Chao-chen Chen
National Taiwan Normal University, Taiwan

Abstract

This chapter describes metalogy, an XML/metadata framework that can handle several different metadata formats. Metalogy was developed under the Digital Museum Project funded by the National Science Council of Taiwan. It is common to have different data types and catalog formats even within one organization. In order to accommodate a variety of objects, it is often necessary to adopt several metadata formats. Thus, when designing a metadata management system, one needs to be able to handle heterogeneous metadata formats. XML, being a standard gaining increasing popularity, is also often used as data format so that exchange between data can be done in a uniform way.

Introduction

The rapid advancement of information technologies has led to new architecture and format for managing all disciplines. This significantly enhances the performance of the operation and management. However, different formats may crucially affect system integration and information sharing among different institutions. Although current information structure can serve the need of printing and audio/video media, its scope should be much broader because of the evolutional changes of applications and development of electronic publication, user interface, and information media. It is therefore necessary to develop a new information operation model that can effectively reduce the cost of system development and automate data management.

Metadata, a traditional tool of libraries, is playing a fundamental role of information organization of digital content. It has, therefore, become an important part of the global information construction in planning, processing, restoring, and managing.

A number of metadata tools are presented in IFLANET (IFLA, 2003). By using these metadata tools, the metadata of heterogeneous documents can be input and managed. These tools are listed below:

- Distributed Systems Technology Center (DTSC). Reggie - The Metadata Editor. URL: *http://metadata.net/dstc/*.

- Interleaf. URL: *http://www.interleaf.com/products/*.

- Jenkins, Charlotte. Automatic RDF Metadata Generator. URL: *http://scitsd.wlv.ac.uk:8080/metadata.html*.

- MARC.pm. URL: *http://marcpm.sourceforge.net*.

- MetaManage. URL: *http://www.metamanage.com/*.

- Nordic Metadata Project. Dublin Core Metadata Template. URL: *http://www.lub.lu.se/metadata/DC_creator.html*.

- SafeSurf. Meta Generator. URL: *http://www.safesurf.com/classify/index.html*.

- U.K. Office for Library and Information Networking (UKOLN). DC-dot. Dublin Core Generator. URL: *http://www.ukoln.ac.uk/metadata/dcdot*.

- U.K. Office for Library and Information Networking (UKOLN). Metadata Software Tools. URL: *http://www.ukoln.ac.uk/metadata/software-tools*.

The Dublin Core Metadata Initiative Web site further classifies metadata tools into following categories (DCMI, 2004):

- Creating Metadata (Templates)
- Tools for the Creation/Change of Templates
- Automatic Extraction/Gathering of Metadata
- Automatic Production of Metadata
- Conversion Between Metadata Formats
- Integrated (Tool) Environments
- Commercially Available Software

It is common to have different data types and catalog formats even within one organization. In order to accommodate a variety of objects, it is often necessary to adopt several metadata formats. The co-existence of different metadata formats and the need to deal with them is an important difference between a digital library and a conventional library.

In order to manage the integration and exchange of objects with different metadata formats, our studies use XML as the data format. Through a complete hierarchical tree structure, we use several XML schemas to define the attributes of the internal data elements, and to solve the problem of storing heterogeneous metadata in a relational database. This method also allows us to provide uniform retrieval as well as authority control.

Concept and Characteristics

In 1997, the National Taiwan University (NTU) initiated a metadata research project, ROSS (*http://ross.lis.ntu.edu.tw*), under the National Taiwan University Digital Library/Museum (NTUDL/M) Project to study metadata interchange for Chinese information (MICI). Its research purpose contains the following (Chen et al., 2001):

- To study existing metadata formats both domestically and internationally;
- To understand the history and features of collections;
- To understand the relation among different metadata, database and system framework; and
- To understand the information needs and retrieval behavior of potential users.

At that time, most digital collections and archives of NTUDL/M were historical documents. Besides historical documents, ROSS began work on metadata for other resource types (objects, ancient maps, photos/pictures, and butterfly specimens) in November 1998. During the process of metadata development, in addition to frequent discussions with experts and scholars, we studied how similar digital museums cataloged their collections. In the first year, ROSS was responsible for metadata development for two of the National Science Council (NSC) topic-based projects, *Discovery of the Tamsui River* and *Butterfly Ecology*. In the second year, the main task of ROSS was to develop a management system capable of handling various types of metadata for all topic-based projects. This system is called "Metalogy" (Chen et al., 2002).

In this section, we will discuss issues related to the development of "Metalogy" systems based on XML Schema to control and manage the different types of metadata. The main design points are focused on structure, authority control, depth, scope, and database technical requirements. The design concept and principles are described as follows (Yu et al., 2003).

Structure

Metadata is employed to describe the resources. In cross-referring most of the currently used or recognized metadata definitions, it is found that they contain almost the same kind of structure. The only differences among metadata are the complexity and the design point of view. The major execution capabilities of handling metadata include functionality of parser for well-formed XML and an authoring tool for editing and validating the XML Schema structure.

Authority Control

Traditionally, the purpose of authority control has been to bring consistency to library catalogs. The authority control process is directed at the access points contained in catalog records, that is, names, titles, and subjects. It ensures that these access points are unique and consistent in content and form, and provides a network of linkages for variant and related headings in the catalog. It supports the finding task by ensuring that each entity has a unique name, only one name is used for each entity, variant name forms are represented and linked in some way, and that related names, titles, and subjects are collocated in the catalog (Vellucci, 2000).

Depth

Metadata describes the attributes and characteristics of the resource. It differs little from the purposes of the library category. Fields are based on hierarchical structure and subdivided downward. It builds up the subordinate relationships between elements and sub-elements. Each element's character relies on the attribute value. Basically, there are two sorts of fields: fixed-length fields and variable fields. Fixed-length fields include general types (e.g., ID number, ISBN, ISSN) and character-indication types (e.g., MARC 21's 008 "GENERAL INFORMATION" tag. Each character position contains its special meaning and range.) Sub-field of a field be it fixed-length fields or variable fields, shall allow both fixed-length and variable fields. According to the reason above, the process ability of the system must cover the situations.

Scope

Metadata not only describes the information resource, but more important it marks the relationship between objects. Metadata emphasizes on the description of the data instance itself and also explains the relationship among different metadata. The cascading connections must evolve from a simple object to time, space, people, and event. Thus, the "Metalogy" system must consider the scope of different applications:

- *Various formats of metadata.* Single metadata cannot meet the needs of digital archive application. The single data recording method cannot even cover the basic needs of the library category. For handling various metadata formats, it needs a super-metadata system to do this. The system analysis of "Multiple Metadata Co-existence" is based on this demand.

- *Various types of users.* Generally, users only wish to know what objects (resources) they can obtain. Nevertheless, users performing searches might retrieve extended documents. The system analysis of "User Inter-face" is based on this demand.

- *Various types of resources.* Some resources may have the constraints of time and space. For example, a certain resource may only be effective in a very short time period, like weather information. Some resources are used only for research institutions and some only for business companies. Some are simple and some are extremely complicated. All these different types of resources may be recorded in the same system according to their practical needs. The system analysis of "Authority Control" is based on this demand.

- *Various data suppliers.* Different institutions of digital archives produce various data, which need to be digitalized. The metadata, built among institutions, should be exchangeable among each other. Therefore, a system must keep the structure of metadata and supply channels for exchange or connection to outside resources. The system analysis of "Import/Export" is based on this demand.

Database Technical Specification

The XML and XML Schema use a hierarchical structure. A relational database system is based on the relationship between tables. Thus, the database structure of this system building the relational tables shall meet the following three criteria:

- Relational database tables with the ability to store hierarchical structure through XML and XML Schema.
- Index tables for different access points while restoring and managing metadata.
- Tables for authority control with different access points.

The methodology of database design is using a linked list structure (Kruse et al., 1997). The idea of a linked list, for every metadata in the list, is to put a pointer into the structure giving the location of the next structure in the list. In this way, metadata can remain in columns of tables in databases to fulfill the hierarchical structure, and every field of metadata can link to another metadata.

System Design Notation: UML

Software inspection is regarded as one of the most effective methods for software quality improvement. To fully fulfill this role, however, a software inspection must involve a thorough and detailed examination of the inspected document. This requires reading techniques that tell inspection participants what to look for and how to scrutinize software documents in a systematic manner. Unfortunately, few reading techniques are available for defect detection in documents created according to object-oriented principles.

Unified Modeling Language (UML) is a modeling language that can be used for both business modeling and software engineering. It is a graphical language for visualizing, specifying, constructing, and documenting the artifacts of a software-intensive system. The UML was adopted as a standard by the Object

Management Group (OMG) in November 1997 and now serves as the standard language of blueprints for software (Booch et al., 1999).

UML is now the object-oriented industry standard modeling language. It started out as collaboration among three outstanding methodologists: Grady Booch, Ivar Jacobson, and James Rumbaugh (Kobryn, 1999). In the past, there was no common object-oriented industry standard in analysis and design for software engineering. Because of the size and complexity of modern software systems, software development is a team endeavor. Larger teams face aggravated communication challenges especially when the teams are geographically scattered or use different standards. UML provides a single, common modeling language that is usable across many technologies, for the entire lifecycle, and in different implementation methods. It facilitates communications with all members of the development team.

As shown in *Figure 1*, because different participants (e.g., the system analysts, the designers, the end users, etc.) have different concerns and because the system is quite complex, multiple views are required to represent architecture adequately. An architectural view is a simplified description of a system from a particular perspective or advantage point, covering particular concerns, and omitting entities that are not relevant to this perspective. Thus, UML identities use five views as a standard set: Logical view, Implementation view, Process view, Deployment view, and Use-Case view. In addition, there are nine key diagrams included in these views (Hunt, 2000):

1.   *Class diagram:* Describes the structure of a system. The structures are built from classes and relationships. The classes can represent and structure information, products, documents, or organizations.

Figure 1. UML provides rich notation that includes nine key diagram in five views

Logical view	Implementation view
Class diagram Object diagram	Component diagram

User view
User case diagram

Process view	Deployment view
Sequence diagram Collaboration diagram State diagram Activity diagram	Deployment diagram

2. *Object diagram:* Expresses possible object combinations of a specific class diagram. It is typically used to exemplify a class diagram.

3. *State diagram:* Expresses possible states of a class (or a system).

4. *Activity diagram:* Describes activities and actions taking place in a system.

5. *Class diagram:* Describes the structure of a system. The structures are built from classes and relationships. The classes can represent and structure information, products, documents, or organizations.

6. *Object diagram:* Expresses possible object combinations of a specific class diagram. It is typically used to exemplify a class diagram.

7. *State diagram:* Expresses possible states of a class (or a system).

8. *Activity diagram:* Describes activities and actions taking place in a system.

9. *Sequence diagram:* Shows one or several sequences of messages sent among a set of objects.

10. *Collaboration diagram:* Describes a complete collaboration among a set of objects.

11. *User-case diagram:* Illustrates the relationships between user cases. Each user case, typically defined in plain text, describes a part of the total system functionality.

12. *Component diagram:* A special case of class diagram used to describe components within a software system.

13. *Deployment diagram:* A special case of class diagram used to describe hardware within a software system.

A model is a complete description of a system from a particular perspective. UML provides diagram for visualizing and describing models. Through these diagrams the three important aspects of systems are captured: structure, behavior, and functionality.

Integrating Mechanism

To meet the above requirements, we construct a multi-XML Schema emulating the hierarchy structure of XML as the schema resource of the data structure. It aims at the compatibility of various metadata schemas by XML framework. To integrate different metadata system, a database, containing the tables of Schema, Mapping, META, and Authority Control, is employed. *Figure 2* describes the relationships and working principles of these tables.

- *Schema tables*: Define the metadata structure of the system (for actual consideration, this system can handle XML Schema and DTD).

- *Mapping tables*: Integrate the XML Schema/DTD and define the access point of each element.

- *META tables (parameter files)*: Combine the Mapping table and XML Schema to generate the source parameters for metadata editing in cataloging module.

- *Authority control tables*: Support the finding task by ensuring that each entity has a unique name, and support the "see," "see also," and "see from" function among entities.

We divide these tables and blocks into four layers (groups) in order to support the process of system management operation, data management operation, inquiry module, and schema construct module.

Information Organization

In the designing phase, the information organization is an important initial step. The method of information arrangement determines the system database structure. In this study, the system design based on the principle of UML is divided into five groups: Pre-work, System, Cataloging, Indexing, and Retrieval. *Figure 3* describes the working process of a system activity according to the above classifications. The designer can allocate these groups to relative objects for follow-up analysis.

Operation/Module Architecture

According to the analysis of information organization mentioned in *Figure 3*, this study employs the following modules to construct the proposed model. All these modules are based on the XML in designing the structure of processing documents and the type definition (XML Schema/DTD).

1. *Schema Construct Module:* supplying XML Schema input and transforming into the function of system schema structure. The major process uses DOM (Document Object Module) (W3C, 2002) function to parser XML Schema. We must reconstruct into relational databases due to the XML and XML Schema hierarchical data structure. *Figure 4* shows the tables of

Figure 2. Majority of four-table layer reflecting the operations/modules of the system

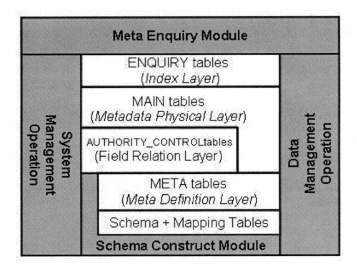

XML Schema (save into XSCHEMA table) and mapping tables combined into Meta tables, which uses a linked list to archive hierarchical structures of XML Schema.

2. *Data Management Operation:* including the record maintenance functions of insert/update/delete for Authority Control, metadata and other parameters of system (ID of institution, operator, Privilege of function, Classification of Index, Multi-lingual Message, etc.). The technique of relational database to handle and store metadata is to use a linked list. As shown in *Figure 5*, we designed recursive tables in order to demonstrate that one metadata can link to another metadata. Each metadata can use a linked list to link all elements that belong to this metadata, and each element can link all attributes that belong to this element. *Figure 6* illustrates how one element of metadata needs to use another metadata to describe itself. This element can use this recursive structure to link to another metadata.

3. *System Management Operation:* including entire system control, Metadata Import/Export Module, in which using XML as the basic format for Import/Export, declaring Well-formed or Valid XML.

4. *Inquiry Module:* including Web and Open Public Access Catalog (OPAC) interface for retrieving metadata in this system.

Figure 3. System activity diagram

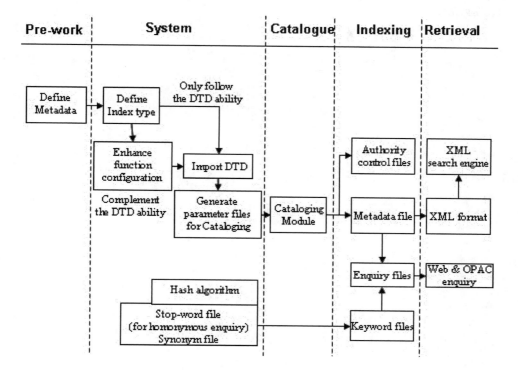

Inquiry Function

To meet the increasing requirements of the integrated retrieval of distributed information system, the retrieval function of the system offers integrated, fast, and exact searching for metadata documents. It also offers deeper and broader information for presenting the value of metadata. Though access method and the query method may be different and data files may have various structures, the basic principle of retrieval is similar, particular in database retrieval through the standard interface of structured query language (SQL). While the system processing metadata, the differential searching between English and CJK (Chinese, Japanese, and Korean) is of the major concern (Yu et al., 2003):

- Besides Unicode character, English character is processed by only one byte; CJK character is processed by at least double-bytes.
- The length of English vocabulary is not fixed, but CJK vocabulary is fixed

Figure 4. Subject of meta definition: combine XML Schema and mapping tables into META tables

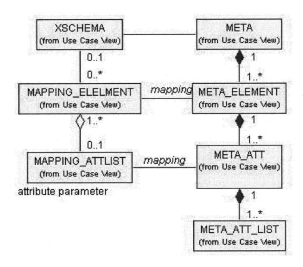

Figure 5. Table structure of metadata

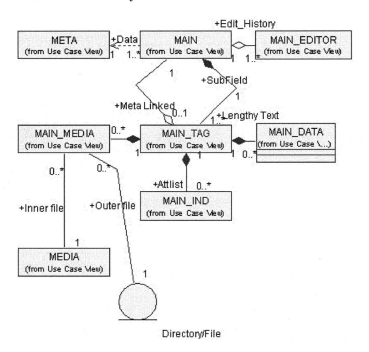

Figure 6. One element of metadata uses this recursive structure to link to another metadata

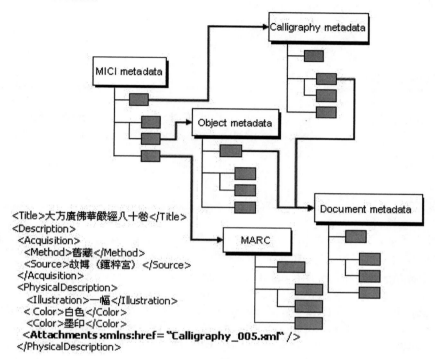

```
<Title>大方廣佛華嚴經八十卷</Title>
<Description>
  <Acquisition>
    <Method>書藏</Method>
    <Source>故博（鍾粹宮）</Source>
  </Acquisition>
  <PhysicalDescription>
    <Illustration>一幅</Illustration>
    <Color>白色</Color>
    <Color>墨印</Color>
    <Attachments xmlns:href="Calligraphy_005.xml" />
  </PhysicalDescription>
```

- English vocabularies often use space as delimiter, but CJK vocabulary doesn't.

- English vocabularies are arranged by alphabetical order. CJK are sorted by stroke-count, strokes, and radicals.

Based on the above differences in word processing, English and CJK vocabularies in metadata document content shall be separated and indexed. The main designing rules are described as follows:

- Vocabulary retrieval is for English, phrase retrieval for CJK.

- Fault-tolerance retrieval is necessary for English, for example, sounded search.

- English vocabulary has the characteristic of singular, plural, third person, and tense.

- CJK phrase needs to be accessed by truncated retrieval.

- Space phrase and wrap lines phrase retrievals are necessary for CJK.
- Phrase segmentation retrieval is necessary for CJK.

Implementation

The "Metalogy" system is composed of the following modules: Schema Constructor, Cataloging, Metadata Import/Export, and Inquiry. The main functions of these modules are described below.

Schema Construct Module

The Schema Constructor provides the function for importing XML Schema and establishing the system schema. It contains three main execution parts:

1. *Storing mechanism:* a database is employed to store the information of imported XML Schema. It is a nested structure similar to the tables of object-oriented database. The XML Schema file should be decomposed into tables before importing into the system. This mechanism simplifies the complexity of front-end software development and rear-ends database accessibility by using the relational database tables as physical structure.

2. *Mapping mechanism:* as shown in *Figure 7*, owing to the XML Schema, declaration does not include the field definitions of access point, extra function, input length, the item of authority control, and default value. The system operators must do some exceptional operations for the imported XML Schema such as transformation, integration, and use partial. To meet these requirements, this system supplies a set of mapping tables as the intermediary files for XML Schema definition transfer.

3. *Verifying mechanism:* usually, mapping tables can be generated automatically while importing XML Schema. However, the system operator needs to manually examine the data format, extra function, input length, item of authority control, and index of every element. Occasionally, it must be edited before importing XML Schema.

Based on the results of comparing the original definitions of XML Schema and the mapping table, the system produces the internal meta-structure. This is the source parameter for metadata editing in cataloging module.

Cataloging Module

Cataloging Module provides the function of cataloging for different metadata and authority control. The activity diagram depicted in *Figure 8* shows the flow procedure of activity within overall cataloging function, and it also presents the interior process behavior and the flow of control among objects. This module contains two sub-functions: Data Input and Authority Control.

Data Input Function

This function provides capability of metadata editing. The XML Schema imported previously decides the editable metadata permitted by the framework, which was developed by this study; that is, how many XML Schemas are imported and then how many metadata can be administrated.

As shown in *Figure 9*, the system generates corresponding META tables (schema parameter tables) while loading an XML Schema. Operators can catalog the metadata by selecting the meta-group where the metadata belongs. The system provides the functions of duplicating, deleting, inserting sub-field, coding, and connecting multimedia files to each field of metadata. Operators can also use the inquiry function during cataloging and copying metadata that was previously edited. If operators consider the subject heading check unnecessary, or need to simplify the processing of cataloging, operators can work off-line and use any text-editor to edit records, and then batch import these records by full-text editor.

Authority Control Function

In the "Metalogy" system, while loading an XML Schema, if the operator decides the XML Schema is imported for authority control, the system will generate the mapping META table of authority control. When Operators catalog the metadata, the system will check the parameters of authority control (such as name, subject, era, or geographical name fields) to automatically proceed with the field linking. Operators can, if necessary, add the same entity but with a different subject heading in the authority control records, then the system will generate relative authority control records. The system executes the functions below according to the META table imported to the database.

1. Importing the authority control records built by other system.

2. Using XML as the syntax of authority control in import and export.

Figure 7. Mapping table configuration – to supply the extended definitions of each element

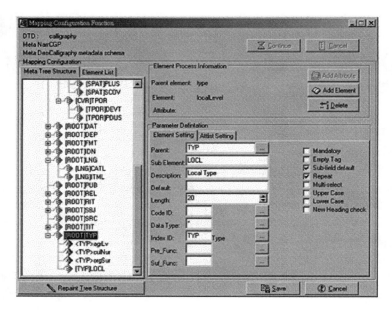

3.   Adding and modifying metadata records will also change the linked authority control records.

4.   Display the same or similar authority control records for operators to choose.

5.   Authority control records can be used for the expanded index for inquiry.

Metadata Import/Export Module

Metadata import/export module offers the system to exchange the data with other systems by XML. Operators can export certain data by inquiry, or assign certain range for batch-export. Exporting metadata supports one or more records in a file to export, but does not support one file containing different metadata. Another purpose of this module is to provide metadata sharing online. The Open Archives Initiative (OAI) develops and promotes an easily implemented protocol called Open Archives Initiative Protocol for Metadata Harvest-

Figure 8. The activity diagram of cataloging module

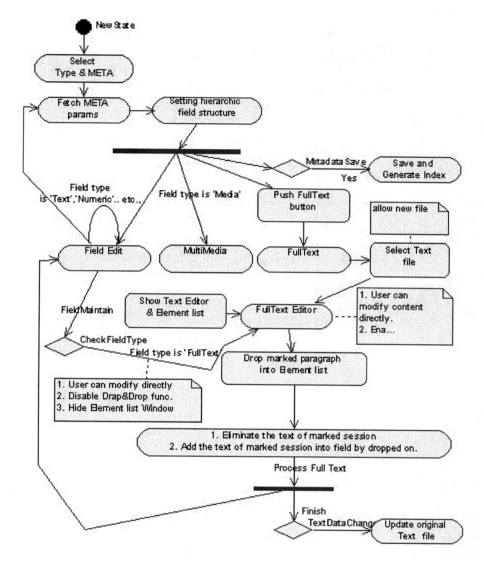

ing (OAI-PMH). This enables data providers to expose their information and for service providers to access and use it (OAI protocol, 2002). As depicted in *Figure 10*, we used and developed CGI programs on the Web server site that provided the Web inquiry and OAI-PMH exposed metadata, but this project is still under development (please see "Future Work" section).

Figure 9. Operators can choose the cataloging format of data according to the amount of imported XML Schema

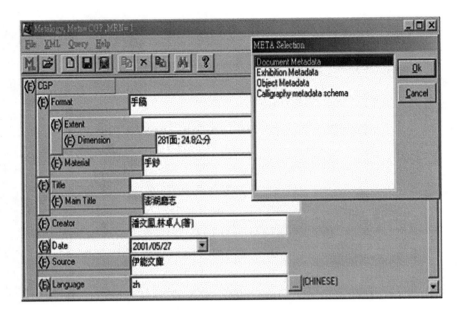

Inquiry Module

With this module, users can search the cataloging data in the status of maintenance or export. Inquiry module can display the result with the formats pre-set by parameters, such as main display, brief display, and detailed display. Users can make a general or authority-data inquiry on the metadata of one single meta-group or the metadata of all meta-group. For the related characteristics of metadata fields, the system can integrate more index items into one access point (or "search item," "search field name"), and combine similar field attributes, to obtain better search results. By this way, it offers more flexibility to user inquiries. For example, users can set the index items with title, sub-title, and other titles, but choose the "title" as the real access point to make inquiries in one step by using the above index (Yu, 1997).

Discussion and Conclusion

Metadata is the media used to describe the management and storing knowledge for digital library/museum systems, and XML is the most popular syntax for metadata. Major types of metadata formats in use include EAD, GILS, DGDC, MARC, CIMI, TEI, DC, and others. One institution may hold different types of resources and use different types of metadata formats. Thus, when designing a metadata management system, one should not base it on a particular format. Rather, it is more appropriate for the system designers to use XML as a core that would be capable of handling various metadata formats. With the compatibility of various metadata, the proposed system is a useful tool in creating a knowledge system by integrating the related knowledge. This will efficiently enhance the performance of data processing and sharing.

This study not only designed a metadata management system for Digital Library/ Museum, but also constructed a metadata system using the XML framework compatible with various metadata schemas. Employing the XML Schema to define the system schema structure allows a system to exist with multiple XML Schemas and to meet the demands of concurrent processing of multiple different types of metadata in import and export. The users can easily retrieve various types of metadata through the integration of multi access points and the consistent inquiry function of the system. More important, the metadata can be accessed by other systems. Based on this framework, libraries, museums, culture centers, education institutions, or enterprises can depend on a well-integrated user interface to achieve a complete system.

Figure 10. Export function provides the process ability of OAI-PMH for metadata sharing online

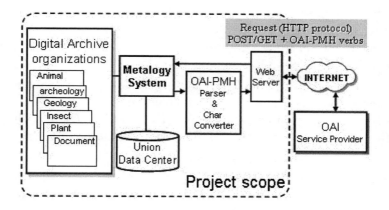

Future Works

On January 1, 2002, the National Science Council (NSC) of Taiwan launched a follow-up project National Digital Archives Program (NDAP), which is a major policy concerning digital content after the proposal of knowledge economy by the Taiwan government. Many universities and research organizations participated in this program, and the Institutional Project of National Taiwan University is one of its institutional projects. With seven sub-projects in this project, it is urgent to build an interoperable mechanism to share and conserve all valuable collections, retrieve the digital collections of these content holders via a union interface, and allow the general public to access the digital collections. For this reason, this project will utilize the OAI-PMH to carry out related studies and implement the system.

Acknowledgments

The work described in this paper was partially sponsored by the National Science Council of the Republic of China under the NSC grant number NSC 89-2750-P-002-012 & NSC-89-2750-P-002-013.

References

Chen, C.C., Chen, H.H., & Chen, K.H. (2001). The design of metadata interchange for Chinese information and implementation of metadata management system. *Bulletin of the American Society for Information Science and Technology, 27*(5), 21-27.

Chen, C.C., Chen, H.H., Chen, K.H., & Hsiang, J. (2002). The design of metadata for the digital museum initiative in Taiwan. *Online Information Review, 26*(5), 295-306.

Chen, C.C., Yu, S.C., & Chen, H.H. (2002). The design and implementation of dynamic metadata management system. In *Proceedings of Digital Library 2002-IT Opportunities and Challenges (DLOC) in the New Millennium*, July 8-12, 2002. Beijing, China: National Library of China.

DCMI. (2004). *Dublin Core Metadata Initiative Tools and Software*. Retrieved from the World Wide Web: *http://dublincore.org/tools/*

Grady B., Rumbaugh, J., & Jacobson I. (1999). *The unified modeling language user guide*. Boston: Addison-Wesley.

Hunt, J. (2000). *The unified process for practitioners: Object-oriented design, UML and Java*. London: Springer.

IFLA. (2003). *Digital Libraries: Metadata Resources*. Retrieved from the World Wide Web: *http://www.ifla.org/II/metadata.htm#tools*

Kobryn, C. (1999). UML 2001: A standardization odyssey. *Communications of the ACM, 42*(10), 29-37.

Kruse, R.L., Leung, B.P., & Tondo, C.L. (1997). *Data structures and program design in C* (2nd ed). NJ: Prentice-Hall.

OAI. (2002). *The Open Archives Initiative Protocol for Metadata Harvesting*, v.2.0. Retrieved from the World Wide Web: *http://www.openarchives.org/OAI/2.0/openarchivesprotocol.htm*

Vellucci, S.L. (2000). Metadata and authority control. *Library Resources & Technical Services, 44*(1), 33-43.

W3C. (2002). *Document Object Model (DOM)*. Retrieved from the World Wide Web: *http://www.w3.org/DOM/*

Yu, S.C. (1997). Study of hetero-MARC databases in the application of cataloging and retrieving. Taipei: Sino-American.

Yu, S.C., Lu, K.Y., & Chen, R.S. (2003). Metadata management system: Design and implementation. *The Electronic Library, 21* (2), 154-164.

Chapter V

Information Filtering and Personalization Services

Chunxiao Xing
Tsinghua University, China

Chun Zeng
Tsinghua University, China

Zhiqiang Zhang
Tsinghua University, China

Lizhu Zhou
Tsinghua University, China

Abstract

Personalization service is becoming one of the core services in digital libraries, and an exciting and challenge research area. In this chapter, we analyze several key technologies and the related works in information filtering and personalized services, and then present a content-based personalized searching algorithm and a probabilistic model to represent user interests, which is more effective than the vector space model by the experiments. To solve the data sparsity and scalability problems in collaborative filtering, we present new methods for similarity computation and instance selection. The experiments show it is higher predicted precision and performance than the others. Based on the above research results, we design and develop a prototype, TH-PASS, which provides personalized searching and recommending services.

Introduction

With the rapid advancement of information technology and the knowledge economy, digital libraries (DLs) have emerged as the large scale and distributed information and knowledge environment and infrastructure to bring together collections, services, and people in support of the full life cycle of creation, dissemination, use, storage, and preservation (Xing et al., 2002).

To quickly and easily gather useful knowledge and to alleviate information overload problems, it has therefore become necessary to provide users with active and personalized service mechanisms that automatically extract only relevant information. To overcome the above challenge, one of the exciting and hot research areas is personalized active service that can route, recommend, rank and filter documents based on users' interest profiles. This service is becoming one of the core services in the future DLs, and it relies on many established techniques applied in information retrieval (IR), information filtering (IF), user modeling and machine learning, and etcetera.

In this chapter, we mainly focus our attention on information filtering technology and its application on personalization service: (1) Exploring the basic problems of content-based filtering including feature selection, representation and revision of user profile; (2) Tracking, studying and representing users' interests based on information filtering technology; (3) Analyzing the performance of several feature selection methods and comparing the different representation of user interests; (4) Researching the collaborative filtering to solve the data sparsity and scalability problems in collaborative filtering; (5) Presenting a class-based method for similarity computation and an approach for instance selection; (6) Comparing the performance of several collaborative filtering algorithms and giving the experiment results; (7) Building a prototype system to provide the users personalized filtering and notification service based on user modeling and profile learning.

The rest of the chapter is organized as follows. The second section gives a brief overview of related works. The third section discusses the representation of document and user interest, analyzes the methods of user interests' revision, and provides a content-based filtering personalized service algorithm. The fourth section then provides the problem description in collaborative filtering algorithms, discusses our method for similarity measure, and describes the technique of instance selection. In addition, we propose the class-based collaborative filtering algorithm. In the third and fourth sections we also give the experimental evaluation, including dataset, metrics and experimental results. In the fifth section we design the framework of TH-PASS prototype and implement the functions of main components. The chapter gives a preview of our future trends and concludes in the last section.

The Related Works

Personalization service is a very active and broad area of research with many applications, such as e-business, DL, and news delivery. Many personalization systems put forward many ideas to implement personalized services (Pretschner, 1999; Zeng, Xing, & Zhou, 2002). Information filtering is a popular way to realize personalization, which can be classified into content-based filtering and collaborative filtering. Content-based filtering systems, such as CiteSeer, ELFI, ifWeb, Letizia, Personal WebWatcher, PVA, SIFTER, Syskill & Webert, WebACE, WebMate and WebPersonalizer (Bollacker, Lawrence, & Giles, 2000; Schwab, Pohl, & Koychev, 2000; Mladenic, 2000; Chen, 2001; Han, 1998; Chen & Sycara, 1998; Mobasher, Cooley, & Srivastava, 2000), associate every user with profiles to filter contents. Content-based filtering is direct and simple, but it depends on the quality and validity of user profiles. In addition it cannot discover new interesting information for users. Collaborative filtering systems, such as Firefly, GroupLens, Let's Browse, LikeMinds (www.macromedia.com), SE-LECT, SiteSeer and WebWatcher (Shardanand & Maes, 1995; Konstan et al., 1997; Lieberman, Dyke, & Vivacqua, 1999; Alton-Scheidl et al., 1999; Rucker & Polanco, 1997; Joachims, 1997), utilize the similarity among profiles of users to recommend interesting material.

Collaborative filtering has been very successful in both research and applications such as information filtering and e-commerce. The k-Nearest Neighbor (KNN) method is a popular way for its realization. Its key technique is to find k nearest neighbors for a given user to predict his interest. However, this method suffers from two fundamental problems: sparsity and scalability. Sparsity refers to the fact that most users do not rate most items and hence a very sparse user-item rating matrix is generated. As a result the accuracy of the method will be poor. Scalability problem means the nearest neighbor algorithm fails to scale up its computation with the growth of both the number of users and the number of items. To solve the first problem, Balabanovic & Shoham (1997) and Claypool et al. (1999) put forward a content-based collaborative filtering method, which utilizes the contents browsed by users to compute the similarity among users.

Sarwar et al. (2000) uses Latent Semantic Indexing (LSI) to capture the similarity among users and items in a reduced dimensional space. Yu et al. (2001) uses a feature-weighting method to improve the accuracy of collaborative filtering algorithms. For the second problem, many studies bring forward model-based methods that use the users' preferences to learn a model for predication. Breese, Heckerman & Kadie (1998) utilizes clustering and Bayesian network approaches. Their study shows that the clustering-based method is efficient but with poor accuracy. The Bayesian networks may prove practical for environments in which knowledge of user preferences changes slowly with respect to the time needed to build the model, but are not suitable for environments in which user preference models must be updated rapidly or frequently. Sarwar et al. (2001) put forth an item-based collaborative filtering algorithm that makes use of a pre-computed model of item similarity to increase the online scalability of item-based recommendations. Sarwar et al. (2000) presents a rule-based approach using association rule discovery algorithms to find association between relevant items and then generates item recommendation based on the strength of the association between items. Yu et al. (2002) solves the second problem from another point of view. They adopt a technique of instance selection to remove the irrelevant and redundant instances from the training set. Experimental results show that this technique improves not only accuracy but also performance of the collaborative filtering algorithm.

Content-Based Filtering

Content-based filtering recommends documents to users according to the similarity between users and documents. Its researches focus on feature selection, representation and revision of user interests and similarity measure methods. Tracking, studying and representing users' interests is a basic and challenging task because users' interests are diverse.

Representation of Document and User Interest

The representation of user interests is consistent to the representation of documents. The traditional way of representing documents is vector space model. Vector space model cannot embody the diversity of user interests. So we present a probability model, which builds a domain classification model in advance, and then computes all documents and users interests' probabilistic distribution over this domain. Because the number of classes is far less then that of key phrases, the performance and precision of content-based filtering are improved. We adopt Naïve Bayes method to train domain classification model (Joachims, Freitag, & Mitchell, 1997). It is assumed that $C = \{c_1, c_2, \ldots c_K\}$ is the set of domain structure, where c_k is the kth domain, K is the size of model. The distribution of document d over domain structure C is defined as: $d=<p(c_1 \mid d), p(c_2 \mid d), \ldots, p(c_K \mid d)>$.

Revision of User Interests

Usually, a personalized service will modify users' interests dynamically by tracking their actions. *Table 1* shows the meaning of different user actions.

A user's interests are represented as a vector of probability distribution over the domain structure. We can also modify each conditional probability according to the actions after recommending documents to users.

$$p(c_k \mid u) \leftarrow \frac{p(c_k \mid u) + \eta w_a p(c_k \mid d)}{1 + \eta w_a} \tag{3.1}$$

Content-Based Filtering Personalized Algorithm

The traditional similarity computation method of vector space model is cosine similarity computation. For instance, the similarity between user u and document d can be defined as:

$$Sim(u,d) = \frac{u \cdot d}{\| u \| \cdot \| d \|} \tag{3.2}$$

Table 1. Meaning of users actions

User Action	Meaning
Add a bookmark	Very high positive
Download a paper	High positive
View details of a paper	Moderate positive
Ignore a paper	Low negative or set to zero
Delete a bookmark	High negative

We present a method to compute the similarity between probability distributions (Hofmann, 1999). The classification model is $C= \{c_1, c_2, ..., c_K\}$, user u is independent to document d, the recommendation probability of document d to user u can be defined as:

$$p(u \mid d) = p(u)\sum_{c \in C} \frac{p(c \mid u)p(c \mid d)}{p(c)} \qquad (3.3)$$

Content-based filtering can be implemented by reordering search results using equation (3.3). We need not compute $p(u)$ in equation (3.3) because it does not influence the comparison between recommendation probabilities.

Algorithm 3.1 shows the details of a new content-based filtering algorithm. This algorithm is actually based on another search engine. If we compute all documents' probabilistic distributions in advance, then the performance of this algorithm will be improved (Zeng, Xing, & Zhou, 2002).

Experimental Results

We design and implement a prototype to test the performance and precision of personalized search algorithm. The experiment data set is from INSPEC database, which has clear classification architecture. To narrow the scope of experiment, we only select the topic of computer software, which includes 45 classes. We collect about 2,000 document abstracts of computer science to create the domain structure. The experiment metrics is precision and recall.

Algorithm 3.1. Content-based filtering personalized algorithm

```
Input: domain structure, a user, keywords, a search engine
Output: results of personalized searching
        Save the result of searching keywords from the search engine into X;
        For each document in X do
        Begin
             Compute the document's probabilistic distribution over the domain structure using
                     Naïve Bayes method;
             According to equation (3.3), compute the recommendation probability of the
                     document to the current user and add the value of probability into list Y;
        End-for
        Reorder the result of search engine according to list Y;
```

$$\Pr ecision = \frac{\# \text{of relevant documents}}{\# \text{of searching results}} \qquad (3.4)$$

$$\text{Re} call = \frac{\# \text{of relevant documents}}{\# \text{of all documents}} \qquad (3.5)$$

We compute the precision for recall 0.2, 0.4, 0.6, 0.8 and 1. The mean precision is defined as the average precision over these five points. The experiment curve is similar to ROC (Receiver Operating Characteristic), which means the larger the area under the curve, the higher the precision of the algorithm.

We utilize vector space model and probability model to represent user interests. *Figure 1* shows the result of comparison between vector space model and probability model. In contrast with the vector space model, the probability model is more effective. In fact, vector space model pays attention to strictly match between words using cosine measure. To avoid strict matching, we compute the relevance between probabilistic distributions over a domain structure. In this experiment, the mean precision of the probability model is 68%, while that of the vector space model is 7%.

Collaborative Filtering

There are two fundamental problems: sparsity and scalability in collaborative filtering. In this section, we propose a matrix conversion method and a new instance selection method (Zeng, Xing, & Zhou, 2003).

Problem Description

User-based collaborative filtering algorithm is very popular in practice. Its key technique is to find k nearest neighbors of the active user to predict his interest. It has the advantages of being able to rapidly incorporate the most up-to-date information and relatively accurate prediction. The detailed description of this algorithm is shown in Algorithm 4.1 (Herlocker et al., 1999).

The key problem of neighbor searching is computing the similarity between users. The time complexity of the user-based collaborative filtering algorithm is $O(NM)$, where N is the size of the training set and M is the number of items.

Algorithm 4.1. User-based collaborative filtering algorithm

Input: a training set, a test set, a target item
Output: mean absolute error of the algorithm
    For each user *a* in the test set do
    Begin
        Compute the similarity of user *a* with all users in the training set;
        Select k neighboring users that have the highest similarity with the target user;
        Predict the voting of user *a* on the target item from a combination of the selected neighboring users'
            ratings;
    End-for
    Compute the mean absolute error of the algorithm and output;

Similarity between user *a* and user *b* is computed using Pearson correlation coefficient, defined by:

$$w_{a,b} = \frac{\sum_{i=1}^{M}(v_{a,i} - \bar{v}_a)(v_{b,i} - \bar{v}_b)}{\sqrt{\sum_{i=1}^{M}(v_{a,i} - \bar{v}_a)^2 \sum_{i=1}^{M}(v_{b,i} - \bar{v}_b)^2}} \qquad (4.1)$$

Where M is the number of items, $v_{a,i}$ is the rating given to item i by user a, $\bar{v}_a$ is the mean rating given by user a, $w_{a,b}$ is the similarity between user a and user b. Predictions are computed as the weighted average of deviation from the neighbor's mean:

$$p_{a,j} = \bar{v}_a + \frac{\sum_{b=1}^{n}(v_{b,j} - \bar{v}_b) \times w'_{a,b}}{\sum_{b=1}^{n} w'_{a,b}} \qquad (4.2)$$

Where n is the number of neighbors of user a, $p_{a,j}$ is the prediction of the active user a on the target item j.

Similarity Measure

We observe that items can be classified into classes. These classes can be used to convert the user-item matrix into a user-class matrix. Unlike the user-item matrix, where the rating of every user for every item is recorded, the user-class matrix only stores the rating of a user to classes. In user interested item prediction, we use user-class matrix to replace user-item matrix. As the number of classes is far less than the number of items, this user-class matrix overcomes the sparsity problem of user-item matrix method. The value of an element of the user-class matrix is the sum of ratings of user u on items belonging to the same class divided by the total ratings of user u on all items:

$$v_{u,c} = \frac{\sum_{\text{item } i \text{ belonging to class } c} v_{u,i}}{\sum_{\text{all item } i} v_{u,i}} \tag{4.3}$$

Where $c \in C = \{c_1, ..., c_K\}$, K is the number of classes, $v_{u,c}$ is the rating of user u on class c, $v_{u,i}$ is the rating of user u on item i.

The similarity between users based on the user-class matrix can still be measured by computing Pearson correlation. We observe that the target item is relevant to some classes. So we adopt a weighting method:

$$w_{a,b} = \frac{\sum_{k=1}^{K} w_k^2 (v_{a,k} - \bar{v}_a)(v_{b,k} - \bar{v}_b)}{\sqrt{\sum_{k=1}^{K} w_k^2 (v_{a,k} - \bar{v}_a)^2 \sum_{k=1}^{K} w_k^2 (v_{b,k} - \bar{v}_b)^2}} \tag{4.4}$$

Where K is the number of classes, w_k represents $P(c_k|j)$, which is the probability of the target item j belonging to class c_k. $\bar{v}_a$ is the mean rating given by user a on all classes.

Instance Selection

An important step of the user-based collaborative filtering algorithm is to search neighbors for the active user. The traditional method is to search the whole database. Apparently this method suffers from poor scalability when more and more users and items are added in the database. To handle this problem, indexing techniques might be considered. However recent results (Weber, Schek, & Blott, 1998) show that a simple sequential scan of the whole data outperforms any of the indexing methods when the dimensionality exceeds around 10. Usually, the dimension of the data of the collaborative filtering algorithm is more than 1,000, so the method of indexing is impractical. The practical method is instance selection that selects appropriate instances from the whole database for the filtering algorithm. Those irrelevant instances have a significant impact on the prediction quality (Yu et al., 2001; Yu et al., 2002). We can adopt a technique of instance selection to remove the irrelevant and redundant instances from the training set. This method improves not only the accuracy but also the performance of the collaborative filtering algorithm.

According to equation (3.3), if user u and item i are independent, then the relevancy between user u and item i can be represented as:

$$p(i \mid u) = p(i) \sum_{c \in C} \frac{p(c \mid u) p(c \mid i)}{p(c)} \qquad (4.5)$$

Equation (4.5) depicts the relevancy of user u to item i based on a latent class model. According to the above analysis, we use equation (4.5) to rank the relevancy of users to a target item. In this equation, we can ignore $P(i)$ because it has no impact on the ranking of the relevancy between users and the target item. For text items, we can use the Naive Bayes classification method to compute $P(c \mid i)$. For multimedia items, we can classify them manually in practice or impose appropriate methods. We utilize the rating of user u on class c divided by the total rating of the user on all classes to represent $P(c \mid u)$, which can be written as:

$$P(c \mid u) \approx \frac{v_{u,c}}{\sum_{k=1}^{K} v_{u,k}} \qquad (4.6)$$

Where K is the number of classes, $v_{u,c}$ is the rating of user u on class c, $v_{u,k}$ is the rating of user u on class c_k.

$P(c)$ is represented as the number of items belonging to class c divided by the total number of items belonging to all classes:

$$P(c) \approx \frac{N_c}{\sum_{k=1}^{K} N_k} \qquad (4.7)$$

Where K is the number of classes, N_c is the number of items belonging to class c, N_k is the number of items belonging to class c_k.

Class-Based Collaborative Filtering Algorithm

On the basis of these two methods mentioned above, we introduce an improved collaborative filtering algorithm, called class-based algorithm shown in Algorithm 4.2. Because this algorithm can narrow the scope of neighbors searching, it can improve performance and reduce time complexity.

Experimental Results

We use EachMovie data set (EachMovie, 2001) to evaluate the performance of improved algorithm. The EachMovie data set is provided by the Compaq System Research Center, which ran the EachMovie recommendation service for 18 months to experiment with a collaborative filtering algorithm. The information they gathered during that period consists of 72,916 users, 1,628 movies, and 2,811,983 numeric ratings ranging from 0 to 5. To speed up our experiments, we only use a subset of the EachMovie data set. For every experiment, we randomly select 5,000 users who had rated 30 or more items and then divide them into a training set (90% users) and a test set (10% users). We have about 380,000 ratings for all movies, and the data density is 4.8%. All movies have already been classified manually into 10 types by the EachMovie recommendation service: action, animation, art or foreign, classic, comedy, drama, family, horror, romance, and thriller. In the experiments, a movie might belong to more than one genre. To measure the impact of classification, we reclassify all movies into 19 genres according to the method of IMDB (*www.imdb.com*).

Algorithm 4.2. Class-based collaborative filtering

Input: training set, test set, a target item, and a given selection rate $r\%$
Output: mean absolute error of prediction
    Preprocess training data set and remove rare rated items whose frequency
        is less than the given threshold;
    Convert the user-item matrix into the user-class matrix;
    Select top $r\%$ instances relevant to the target item into X;
    For each instance in the test set do
    Begin
        Search neighbors from X ;
        Compute a prediction for the target item;
    End-for
    Compute the mean absolute error of prediction and output.

We use Mean Absolute Error (MAE), a statistical accuracy metrics, to report prediction experiments, for it is most commonly used and easy to understand:

$$MAE = \frac{\sum_{a \in T} |v_{a,j} - p_{a,j}|}{|T|} \qquad (4.8)$$

Where $v_{a,j}$ is the rating given to item j by user a, $p_{a,j}$ is the predicted value of user a on item j, T is the test set, $|T|$ is the size of the test set.

As in Breese, Heckerman & Kadie (1998), we also employ two protocols, All but 1, and Given K. In the first class, we randomly withhold a single randomly selected vote for each test user, and try to predict its value given all the other votes the user has voted on. The All but 1 experiments measure the algorithms' performance when given as much data as possible from each test user. The second protocol, given K, randomly selects K votes from each test user as the observed votes, and then attempts to predict the remaining votes. It looks at users with less data available, and examines the performance of the algorithms when there is relatively little known about an active user.

We analyze the impact of matrix conversion, the sensitivity of instance selection on experimental results, and conclude by giving the comparison result in accuracy and performance for five representative algorithms.

Impact of Matrix Conversion

To determine the impact of matrix conversion, we carried out an experiment to compare the accuracy of prediction before and after matrix conversion. The experiments were conducted for training set with 1,000, 2,000, 3,000, 4,000 and finally 5,000 users. The data density of the training set increases after matrix conversion. For instance, when the size of training set is 5,000, the initial data density is 4.8% before data preprocessing. After data preprocessing and matrix conversion, the data density becomes 91.8%. *Figure 2* shows the experimental results. It can be observed that the proposed method outperforms the traditional user-based collaborative filtering algorithm. In addition, the results show that the accuracy of matrix conversion with 19 genres is more than that of matrix conversion with 10 genres. So we choose matrix conversion with 19 genres for the rest of our experiments.

Figure 1. Comparison of user interests representation

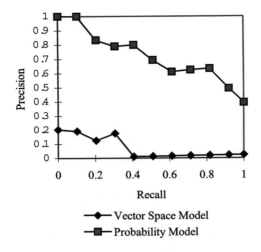

Recall

Vector Space Model
Probability Model

Figure 2. Impact of matrix conversion

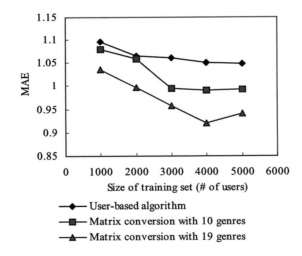

Size of training set (# of users)

User-based algorithm
Matrix conversion with 10 genres
Matrix conversion with 19 genres

Sensitivity of Instance Selection

Those irrelevant instances have a significant impact on the prediction quality. We evaluated the quality of our method of selecting relevant instances. The outcomes are given in *Figure 3*. We sort users in descending order of their

Figure 3. Sensitivity of instance selection

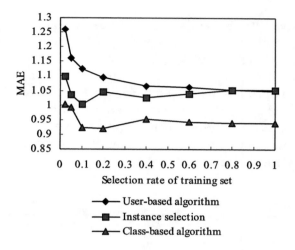

Figure 4. Comparison of accuracy between five algorithms

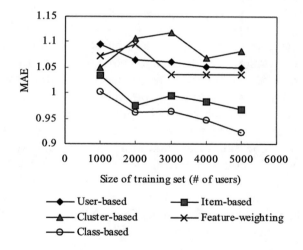

relevancy to each movie, and select highly relevant users for the prediction in different selection rates of 2.5%, 5%, 10%, 20%, 40%, 60%, 80% and 100%. The results are compared with the outcomes of random sampling. The proposed method outperforms random sampling in accuracy, and the combination with other techniques results in further 10% improvement of accuracy. Moreover, these techniques remain effective even if the selection rate is equal to 0.1.

Comparison Experiments

We implemented five different collaborative filtering algorithms: user-based algorithm, item-based algorithm (Sarwar et al., 2001), cluster-based algorithm (Breese, Heckerman, & Kadie, 1998), feature-weighting algorithm (Yu et al., 2001), and our class-based algorithm. The results of comparison of accuracy between these five algorithms are shown in *Figure 4*. Our algorithm shows its satisfactory results. The selection rate of our algorithm is 0.1. If we take the user-based algorithm as the baseline, then we can see that the clustering-based algorithm is the worst, and the class-based algorithm is better than both the feature-weighting algorithm and the item-based algorithm.

Performance Results

We also carried out an experiment to compare the performance of these five algorithms. *Figure 5* shows the results of comparison of training time between these five algorithms. In this figure, we observe that the training time of the cluster-based algorithm is more than other four algorithms on average. The training time of the feature-weighting algorithm is relatively long because it spends much time on computing the mutual information between the target item and other items. The training time of the class-based algorithm is short because the time of matrix conversion and instance selection is not too much. The training time of the user-based algorithm and the item-based algorithm are short as well because these two algorithms load all data into memory without any processing. *Figure 6* shows the results of comparison of predicting time between these five algorithms. We observe that the predicting time of the user-based algorithm is more than other four algorithms on average and is subject to the number of users. The predicting time of the cluster-based algorithm is the shortest because it finds neighbors from clusters. The predicting time of the item-based algorithm is short and it doesn't change significantly with the size of the training set because it is based on items rather than the number of users. The predicting time of the feature-weighting algorithm and the class-based algorithm are very close to item-based algorithm because these two algorithms select appropriate user instances from the training set with much smaller size.

Personalized Service System

In this section, we briefly introduce a personalized services system TH-PASS. In TH-PASS the major components have been developed as separate modules based

Figure 5. Comparison of training time

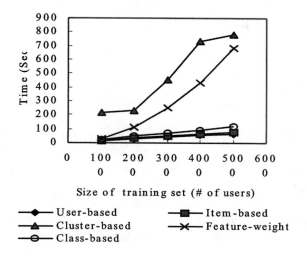

Figure 6. Comparison of predicting time

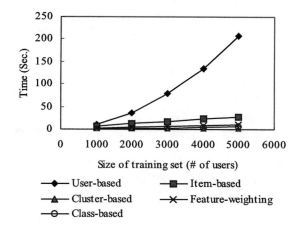

on intelligent agents. The framework consists of major components of User Interface/WWW Browsers, TH-PASS Proxy Server, Information Filtering Agent, Learning/Discovering Agent, User Model & User Profile, MetaSearch Engine, Metadata Extraction, Monitor Agent/Notification Agent, Notification Agent, and Distributed information Source. The prototype system has provided a general architecture to represent, filter, and recommend relevant information based on dynamic profiles of the users and combined a five-stage process successfully:

collections construction, feature extraction, user modeling and user profile learning, personalized filtering, and personalized adaptation and notification of new interesting research and trends.

Conclusion

Personalized services are very important services in the construction of digital libraries. In this chapter, we first compare some traditional feature selection approaches and a model-based approach, and then present a new method for representing users' interests by means of the probability distribution over a domain structure. To solve the data sparsity and scalability problems in collaborative filtering, we present class-based method for similarity computation by means of the characteristics of classification of resources, which can discover the implicit similarity between users.

We design and implement a prototype system TH-PASS. This system adopts client/server architecture. It provides several management functions for personal profile, such as interests and bookmarks. It learns users' interests by tracking their behaviors and provides personalized searching and recommending services. The work of TH-PASS is preliminary towards this goal. Our team will undertake more research in this direction.

Acknowledgments

Our work is partially supported by the National Natural Science Foundation of China under Grant No. 60473078 and the National Grand Fundamental Research 973 Program of China under Grant No. G1999032704.

References

Alton-Scheidl, R. et al. (1999). SELECT: Social and collaborative filtering of web documents and news. In *Proceedings of the 5th ERCIM Workshop on User Interfaces for All: User-Tailored Information Environments* (pp. 23-37).

Balabanovic, M., & Shoham, Y. (1997). Fab: Content-based, collaborative recommendation. *Communications of the ACM, 40* (3), 66-72.

Bollacker, K.D., Lawrence, S., & Giles, C.L. (2000). Discovering relevant scientific literature on the Web. *IEEE Intelligent Systems, 15* (2), 42-47.

Breese, J. S., Heckerman, D., & Kadie, C. (1998). Empirical analysis of predictive algorithms for collaborative filtering. In *Proceedings of the 14th Conference on Uncertainty in Artificial Intelligence* (pp. 43-52).

Chen, C.C., Chen, M.C., & Sun, Y.S. (2001). PVA: A self-adaptive personal view agent system. In *Proceeding of the 7th ACM SIGKDD International Conference on Knowledge Discovery and Data Mining* (pp. 257-262). New York: ACM Press.

Chen, L., & Sycara, K. (1998). WebMate: A personal agent for browsing and searching. In *Proceedings of the 2nd International Conference on Autonomous Agents* (pp. 132-139). New York: ACM Press.

Claypool, M. et al. (1999). Combining content-based and collaborative filters in an online newspaper. In *ACM SIGIR Workshop on Recommender Systems*. Berkeley, CA.

EachMovie. (2001). *EachMovie data set*. Retrieved from the World Wide Web: *http://research.compaq.com/SRC/eachmovie*

Han, E.H. et al. (1998). WebACE: A Web agent for document categorization and exploration. In *Proceeding of the 2nd International Conference on Autonomous Agents* (pp. 408-415). New York: ACM Press.

Herlocker, J., Konstan, J., Borchers, A., & Riedl, J. (1999). An algorithmic framework for performing collaborative filtering. In *Proceedings of the 22nd Annual International ACM SIGIR Conference on Research and Development in Information Retrieval* (pp. 230-237).

Hofmann, T. (1999). Probabilistic latent semantic analysis. In *Proceedings of the Fifteenth Conference on Uncertainty in Artificial Intelligence* (pp. 289-296). San Francisco: Morgan Kaufmann Publishers.

Joachims, T. (1997). A probabilistic analysis of the Rocchio Algorithm with TFIDF for text categorization. In *Proceedings of the 14th International Conference on Machine Learning* (pp. 143-151). San Francisco: Morgan Kaufmann Publishers.

Joachims, T., Freitag, D., & Mitchell, T. (1997). WebWatcher: A tour guide for the World Wide Web. In *Proceedings of the International Joint Conference on Artificial Intelligence* (pp. 770-777). Menlo Park, CA: AAAI Press, San Francisco: Morgan Kaufmann Publishers.

Konstan, J. et al. (1997). GroupLens: Applying collaborative filtering to usenet news. *Communications of the ACM, 40* (3), 77-87.

Lieberman, H., Dyke, N.V., Vivacqua, A. (1999). Let's browse: A collaborative Web browsing agent. In *Proceedings of the International Conference on Intelligent User Interfaces* (pp. 65-68). Los Angeles: ACM Press.

Mladenic, D. (2000). Machine learning for better Web browsing. In *AAAI 2000 Spring Symposium Technical Reports on Adaptive User Interfaces* (pp. 82-84). Menlo Park, CA: AAAI Press.

Mobasher, B., Cooley, R., & Srivastava, J. (2000). Automatic personalization based on Web usage mining. *Communications of the ACM, 43* (8), 142-151.

Pretschner, A. (1999). *Ontology based personalized search* [Master Thesis]. Lawrence, KS: University of Kansas.

Rucker, J., & Polanco, M.J. (1997). Siteseer: Personalized navigation for the web. *Communications of the ACM, 40* (3), 73-75.

Sarwar, B. et al. (2001). Item based collaborative filtering recommendation algorithms. In *Proceedings of the 10th International World Wide Web Conference* (pp. 285-295).

Sarwar, B. M. et al. (2000). Application of dimensionality reduction in recommender system: A case study. In *ACM WebKDD 2000 Web Mining for E-Commerce*.

Sarwar, B. M., Karypis, G., Konstan, J. A., & Riedl, J. (2000). Analysis of recommendation algorithms for e-commerce. In *Proceedings of the ACM EC'00 Conference* (pp. 158-167). Minneapolis, MN.

Schwab, I., Pohl, W., & Koychev, I. (2000). Learning to recommend from positive evidence. In *Proceedings of the International Conference on Intelligent User Interfaces* (pp. 241-247). New York: ACM Press.

Shardanand, U., & Maes, P. (1995). Social information filtering: algorithms for automating word of mouth. In *Proceedings of the ACM CHI'95 Conference on Human Factors in Computing Systems* (pp. 210-217). New York: ACM Press.

Weber, R., Schek, H. J., & Blott, S. (1998). A quantitative analysis and performance study for similarity-search methods in high-dimensional spaces. In *Proceedings of the International Conference on Very Large Databases* (pp. 194-205).

Xing, C.X. et al. (2002). Developing Tsinghua University architecture digital library for Chinese architecture study and university education. In *Proceedings of the 5th International Conference on Asian Digital Libraries* (pp. 206-217). Singapore.

Yu, K. et al. (2001). Feature weighting and instance selection for collaborative filtering. In *Proceedings of the 2nd International Workshop on Management of Information on the Web: Web Data and Text Mining*.

Yu, K., Xu, X., Tao, J. et al. (2002). Instance selection techniques for memory-based collaborative filtering. In *Proceedings of the 2nd SIAM International Conference on Data Mining*.

Zeng, C., Xing, C.X., & Zhou, L.Z. (2002). A survey of personalization technology. *Journal of Software*, *3* (10), 1952-1961.

Zeng, C., Xing, C.X., & Zhou, L.Z. (2003). Personalized search algorithm using content-based filtering. *Journal of Software*, *14* (5), 997-1002.

Zeng, C., Xing, C.X., & Zhou, L.Z. (2003). Similarity measure and instance selection for collaborative filtering. In *Proceedings of the 12th International World Wide Web Conference* (pp. 652-658). Budapest.

Section III

Implementation Issues
and Challenges

Chapter VI

Implementation of Next Generation Digital Libraries

Ee-Peng Lim
Nanyang Technological University, Singapore

San-Yih Hwang
National Sun Yat Sen University, Taiwan

Abstract

To implement the next generation digital libraries, one has to examine both the data *and* functional *aspects of the digital library requirements and understand the existing available technologies. In this chapter, we outline the major implementation issues of next generation digital libraries and review existing standards, tools and related research topics. Due to new kinds of content and metadata, as well as domain- and task-specific usage, the next generation digital libraries will need to handle the representation and storage scheme of metadata and content. Unlike the brick-and-mortar libraries, there are new challenges in metadata harvesting, search and retrieval that require standardized protocols to be adopted across different digital libraries. Finally, some advanced digital library services are also discussed.*

Introduction

In recent years, there has been a flurry of new efforts developing different kinds of digital libraries that meet the needs of a wide range of users. Some of these efforts simply involve turning the conventional online catalog search systems into some Web-based systems. The other efforts, which are also the main focus of this chapter, require the development of both novel *content* and advanced *services* for users with information needs that could not met by the *brick-and-mortar libraries* [see Chan (2004) for a good discussion on how a university library embarks on a digital library development effort to manage digital content contributed by its users.]. We call these the *next generation digital libraries*. In this chapter, we will review some of the implementation challenges faced by the next generation digital libraries, and provide some pointers to the standards, tools and methods that address these challenges.

Like any other software application, we can dissect a next generation digital library system into two main components: the *data component* and *functional components*. The data component refers to the digital content and other information managed by the digital library. This mainly includes a collection of raw data content and the corresponding metadata. User profiles covering the user identities, interests and usage patterns are also part of the data component when such information is required to provide personalized services to the library users. The functional components refer to the range of services provided by the digital library system. Other than the standard search and retrieval facilities, new services are often required in a next generation digital library for the following reasons:

- New operations are required to cope with the visualization and manipulation requirement of new types of digital content. For example, the usual text and attribute based search and retrieval facilities are inadequate for a collection of map images or music audio files.

- When the use of a digital library is closely coupled with user tasks, for example, e-learning, new services that provide seamless integration of digital library accesses with user tasks will be required. For example, an e-learning system may require a digital library to flexibly organize reference materials by course topics in order to facilitate learning.

- Due to advances in Web and media technologies, the next generation digital libraries are likely to manage massive amount of digital content. If there are no effective methods and tools to help users locating the relevant information, users are likely to be overloaded with too much information, causing the *information overload* problem.

- To leverage on the content and services provided by different next generation digital libraries, *interoperability* of metadata and services among different digital libraries must be supported.

In this chapter, we will give an overview of a set of rather new methods, standards and tools for realizing a next generation digital library. This overview will also serve as an introduction to the series of articles covered by the book section on digital library implementation issues and challenges. While the intent is to cover as much information as possible, some of the relevant implementation issues will be omitted in this chapter due to space limitation. Nevertheless, it is hoped that, by reading this chapter, readers are able to acquire an overall strategy of implementing next generation digital libraries and filling in the missing gaps with information from other sources.

Metadata Representation and Storage

Metadata in a digital library is similar to the library catalog records in the brick-and-mortar libraries. They are the data about data. Metadata together with the raw digital content constitute the *core data component* of the next generation digital libraries. Unlike the library catalog records, metadata in the next generation digital libraries has to provide a few unique features:

- Since the raw content are digitized and are likely to be available online, it is necessary for their corresponding metadata records to incorporate references to the original content. This differs from the existing library catalogs that store only the Dewey numbers (or other similar ids) of library materials organized in physical stacks[1].

- The next generation digital libraries will need to share metadata among themselves to avoid the costly process of metadata creation and maintenance. This sharing of metadata is only possible if there is a common metadata standard adopted by all these digital libraries.

- The raw content of a digital library may be stored in one centralized local repository or may originate from distributed and autonomous sources. When a digital library involves only content from non-local autonomous sources, they are known as the *virtual digital libraries*. As the metadata formats required for the content from different sources could be different, one will have to adopt some flexibility in designing the metadata format.

- To support task-oriented access to the digital library content, we need to custom-design the metadata format to store attributes required by the tasks. For example, to visualize the metadata of a digital library comprising map files as raw content, we need to store the geometrical shapes and locations of map objects within their metadata.

Indeed, the above features have been considered by several metadata standards that have been developed in recent years. These standards include the *Dublin Core* (Dekkers, 2003) and *Resource Descriptive Framework* (World Wide Web Consortium, 2003).

Dublin Core Metadata Initiative is an effort to promote a single metadata standard for resource sharing and discovery on the Web. The most important product of this effort is the *Dublin Core Metadata Element Set*, which has been adopted as an international standard known as ISO15836. Dublin Core Metadata Element Set consists of 15 elements (or attributes), namely:

- *Title:* Name given to the resource.

- *Creator:* An entity primarily responsible for making the content of the resource.

- *Subject:* The topic of the content of the resource.

- *Description:* An account of the content of the resource.

- *Publisher:* An entity responsible for making the resource available.

- *Contributor:* An entity responsible for making contributions to the content of the resource.

- *Date:* A date associated with an event in the life cycle of the resource.

- *Type:* The nature or genre of the content of the resource.

- *Format:* The physical or digital manifestation of the resource.

- *Identifier:* An unambiguous reference (e.g., URI, URL, DOI and ISBN) to the resource within a given context.

- *Source:* A reference to a resource from which the present resource is derived.

- *Language:* A language of the intellectual content of the resource.

- *Relation:* A reference to a related resource.

- *Coverage:* The extent or scope of the content of the resource.

- *Rights:* Information about rights held in and over the resource.

The above elements represent the most essential metadata attributes to be represented. Compared to the traditional library catalog format (e.g., USMARC),

Dublin Core Metadata Element Set has much fewer core elements, making it easy for all digital libraries to adopt the standard. Among them, *source* captures the reference to the original resource content. To further cope with other requirements, Dublin Core Metadata Element Set allows for element refinements (also known as qualifiers) into the standard to define the syntax or to refine the semantics of the 15 elements. For example, one can refine the *Description* element to include an *Abstract* or *Table of Content* of a resource. A Dublin Core metadata record can be stored together with its referenced resource or separately expressed using the HTML meta-tags or XML (EXtensible Markup Language).

The 15 elements of Dublin Core Metadata Element Set enable broad adoption but may be too restrictive for specialized digital libraries that require more domain- or task-specific metadata elements. It is, therefore, crucial to have other metadata standards to co-exist with Dublin Core. *Resource Description Framework* (RDF), an initiative by the W3 consortium, on the other hand, provides a way to accommodate Dublin Core metadata with other metadata of other formats. Using RDF, a resource can have both Dublin Core metadata elements and other domain- or task- specific elements expressed in XML. More details about RDF can be found in World Wide Web Consortium (2003).

Metadata Harvesting/Dissemination

In the context of brick-and-mortar libraries, library catalog records are the metadata specially created by the library community to support OPAC searches. Library catalog records are usually created one at a time in a controlled manner by professional catalogers. Such a manual approach to create metadata records is, however, not efficient in the context of next generation digital libraries. While there is some research on automated approaches to derive metadata elements from Web page content using some classification methods (Jenkins & Inman, 2000), such approaches are not always feasible. A more practical approach is therefore to facilitate automatic or semi-automatic metadata harvesting when the metadata of the digital content can be drawn from other digital libraries. In this way, much of the metadata creation efforts can be shared across digital libraries in an automated manner, thus reducing the overhead of metadata maintenance.

The *Open Archives Initiative* (OAI) (Open Archives Initiative, 2003) addresses the above metadata harvesting and dissemination issues by offering a simple and easy-to-implement protocol for *metadata providers* to share their metadata with different *service providers*. The currently implemented OAI protocol, known as *Open Archives Initiative Protocol for Metadata Harvesting* (OAI-PMH), uses HTTP-based request-response communication to obtain metadata encoded in XML from the metadata providers and delivers them to the service providers (Lagoze & Sompel, 2000). All metadata providers must support the Dublin Core Metadata Element Set. To avoid harvesting the same metadata records from a provider site multiple times, OAI-PMH is able to selectively harvest records based on their date stamps or their groupings.

The OAI-PMH request is formatted as a HTTP message with a GET command. The GET command includes a *base URL* specifying the OAI-PMH request type, and a list of input arguments expressed in *key-value pairs*. There are six OAI-PMH request types, namely:

- *GetRecord*: To retrieve a single metadata record.

- *Identify*: To retrieve information about the collection of metadata maintained by the metadata provider.

- *ListIdentifier*: To retrieve the record ids from the metadata collection of the provider.

- *ListMetadataFormats*: To retrieve metadata formats supported by the provider.

- *ListRecords*: To return metadata records from the provider.

- *ListSets*: To retrieve the set structure in the provider's metadata collection.

Note that a metadata provider under the OAI-PMH protocol can support other metadata formats co-existing with Dublin Core. The *ListMetadataFormat* request is designed to discover the metadata format supported by the metadata provider. By specifying the *metadataPrefix* input argument of the *ListRecords* request, the service provider can obtain metadata records of the desired format.

OAI-PMH protocol has been adopted in several digital libraries including ePrints.org (Liu, Brody, Carr, Zubair & Nelson, 2002) and DLESE (DLESE, 2003). There are also several digital library tools developed based on the protocol. For example, DP6 is a gateway that enables Web search engines such as Google to harvest and index records from metadata providers (Liu, Brody, Carr, Zubair & Nelson, 2002).

Search and Retrieval Facilities

Once the metadata collection is constructed, whether by manually creating them from the original digital content or automatically harvesting from other digital libraries, search and retrieval facilities can be developed on both the local metadata collection and the original content. To distinguish the two, we call them the *metadata search/retrieval* and *content search/retrieval* facilities respectively. The former allows users to specify search criteria against the metadata elements, while the latter supports queries on features that can be extracted from the original digital content. The search and retrieval facilities often include the following components:

- *Collection indexing*: This refers to indexing the metadata elements or content features to enable fast searching on large collections of metadata records or digital content.

- *Search engine*: Once an index is built, a search engine can be deployed to evaluate search queries.

- *Search/retrieval interface*: A user-friendly, Web-based user interface is required to simplify the process of formulating search queries and viewing the returned results.

Search and retrieval facilities usually can be implemented using off-the-shelf digital library tools. For example, Greenstone is an open source suite of digital library tools that supports both metadata and text content search/retrieval (Witten, Bainbridge, & Boddie, 2001) [Please refer to Chapter X by Nichols et al. (2004) for more detailed description about Greenstone.] For non-text content (e.g., video, image, and audio) collections, more specialized indexing and search/retrieval tools will be required. The Informedia project is one example that indexes video files and supports advanced search functions on the video objects (Wactlar, Christel, Gong, & Hauptmann, 1999). IBM's Query By Image Content (QBIC) system is another example that supports search queries on a collection of images using image features such as color and texture (Flickner, Sawhney, Niblack, Ashley, Huang, & Dom, 1995).

Apart from searching local collections, some next generation digital libraries will have to cater for remote collection search queries when the metadata or information required could only be derived from sites that do not permit metadata harvesting or content replication. Often, these sites support some form of networked query interfaces on their collections, either for free or some fee. These query interfaces may be HTTP-based and can be invoked using the standard HTTP Get and POST requests. In other cases, the query interfaces may only be accessed via some other Internet protocols. For example, Z39.50 is a well-established application level (ANSI/NISO) protocol adopted by many brick-and-mortar libraries to provide access to their online catalog collections (Hammer & Favaro, 1996). The present Z39.50 protocol however can only support limited types of metadata formats although there are some discussions on decoupling its communication aspect from the metadata format.

When a digital library allows multiple remote digital libraries to be searched for a given user query, we call this the *federated search query* (or *metasearch query*). For example, in the implementation of NDLTD (Network Digital Library of Thesis and Dissertations) (Fox, Gonçalves, McMillan, Eaton, Atkins, & Kipp, 2002), both federated search and harvested metadata search are supported. The ability to federate a search query and draw information from different sources simultaneously leads to both advantages and new challenges. The main advantages include up-to-date results from the sites, and no storage required for harvested information. As the overheads of searching multiple sites may be very high, the problem of selecting relevant sites to be searched will have to be addressed. Furthermore, the federated approach will also be affected when some sites are not available due to site maintenance or temporary network disconnections.

Other Advanced Digital Library Services

The services provided by the next generation digital libraries are not limited to metadata creation, metadata maintenance, metadata harvesting, search and retrieval. Several new advanced services are expected to be added to the list to enhance the usability of the digital libraries. In the following, a few of such services will be described.

Automated Summarization

Information overloading is a common phenomenon found in the next generation digital libraries. One way to reduce the amount of information to be processed by users is to give them summaries of search and retrieval results instead of the original large-sized results. This automatic summarization service is particularly useful in a text content search that returns a large number of text documents that could not be digested within a short time. By condensing the documents into short abstracts or key sentences, the user can quickly determine the relevance of each document and decide whether to delve into the document details. Automatic summarization is usually done one document at a time. Min-Yen Kan (Kan, 2004) in Chapter VII introduces a new summarization method that considers similar content across different documents and derives the summarized content accordingly. This method has been implemented in the Centrifuser system. Instead of giving a summary, which usually consists of a few well-formed sentences, it is also possible to just extract a few key phrases from a given document to describe its content. For example, in the KEA system, key phrases can be automatically picked up using some machine learning method with some training samples. This system will be described in Chapter VIII (Witten, Paynter, Frank, Gutwin, & Nevill-Manning, 2004).

Annotations

Increasingly, the success of a digital library depends on the community of users it serves. In next generation digital libraries, users will play a paramount role not only in using library services, but also contributing resources. Unlike the controlled and well-regulated metadata and content maintained by the professional librarians, the user-contributed information is less rigorous and usually comprises comments or additional pieces of knowledge that are added for future references or for sharing with other users. Such contributed information is generally known as annotations. Annotation service has been studied in the context of electronic text and hypertext systems (Marshall, 1997). There are several issues to be addressed when annotations are to be supported within the next generation digital libraries. Firstly, an *annotation data model* describing the kinds of objects to be annotated and the annotation data structure used to represent annotation information must be designed. Secondly, one must develop the storage scheme and access methods of the annotation information. Lastly, when annotations are treated as first class objects, other digital library services previously applicable to metadata and library content will have to be extended to annotations. For example, a user may want to query annotations or provide further annotations to the existing annotations.

Multi-Cultural and Multi-Lingual Support

While most digital libraries today are English-based, the next-generation digital libraries are more likely to be *multi-cultural* and *multi-lingual*. For example, a digital library for music artifacts may include music works from different cultures written in different kinds of musical notations with unique musical forms. The intrinsically multi-lingual descriptions of these works require the digital library services to support multiple languages. In the simplest monolingual scenarios, depending on the language used in the description, the same language is required for invoking the services. Instead of taking such a restrictive monolingual approach, a *cross-lingual approach* whereby users are free to use any language to access content of any languages will be ideal. Yang & Li (2004) in Chapter IX discuss several research issues in cross-lingual information retrieval.

Recommendation and Personalization

The massive amount of information managed by a next generation digital library imposes an urgent need to remedy the information overload problem. Indeed, most users are incapable of specifying precisely their needs in queries, and a search condition often matches a large number of digital objects, among which only a small subset are of interest to the users. Personalization techniques, with its origin in information filtering (Loeb & Terry, 1992), (statically or dynamically) create a user profile for each library user and subsequently recommend a small number of digital objects that meet users' interests without requiring the specification of ad-hoc queries.

A user profile is used to record a user's *long-term* interests and/or *short-term* interests. The long-term interest of a scholar, for example, may include the specific topics that s/he has been persistently working on and that will not change abruptly. The most straightforward approach to generating a long-term interest profile is to ask the user to explicitly specify it. Such a user-created long term interest profile is much like a query that consists of a set of key terms connected by logical connectives such as AND, OR, and NOT. Then the profile acts as a *persistent query*, which is periodically evaluated against updates to the digital library. The digital objects contained in the result of each query evaluation are then summarized and disseminated (typically through e-mails) to the user. This approach, often called *selective dissemination of information* (SDI), has been widely used by traditional library automatic systems and existing literature digital libraries for keeping their patrons updated about the newest developments in their areas.

With the advent of the World Wide Web and the rapid growth of e-commerce, new types of personalization techniques have emerged and been radically applied to a wide spectrum of domains not limited to digital information products. These techniques maintain for each user a set of ratings assigned to products that indicate the degrees to which s/he likes the products and subsequently learn the user's interest profile. These ratings can be explicitly provided by users or implicitly derived by observing users' actions. For example, Pennock et al. (2000) examined users' actions to Citeseer, a digital library for scientific literatures, and gave 1 point for adding an article to profile, 0.5 point for downloading an article, and -1 point for ignoring a recommended article. Two broad classes of recommendation approaches that are commonly used by today's recommender systems are *content-based filtering* and *collaborative filtering*. The content-based filtering approach establishes a user's interest profile by analyzing the metadata or the content of his/her rated objects. Each object is represented by a set of content features, and a rating is seen as a label.

Thus, the problem of constructing a user's interest profile is formulated as a classification problem. The resultant classification model will predict the user's rating of an un-rated digital object based on its metadata or content. Many classification techniques, such as Bayesian classifier, linear regression or SVM, decision tree, and neural network, serve the purpose of building a classification model.

Unlike the content-based filtering which considers only a given user's preference in making recommendation, the collaborative filtering recommends objects to a user by taking into account other users' preference. Preferences of un-rated objects are predicted for a user based on a combination of known ratings from other users. There are two broad approaches for estimating the preference of an unseen object to a user: *memory-based* and *model-based* (Breese, Heckerman, & Kadie, 1998). The memory-based approach computes a weighted sum on rows or columns of the rating matrix for predicting the liking of a user to an object. Possible weighting schemes include correlation, cosine and regression. The model-based approach uses the set of ratings to learn a probabilistic model and then applies this model to predict the probability of a user likes an object. Many classification schemes, such as those mentioned above, can be deployed to learn the model. Due to the simplicity and the effectiveness concluded by some empirical studies (Pazzani, 1999), collaborative filtering is by far the most popular approach used in today's recommender systems.

A short-term interest of a user is referred to as the immediate information need for the task at hand, which may or may not relate to his/her long-term interest. Thus, it is inadequate to derive a user's task profile from historical data. In contrast, a task profile should be dynamically specified by a list of example objects that are related to the task. In its simplest form, the task profile of a user can be regarded as a single object that the user is currently looking at. When a user chooses to browse a digital object A, those objects that are either similar to A in their content or often accessed together with A by other users are recommended. Such a function has already been provided by many literature digital libraries. The task profile of a user can be extended to include a set S of objects that the user recently accessed, and the goal becomes to recommend a set of objects whose contents are similar to and/or that are often accessed together with the objects in S. Based on Web usage log, Mobasher et al. derived clustering based approaches that recommend a set of Web pages to a user that are often accessed together with the set of Web pages s/he has just browsed (2000). Similar approaches were adopted to recommend articles in literature digital libraries (Hwang, Hsiung, & Yang, 2003).

Conclusion

The opportunities and challenges of next generation digital libraries provide software developers and researchers much room for system design and implementation. Almost all the existing library services will be extended to cope with the new operating environments and content. Metadata representation, metadata storage, search and retrieval are among them. At the same time, new services will also be required to provide better support to the library users and user communities. This chapter attempts to describe the new implementation requirements and cover the various available standards and tools. While many of these are already mature technologies, there are also some that are in prototyping stage in the laboratories. We hope that this chapter will lay the foundation for a good understanding of the various technological issues of the next generation digital libraries and the pursuits for their solutions.

References

Breese, J. S., Heckerman, D., & Kadie, C. (1998, October). *Empirical analysis of predictive algorithms for collaborative filtering*. Technical Report, MSR-TR-98-12. Microsoft Research.

Chan, S.S., & Tan, C.W. (2004). Chapter Article: Development and Management of Nanyang Technological University E-Document.

Dekkers, M., & Weibel, S. (2003, April). State of the Dublin Core Metadata Initiative. *D-Lib Magazine, 9* (4).

DLESE. (2003). *Digital Library for Earth System Education.* Retrieved from the World Wide Web: *http://www.dlese.org/*

Flickner, M., Sawhney, H., Niblack, W., Ashley. J., Huang, Q., & Dom, B. et al. (1995). Query by image and video content: The QBIC System. *IEEE Computer, 28* (9), 23-32.

Fox, E.A., Gonçalves, M.A., McMillan, G., Eaton, J., Atkins, A., & Kipp, N. (2002, Spring). The networked digital library of theses and dissertations: Changes in the university community. Special issue on "Information Technology and Educational Change." *The Journal of Computing in Higher Education, 13* (2), 3-24.

Hammer, S., & Favaro, J. (1996, March). Z39.50 and the World Wide Web. *D-Lib Magazine.*

Hwang, S.Y., Hsiung, W.C., & Yang, W.S. (2003). A prototype WWW literature recommendation system for digital libraries. *On-line Information Review, 27* (3), 169-182.

Jenkins, C., & Inman, D. (2000). Server-side automatic metadata generation using qualified Dublin Core and RDF. In *Kyoto International Conference on Digital Libraries 2000* (pp. 245-253).

Kan, M.Y. (2004). Chapter Article: Using multi-document summarisation to assist in semi-structured literature retrieval: A case study in consumer healthcare.

Lagoze, C., & Sompel, H.V.D. (2000). The Open Archives Initiative: Building a lower-barrier interoperability framework. In *ACM Digital Library Conference*.

Liu, X., Brody, T., Carr, L., Zubair, M., & Nelson, M.L. (2002, November). A scalable architecture for harvest-based digital libraries. *D-Lib Magazine, 8* (11).

Loeb, S., & Terry, D. (1992, December). Special issue on information filtering. *Communications of the ACM, 35* (12).

Marshall, C.C. (1997). Annotation: From paper books to the digital library. *ACM Digital Libraries*, pp. 131-140.

Mobasher, B., Dai, H., Luo, T., Nakagawa, M., & Witshire, J. (2000). Discovery of aggregate usage profiles for Web personalization. In *Proceedings of the WebKDD Workshop 2000*.

Nichols, D. et al. (2004). Chapter Article: Evolving Tool Support for Digital Librarians.

Open Archives Initiative. (2003). Retrieved from the World Wide Web: *http://www.openarchives.org/*

Pazzani, M. J. (1999). A framework for collaborative, content-based and demographic filtering. *Artificial Intelligence Review*, 13 (5-6), 393-408.

Pennock, D.M., Horvitz, E., Lawrence, S., & Giles, C. L. (2000). Collaborative filtering by personality diagnosis: A hybrid memory- and model-based approach. In *Proceedings of the 6th Conference on Uncertainty in Artificial Intelligence* (UAI-2000) (pp. 473-480).

Wactlar, H., Christel, M., Gong, Y., & Hauptmann, A. (1999). Lessons learned from building a terabyte digital video library. Computer, *32* (2), 66-73.

Witten, I.H., Bainbridge, D., & Boddie, S.J. (2001, October). Greenstone open-source digital library software. *D-Lib Magazine, 7* (10).

Witten, I.H., Paynter, G.W., Frank, E., Gutwin, C., & Nevill-Manning, C.G. (2004). Chapter Article: KEA: Practical automatic keyphrase extraction.

World Wide Web Consortium. (2003). *Resource description framework (RDF)*. Retrieved from the World Wide Web: *http://www.w3.org/RDF/*

Yang, C., & Li, K.W. (2004). Chapter Article: Cross-lingual information retrieval: The challenge in multilingual digital libraries.

Endnotes

[1]   Library records in MARC format can actually accommodate digital references to the original digital content. This feature however has rarely been used in the brick-and-mortar libraries.

Chapter VII

Using Multi-Document Summarization to Facilitate Semi-Structured Literature Retrieval:
A Case Study in Consumer Healthcare

Min-Yen Kan
National University of Singapore, Singapore

Abstract

This chapter examines the techniques behind a user interface that computes a multi-document summary of documents retrieved by a search. As a user's query can retrieve thousands of relevant documents, it is paramount that they be logically organized. In digital libraries, documents are traditionally represented as a ranked list of documents ordered by computed relevance and do not take into account presentation techniques used by information professionals (such as librarians) in the physical library. This chapter examines a framework used in a consumer healthcare digital library that incorporates techniques used by librarians. It brings together commonalities between documents and highlights their salient differences to target the needs of users using the browsing and searching modes of information seeking. It achieves this by discovering common and unique topics among its input from a combination of structural and lexical cues.

Introduction

A digital library implementation involves many components, including ones that display retrieved results. As a query in a digital library can retrieve thousands of relevant documents, sorting out which documents are useful can be a daunting task. This chapter presents the design and implementation of a novel user interface and backend support that helps cope with this information overload.

While this book concerns the design and usability of *digital* libraries, the same issues exist in traditional physical libraries. In this chapter, we analyze how people deal with information overload in traditional libraries, and how the analysis can offer solutions for the digital medium. We present guidelines that are distilled from this analysis in the first portion of the chapter.

To implement the guidelines, we use automatic multi-document text summarization, which attempts to remove redundancies across texts and identify key differences. Our implementation, called Centrifuser, also recognizes that documents in the digital library are often structured and composed of mixed media, involving nested headers, tables and images. A key observation in this chapter is that the documents retrieved by a query are often structurally similar. We utilize this structural regularity to organize and build the summary. In the second half of the chapter, we will detail the implementation of Centrifuser and present examples of how the system presents healthcare information from a medical digital library meant for laypersons.

Informal Seeking in Traditional Library

In the traditional physical library, users with questions interact with librarians in two primary scenarios. Librarians can interact with users during a reference interview, in which the user comes to the librarian for assistance. Librarians can also assist users by compiling finding aids (such as subject guides and bibliographies) that users can consult at will. We describe these two scenarios in more detail and distill design guidelines for the user interface from each approach.

Reference Interviews

When presented with an in-depth research question during a reference interview, librarians undertake a process to answer the question as well as possible. This process consists of four sequential steps (Katz, 1987), of which two are pertinent to the discussion at hand:

1. *Communicating the information need*: Users often do not specify fully what they are looking for. This results in a gap between the user's need and the librarian's understanding of it. Librarians are trained to recognize this cognitive gap and to gently ask the user for clarification. This problem often arises when users: (a) make a tacit assumption that the librarian understands the specifics implied by their request; or (b) lack the terminology to correctly express their information need. Belkin et al. (1994) phrase the latter problem as an Anomalous State of Knowledge: naïve users lack the knowledge of the correct terminology that will enable them to find the relevant material.

2. *Provide structure to initial results*: In the course of searching a library and obtaining partial results, the librarian may need to help the user evaluate preliminary results. In this regard, the librarian often acts as an information filter, by grouping preliminary search results by content or narrowing the choices down to a manageable set of alternatives (often two to five sources).

Finding Aids

When no librarian is present to actively assist users in fulfilling their information needs, users can consult passive resources for assistance. These compiled finding aids can be viewed as a written form of the information retrieval (IR) process, which are static and non-interactive. Two additional characteristics that emerge from an analysis of these resources are useful to note:

3. *Descriptive metadata that assist relevance judgments*: The *Guide to Reference Books* (Balay, 1996) states that its "… contributors were asked to consider a [book]'s purpose, audience, scope, coverage, arrangement and special features…" in creating annotations. This description shows that such metadata are important features in providing a description for the user (even when the user is a librarian herself). Earlier work has also shown

that these and other descriptive metadata are relevant for retrieval but differ according to the domain and genre of the resource (Kan, 2003).

4. *Clearly differentiated bibliographic items that route users to relevant information*: Lubetzky (1953) requires "...the cataloguer to relate the given work to the other works of the author and the other editions of the work... so that he could select the edition most useful or suitable for his purposes...." A finding aid entry is not independent of its surrounding entries; it needs to be differentiated and interrelated with other entries. The quality of the finding aid as a whole can be judged by its coverage of the subject and how well it routes users to the appropriate resource.

Performance of the Standard Ranked List

Although many alternative, graphical user interfaces have been proposed for information retrieval applications, the standard ranked list of documents still dominates as the most familiar interface and is one of the most usable. In this interface, documents are ranked by their prestige and/or similarity to the user's query, and several highly ranked documents are listed in descending order. Typically the page's title, file size, URL and date indexed are provided for each entry, along with a short summary.

While the standard ranked list is straightforward to understand and use, it only provides minimal support for the strategies uncovered in our analysis. No explicit support is given to help users revise or edit their queries. Aside from removing duplicate materials found on mirrored sites, little is done to group or filter preliminary results. Traditional descriptive metadata that would be accessible in the digital library are not displayed. Its short summaries are often built by highlighting query words in context or by extracting the beginning words of the document. Neither of these approaches takes the other relevant documents into consideration when constructing summaries.

Centrifuser: Multi-Document Summarization Using Similarities and Differences

The shortcomings of the ranked list motivated us to construct an alternative user interface that explicitly supports the strategies distilled from our study. The result of our effort is encapsulated in the Centrifuser user interface. It implements the reference librarian's strategies by using automatic multi-document summarization that capitalizes on regularities in document structure.

Table 1. Summary of physical library strategy support in the standard ranked list interface, compared with the Centrifuser system

Physical library strategy	Explicit support in ranked list?	Explicit support in Centrifuser?
1. Clarify information need	No.	Yes. Navigation bar provides context to the user and assists in exploring related and more detailed topics.
2. Group or filter preliminary results	No.	Yes. Constructs an overview of similarities to assist browsers.
3. Include descriptive metadata	Limited.	Yes. Includes salient document metadata when differing from others.
4. Differentiate Items	No.	Yes. Reports salient differences to route searchers to specific documents.

The system is built as a post-processor to a standard information retrieval system: taking relevant documents as input and synthesizing different summary components as output. Although the approach used in Centrifuser is domain-independent, we will limit our examples to ones in the consumer healthcare domain. *Figure 1* shows a Centrifuser summary for a consumer healthcare query on angina (chest pain).

Centrifuser computes three distinct summary components that form an *overview plus details* user interface: (a) navigation links that allow the user to move directly to related topics; (b) an informative extract that pools together the commonalities of input documents; and (c) indicative group summaries which group search results into several text bullets. Centrifuser is a fully automated system and authors these components using a combination of information extraction and natural language generation techniques.

Figure 2 shows the architecture of Centrifuser. We describe the central data structure (the topic tree) used in Centrifuser along with the off-line preprocessing steps first.

Topic Trees

Expository documents, such as those stored in digital libraries, are often well structured. They can consist of nested topics and subtopics, which can be visualized as a hierarchy or tree. In Centrifuser, documents are analyzed at the topical level: each document is represented by its corresponding document topic tree (DTT). We define a DTT as a tree of topics, where each topic contains its

Figure 1.   Centrifuser summary in response to the query "What is angina?"

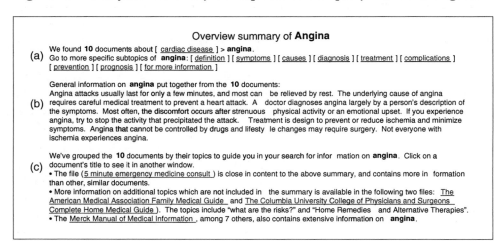

Overview summary of **Angina**

(a) We found **10** documents about [cardiac disease] > **angina**.
Go to more specific subtopics of **angina** : [definition] [symptoms] [causes] [diagnosis] [treatment] [complications]
[prevention] [prognosis] [for more information]

(b) General information on **angina** put together from the **10** documents:
Angina attacks usually last for only a few minutes, and most can   be relieved by rest. The underlying cause of angina
requires careful medical treatment to prevent a heart attack. A   doctor diagnoses angina largely by a person's description of
the symptoms. Most often, the discomfort occurs after strenuous   physical activity or an emotional upset. If you experience
angina, try to stop the activity that precipitated the attack.   Treatment is design to prevent or reduce ischemia and minimize
symptoms. Angina that cannot be controlled by drugs and lifesty le changes may require surgery. Not everyone with
ischemia experiences angina.

(c) We've grouped the **10** documents by their topics to guide you in your search for infor mation on **angina**. Click on a
document's title to see it in another window.
• The file (5 minute emergency medicine consult) is close in content to the above summary, and contains more in formation
than other, similar documents.
• More information on additional topics which are not included in   the summary is available in the following two files: The
American Medical Association Family Medical Guide   and The Columbia University College of Physicians and Surgeons
Complete Home Medical Guide). The topics include "what are the risks?" and "Home Remedies   and Alternative Therapies".
• The Merck Manual of Medical Information , among 7 others, also contains extensive information on **angina** .

Figure 2.   Centrifuser architecture (preprocessing steps are shown in the lower left rounded box)

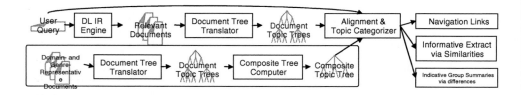

subordinating text (i.e., associated paragraphs and sentences), pointers to any nested topics, and a text label (e.g., "symptoms").

Document topic trees, variously known as logical structure trees (Summers, 1998) and topic maps (*http://www.xtm.org*) can be easily obtained from most richly-formatted documents, such as those encoded in TEI or HTML format. Nested headers in such texts indicate the scope and boundaries of topics and serve as text labels. In less richly formatted documents, hierarchical text segmentation (Yaari, 1999) can be used with headline generation (Zajic et al., 2002) to automatically derive DTTs.

Documents that discuss similar topics are often similar in their structure. Recovering the common structure as a composite topic tree is a necessary step in Centrifuser, as it allows the system to align topics across documents in an efficient manner and assess each topic's importance. Examples of this shared structure are apparent in consumer healthcare leaflets, biographies, company annual reports and travel brochures. This phenomenon has been explored and quantified in the literature as being dependent on text genre (Hoffman, 1991) and knowledge domain (Kittredge et al., 1991).

Shared structure is often also found in the documents returned by a user's search. When searches are ambiguous or polysemous, the retrieved documents may belong to different domains and genres, with different topical structures. In this chapter, we limit our discussion to queries that retrieve documents of the same text genre and knowledge domain, and hence the same topical structure.

Shared topical structure is captured in Centrifuser by a data structure called a composite topic tree (CTT). This structure is manifested across documents in three ways: (1) similar topical content; (2) similar ordering among topics (e.g., symptom information before treatment); and (3) similar notion of importance among topics (e.g., information on symptoms is more commonly seen than information on complications).

Our algorithm for constructing a CTT captures these three aspects by iteratively merging a set of authoritative, sample DTTs. *Figure 3* shows a detail of a CTT built from healthcare Web pages as inputs. The algorithm enriches the DTT structure by adding frequency and variant text label information to each topic in the DTT. As topics across documents are found to be equivalent, the authoritative DTTs are joined together, allowing more correspondences to be found.

The construction algorithm begins with a set of DTTs that represent information on related topics from the same knowledge domain and text genre. In our example, documents about diabetes, heart failure and angina (chest pain) written for laypersons constitute a set of representative DTTs. Note that these docu-

Figure 3. Automatically constructed composite topic tree for the consumer healthcare domain

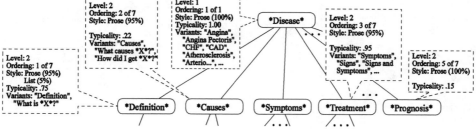

ments can exhibit different levels of granularity: some documents might discuss several different medical conditions (e.g., a book on cardiac diseases), other documents might discuss only one condition (e.g., a pamphlet on angina), and other may focus only on some specific aspects of one condition (e.g., an article on treatments for angina). These differing levels of granularity are handled by the full construction algorithm given in Kan (2003), ChapterIV4. For succinctness, we limit our discussion to the specific case where input DTTs discuss a single topic.

A Top-Down CTT Construction Algorithm

To construct the CTT, we have modified a baseline iterative approach that fuses the two most similar topics from different DTTs into a single multi-document topic. This process repeats until the similarity between the two most similar topics falls below a threshold. Our algorithm limits what topics can be joined during an iteration and improves on the similarity calculation.

The algorithm notes that the top levels of DTTs tend to exhibit more structural similarity than the bottom ones. To capture this intuition, we use a top-down approach, shown in Figure 4. A link between two parent topics is evidence that their children might also be similar. The system first attempts to merge similar root topics among the input DTTs. When two topics merge, their subtopics become candidates for subsequent merging. The process continues until all topics are candidates for merging but none meet the required similarity threshold.

The second improvement targets the similarity computation. We note that the metric should consider structural similarity as well as word overlap. Similarity

Figure 4. Two steps in the top-down construction of the composite topic tree: A merge at level two (left) and a subsequent merge at level three (right)

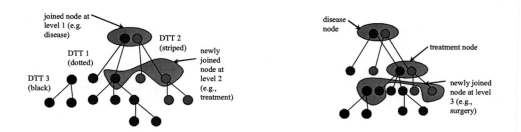

between two topics' text labels, tree depth, tree ordering and parent topics are first calculated separately. Similarity calculations for numeric fields, such as order and depth, and parent topic are straightforward: it is the absolute difference between the two topics' depth or order values. Parent topics are deemed unit similar if they are identical. Text label similarity is more complicated. When topics are merged, the resulting text label often combines two or more similar but non-identical strings. The text similarity metric takes these variations into account, computing the maximum word overlap between all variant forms for each topic. We also substitute a slot holder for any strings corresponding to topic instances (e.g., the various disease names: *symptoms of angina*, and *angina treatments* become *symptoms of <disease>* and *<disease> treatments*). These components are linearly combined to form a single similarity metric, in which the weights for each of the text label, order, parent and depth are empirically determined. In this way, when two topics' structural similarity is very high, we can merge two topics, such as *indicators* and *symptoms*, even when the text labels of the topics do not overlap at all. The resulting procedure is used to construct CTTs for each domain and text genre handled by the digital library.

Computing Summary Components

As in *Figure 2*, the online process begins with a user's query retrieving a set of relevant input documents. These documents would be pre-classified to a particular domain and genre, which causes the corresponding CTT to be retrieved as well. DTTs are then created for each relevant input documents. We employ the aforementioned CTT similarity metric to align the input DTTs with their corresponding CTTs, and use it to align the user's pure-text query to the CTT and DTTs. Once the alignment is complete, Centrifuser creates each summary component independently.

Each summary component is designed to enable the browsing or searching of the input documents in an effective manner. The component algorithms implement the recommendations distilled from the reference librarian's strategies. Furthermore, each component can adjust its output for length constraints. This allows Centrifuser to author short summaries (for use with small form-factor devices, such as PDAs) or longer ones, and enables Centrifuser to tune the interface to favored features at the cost of and vice versa. We begin our discussion of these summary components by examining the components that are provided for browsing support.

Supporting Browsing with Navigation Links and Extracted Similarities

Browsing is a methodology for exploring an information space. It can be utilized by a user exploring a new area or a domain or seeking to learn more about tangential areas of interest. In contrast with searching, which relies on the user to express his need, browsing often gives explicit suggestions on carrying out subsequent actions (e.g., click on a hyperlink or look at resources on the same shelf). An information-seeking interface should support this strategy, as browsing has also been shown to place less cognitive load on the user (Marchionini, 1992). Browsing is supported in Centrifuser by the first two summary components.

Navigation Bar

Centrifuser automatically builds a navigation bar consisting of links to topics related to the user's query. The links on the navigation bar are a corollary to a librarian's responses during the query clarification phase. For example, when asked about the general topic of angina, a librarian may ask whether the user is interested in angina's symptoms, diagnosis or treatments. Centrifuser mimics this behavior by creating links to such topics by using information from the query-aligned CTT. The created links allow the user to browse topics related to her original query. Clicking on a link re-invokes the entire Centrifuser pipeline – the related topic is sent to the search engine and Centrifuser is called on the resulting ranked list of documents to post-process the results.

To build the navigation bar, the aligned query topic in the CTT is first used to define a browsing region. Topics in this region are related to the user's query and are instantiated as a link in the Centrifuser display. This browsing region centers on the query node and is defined as all the sibling topics of the query, the ancestor topics of the query, as well as the children of the topic. The parent and children links allow a query to be broadened or narrowed while the sibling links allow navigation to related topics. The resulting navigation bar for an actual user query on hypertension (high blood pressure) is shown in *Figure 5*.

Informative Synopsis Based on Similarities

The component in the middle of *Figure 1* is a synopsis that gives an overview of the query topic, presenting general, high-level information culled from similar texts in multiple input DTTs. This synopsis is constructed to cover a wide range

Figure 5. (l) CTT with the browsing region defined and (r) its instantiated navigation links for a summary. The query topic hypertension (in black), is an instantiation of the *Disease* CTT node.

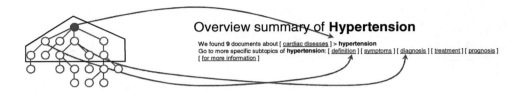

of information related to the query. Users who are browsing for general information rather than seeking details can be satisfied with such a summary, and would save time that would otherwise be needed to retrieve the information from an actual document. In this component, we make the simplifying assumption that important facts tend to be repeated across related documents (Barzilay et al., 1999; Mani & Bloedorn, 1999; Monz, 2001).

The synopsis is composed of sentences extracted from the text of the individual documents in the result set. The process begins by identifying appropriate topics for a summary. Similar to the region used to create navigation links, the query topic defines a region of relevant topics in the CTT. Where the navigation region is used to define which topics to offer as options for the user's next move, the definition of the relevant region indicates which topics should be used to produce the summary. This relevant region is defined as a tree rooted at the query topic, encompassing descendant topics up to some depth away from the query topic. Figure 6 gives some examples of the relevant region.

Each topic is first allocated a sentence to ensure maximum coverage of the summary. Additional sentences are distributed to topics in proportion to their frequency, as described by the frequency information encoded in the CTT until the user-defined summary length is met. This is done to ensure that the important (i.e., typical) topics are adequately captured in proportion to the space constraints.

To choose sentences for each topic, we follow an approach similar to diversity-based summarization (Carbonell & Goldstein, 1998; Nomoto & Matsumoto, 2001). For each topic, we first cluster all of the topic's text in the aligned DTTs using the SimFinder utility (Hatzivassiloglou et al., 2001). This process results in clusters of sentences that express similar information. We extract a representative sentence from each collection, using the standard heuristics of sentence length and position. To order the selected sentences into the resulting synopsis,

Figure 6. (l) A relevant region with the query in black as the root (e.g., "angina"), (c) with the query at the second level (e.g., a follow-up query "symptoms of angina").   (r) a region with a larger depth limit.

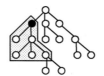

we use the topic order as defined by the CTT for inter-topic ordering. For intra-topic order, sentences that come earlier in the document are ordered first.

The finished synopsis represents an instantiation of the CTT, created from component sentences found in the documents of the result set. Unlike an indicative summary, it gives a miniature version of a prototypical document, excerpting main ideas from each topic. This can be seen in *Figure 1 (b)* for the query on *angina* and below in *Figure 7* in the longer summary for the query on *hypertension*.

Supporting Searching with Generated Indicative Differences

Aside from browsing, searching is the other main information seeking paradigm. In many IR interfaces, search is usually facilitated by an input box for the user's query. When the resulting ranked list of documents is returned, the user may want to select a document for the retrieval of more information. Which document is selected is determined by the information returned by the retrieval engine, such as the URL, title and page summary. To ensure that the user is well informed to perform the selection process, it is vital that the information returned includes discriminatory information for the user to make a selection.

To support this process, Centrifuser attempts to identify the distinguishing aspects of each page. In contrast to existing search systems, which create page summaries independent of each other, the contents of Centrifuser's page summaries are strongly influenced by the presence of their peer pages in the relevant set of documents. This approach implements the librarian's strategy of clearly differentiating items in a listing. Centrifuser also attempts to report only distinguishing characteristics that are relevant to the user's query.

The process begins with the categorization of topics in a document. We start from the definition of each DTT's relevant region, as defined earlier for the

Figure 7. An example of a multi-document synopsis (longer than the one presented in Figure 2). As this summary component is allowed to be longer than the one in Figure 2, the system has chosen additional sentences to represent the subtopic of treatment, diet (shown in italics).

General information on **hypertension** from the **10** documents:
Hypertension, or high blood pressure, is a very common condition that affects 1 out of 4 adults. High blood pressure has no symptoms, so it is very important to have it checked regularly and closely follow the treatment plan recommended by your doctor. The exact causes of hypertension are not known. If you have mild HBP, your doctor may suggest that you lose weight and keep it off, eat less salt, cut down on alcohol, and get more exercise. If blood pressure goes above 140/90, however, some form of treatment diet or drugs may be needed. *Diet changes include eating less table salt and less fat.* For more information on HBP, contact: National Heart, Lung, and Blood Information Center P.O. Box 30105 Bethesda, MD 20824-0105 301-251-1222.

informative summary. The topics in the relevant region are further refined as either *rare* or *typical*, depending on their frequency as given in the CTT. Topics that are more frequent than a given threshold are *typical*, otherwise they are considered *rare*. We further categorize the non-relevant topics as either too *intricate* in detail (too distant a descendant of the query node; in our examples we use a distance of two) or *irrelevant* (outside the subtree defined by the query node). The categorization exhaustively labels each topic in a DTT with one of the four labels, as shown in *Figure 8*.

Document Categories

The documents themselves are then grouped into seven document categories by Centrifuser according to their distribution of the four topic types. Centrifuser uses natural language generation to generate a short indicative summary of each category containing at least one document. The length of the description is controlled by the user. The generated descriptions vary in content and detail according to the number of documents placed in the category. As there are only seven categories and as a single description is generated per category (regardless of the number of documents belonging to it), it is possible to compress a ranked list of many documents into a single screen.

To decide exactly what information to generate in the textual description, we conducted a study of indicative online public access catalog summaries from the Library of Congress, described in further detail in Kan et al. (2001). The main finding is that topical information is most important, but distinguishing metadata also plays an important role in indicative summaries. This leads us to include information about distinguishing descriptive metadata where space allows (e.g., *Content Types* ("does the document contain pictures or tables") or *Audience*

Figure 8. Categorization of topics in a sample DTT into rare, typical, intricate and irrelevant topics. Frequency of the topic from the CTT is given for each topic in the relevant region.

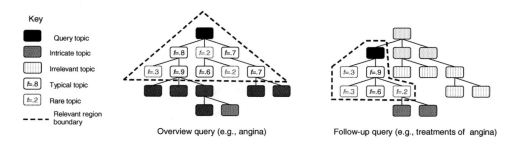

("does it target medical students") in addition to the obligatory topical information. The resulting summary for the query on *angina* is shown in *Figure 1 (c)* and for *hypertension,* in *Figure 9*.

Future Trends

The user interfaces of legacy IR systems put the computer and programmer first, requiring users to remember esoteric command line abbreviations and switches to formulate and execute searches as well as navigate documents. With digital libraries housing terabytes and larger scale data, precise and effective information seeking is no longer a luxury but a necessity.

We see information retrieval as a broad spectrum, with the highly successful science of document retrieval at its midpoint. At one end of the continuum is the support of information seeking at large, involving user modeling and enterprise knowledge management and organization. In digital library research and development, we envision progress at the other end: more exact search and browse using techniques such as passage retrieval, question answering and text summarization. We feel that these technologies will bring the scale of information retrieval to the small, with fragments of text being combined to synthesize an appropriate answer to a user's question (Carbonell et al., 2000). There are a myriad of possible ways to address these issues, but we feel that the careful consideration of interface usability will guide the design of the best approaches.

Table 2. Document typing criteria based on topic type distribution

Document Type	Topic Distribution	Description
Prototypical	· ≥ 50% of summary region topics are typical, and · ≥ 50% of all topics exceed α in frequency	The document has a topic distribution that matches the distribution of topics in the CTT.
Comprehensive	· ≥ 50% of summary region topics are typical	The document contains typical content relevant to the user's query, but also rare information outside of the user's current interest.
Specialized	· ≥ 50% of all topics exceed α in frequency	The document is typical, but contains rare topics of interest to the user's query.
Atypical	· ≥ 50% of all topics are rare	The document contains information on special cases or exceptions.
Deep	· ≥ 50% of all topics are intricate	The document contains not just relevant information on the query topics but also detailed information good for follow-up and narrowing queries.
Irrelevant	· ≥ 50% of all topics are irrelevant	The document contains information outside the scope of interest for the query.
Generic	Everything else	The document displays no particular distribution of information.

Figure 9. Indicative differences generated for a query on hypertension. Sentences that use descriptive metadata are given in italics.

We've grouped the **10** documents by their topics to guide you in your search for information on **hypertension**. Click on a document's title to see it in another window.
• High Blood Pressure and MEDLineplus: High Blood Pressure contain information on rare topics. Topics include "high blood pressure", "specific conditions/aspects", "treatment" and "latest news".
• 5 documents (such as How To Prevent High Blood Pressure) are generally related to your query. They discuss topics such as "hypertension" and "causes". *Some of the these files are longer than usual. The example file contains more figures and tables than usual.*
• Files High Blood Pressure Message Board, High Blood Pressure and High Blood Pressure Foundation don't seem to be related to the main sense of your query. *The first file is longer than usual.*

Conclusion

In this chapter, we have addressed the problem of designing a usable information retrieval interface suitable for the vast collections handled by digital libraries. The library community has approached this problem by bringing their expertise online: reference librarians can now often be consulted as part of the virtual reference desk available to users at their convenience (Lankes et al., 2000). Our approach complements this approach by providing an automated solution that implements the librarian's strategies with the use of automatic text summarization. We differ from other text summarization approaches by exploiting the rich text structure present in the majority of digital library materials, embodied by the topic tree data structures that are central to the algorithms in Centrifuser.

Topic trees provide a foundation for succinctly capturing the logical structure of documents. In this chapter, we have also illustrated how a simple merging algorithm allows Centrifuser to capture the prototypical structure of domain- and genre-specific documents from a representative set of sample trees. This composite topic tree structure is leveraged in Centrifuser's online processes to efficiently align documents with each other and rank the importance of individual topics.

Centrifuser ties summary construction directly with the two primary modes of information seeking in a flexible, tunable system consisting of three distinct components: automatically computed navigation links attempt to clarify the user's information need for broadening and narrowing follow-up queries. To support browsing, Centrifuser builds an informative summary consisting of sentences extracted from the most salient topics. To support searching, Centrifuser clusters input documents by topical content and actively seeks to differentiate each cluster in a maximal way using a combination of content and descriptive metadata facets.

References

Balay, R. (ed.). (1996). *Guide to reference books* (11th ed.). Chicago: American Library Association.

Barzilay, R., McKeown, K., & Elhadad, M. (1999). Information fusion in the context of multi-document summarization. In *Proceedings of the Association for Computational Linguistics (ACL-99)*.

Bates, M. (1979). Information search tactics. *Journal of the American Society for Information Science, 30* (7), 205-214.

Belkin, N., Oddy, R., & Brooks, H. (1982). ASK for information retrieval: Part I. Background and theory. *Journal of Documentation, 38* (2), 61-71.

Carbonell, J., & Goldstein, J. (1998). The use of MMR, diversity-based reranking for reordering documents and producing summaries. In *Proceedings of the Association of Computational Machinery Conference on Information Retrieval (SIGIR-98)*. Melbourne, Australia.

Carbonell, J., Harman, D., Hovy, E., Maiorano, S., Prange, J., & Sparck-Jones, K. (2000, April). *Vision statement to guide research in question & answering (Q&A) and text summarization* (Final Version 1). National Institute of Science and Technology Publication.

Chen, H., Hu, J., & Sproat, R. (1999). Integrating geometrical and linguistic analysis for e-mail signature block parsing. In *Association for Computational Machinery Transactions on Information Systems (TOIS)*.

Cutting. D. (1997). Real life information retrieval: Commercial search engines (Part of a panel discussion at SIGIR 1997). In *Proceedings of the Association for Computational Machinery Conference on Information Retrieval (SIGIR-97)*.

Hatzivassiliglou, V., Klavans, J., Holcombe, M., Barzilay, R., Kan, M., & McKeown, K. (2001). SimFinder: A flexible clustering tool for summarization. In *Proceedings of the North American Association for Computational Linguistics Workshop on Automatic Summarization*.

Hoffman, L. (1991). Texts and text types in LSP. In H. Schröder (ed.), *Subject-Oriented Texts: Languages for Special Purposes and Text Theory, Research in Text Theory* (pp. 158–166). Berlin: Walter de Gruyter.

Kan, M. (2003). Automatic text summarization as applied to information retrieval: Using indicative and informative summaries. (Doctoral dissertation, Columbia University, 2003). *Dissertation Abstracts International, 63* (11).

Kan, M., McKeown, K., & Klavans, J. (2001). Domain-specific informative and indicative summarization for information retrieval. In *Proceedings of the Document Understanding Conference (DUC)* (pp. 19–26). New Orleans.

Katz, W. (ed.). (1987). *Introduction to reference work* (5th edition). McGraw-Hill.

Kittredge, R., Korelsky, T., & Rambow, O. (1991). On the need for domain communication knowledge. *Computational Intelligence, 7* (4).

Kushniruk, A., Patel, V., & Cimino, J. (1997). Usability testing in medical informatics: Cognitive approaches to the evaluation of information systems and user interfaces. In *Proceedings of the American Medical Informatics Association Annual Fall Symposium*.

Lankes, R., Collins, J., & Kasowitz, A. (eds.). (2000). *Digital reference service in the new millennium: Planning, management, and evaluation*. New York: Neal-Schuman Publishers, Inc.

Lubetzky, S. (1953). *Cataloging rules and principles: A critique of the A.L.A. rules for entry and a proposed design for their revision*. Washington, D.C.: Processing Department, Library of Congress.

Mani, I., & Bloedorn, E. (1999). Summarizing similarities and differences among related documents. *Information Retrieval, 1* (1-2), 35–67.

Marchionini, G. (1992). Interfaces for end-user information seeking. *Journal of the American Society for Information Science, 43* (2), 156–163.

Monz, C. (2001). Document fusion for comprehensive event description. In *Proceedings of the Association for Computational Linguistics / Euro-*

pean Association for Computational Linguistics Workshop on Human Language Technology and Knowledge Management.

Nomoto, T., & Matsumoto, Y. (2001). A new approach to unsupervised text summarization. In *Proceedings of the Association for Computational Machinery Conference on Information Retrieval (SIGIR-01)* (pp. 26–34).

Rose, D., & Cutting, D. (1996). *Ranking for usability: Enhanced retrieval for short queries*. Apple Technical Report #163. Cupertino: Apple Computer, Inc.

Summers, K. (1998). Automatic discovery of logical document structure. (Doctoral dissertation, Cornell University, 1998). *Dissertation Abstracts International*, 59 (07).

Yaari, Y. (1999, April). The Texplorer. (Doctoral Dissertation). Israel: Bar Ilan University.

Zajic, D., Dorr, B., & Schwartz, R. (2002). Automatic headline generation for newspaper stories. In *Proceedings of the Association for Computational Linguistics 2002 Workshop on Text Summarization*, Philadelphia.

Chapter VIII

KEA:
Practical Automatic
Keyphrase Extraction

Ian H. Witten
University of Waikato, New Zealand

Gordon W. Paynter
University of Waikato, New Zealand

Eibe Frank
University of Waikato, New Zealand

Carl Gutwin
University of Saskatchewan, Canada

Craig G. Nevill-Manning
Google, Inc., USA

Abstract

Keyphrases provide semantic metadata that summarize and characterize documents. This chapter describes Kea, an algorithm for automatically extracting keyphrases from text. Kea identifies candidate keyphrases using lexical methods, calculates feature values for each candidate, and uses a machine-learning algorithm to predict which candidates are good keyphrases. The machine-learning scheme first builds a prediction model using training documents with known keyphrases, and then uses the model to find keyphrases in new documents. We use a large test corpus to evaluate

Kea's effectiveness in terms of how many author-assigned keyphrases are correctly identified. The system is simple, robust, and available under the GNU General Public License; the chapter gives instructions for use.

Introduction

Keyphrases provide a brief summary of a document's contents. As large document collections such as digital libraries become widespread, the value of such summary information increases. Keywords and keyphrases[1] are particularly useful because they can be interpreted individually and independently of each other. They can be used in information retrieval systems as descriptions of the documents returned by a query, as the basis for search indexes, as a way of browsing a collection, and as a document clustering technique.

In addition, keyphrases can help users get a feel for the content of a collection, provide sensible entry points into it, show how queries can be extended, facilitate document skimming by visually emphasizing important phrases, and offer a powerful means of measuring document similarity (e.g., Gutwin et al., 1999; Witten, 1999).

Keyphrases are usually chosen manually. In many academic contexts, authors assign keyphrases to documents they have written. Professional indexers often choose phrases from a predefined "controlled vocabulary" relevant to the domain at hand. However, the great majority of documents come without keyphrases, and assigning them manually is a tedious process that requires knowledge of the subject matter. Automatic extraction techniques are potentially of great benefit.

There are two fundamentally different approaches to the problem of automatically generating keyphrases for a document: *keyphrase assignment* and *keyphrase extraction*. Both use machine learning methods, and require for training purposes a set of documents with keyphrases already attached.

Keyphrase assignment seeks to select the phrases from a controlled vocabulary that best describe a document. The training data associates a set of documents with each phrase in the vocabulary, and builds a classifier for each phrase. A new document is processed by each classifier, and assigned the keyphrase of any model that classifies it positively (e.g., Dumais et al., 1998). The only keyphrases that can be assigned are ones that have already been seen in the training data.

Keyphrase extraction, the approach used here, does not use a controlled vocabulary, but instead chooses keyphrases from the text itself. It employs lexical and information retrieval techniques to extract phrases from the document text that are likely to characterize it (Turney, 2000). In this approach, the training data is used to tune the parameters of the extraction algorithm.

This chapter describes the *Kea* keyphrase extraction algorithm. It is simple and effective, and performs at the current state-of-the-art (Frank et al., 1999). It uses the Naïve Bayes machine-learning algorithm for training and keyphrase extraction. An implementation is available from the New Zealand Digital Library project (*http://www.nzdl.org/*).

Kea builds on work by Turney (2000), who was the first to treat this problem as a problem of supervised learning from examples. Others had previously used heuristics to extract keyphrases from a document (Krulwich & Burkey, 1996), or methods such as neural networks (Munoz, 1996), or the mutual information heuristic (Steier & Belew, 1993), to discover a large list of two-word phrases. There has also been a great deal of related research on generating or extracting summary information from text (e.g., Brandow et al., 1994; Johnson et al., 1993; Kupiec et al., 1995), but this, in general, attempts to extract complete sentences rather than keywords or keyphrases.

Kea's output is illustrated in *Table 1*, which shows the titles of three research articles and two sets of keyphrases for each article. One set gives the keyphrases assigned by the author; the other was determined automatically from the article's full text. Phrases in common between the two sets are italicized.

In each case, the author's keyphrases and the automatically extracted keyphrases are quite similar, but it is not too difficult to guess which phrases are the author's.

Table 1.   Titles and author- and machine-assigned keyphrases, for three papers

Protocols for secure, atomic transaction execution in electronic commerce		Neural multigrid for gauge theories and other disordered systems		Proof nets, garbage, and computations	
anonymity	*atomicity*	disordered systems	disordered	*cut-elimination*	cut
atomicity	auction	*gauge fields*	gauge	linear logic	*cut elimination*
auction	customer	multigrid	*gauge fields*	*proof nets*	garbage
electronic commerce	*electronic commerce*	neural multigrid	interpolation kernels	sharing graphs	*proof net*
privacy	intruder	neural networks	length scale	typed lambda-calculus	weakening
real-time	merchant		*multigrid*		
security	protocol		smooth		
transaction	*security*				
	third party				
	transaction				

Table 2. Author- and machine-assigned keyphrases for three abstracts in German

Kompensation oder Konflikt? Zur Erklärung negativer Einstellungen zur Zuwanderung		Gewalt als Reaktion auf Anerkennungs-defizite? Eine Analyse bei männlichen deutschen, türkischen und Aussiedler-Jugendlichen mit dem IKG-Jugendpanel		Ausländer, Eingebürgerte und das Problem einer realistischen Zuwanderer-Integrationsbilanz	
Anomie	Erklärung	Befragung	*Gewalt*	Arbeitsmarkt	Ausländer
Autorität	*Einstellungen*	Desintegrations-ansatz	*Jugendlichen*	Bildung	*Eingebürgerter*
Einstellungen	Erklärung negativer Einstellungen	*Gewalt*	männlichen	*Einbürgerung*	juristische
Fremden-feindlichkeit		*Jugend*	türkischen	Einkommen	sozialwissen-schaftliche
Konflikt	*Konflikt*	Multivariate logistische Regression		Integration	*Zuwanderer*
Kompensierung	*Kompensation*			Sprachkenntnisse	
Rechtsextremis-mus				*Zuwanderung*	
Zuwanderung					

The giveaway is that Kea, in addition to choosing several good keyphrases, also chooses some that authors are unlikely to use—for example, *gauge, smooth*, and especially *garbage*! Despite these anomalies, the automatically extracted lists seem to provide a reasonable description of the three papers. In the case where no author-specified keyphrases were available, Kea's choices would be a valuable resource to someone encountering these three articles for the first time.

The Kea algorithm is language-independent (although a stemmer and a stopword list are used, both of which do depend on the language). *Table 2* shows an example in the German language. In this case the documents are abstracts of papers in a German sociology journal. Again the first list in each pair gives the author's keyphrases; the second gives Kea's; and phrases with a common stem are italicized. Most of the authors' phrases are single words, and this relative lack of multiword phases is probably characteristic of the German languages, where compound words often serve the role of phrases in English. Also, because in this example only abstracts were available, rather than full articles, the extracted keyphrases have a somewhat lower correspondence with the authors' ones than can be seen in *Table 1*.

Our goal with Kea is to provide useful metadata where none existed before. Although we evaluate Kea's performance by comparing with the author's own keyphrases, we do not expect to equal them. If we can extract reasonable summaries from text documents, we give a valuable tool to the designers and users of digital libraries. The remainder of this paper describes Kea. The next section details the design of the algorithm. We then give an example of the prediction model generated by Kea and show how it is used to assess a candidate keyphrase. Following that, we report on several experiments designed to test Kea's effectiveness and to explore the effects of varying parameters in the extraction process. An Appendix describes how to download and run the Kea system.

The Kea Algorithm

Kea's extraction algorithm has two stages:

1. *Training:* create a model for identifying keyphrases, using training documents where the author's keyphrases are known.
2. *Extraction:* choose keyphrases from a new document, using the above model.

The process is outlined in *Figure 1*. Both stages choose a set of *candidate phrases* from their input documents, and then calculate the values of certain attributes (called features) for each candidate. We describe these two steps first, and then outline the training and extraction stages in more detail.

Candidate Phrases

Kea chooses candidate phrases in three steps. It first cleans the input text, then identifies candidates, and finally stems and case-folds the phrases.

Input cleaning

ASCII input files are filtered to regularize the text and determine initial phrase boundaries. The input stream is split into tokens (sequences of letters, digits and internal periods), and then several modifications are made:

*   Punctuation marks, brackets, and numbers are replaced by phrase boundaries.
*   Apostrophes are removed.
*   Hyphenated words are split in two.
*   Remaining non-token characters are deleted, as are any tokens that do not contain letters.

The result is a set of lines, each a sequence of tokens containing at least one letter. Acronyms containing periods, like *C4.5*, are retained as single tokens.

Phrase Identification

Kea then considers all the subsequences in each line and determines which of these are suitable candidate phrases. We have investigated several methods for determining suitability, such as looking for noun phrases, but we have found that the following rules are both simple and effective:

1. Candidate phrases are limited to a certain maximum length (usually three words).

2. Candidate phrases cannot be proper names (i.e., single words that only ever appear with an initial capital).

3. Candidate phrases cannot begin or end with a stopword.

The stopword list contains 425 words in nine syntactic classes (conjunctions, articles, particles, prepositions, pronouns, anomalous verbs, adjectives, and adverbs). For most of these classes, all the words listed in an online dictionary were added to the list. However, for adjectives and adverbs, we introduced several subclasses, and words from the subclasses were added only if they overlapped the 60 most common words in the Brown corpus (Kucera & Francis,

Figure 1. Training and extraction processes

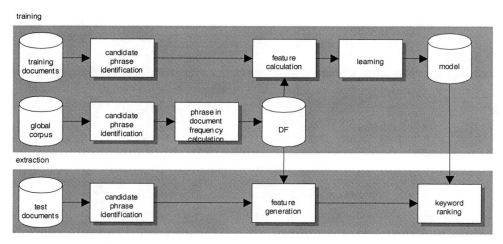

1967). Furthermore, we only added frequently occurring words from these subclasses.

All contiguous sequences of words in each input line are tested using the three rules above, yielding a set of candidate phrases. Note that subphrases are often candidates themselves. Thus, for example, a line that reads *the programming by demonstration method* will generate *programming, demonstration, method, programming by demonstration, demonstration method*, and *programming by demonstration method* as candidate phrases, because *the* and *by* are on the stopword list.

Case-Folding and Stemming

The final step in determining candidate phrases is to case-fold all words and stem them using the iterated Lovins method. This involves using the classic Lovins stemmer (1968) to discard any suffix, and repeating the process on the stem that remains until there is no further change. So, for example, the phrase *cut elimination* becomes *cut elim*.[2]

Stemming and case-folding allow us to treat different variations on a phrase as the same thing. For example, *proof net* and *proof nets* are essentially the same, but without stemming they would have to be treated as different phrases. In addition, we use the stemmed versions to compare Kea's output to the author's keyphrases. We consider an author-specified keyphrase to have been success-fully identified if, when stemmed, it is the same as a machine-generated keyphrase, also stemmed. That is why in *Table 1* the phrases *cut-elimination* and *cut elimination*, and *proof nets* and *proof net*, are considered equivalent.

We retain the unstemmed words for each phrase, in their original capitalization, for presentation to the user in case the phrase does turn out to be a keyphrase. When several different capitalizations occur, the most frequent version is chosen.

Feature Calculation

Two features are calculated for each candidate phrase and used in training and extraction. They are: *TFxIDF*, a measure of a phrase's frequency in a document compared to its rarity in general use; and *first occurrence*, which is the distance into the document of the phrase's first appearance.

TFxIDF

This feature compares the frequency of a phrase's use in a particular document with the frequency of that phrase in general use. General usage is represented by *document frequency*—the number of documents containing the phrase in some large corpus. A phrase's document frequency indicates how common it is (and rarer phrases are more likely to be keyphrases). Kea builds a document frequency file for this purpose using a corpus of documents. Stemmed candidate phrases are generated from all documents in this corpus using the method described above. The document frequency file stores each phrase and a count of the number of documents in which it appears.

With this file in hand, the TFxIDF for phrase P in document D is:

$$\text{TFxIDF} = \frac{\text{freq}(P, D)}{\text{size}(D)} \times -\log_2 \frac{\text{df}(P)}{N}, \text{ where}$$

1.   freq(P, D) is the number of times P occurs in D.
2.   size(D) is the number of words in D.
3.   df(P) is the number of documents containing P in the global corpus.
4. N is the size of the global corpus.

The second term in the equation is the log of the probability that this phrase appears in any document of the corpus (negated because the probability is less than one). If the document is not part of the global corpus, df(P) and N are both incremented by one before the term is evaluated, to simulate its appearance in the corpus.

First Occurrence

The second feature, first occurrence, is calculated as the number of words that precede the phrase's first appearance, divided by the number of words in the document. The result is a number between 0 and 1 that represents how much of the document precedes the phrase's first appearance.

Discretization

Both features are real numbers, which we convert to nominal data for the machine-learning scheme. During the training process, a discretization table for each feature is derived from the training data. This table gives a set of numeric ranges for each feature, and values are replaced by the range into which the value falls. Discretization is accomplished using the supervised discretization method described by Fayyad & Irani (1993).

Training: Building the Model

The training stage uses a set of training documents for which the author's keyphrases are known. For each training document, candidate phrases are identified and their feature values are calculated as described above. To reduce the size of the training set, we discard any phrase that occurs only once in the document. Each phrase is then marked as a keyphrase or a non-keyphrase, using the actual keyphrases for that document. This binary feature is the *class feature* used by the machine-learning scheme.

The scheme then generates a model that predicts the class using the values of the other two features. We have experimented with a number of different machine learning schemes; Kea uses the Naïve Bayes technique (e.g., Domingos & Pazzani, 1997) because it is simple and yields good results. This scheme learns two sets of numeric weights from the discretized feature values, one set applying to positive ("is a keyphrase") examples and the other to negative ("is not a keyphrase") instances. An example model is described in the third section.

Extraction of New Keyphrases

To select keyphrases from a new document, Kea determines candidate phrases and feature values, and then applies the model built during training. The model determines the overall probability that each candidate is a keyphrase, and then a post-processing operation selects the best set of keyphrases.

When the Naïve Bayes model is used on a candidate phrase with feature values t (for TFxIDF) and d (for distance), two quantities are computed:

$$P[yes] = \frac{Y}{Y+N} P_{TFxIDF}[t \mid yes] \ P_{distance}[d \mid yes] \tag{1}$$

and a similar expression for P[*no*], where Y is the number of positive instances in the training files—that is, author-identified keyphrases—and N is the number of negative instances—that is, candidate phrases that are not keyphrases. (The Laplace estimator is used to avoid zero probabilities. This simply replaces Y and N by $Y+1$ and $N+1$.)

The overall probability that the candidate phrase is a keyphrase can then be calculated:

$$p = \text{P}[yes] \ / \ (\text{P}[yes]+\text{P}[no])   \tag{2}$$

Candidate phrases are ranked according to this value, and two post-process steps are carried out. First, TFxIDF (in its pre-discretized form) is used as a tie-breaker if two phrases have equal probability (common because of the discretization). Second, we remove from the list any phrase that is a subphrase of a higher-ranking phrase. From the remaining ranked list, the first r phrases are returned, where r is the number of keyphrases requested.

Keyphrase Extraction Example

To illustrate the Naïve Bayes modeling method, we exhibit a model for keyphrase extraction that was learned in one experiment, and show its application to a particular phrase.

Sample Model

Table 3 shows the model. For this training set, TFxIDF was discretized into five fixed levels, and first occurrence into four levels. The discretization boundaries are given at the top of *Table 3*.

Using this discretization, there are nine feature weights for positive examples and nine for negative ones. For example, $\text{P}_{TFxIDF}[1 \mid yes]$ is the proportion of positive examples that have a discretized TFxIDF value of 1. The values learned for these weights are shown in the middle of *Table 3*.

The final component of the learned model is the number of positive and negative instances in the training set, shown at the bottom of *Table 3*. These determine the prior probability of a candidate phrase being a keyphrase, in the absence of any other information.

Application of the Model

As an example of keyphrase assignment, the phrase *cut elimination*, with stem *cut elim*, appears 16 times in the third paper of *Table 1*. The size of this paper is 5114 words; the phrase first appears at word 130. There are 132 documents in the global

Table 3. A particular learned model for keyphrase identification

Discretization table	Feature	Discretization ranges				
		1	2	3	4	5
	TFxIDF	< 0.0031	[0.0031, 0.0045)	[0.0045, 0.013)	[0.013, 0.033)	≥ 0.033
	distance	< 0.0014	[0.0014, 0.017)	[0.017, 0.081)	≥ 0.081	

Class probabilities	Feature	Values	Discretization ranges				
			1	2	3	4	5
	TFxIDF	P[TFxIDF | yes]	0.2826	0.1002	0.2986	0.1984	0.1182
		P[TFxIDF | no]	0.8609	0.0548	0.0667	0.0140	0.0036
	distance	P[distance | yes]	0.1952	0.3360	0.2515	0.2173	
		P[distance | no]	0.0194	0.0759	0.1789	0.7333	

Prior probabilities	Class	Training instances	Prior probability
	yes	493	P(yes) = Y/ (Y+N) = 0.0044
	no	112183	P(no) = N/ (Y+N) = 0.9956

corpus, and *cut elim* appears in just one, but this paper is not in the global corpus, so these counts are incremented by 1. This gives *cut elim* the feature values TFxIDF = 0.0189, distance = 0.0254. After discretization, these become 4 and 3.

The a posteriori likelihoods of this phrase being in the *yes* and *no* classes are calculated from Equation (1), and the overall probability for it being a keyphrase is calculated from Equation (2) as 0.0805. This makes it the fifth candidate phrase in the probability ordered list, so it will be returned as a keyphrase provided five or more are requested.

The individual words *cut* and *elim* are also candidate phrases. Although *cut* has the same probability as *cut elimination*, it is ranked higher because its (undiscretized) TFxIDF value is greater; thus it will also appear as a keyphrase. On the other hand, *elim* will never be chosen as a keyphrase, no matter how many are sought, because its probability is lower than that of its superphrase.

Evaluation

We carried out an empirical evaluation of Kea using documents from the New Zealand Digital Library. Our goals were to assess Kea's overall effectiveness, and also to investigate the effects of varying several parameters in the extraction process. We measured keyphrase quality by counting the number of matches between Kea's output and the keyphrases that were originally chosen by the document's author. The following sections outline our experimental methodology and report the results.

Methodology

Procedure

Kea was evaluated using the Computer Science Technical Reports (CSTR) collection of the NZDL. From the 46,000 documents in this corpus, we chose 1,800 where the author had supplied keyphrases. From these 1,800, we randomly chose a test set of 500 documents, leaving 1,300 as a pool from which to select training documents. The large test set reduces measurement error, so our results will closely approximate the expected values for any particular document. Finally, a further set of documents were chosen at random from the remainder of the CSTR as our global corpus, used to build the document-frequency file.

We then carried out four experiments to determine:

- Kea's overall effectiveness.

- The effect of changing the size and source of the global corpus.

- The effect of changing the number of training documents.

- Kea's performance using abstracts rather than full text.

Results from each of these experiments are given below; first, however, we describe our quality measures, and discuss the advantages and disadvantages of using author-specified keyphrases as a standard.

Measures

We assess Kea's effectiveness by counting the keyphrases that were also chosen by the document's author, when a fixed number of keyphrases are extracted. We use this measure instead of the more common information-retrieval metrics of *precision* and *recall* for three reasons. First, a single overall value is more easily interpreted than two values. Second, precision and recall can be misleading, for it is easy to maximize precision at the expense of recall (by returning the single most promising candidate phrase), or recall at the expense of precision (by returning all candidates). Third, our measure fits well with the expected behaviour of end-users, who will likely ask for a certain number of keyphrases for a document. If required, however, precision can be calculated by dividing our measure by the number of phrases retrieved.

We chose to measure Kea against the choices of the document's author for several reasons: this method of evaluation is simple, can be carried out automatically, and allows the comparison of different extraction schemes. However,

Figure 2. Overall performance

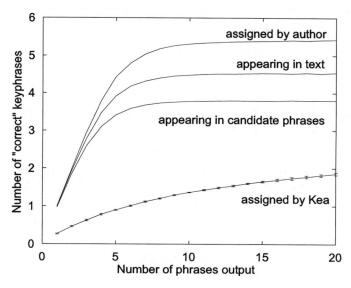

Table 4. Overall performance

Key phrases extracted	Average matches with author key phrases
5	0.93
10	1.39
15	1.68
20	1.88

there are several disadvantages to using author keyphrases as a standard—primarily that authors do not always choose keyphrases that best describe the content of their paper. Authors might choose phrases to slant their work a certain way, or to maximize its chance of being noticed by particular searchers. Also, keyphrases are often chosen hastily, just before a document is finalized. Finally, one can argue that authors are in any case poorly qualified to choose phrases to describe their work for others.

This problem raises two issues. First, the variance in author choices makes it more difficult for an automatic extraction scheme to perform well. Second, Kea's incorrect choices (those that did not match an author choice) are not necessarily poor keyphrases. A more revealing approach might be to use human judges to independently assess the quality of Kea's phrases, without using the original author's choices at all (Jones & Paynter, 2002).

Results

Overall Effectiveness

Our first experiment assessed Kea's overall effectiveness, when extracting up to 20 keyphrases per test document. This experiment used 50 training documents, the standard 500-document test set, and a global corpus of 100 documents. Selected results are shown in *Table 4*, and illustrated in *Figure 2*.

In *Figure 2*, the lowest line shows the average number of correct identifications. The upper lines show three limits on possible performance. The first shows how many keyphrases the author assigned: clearly it is not possible for any algorithm to do better than this using our measure of success. The asymptote shows that the test set has an average of 5.4 author-assigned keyphrases per document. The second line from the top indicates the number of keyphrases that appear in the document's text. No method of keyphrase *extraction* (as opposed to *assignment*) can possibly identify keyphrases that do not appear in the text. The third gives the number of keyphrases appearing within the *candidate* phrases (see Section 2.1).

Figure 2 thus illustrates where Kea loses ground. The difference between the two middle lines represents how many keyphrases are not selected by the candidate selection process. The difference between the bottom two lines represents how much better the machine-learning scheme could conceivably do in finding the authors' keyphrases from among the candidates.

The error bars on the lowest line (which are so small as to be barely visible) represent variance due to the choice of training documents. If one considers the population of all training sets of size 50, there is a 99% chance that the population mean lies within the error bar. Using training sets of only 50 documents represents the realistic situation where there are not many documents available with known keyphrases. Although the results for any given training set will differ, we can be 99% sure that *Figure 2* accurately portrays the expected result over different training sets.

Effect of Size and Source of Global Corpus

We carried out a series of tests to determine how the size and source of the global corpus affect performance. As described in Section 2.2, the global corpus is used to build a document frequency file used in TFxIDF calculations. We were interested in the corpus' size since a larger global corpus will more closely approximate a phrase's true frequency in general use. We were also interested in the source of the global corpus' documents—in particular, whether the

Figure 3. Effect of number of documents used when calculating TFxIDF

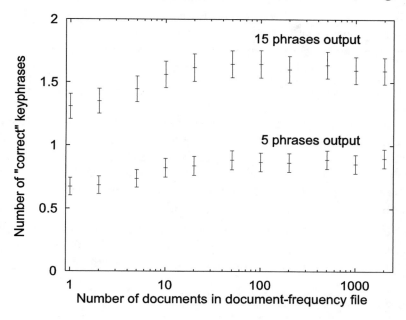

Figure 4. Performance against number of training files

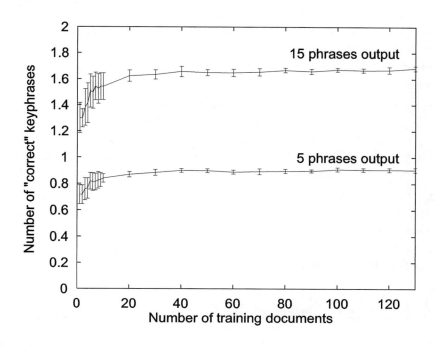

similarity of these documents to the test documents would affect performance.

To test the effect of the source, we built different global corpuses from: an independent set of similar documents, the training set, the training and test sets, the test set alone, and a set of documents containing a different kind of material. In our trials, no one global corpus significantly outperformed the others.

To test the effect of global corpus size, we tested Kea using corpuses of different sizes. For these trials, we used a training set of 130 documents, and the standard 500-document test set. All global corpuses were formed randomly from the CSTR documents without author-assigned keyphrases. As shown in *Table 5* and in *Figure 3*, there is little to be gained by increasing the size of the global corpus beyond about ten documents, and after 50 documents, there is no further improvement. However, the document-frequency file is crucial for good results: without one, performance drops off dramatically.

Figure 3 plots the number of keyphrases matched against the size of the global corpus. The error bars give 95% confidence intervals for the number of correct keyphrases extracted from a test document, given the particular training set.

Effect of Training Set Size

Our third experiment investigated whether the number of training documents (those with keyphrases identified) affects performance. We were interested in the practical problem of how many training documents are necessary for good results. In this experiment, we use a standard global corpus of 100 CSTR documents, and the standard test set. We varied the size of the training set from one to 130 documents, and tested Kea's performance with each set.

Our results (*Table 6* and *Figure 4*) show that performance improves steadily up to a training set of about 20 documents, and smaller gains are made until the training set holds 50 documents. *Figure 4* plots the number of correctly identified keyphrases, when five and 15 phrases are extracted, against the number of documents used for training. The error bars show 99% confidence limits.

These results indicate that good extraction performance can be had with a relatively small set of training documents. In a real-world situation where a collection without any keyphrases is to be processed, human experts need only read and assign keyphrases to about 25 documents in order to extract keyphrases from the rest of the collection.

Effect of Document Length

Our final experiment considered whether Kea's performance suffers when it only uses the abstracts of documents to extract keyphrases, and compares it to

Table 5. Effect of varying global corpus size

Documents in corpus	Average # matches (5 extracted)	Average # matches (15 extracted)
0	?	?
1	0.674	1.307
5	0.738	1.445
10	0.822	1.560
50	0.884	1.644
100	0.868	1.644
1000	0.854	1.596

Table 6. Effect of varying training set size

Training documents	Average # matches (5 extracted)	Average # matches (15 extracted)
0	0.684	1.266
1	0.717	1.301
5	0.819	1.508
10	0.840	1.542
20	0.869	1.625
50	0.898	1.650
100	0.908	1.673

Table 7. Effect of varying document length

Document length	Average # matches (5 extracted)	Average # matches (15 extracted)
Full text	0.909	1.712
Abstracts	0.655	1.028

performance on the full text. This experiment used the standard training, testing, and global corpus sets, except that documents with no abstract were ignored (leaving 110 training documents and 429 testing documents).

Table 7 shows the number of correct keyphrases extracted using both the short and full documents. As expected, Kea extracts fewer keyphrases from abstracts than from the full document text.

Figure 5 plots curves for the short document trial only. The four solid lines, from top to bottom, indicate: the number of keyphrases assigned by the author, the number appearing in the shortened document, the number that appear in the candidate list, and the number that are correctly identified by Kea. The dashed line is the number of correct keyphrases identified when using the full document text. The main reason for the reduced performance when using abstracts seems to be that—not surprisingly—far fewer of the author's keyphrases appear in the abstract than can be found in the entire document.

Conclusion

We have described and evaluated an algorithm for automatically extracting keyphrases from text. Our results show that Kea can on average match between one and two of the five keyphrases chosen by the average author in this collection. We consider this to be good performance. Although Kea finds less than half the author's phrases, it must choose from many thousands of candidates; also, it is highly unlikely that even another human would select the same set of phrases as the original author.

Figure 5. Number of correct keyphrases against number of phrases extracted

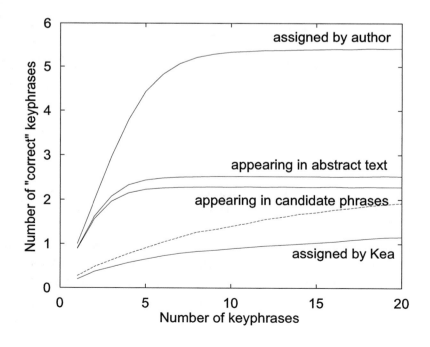

At present, Kea's performance is sufficient for the applications it was designed for: providing support for summarizing, browsing, searching and clustering in cases where manual keyphrase assignment is infeasible. It can and will greatly assist designers and users of large document collections.

Acknowledgments

We would like to thank Peter Turney for sharing his datasets, discoveries, and experiences.

References

Brandow, R., Mitze, K., & Rau, L.R. (1994). The automatic condensation of electronic publications by sentence selection. *Information Processing and Management, 31* (5).

Caumanns, J. (1999). *A fast and simple stemming algorithm for German words*. Technical Report B99-16 Berlin: Center für Digitale Systeme, Freie Universität Berlin.

Domingos, P., & Pazzani, M. (1997). On the optimality of the simple bayesian classifier under zero-one loss. *Machine Learning, 29* (2/3), 103–130.

Dumais, S. T., Platt, J., Heckerman D., & Sahami M. (1998). Inductive learning algorithms and representations for text categorization. In *Proceedings of ACM-CIK International Conference on Information and Knowledge Management* (pp 148–155).

Fayyad, U.M., & Irani, K.B. (1993). Multi-interval discretization of continuous-valued attributes for classification learning. In *Proceedings of IJCAI'93* (pp. 1022–1027).

Frank, E., Paynter, G.W., Witten, I.H., Gutwin, C., & Nevill-Manning, C.G. (1999). Domain-specific keyphrase extraction. In *Proceedings of the Sixteenth International Joint Conference on Artificial Intelligence* (pp. 668-673). San Francisco: Morgan Kaufmann Publishers.

Gutwin, C., Paynter, G.W., Witten, I.H., Nevill-Manning, C.G., & Frank, E. (1998, November). Improving browsing in digital libraries with keyphrase indexes. *Journal of Decision Support Systems, 27* (1-2), 81-104.

Johnson, F.C., Paice, C.D., Black, W.J., & Neal, A.P. (1993) The application of linguistic processing to automatic abstract generation. *Journal of Documentation and Text Management, 1.*

Jones, S., & Paynter, G.W. (2002). Automatic extraction of document keyphrases for use in digital libraries: Evaluation and applications. *Journal of the American Society for Information Science and Technology (JASIST), 53* (8), 653-677.

Krulwich, B., & Burkey, C. (1996, March). Learning user information interests through the extraction of semantically significant phrases. In *AAAI Spring Symposium on Machine Learning in Information Access*, Stanford, CA.

Kucera, H., & Francis, W.N. (1967). *Computational analysis of present-day American English.* Providence, R.I.: Brown University Press.

Kupiec, J., Pedersen, J., & Chen, F. (1995). A trainable document summarizer. *Proceedings of SIGIR* (pp. 68–73). ACM Press.

Lovins, J.B. (1968). Development of a stemming algorithm. *Mechanical Translation and Computational Linguistics, 11,* 22–31.

Munoz, A. (1996). Compound key word generation from document databases using a hierarchical clustering ART model. *Intelligent Data Analysis, 1* (1).

Steier, A.M., & Belew, R.K. (1993). Exporting phrases: A statistical analysis of topical language. In *Proceedings of the Symposium on Document Analysis and Information Retrieval* (pp. 179-190).

Turney, P.D. (2000). Learning algorithms for keyphrase extraction. *Information Retrieval, 2* (4), 303-336.

Witten, I.H. (1999). Browsing around a digital library. In *Proceedings of the Australasian Computer Science Conference* (pp. 1–14). Auckland, New Zealand.

Witten, I.H., & Frank, E. (2000). *Data mining: Practical machine learning tools and techniques with Java implementations.* Morgan Kaufmann, San Francisco.

Endnotes

[1]   Throughout this document we use the latter term to subsume the former.

[2]   For German, we used the stemmer described in Caumanns (1999).

Appendix: Using Kea

The latest version of Kea is Kea-3.0, a Java implementation that basically follows the ideas presented above. It differs slightly from the version described above in the pre-processing step (i.e., in how candidate keyphrases are generated). Also, the global frequencies are based on the training data rather than a separate corpus. The online documentation gives more detailed information.

Kea is distributed under the GNU General Public License, and can be downloaded from http://www.nzdl.org/Kea/. It includes a cut-down version of WEKA (Witten & Frank, 2000), a widely-used machine learning workbench whose full form is available from http://www.cs.waikato.ac.nz/ml/weka, also under the GNU General Public License.

Installation

To install Kea, download the archive file and use the *jar* utility included in every standard Java distribution to expand it. This creates a directory called *Kea-3.0*.

Kea is implemented as a set of Java classes. To run it, first tell the Java Virtual Machine where to look for the classes. One way of doing this is to add *Kea-3.0* (the directory containing the Kea code) to the CLASSPATH environment variable that is used by the Java Virtual Machine.

Under Linux, do this:

a)   Set KEAHOME to Kea-3.0.

b)   Add $KEAHOME to your CLASSPATH environment variable.

The online documentation, generated automatically from the source code, is located in a directory called *doc*. To have the documentation handy,

c)   Bookmark $KEAHOME/doc/packages.html in your Web browser.

Getting Started

Building a Keyphrase Extraction Model

To extract keyphrases for new documents, you must first build a keyphrase extraction model from a set of documents for which you have author-assigned keyphrases. Preferably these documents will be from the same domain as those from which you intend to extract keyphrases.

a)   Create a directory containing the documents to be used to train Kea.

b)   Rename the document files in that directory so that they end with the suffix ".txt".

c)   Delete the author-assigned keyphrases from those documents and put them into separate ".key" files. For example, for a document file called *doc1.txt*, move its keyphrases into a new file called *doc1.key*. Each keyphrase must be on a separate line.

d)   Build the keyphrase extraction model by running the KEAModelBuilder:

   java KEAModelBuilder –l <name_of_directory> –m <name_of_model>

This uses the documents in <name_of_directory> to build a keyphrase extraction model, and saves it in <name_of_model>.

KEAModelBuilder has several other options, shown in *Table 8* (run it with no arguments to see the list).

The –e option specifies a different character encoding supported by Java. For example, to extract keyphrases from Chinese documents encoded using GBK, specify "–e GBK". The –d option generates some output that shows the progress of the model builder.

If –k is set, the keyphrase frequency attribute is used in the model (Frank et al., 1999). This can improve accuracy if the training and test documents come from the same domain. For example, to extract keyphrases from papers on radiology, where the training documents are about radiology, use this option.

If –p is set, KEA does not consider phrases with internal periods as candidate keyphrases. It is important to use this if a full stop is not always followed by white space in the documents.

The last three options, –s, –t and –n allow Kea to be adapted for different languages by changing the list of stopwords, the stemmer, and the policy for whether capitalized words can be keywords.

Extracting Keyphrases

To extract keyphrases, place the documents in an empty directory and rename them to end with the suffix ".txt". A previously built keyphrase extraction model can be applied to the new documents using:

   java KEAKeyphraseExtractor –l <name_of_directory> –m <name_of_model>

Table 8. Options for KEA ModelBuilder

Option	Meaning
–l <directory name>	Specifies name of directory
–m <model name>	Specifies name of model
–e <encoding>	Specifies encoding
–d	Turns debugging mode on
–k	Use keyphrase frequency statistic
–p	Disallow internal periods
–x <length>	Sets the maximum phrase length (default: 3)
–y <length>	Sets the minimum phrase length (default: 1)
–o <number>	The minimum number of times a phrase needs to occur (default: 2)
–s <name of stopwords class>	The list of stopwords to use (default: StopwordsEnglish)
–t <name of stemmer class>	The stemmer to use (default: IteratedLovinsStemmer)
–n	Do not check for proper nouns

For each document in the directory, this creates a *.key* file containing five extracted keyphrases. However, existing *.key* files will not be overwritten. Instead, the keyphrases present in that file will be used to evaluate the extraction model. To do this, KEAKeyphraseExtractor compares the stemmed extracted phrases with the stemmed versions of the phrases in the *.key* file and reports the number of hits among the total number of extracted phrases for those documents that have associated *.key* files.

Table 9 shows the options for KEAKeyphraseExtractor.

To get good results, the input text for Kea should be as "clean" as possible. For example, HTML tags, etcetera, in the input documents should be deleted before the model is built and before keyphrases are extracted from new documents.

Examples

The Kea archive file contains two small example collections, each split into train and test directories. Note that these collections are only included to show how the system can be applied to actual documents. Due to lack of data, the accuracy is low on both examples.

Table 9. Options for KEAKeyphraseExtractor

Option	Meaning
–l <directory name>	Specifies name of directory
–m <model name>	Specifies name of model
–e <encoding>	Specifies encoding
–n	Specifies number of phrases to be output (default: 5)
–d	Turns debugging mode on
–a	Also write stemmed phrase and score into ".key" file

Collection A

This is a collection of abstracts of computer science technical reports. To build a model from the training data, use:

java KEAModelBuilder –l CSTR_abstracts_train –m CSTR_abstracts_model

To evaluate that model on the test data, use:

java KEAKeyphraseExtractor –l CSTR_abstracts_test –m
    CSTR_abstracts_model

Collection B

This is small collection of Chinese documents in GBK encoding. To build a model from the training data, use:

java KEAModelBuilder –l Chinese_train –m Chinese_model –e GBK

To evaluate that model on the test data, use:

java KEAKeyphraseExtractor –l Chinese_test –m Chinese_model –e GBK

Chapter IX

Cross-Lingual Information Retrieval:
The Challenge in Multilingual Digital Libraries

Christopher Yang
The Chinese University of Hong Kong, China

Kar Wing Li
The Chinese University of Hong Kong, China

Abstract

Structural and semantic interoperability have been the focus of digital library research in the early 1990s. Many research works have been done on searching and retrieving objects across variations in protocols, formats, and disciplines. As the World Wide Web has become more popular in the last ten years, information is available in multiple languages in global digital libraries. Users are searching across the language boundary to identify the relevant information that may not be available in their own language. Cross-lingual semantic interoperability has become one of the focuses in digital library research in the late 1990s. In particular, research in cross-lingual information retrieval (CLIR) has been very active in recent conferences on information retrieval, digital libraries, knowledge management, and information systems. The major problem in CLIR is how to build the bridge between the representations of user queries and documents if they are of different languages.

Cross-Lingual Information Retrieval

Information retrieval is a process by which users seek to locate documents that contain information about the subject of their query. The information retrieval process is distinguished from the conventional database access paradigm by the user's desire to find documents about a subject rather than data that directly answers the query (Oard & Dorr, 1996). Lancaster (1968) defined that an information retrieval system does not inform (i.e., change the knowledge of) the user on the subject of his inquiry but it merely informs on the existence (or non-existence) and whereabouts of documents relating to his request. *Figure 1* depicts a typical information retrieval system.

With the advance of technologies in World Wide Web and digital libraries, the traditional discipline of information retrieval has been extended to multimedia including image, graphics, video, and speech, and multi-languages, including European, Asian and other languages. Users expect to submit a textual query to the digital library in one language and obtain all the relevant information in all media and languages. In this chapter, our focus is the challenge of cross-lingual information retrieval in digital libraries.

The followings are some scenarios of the application of CLIR in digital libraries:

a.   The digital library has a collection of monolingual documents but it supports users who speak different languages. In this case, the queries may be of

Figure 1. A typical information retrieval system

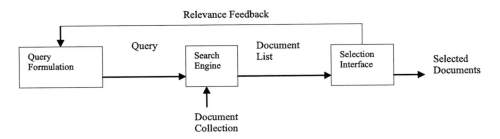

different languages. The queries must be translated into the document language before retrieval.

b.   The digital library has a collection of parallel documents. Users who know only one language may search in the digital library using his language and obtain the relevant documents in the same language. The corresponding documents in other languages that are parallel to retrieved documents are also extracted. In this case, the digital library must be able to align the parallel documents if the documents do not come in pairs from the source.

c.   The digital library has a collection of multi-lingual documents. Documents can be written in any language. Multiple languages may exist in an individual document. In this case, the digital library must be able to identify the languages in the documents and represent the documents in a way that retrieval can be processed in regardless to the language of the queries.

Once documents are retrieved, users may translate the retrieved documents manually or automatically.

Cross-lingual information retrieval refers to the ability to process a query for information in one language, search a collection of objects, including text, images, audio files, etcetera and return the most relevant objects, translated into the user's language if necessary (Klavans et al., 1999; Oard & Dorr, 1996).

Information Retrieval Model

An information retrieval model has two major components, (i) representation of queries and documents, and (ii) comparisons of these representations. The objective of an information retrieval system is to automate the process of examining documents by computing the comparisons between the representations of queries and documents (Turtle & Croft, 1991; van Rijsbergen, 1979). The model is good if its performance is similar to those produced by human experts. *Figure 2* depicts the representation and comparison processes in an information retrieval model.

In an ideal information retrieval system, the comparison function, as depicted in *Figure 2*, can perfectly replicate the human judgement.

$$c(q(query), d(doc)) = j(query, doc), \qquad \forall query \in Q, \ \forall doc \in D$$

Figure 2. Representation and comparison processes in an information retrieval model

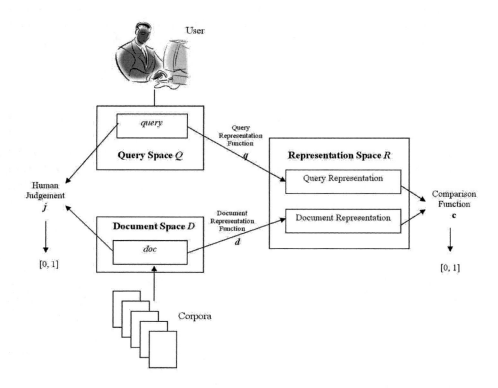

where *j: Q x D → [0,1]* represents the user's judgment on some relationship between two texts, measured on a single ordinal scale (e.g., content similarity) (Oard & Dorr,1996).

In CLIR, the queries and documents are of different languages. As a result, the query representation and document representation directly obtained from the queries and documents are of different languages. The research in CLIR is, therefore, concerning the modification of the query and document representation and their comparison functions based on the foundations of monolingual informa- tion retrieval.

There are two major directions of CLIR: (i) controlled vocabulary and (ii) free text. The controlled vocabulary approach simply restricts the use of vocabulary in query and document representations. For this reason, very little research work has been done using this approach. More research work has been developed in the free text approach. It can be further categorized into the knowledge-based approach and the corpus-based approach. In the following sections, we shall discuss these approaches.

Controlled Vocabulary

In the controlled vocabulary approach, documents are manually indexed using a predetermined vocabulary and queries from users are using terms drawn from the same vocabulary (Oard & Dorr, 1996). The systems exploiting such an approach bring queries and documents into a representation space by a multilingual thesaurus to relate the selected terms from each language to a common set of language-independent concept identifiers, where the document selection is based on the concept identifier matching (Davis & Dunning, 1995; Fluhr, 1995; Fluhr & Radwan, 1993; Radwan & Fluhr, 1995). However, it imposes the limitation of the user-employed vocabulary, and the selection of thesaurus highly affects the performance of the retrieval. Although such an approach is widely used in commercial and government applications, it is not practical and becomes less manageable as the number of concepts increases. The performance becomes worse as the collection of documents increases, such as the World Wide Web, because the documents generated from diverse sources cannot be standardized easily. Besides, the training of users to select search terms from the controlled vocabulary is difficult. General users are usually unable to identify the appropriate term to represent their information needs.

Pollitt's team at the University of Huddersfield Centre for Database Access Research has applied the controlled vocabulary approach (Li et al., 1992; Pollitt & Ellis, 1993; Pollitt et al., 1993). Based on their Menu-based User Search Engine (MenUSE) and the European Parliament's multilingual EUROVOC thesaurus, Pollitt's team has developed a query formulation tool, which facilitates visual browsing in the user's preferred language. Pollitt's team has also extended the English thesaurus for the INSPEC database to Japanese and integrated it with MenUSE. Their experience has shown that although the domain knowledge that can be encoded in a thesaurus permits experienced users to form more precise queries, casual and intermittent users have difficulty exploiting the expressive power of a traditional query interface in exact match retrieval systems.

Free Text

The free text approach does not limit the usage of vocabulary but uses the words that appear in the documents. Queries or documents are translated and then retrieval is performed. In most CLIR applications, only the queries are translated because queries are normally short and therefore higher efficiency can be achieved. However, the short queries without much context imply higher translation ambiguity. Many techniques have been proposed to resolve the translation ambiguity problem in the query formulation (Davis & Ogden, 1997), including automatic query expansion before and after translation (Ballesteros & Croft, 1997) and cognate matching for out-of-vocabulary words (Buckley et al., 1997). If the user is not fluent in the language that the document is written in, interactive selection of promising documents from a list can be facilitated using simple translation techniques that are tuned for the semantics of titles and other displayed metadata (e.g., Hayashi et al., 1997).

Free Text Knowledge Based Approach

The knowledge-based approach employs *dictionary* or *ontology* (Ballesteros & Croft, 1997; Hull & Grefenstette, 1996; Oard, 1997; Radwan & Fluhr, 1995). A *dictionary* replaces each term in the query with an appropriate term or set of terms in the target language (Salton, 1970). Ontology is an inventory of concepts, which is organized under some internal structuring principle. A multilingual thesaurus is an example of ontology to organize terminology from more than one language. Complex thesauri, which encode syntactic and semantic information about terms, are used as concept index in automatic text retrieval system (Oard & Dorr, 1996).

The dictionary-based CLIR approach replaces each term in the query with an appropriate term or set of terms in the target language. This approach has two limitations. Firstly, most words have multiple translations, and sometimes the alterative translations have very different meanings. Monolingual text retrieval systems face similar challenges from polysemy. Polysemous words are words that have more than one meaning. The problem is significantly aggravated by translation ambiguity. If every possible translation of the query is used, it can greatly expand the set of possible meanings because some of those translations will introduce additional polysemous word senses in the target language. Besides, the query expansion would make the system or even a human hard to determine the intended meaning from the available context (Oard, 1997). Secondly, the dictionary may not have terms that are essential for a correct interpretation of the query. For example, the query is related to a technical topic or in the form of abbreviation or slang, which is out of the scope of the dictionary. The effect of this limitation is unlikely to be eliminated completely no matter how perfect is the dictionary. It is because the usage of language is a creative activity where new terms are created all the time. There is a natural lag between the introduction of a term and its incorporation into a dictionary.

The multilingual thesaurus-based approach is an alternative to the dictionary-based approach. A multilingual thesaurus is an ontology, which organizes terminology from more than one language. The key feature of every multilingual thesaurus is a specification of cross-linguistic synonymy. Hierarchical concept relationships (broader term, narrower term) and associative relationships (related term, synonymous term) are typically included in more sophisticated thesauri (Oard & Dorr, 1996). In the last 30 years, a lot of effort has been taken to develop the multilingual thesaurus. The International Standards Organization (ISO) drafted the standards for multilingual thesaurus development in 1973 and expanded the draft specification in 1976 (Austin, 1977). ISO 5964 was approved in 1978 and modified in 1985. The standard describes how domain knowledge can be incorporated in multilingual thesauri and identifies alternative techniques for multilingual thesaurus development. The European Parliament's EUROVOC is a recently developed multilingual thesaurus based on ISO 5964 in 1995. EUROVOC includes nine official languages of the European community and portion of it has been translated into other languages (Chmielewska-Gorczyca & Struk, 1994). However, manual development of multilingual thesaurus is expensive and the lag problem in dictionary also exists in multilingual thesaurus.

Machine translation (MT) is a popular technique that utilizes dictionary and/or multilingual thesaurus in CLIR. Maegaard et al. (1999) claimed that machine translation includes any computer-based process that transforms (or help users to transform) written text from one language into another. MT systems usually convert the input text, sentence by sentence, into a series of internal representations, in which sentence-internal relationships are determined and the intended meaning of words is identified. However, high quality of translation is only achievable in limited domain. The semantic accuracy is poor when there is insufficient domain knowledge encoded in the MT system (Fluhr, 1995).

Free Text Corpus-Based Approach

The corpus-based approach overcomes the limitation of the knowledge-based approach by making use of the statistical information of term usage in parallel or comparable corpora to construct an automatic thesaurus. Since it is impractical to construct bilingual dictionary or sophisticated multilingual thesauri manually for large applications, the corpus-based approach uses the term co-occurrence statistics across large document collections to construct a statistical translation model for cross-lingual information retrieval.

Multilingual Corpus

A multilingual corpus is a collection of text in electronic form (written language corpus) where texts in different languages are put together either based on parallelism or comparability. A multilingual corpus constructed based on parallelism and comparability is known as parallel corpus and comparable corpus, respectively. A parallel corpus can be developed using overt translation or covert translation. The overt translation posses a directional relationship between the pair of texts in two languages, which means texts in language A (source text) is translated into texts in language B (translated text) (Rose, 1981). The covert translation is non-directional. Multilingual documents expressing the same content in different languages are generated by the same source (Leonardi, 2000). Therefore, none of the text in each pair of such parallel corpus is marked as translated text or source text. For example, commentaries on a sports event are broadcast live in several languages by a broadcasting organization. None of these commentaries are translated from a source language. Documents generated by covert translation are not bound to a specific culture but enjoyed the status of the original source in the target culture.

A comparable corpus consists of texts in multiple languages composed independently, which shared similar criteria of content, domain, and communicative function (Oard, 1997). Criteria for creating comparable corpora depends on the homogeneity of texts, both with or across languages, in terms of features such as subject domain, author-reader relationship, text origin and constitution, factuality, technicality and intended outcome (Zanettin, 1998).

Although the availability of comparable corpus is higher than the availability of parallel corpus, it is difficult to justify the criteria for constructing comparable corpora. Generating the hypotheses of possible alignments is a complicated task. It is necessary to rely on known or suspected equivalences as heuristics to retrieve similar contexts in another language, providing a specification which is both sufficiently general to recall a range of possibilities, and sufficiently precise to limit the number of spurious hits (Aston, 1999). Verification is required to ensure the citations that have been retrieved are in fact sufficiently similar to those in the source language. These procedures are both time-consuming and error-prone: an expression in one text may occur in a similar context to one in another language text but in fact have a different meaning. Greater certainty as to the equivalence of particular expressions can be obtained by using parallel corpora. If the corpus is aligned, the user can locate all the occurrences of expression together with the corresponding sentences in the other language. Since parallel concordances provide translations of a word, the risk of misinterpretation associated with comparable corpora is diminished.

With regard to parallel corpora, it has been observed that translated texts cannot represent the full range of linguistic possibilities of the target language and that they may reflect the stylistic idiosyncrasies of the source language and of individual translators (Picchi & Peters, 1997). However, the comparison between large numbers of texts and their acknowledged translations can show how equivalence has been established by translators under certain circumstances and provide examples of translation strategies. If such corpora are sufficiently varied and large, by observing recurring linguistic choices made by translators, general patterns can be perceived. Learners can thus notice the translation pattern and generalize from the aggregation of sets of individual instances.

Automatic Generation of Multilingual Corpus

A parallel corpus can be generated by automatic alignment techniques. However, alignment of text from multiple languages possesses several difficulties:

1. A word in Language A can be translated into many words in Language B.
2. Some words may not be translated at all.
3. A word in Language A is not always translated in the same way in Language B.
4. A word in Language A can be translated into morphological or syntactic phenomena rather than a word in Language B.

Identifying the pairs of parallel documents from a multilingual corpus is not easy. Several techniques have been developed to construct parallel corpus automatically from the World Wide Web. In order to extract the parallel corpus from the World Wide Web, a better understanding of the structure of parallel documents based on their links is important. There are three major Web structures for parallel corpus (Resnik, 1999; Yang & Li, 2003a):

1.   Parent page structure: In a Web page (parent), there are two anchor texts, T_1 and T_2. T_1 is linked to Language A version and T_2 is linked to Language B version of the parallel corpus.

2.   Sibling page structure: The Web page in Language A contains a link directly to the translated Web page in Language B and vice versa.

3.   Monolingual sub-tree: It contains a completely separate monolingual sub-tree for each language, with only the single top-level Web page pointing off to the root page of single-language version of the site.

The most prominent system that generates parallel corpus from the World Wide Web is Structural Translation Recognition for Acquiring Natural Data (STRAND), developed by Resnik (1998, 1999), and PTMiner, developed by Chen & Nie (Nie et al., 1999; Chen & Nie, 2000). STRAND consists of three modules, candidate generation module, candidate evaluation module and candidate pair-filtering module. A similar system has also been developed by Nie et al. (1999). PTMiner utilizes five steps to generate English/Chinese corpus: (i) candidate sites searching; (ii) fetching; (iii) host crawling; (iv) pair scanning; and (v) verifying. Potential candidates are identified by search engines, where name patterns are used for filtering. File size, text length, and language/character sets are utilized for filtering and verification. Yang has recently developed a technique for constructing Chinese/English parallel corpus using longest common subsequence and tackling the problem of redundancy (Yang & Li, 2003a). A review of the length-based approach and text-based approach of title alignment can be found in Yang & Li (2004a).

Automatic Generation of Thesaurus from Parallel Corpus

Based on the aligned multilingual corpus, the corpus-based approach of CLIR makes use of the statistical information of term usage in multilingual corpus to generate an automatic thesaurus. The latent semantic indexing is one of the earliest approaches in this research area.

The latent semantic indexing (LSI) was first adopted by Dumais (1994) and Landauer & Littman (1991) to identify important bilingual semantic descriptors. The basic idea of the LSI is to use a matrix decomposition to identify the principal components of the vector space defined by the document collection (Oard & Dorr, 1996). The vectors are then projected into the space spanned by the principal components. The principal components represent important conceptual distinctions.

Dumais (1994, 1996, 1997) used a rank revealing matrix decomposition (the singular value decomposition) to compute a mapping from sparse term-based vectors to short but dense vectors that appear. It captured the conceptual content of each document while suppressing the effect of variation in term usage. The result shows that extending LSI to CLIR is encouraging. Landauer & Littman (1991) have also applied LSI on a parallel corpus of Canadian parliamentary proceedings. Using the English vectors as queries, the top ranked French vector was derived from the translated version of the English paragraph in most of the cases. Berry & Young (1995) have done similar work using the Bible in English and Greek. Using the fine-grained training data set, improved retrieval performance can be obtained simply by using the first verse of each passage to identify the principal components.

After closely examining many previous research works (both in information science and cognitive studies), Chen et al. (1996, 1997) developed an asymmetric clustering algorithm based on a variant of a Hopfield network to create a robust and useful domain-specific thesaurus automatically. The approach was first used in monolingual thesaurus construction and then extended to multilingual thesaurus construction (Lin & Chen, 1996). The concept retrieval approach allows users to retrieve information on the basis of a conceptual topic or meaning of a document. The corpus-based approach tries to overcome the problems of lexical matching by using statistically derived conceptual indices instead of individual words for retrieval. It takes advantage of the implicit structure in the association of terms with documents and estimates variability in word usage across documents. The approach can generate the concept space automatically from a corpus where a concept space is a semantic network consisting of concepts (noun phrases in the textual domain) and related concepts, and is computed based on co-occurrence relationships.

Since the semantic network contains knowledge obtained from the entire collection, the concept space for each term represents the important associative relationships between terms and documents that are not only evident in individual documents. Such approach of automatic thesaurus generation is also known as the concept space approach (Chen et al., 1997) because a meaningful and understandable concept space (a network of terms and weighted associations) could represent the concepts (terms) and their associations for the underlying information space (i.e., documents in the database). The performance shows that these statistically derived concept spaces are more robust indicators of conceptual meaning than individual terms. The thesaurus-like, semantic network knowledge base generated by this approach was tested to be a promising tool to improve users' access to textual materials and understand the users' information needs.

To facilitate English/Chinese cross-lingual information retrieval, Yang (Yang & Luk, 2003; Yang & Li, 2003b; Li & Yang, 2003) applied Lin & Chen's (1996) asymmetric clustering algorithm to construct a bilingual thesaurus. The approach uses the term co-occurrence statistics in parallel corpus to construct a statistical translation model to cross the language boundary. The approach is based on a variant of a Hopfield network. The Hopfield network clusters strongly related terms (concepts) together to form concept spaces and a sigmoid transformation function allowed overlapping clusters to be generated during the parallel clustering process. By controlling various thresholds, a number of meaningful concept spaces are generated. Such a technique has been tested on parallel corpus in law and press releases from police department, government, and commercial banks. The performance is promising. In addition, the online bilingual newswire articles used in this research are dynamic (Li & Yang, 2003). They provide a continuous large amount of information for relieving the lag between the new information and the information incorporated into a reference work. However, the efficiency of the Hopfield network is low. Besides, the Hopfield network is a random process; therefore, the result may not be consistent.

Recently, Yang & Li (2004b) have developed the associate constraint network to overcome the shortcomings of the Hopfield network in constructing the bilingual thesaurus. The problem is modelled as a constraint satisfaction problem, where node consistency is defined for the network. In the associate constraint network, the nodes correspond to the terms in multiple languages and the arcs correspond to the associations between terms. The associate constraint network is satisfied if and only if all the nodes are consistent. Backmarking is developed to solve the constraint satisfaction problem. The result is a cross-lingual concept space. The experimental result shows that the associate constraint network outperforms the Hopfield network.

Conclusion

With the advance of digital library and Internet, the amount of online information is increasing exponentially. The information retrieval systems in a digital library must be capable to manage large volumes of data and information, often written in different languages and stored in different locations. This provides a challenge for *cross-lingual semantic interoperability* since much of this information may be seemingly unconnected. How to generate an overview of this disparate data and information so that it can be analysed, searched, summarized and visualized is problematic.

The *cross-lingual information retrieval* brings an added complexity to the standard *IR* task. Users may have different abilities in different languages, affecting their ability to form queries and interpret results. For example, a user might be proficient in understanding documents in Chinese, but could not find a suitable word to a Chinese query. In this case, the user will need to formulate a query in English, but will want documents returned only in Chinese. Taking the World Wide Web as an example, information in languages other English is growing significantly in recent years. The number of non-English speaking users will exceed the number of English speaking users. This highlights the importance of automated assistance to refine a query in cross-lingual information retrieval.

To alleviate information overload, the controlled vocabulary cross-lingual retrieval systems are clearly able to provide a solution in many libraries. However, the controlled vocabulary approaches normally require a document to share some keywords with the query. In reality, the users may use some keywords that are different from what used in the documents. There are then two different term spaces, one for the users, and another for the documents. How to create relationships for the related terms between the two spaces is an important issue. The problem can be viewed as the creation of a thesaurus. The creation of such relationships would allow the system to match queries with relevant documents, even though they contain different terms.

The techniques for manual thesaurus construction and maintenance are resource-intensive. Although automated tools can improve human productivity, as long as human intellectual activity is required to recognize and organize information, the costs will remain substantial. In fact, with the sustained dramatic decline of computer hardware costs, human activities such as thesaurus maintenance and controlled vocabulary indexing have come to dominate system costs. The construction of a thesaurus becomes economically impractical. This limits both the scalability of existing thesaurus-based systems to accommodate the rapid growth in electronically accessible texts and the generalization of the technique to new domains (e.g., personal document collections).

The corpus-based approach can be viewed as an *automatic thesaurus construction* technique where the relationship between terms is obtained from statistics of term usage. The cross-lingual concept retrieval techniques such as query expansion could exploit information encoded in a thesaurus without human intervention during retrieval. This approach allows users to retrieve information on the basis of a conceptual topic or meaning of a document. Some corpus-based approaches for concept retrieval tried to overcome the problems of lexical matching by using statistically derived conceptual indices instead of individual words for retrieval. It takes advantage of the implicit structure in the association of terms with documents and estimates variability in word usage across documents. The approach can generate the concept space automatically from a corpus, where a concept space is a semantic network consisting of concepts (noun phrases in the textual domain) and related concepts, and is computed based on co-occurrence relationships. Using the concept space approach, a meaningful and understandable concept space (a network of terms and weighted associations) could represent the concepts (terms) and their associations for the underlying information space (i.e., documents in the database). The performance data shows that these statistically derived concept spaces are more robust indicators of conceptual meaning than individual terms.

With the advance development of cross-lingual information retrieval, a global digital library that encompasses digital libraries from all around the world and including information in all languages becomes possible. Users at any corner of the world could submit a query in his language and search through all linked digital libraries. The relevant information in any language will then be extracted and translated to the user language. The information needs of users can be further satisfied by minimizing the obstacles produced by the boundary of languages.

References

Aston, G. (1999). Corpus use and learning to translate. *Textus, 12,* 289-314.

Austin, D. (1977). Progress towards standard guidelines for the construction of multilingual thesauri. In Commission on the European Communities (ed.), *Third European Congress on Information Systems and Networks* (Vol. 1, pp. 341-402). Verlag Dokumentation.

Ballesteros, L., & Croft, W. B. (1997). Phrasal translation and query expansion techniques for cross-language information retrieval. In *Proceedings of the 20th Annual International ACM SIGIR Conference on Research and Development in Information Retrieval* (pp. 84-91). Philadelphia.

Berry, M., & Young, P. (1995). Using latent semantic indexing for multilanguage information retrieval. *Computers and the Humanities, 29* (6), 413-429.

Buckley, C., Mitra, M., Walz, J., & Cardie, C. (1997). Using clustering and SuperConcepts within SMART: TREC 6. In D.K. Harman (Ed.), *The sixth text retrieval conference*. National Institutes of Standards and Technology.

Chen, H. (1998). Artificial intelligence techniques for emerging information systems applications: Trailblazing path to semantic interoperability. *Journal of the American Society for Information Science, 49* (7), 579-581.

Chen, H., Schatz, B., Ng, T., Martinez, J., Kirchhoff, A., & Lin, C. (1996). A parallel computing approach to creating engineering concept spaces for semantic retrieval: The Illinois Digital Library Initiative Project. *IEEE Transactions on Pattern Analysis and Machine Intelligence, 18* (8), 771-782.

Chen, H., Ng, T., Martinez, J., & Schatz, B. (1997). A concept space approach to addressing the vocabulary problem in scientific information retrieval: An experiment on the worm community system. *Journal of The American Society for Information Science, 48* (1), 17-31.

Chen, J., & Nie, J.Y. (2000). Automatic construction of parallel Chinese-English corpus for cross-language information retrieval. In *Proceedings of the Sixth Conference on Applied Natural Language Processing* (pp. 21-28). Seattle.

Chmielewska-Gorczyca, E., & Struk,W. (1994). Translating multilingual thesauri. In P. Stancikova & I. Dahlberg (Eds.), *Proceedings of the First European ISKO Conference* (pp. 150-155). International Society for Knowledge Organization, Indeks Verlag.

Davis, M.W., & Dunning, T.E. (1995). Query translation using evolutionary programming for multi-lingual information retrieval. In *Proceedings of the Fourth Annual Conference on Evolutionary Programming.*

Davis, M.W., & Ogden, W.C. (1997). QUILT: Implementing a large-scale cross-language text retrieval system. In *Proceedings of the 20th Annual International ACM SIGIR Conference on Research and Development in Information Retrieval* (pp. 92-98). Philadelphia.

Dumais, S.T. (1994). Latent Semantic Indexing (LSI) and TREC-2. In *Proceedings of The Second Text Retrieval Conference* (pp. 105-115). Gaithersburg, MD.

Dumais, S.T., Landauer, T.K., & Littman, M.L. (1996). Automatic cross-language retrieval using latent semantic indexing. In G. Grefenstette (Ed.), *Working Notes of the Workshop on Cross-linguistic Information Retrieval.* ACM SIGIR.

Dumais, S.T., Letsche, T.A., Littman, M.L., & Landauer, T.K. (1997). Automatic cross-language retrieval using latent semantic indexing. In *AAAI Symposium on Cross-language Text and Speech Retrieval.* American Association for Artificial Intelligence.

Fluhr, C. (1995). Multilingual information retrieval. In R.A. Cole, J. Mariani, H. Uszkoreit, A. Zaenen, & V. Zue (Eds.), *Survey of the State of the Art in Human Language Technology* (pp. 305-391). Center for Spoken Language Understanding, Oregon Graduate Institute.

Fluhr, C., & Radwan, K. (1993, September). Fulltext database as lexical semantic knowledge for multilingual interrogation and machine translation.

In *Proceedings of the East-West Conference on Artificial Intelligence* (pp. 124-128). Moscow.

Hayashi, Y., Kikui G., & Susaki, S. (1997). TITAN: A cross-linguistic search engine for the WWW *(Cross-Language Text and Speech Retrieval, AAAI Technical Report SS-97-05)*.

Hull, D., & Grefenstette, G. (1996). Querying across languages: A dictionary-based approach to multilingual information retrieval. In *Proceedings of the 19th Annual ACM Conference on Information Retrieval* (SIGIR) (pp. 49-57).

Klavans, J., Hovy, E., Fluhr, C., Frederking, R.E., Oard, D., Okumura, A., Ishhikawa, K., & Satoh, K. (1999). Multilingual (or cross-lingual) information retrieval. In *Multilingual Information Management: Current Levels and Future Abilities* (Ch. 2). Pisa, Italy: Insituti Editoriali e Poligrafici Internazionali.

Lancaster, F.W. (1968). *Information retrieval systems: Characteristics, testing and evaluation*. New York: Wiley.

Landauer, T.K., & Littman, M.L. (1991). A statistical method for language-independent representation of the topical content of text segments. In *Proceedings of the Eleventh International Conference: Expert Systems and Their Applications* (Vol. 8, pp. 77-85). Avignon, France.

Leonardi, V. (2000). Equivalence in translation: Between myth and reality. *Translation Journal, 4* (4).

Li, C.S., Pollitt, A.S., & Smith, M. P. (1992). Multilingual MenUSE: A Japanese front-end for searching English language database and vice versa. In *Proceedings of the 14th BCS IRSG Research Colloquium on Information Retrieval*. Berlin: Springer-Verlag.

Li, K.W., & Yang, C. C. (2003). Automatic construction of cross-lingual networks of concepts from the Hong Kong SAR Police Department. In *Proceedings of the First NSF/NIJ Symposium on Intelligence and Security Informatics* (ISI 2003). Tucson, Arizona.

Lin, C., & Chen, H. (1996). An automatic indexing and neural network approach to concept retrieval and classification of multilingual (Chinese-English) documents. *IEEE Transactions on Systems, Man and Cybernetics, 26* (1), 75-88.

Maegaard, B., Bel, N., Dorr, B., Hovy, E., Knight, K., Iida, H., Boitet, C., Maegaard, B., & Wilks, Y. (1999). Machine translation. In *Multilingual information management: Current levels and future abilities* (Ch. 4). Pisa, Italy: Insituti Editoriali e Poligrafici Internazionali.

Nie, J. Y., Simard, M., Isabelle, P., & Durand, R. (1999). Cross-language information retrieval based on parallel texts and automatic mining of parallel texts from the Web. In *ACM SIGIR '99*. Berkley, CA, U.S.

Oard, D.W. (1997). Alternative approaches for cross-language text retrieval. In D. Hull & D. Oard (Eds.), *AAAI Symposium in Cross-Language Text and Speech Retrieval*. Menlo Park, CA: American Association for Artificial Intelligence.

Oard, D.W., & Dorr, B.J. (1996). *A survey of multilingual text retrieval*. UMIACS-TR-96-19 CS-TR-3815.

Picchi, E., & Peters, C. (1997). Reference corpora and lexicons for translators and translation studies. In A. Trosberg (Ed.), *Text Typology in Translation Studies*. Amsterdam and Philadelphia: John Benjamins Publishing Company.

Pollitt, A.S., & Ellis, G. (1993). Multilingual access to document databases. In *21st Annual Conference Canadian Society for Information Science* (pp. 128-140).

Pollitt, A. S., Ellis, G. P., Smith, M. P., Gregory, M. R., Li, C. S., & Zangenberg, H. (1993). A common query interface for multilingual document retrieval from databases of the European Community institutions. In *Proceedings of the 17th International Online Information Meeting* (pp. 47-61).

Radwan, K., & Fluhr, C. (1995, April). Textual database lexicon used as a filter to resolve semantic ambiguity application on multilingual information retrieval. In *Proceedings of Fourth Annual Symposium on Document Analysis and Information Retrieval* (pp. 121-136).

Resnik, P. (1998). Parallel STRANDS: A preliminary investigation into mining the Web for bilingual text. In *Proceedings of the Third Conference of the Association for Machine Translation in the Americas on Machine Translation and the Information Soup* (pp. 72-82). Langhorne, Pennsylvania.

Resnik, P. (1999). Mining the web for bilingual text. In *Proceedings of the 37th Annual Meeting of the Association for Computational Linguistics* (pp. 527-534). College Park, Maryland.

Rose, M.G. (1981). Translation types and conventions. In M.G. Rose (Ed.), *Translation Spectrum: Essays in Theory and Practice* (pp. 31-33). State University of New York Press.

Salton, G. (1970). Automatic processing of foreign language documents. *Journal of the American Society for Information Science, 21* (3), 187-194.

Schatz, B., & Chen, H. (1999). Digital libraries: Technological advances and social impacts. *IEEE Computer, Special Issue on Digital Libraries, 32* (2), 45-50.

Turtle, H., & Croft, W.B. (1991). Evaluation of an inference network-based retrieval model. *ACM Transactions on Information Systems, 9* (3), 187-222.

van Rijsbergen, C.J. (1979). *Information Retrieval.* Butterworths.

Yang, C.C., & Li, K.W. (2002). Mining English/Chinese parallel documents from the World Wide Web. In *Proceedings of the International World Wide Web Conference.* Honolulu, Hawaii.

Yang, C.C., & Li, K.W. (2003a). Automatic construction of English/Chinese parallel corpora. *Journal of the American Society for Information Science and Technology, 54* (8), 730-742.

Yang, C.C., & Li, K.W. (2003b). Generating cross-lingual concept space from parallel corpora on the Web. In *Proceedings of the International World Wide Web Conference.* Budapest, Hungary.

Yang, C.C., & Li, K.W. (2004a). Building parallel corpora by automatic title alignment using length-based and text-based approaches. *Information Processing & Management.*

Yang, C. C., & Li, K.W. (2004b). Cross-lingual semantics for crime analysis using associate constraint network. In *Proceedings for the Second NSF/ NIJ Symposium on Intelligence and Security Informatics* (ISI2004). Tucson, Arizona, June 10-11.

Yang, C.C., & Luk, J. (2003). Automatic generation of English/Chinese thesaurus based on a parallel corpus in law. *Journal of the American Society for Information Science and Technology, Special Topic Issue on Web Retrieval and Mining: A Machine Learning Perspective, 54* (7), 671-682.

Zanettin, F. (1998). Bilingual comparable corpora and the training of translators. In S. Laviosa (Ed.), *META, 43, (4), Special Issue. The corpus-based approach: A new paradigm in translation studies* (pp. 616-630).

Chapter X

Evolving Tool Support for Digital Librarians

David M. Nichols
University of Waikato,
New Zealand

David Bainbridge
University of Waikato,
New Zealand

Gary Marsden
University of Cape Town,
South Africa

Dynal Patel
University of Cape Town,
South Africa

Sally Jo Cunningham
University of Waikato,
New Zealand

John Thompson
University of Waikato,
New Zealand

Stefan J. Boddie
University of Waikato,
New Zealand

Ian H. Witten
University of Waikato,
New Zealand

Abstract

Usability in digital libraries is often focussed on end-user interactions such as searching and browsing. In this chapter, we describe usability issues that face the digital librarian in creating and maintaining a digital library. The Greenstone digital library software suite is used as an example to examine how to support digital librarians in their work.

Introduction

Usability in digital libraries (DLs) often concentrates on end-user interactions. In this chapter we describe the evolution of tools to support the other important class of DL user: the digital librarian.

As libraries have become more computerised, librarians have had to learn more and more about computer systems, file formats and Web servers. The Greenstone software development team has, over several years, developed a variety of tools to abstract away from these technical details to simplify the tasks of creating and maintaining digital collections.

Tasks supported by these tools include: collection creation, metadata assignment, collection interface design and multilingual interface support. We outline the history of Greenstone, the role of the digital librarian and how the tools have evolved to meet the needs of Greenstone's users.

Background

Greenstone is a tool to simplify the construction of digital libraries (Witten, Boddie, Bainbridge, & McNab, 2000; Witten & Bainbridge, 2003). As with many tools, it hides the complexity of the task from its users. A digital library can be understood at several levels, from a sequence of ones and zeroes to a whole library: as tool designers the problem we face is which levels are appropriate for user interaction. As Greenstone has developed and the user base has expanded the tools have changed to more easily support the work of digital librarians.

Discussions of usability and digital libraries (e.g., Borgman, 2003; Blandford, 2001; Keith, Blandford, Fields, & Theng, 2002) usually focus on the end-users — the users that search the collections for information. The influence of DL creation tools on user studies is rarely discussed, yet the tools completely delimit the possible experiences of the information searchers. If the digital librarians find their tools hard to use then they are unlikely to be able to produce high quality DLs. The problem for the Greenstone developers is thus much harder: design Greenstone so that digital librarians can use it to produce easy-to-use digital libraries.

The earliest versions of Greenstone contained content-based abstractions, such as documents and collections, that are drawn from library and information science (LIS). These concepts have remained relatively static throughout Greenstone's development. In contrast, the DL creation tools have evolved through several versions; largely to enable collection creators to work without using low-level command-line interaction. As the tools have improved the usability of the software, we have observed more institutions and individuals using Greenstone as a vehicle to digitally publish their content.

The Role of the Digital Librarian

"[A digital library is] a collection of digital objects, including text, video, and audio, along with methods for access and retrieval, and for selection, organization and maintenance of the collection." (Witten, Bainbridge & Boddie, 2001, p. 96)

This definition of a digital library shows both the end-user side (access and retrieval) and the librarian side (selection, organization and maintenance). Although most user-oriented research on DLs focuses on the end-users, we concentrate here on the role of the digital librarian (Hastings & Tennant, 1996). Although the term "digital librarian" is gaining in currency, the scope of associated skills is not yet well defined. A typical operational definition is that a digital librarian is a "type of specialist information professional who manages and organizes the digital library" (Sreenivasulu, 2000, p. 12).

Analysis of recruitment trends in LIS confirms that computer-based skills are in greater demand, although few organisations are explicitly hiring "digital librarians": "the evidence points to an increasingly and a rapidly changing automated library environment" (Marion, 2001, p. 148). Librarians have used computers to power online catalogues for many years but, as with other professions, computerisation has now become pervasive for both library staff and library users.

Although their environment is computerised, the core mission of librarians, providing access to information, remains the same (Rice-Lively & Racine, 1997). Greenstone itself is an example of the increasingly computerised environment of the LIS professional and as such has to bring the technology of DLs to digital librarians in a format that doesn't require extensive knowledge of computers.

Although the computerisation of the librarian's role is an important trend there is a further consideration: the empowerment of end-users to become digital librarians. As tools become more sophisticated the range of people wishing to publish information widens. In the case of Greenstone this trend is particularly relevant to our work in developing countries, "in particular by the observation that effective human development blossoms from empowerment rather than gifting

... a more effective strategy for sustained long-term development is to disseminate the capability to create information collections rather than the collections themselves" (Witten et al., 2001, p. 94). This view of DLs looks forward to a future where any user can be a digital librarian — when supported by appropriate tools. Greenstone supports this vision since, as open source software, it is freely downloadable by anyone from *http://greenstone.org*.

Tools for Digital Librarians

Publishing a Greenstone DL involves several steps including: interface design and collection creation which covers source data specification, metadata assignment, and collection design. In this section, we describe graphics tools for performing these two activities.

Supporting Collection Creation

Collection creation is the cornerstone to the Greenstone toolkit: it turns a number of source documents into a DL with browsing structures and full text searching, all accessible via a Web browser or served in the exact same format from CD-ROM. Decisions made during this creative stage dictate what functionality is available to the end-user and how much effort is expended by the digital librarian in maintaining and extending the collection.

In Greenstone, the structure of a particular collection is determined when the collection is set up. This includes such things as the format, or formats, of the source documents, how they should be displayed on the screen, the source of metadata, what browsing facilities should be provided, what full-text search indexes should be provided, and how the search results should be displayed. Fundamentally, all this is expressed through configuration files and by executing command-line programs. In the early days of the software this was the only way to control the creation process, and typically required the involvement of staff with programming skills to establish a new type of collection. Once this had been done, adding new documents became a mostly pedestrian chore—so long as they have the same format as the existing documents, and the same metadata is provided, in exactly the same way—and could be conducted by someone with less specialist computer skills.

Figure 1 shows a typical command-line sequence for building a Greenstone DL: this contrasts sharply with the more supportive graphical environments used for most everyday computing tasks.

Figure 1. Typical command-line sequence to build a Greenstone DL

```
mkcol.pl -creator davidb@cs.waikato.ac.n
demomarc
cd demomarc
cp /archive/catalog.marc import/.
<edit collection configuration file>
import.pl demomarc
buildcol.pl demomarc
mv building/* index/.
<view built collection in Web browser>
```

As unsightly as *Figure 1* may appear, much of the excruciating, sometimes character-by-character specific detail is masked by the entry *<edit collection configuration file>*. *Figure 2* reveals some of this detail, which is an excerpt from a collection configuration file for a DL based on MARC records. The extract shows that the collection creator has to specify many textual elements using syntax that many LIS professionals, and ordinary users, find difficult to use. The "classify" statements produce browsing indices; they use pattern matching called regular expressions (the sequences of punctuation) to identify which items to include. The "format" statements mix HTML elements and conditional programming constructs to determine how items in lists should appear.

Editing highly structured text files is error-prone and even experienced users can easily make mistakes. It is not surprising that many of the requests to the Greenstone mailing lists are for help with aspects of the collection configuration files. The command-line-based interaction was also awkward for users and usability testing showed that a structured Web-based alternative was more effective (Nichols, Thomson, & Yeates, 2001). These tests compared the standard interaction with an early version of the Web-based tool, The Collector; later versions are shown in *Figures 3* and *4*. The Collector provided a more supportive environment for collection creation through making the sub-tasks an explicit part of the interface; always present and constantly reminding the user of the current state (Witten et al., 2001).

The Collector is modeled after popular end-user installation software (such as InstallShield). Frequently called a software "wizard," this interaction style suits less technically-adept users because it simplifies the choices and presents them clearly. The Collector is accessed via a Web-browser and allows a point-and-click style of interaction to create a new DL collection.

Figure 2. An extract from a collection configuration file for a DL collection of MARC records

```
classify        AZCompactList -metadata Title    -mingroup 1 -
removesuffix "(\\s*(\\/|:|;|,|\\.).*)"
classify        AZCompactList -metadata Creator -mingroup 1 -
removesuffix "(b\\.\\s+)?(\\d+(\\-?))(\\d+(\\.)?)?"

classify        AZCompactList -metadata Subject -mingroup 1

collectionmeta collectionname    "MARC-e"
collectionmeta iconcollection    "_httpprefix_/collect/MARC-
e/images/MARC-e.gif"

collectionmeta .document:text    "text"
collectionmeta .document:Title  "titles"

format VList "<td>[link][icon][/link]</td><td>[Title]</td>"

format CL1VList
"<td>[link][icon][/link]</td><td>[Title]{If}{[Creator],
<i>[Creator]</i>}{If}{[Publisher],
<i>[Publisher]</i>}</td><td>{If}{[numleafdocs],<i>([numleafd
ocs])</i>}</td>"
format CL2VList
"<td>[link][icon][/link]</td><td>{If}{[numleafdocs],[Title],
[Creator]; <i>[Title]</i>{If}{[Publisher],
<i>[Publisher]</i>}}</td><td>{If}{[numleafdocs],<i>([numleaf
docs])</i>}</td>"
```

Figure 3 shows an example snaphot of The Collector in use. Styled after the commonly encountered "wizard" helper applications—a term we try to avoid due to its appeal to mystcism and the unexplained—the digital librarian is guided through a sequence of steps, manifest as Web pages, that control the building process. First the user specifies some top-level collection information such as its name, a contact email address and some text describing the focus and purpose of the collection. Next they enter the location of the source documents, which can be both local filenames and URLs to remote sites.

The third page presents the collection configuration file, initially seeded with some meaningful defaults, in a text box that can be freely edited. Once the user is satisfied with this they proceed to the building page, where the necessary Greenstone commands are run, including those necessary to amass all the source documents into one pace. Every five seconds or so this page is updated with the most recently generated text message output by the command line programs, so the digital librarian can monitor progress. The final stage of The Collector is viewing the built collection.

Figure 3. Specifying source data in The Collector

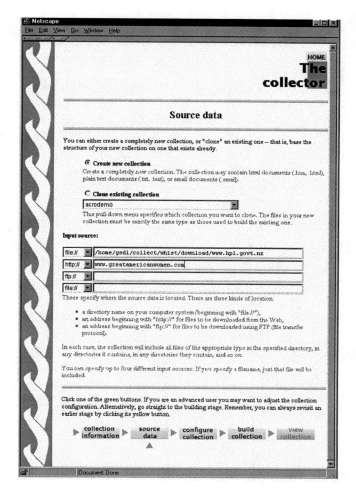

A progress bar at the bottom of every page maps where the digital librarian is within this five-step progress. Once the collection is built, there are other sequences the librarian can choose from in addition to "start a new collection." These are: edit an existing collection, add new documents, and delete a collection.

The aim in developing The Collector was to support the activity of users building modest collections — both in size and complexity — and in this it was successful. Its key attributes are that is substantially lowers the entry cost for someone wanting to learn about collection creation and, by being implemented through

Figure 4. Collection configuration in The Collector

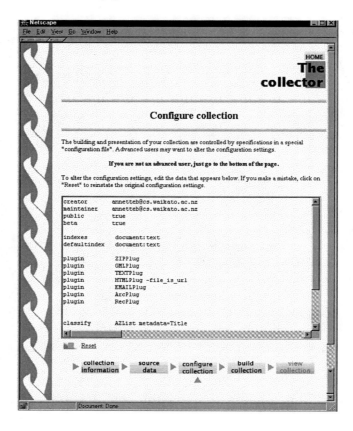

Web forms that are installed as part of the standard Greenstone installation, it is easy to access.

Predictably, as users became more expert with the Web tool, they encountered its limitations and requests started appearing for additional features. Beyond these feature additions, a more fundamental issue in The Collector is the exposure of the collection configuration file in its raw form. The message at the bottom of the page even says this is for advanced users, and most will probably want to skip on to the next page.

One of the most beneficial aspects of The Collector has proved to be the "clone" feature. When a new collection is started, the user can either chose the default collection configuration file, or name an existing collection they want to base their new collection on. This allows for the possibility of a user working with, say, MARC data, seeding the collection configuration settings for their new collection from one that someone else has already developed for a similar purpose.

The Organizer

One of Greenstone's early adopters, SimpleWords of Brasov, Romania, developed The Organizer to assist in the assembly of collections for humanitarian purposes—collections that share a common collection configuration file but have different content. It relies on a substantial amount of metadata that must be manually assigned to each document in the collection. The utility, written using Visual C++, runs standalone and is well tuned for its intended aim.

While The Organizer overcomes the main impediment of command-line only interaction, its tightly focused aim led to some design decisions that are too restrictive when a wider audience for collection creation is taken in to account.

For instance, it is implicitly limited to a particular document model, and users who wish to add metadata not included in this model would have to make manual modifications to the Organizer's results. Also, because it is restricted to Windows, whereas Greenstone runs under Unix and MacOS X too, the Organizer is not fully integrated but works by generating intermediate files that Greenstone uses when building collections. While this loose coupling has some advantages in flexibility, it prevents the full collection-building process from being a single, integrated task.

Mercy Corps Case Study

The Mercy Corps, an international relief and development organization with programmes in over 30 countries and reaching over five million people, has developed a "Metadata Creator" as a support tool for their digital librarian (*Figure 5*). The Mercy Corps uses Greenstone to organize and make available to worldwide Corps workers and consultants a variety of in-house documents, including forms, reports, proposals, and manuals. Externally produced Web documents can also be indexed and included in a collection. The Metadata Creator supports collection maintenance through the full lifecycle of individual documents—from acquisition and addition of a document to the appropriate Greenstone collection(s), to recording updates or modifications to documents, to the removal and/or archiving of obsolete documents.

New documents are submitted for consideration for inclusion in the collection in one of two ways: either by a member in a field office who uses a simple Web-based form to suggest metadata for the document, or—more usually—by the document creator e-mailing the document to a "drop box" address. In either case, the digital librarian supervises the workflow from that point, using the Metadata Creator. The new document is manually checked for correctness, the librarian determines the appropriate collection(s) to which it should be added, and

Figure 5. Metadator Creator from Mercy Corps

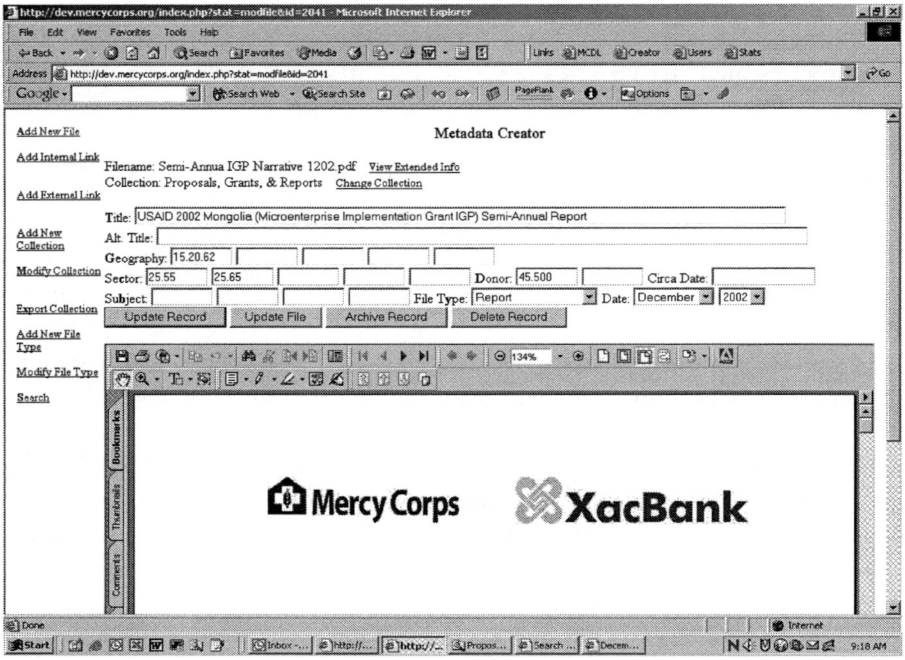

the document's metadata is created. The new document is then made available to users with Internet access after the nightly automatic rebuild of the collections; users with poor Internet connections receive an updated copy of the collections on CD, distributed periodically.

The usability of the Metadata Creator was significantly enhanced by an extensive, cooperative design effort, conducted through focus groups whose members included the digital librarian, a software developer, and potential users of the digital library. Some of the design tweaks suggested by the focus groups sound minor, but have had a major impact on the usability and acceptance of the system: for example, ability to view the document contents within the Metadata Creator (see the bottom portion of *Figure 5*) enables the digital librarian to quickly and easily scan the document when creating metadata, without leaving the Metadata Creator environment. Other changes have taken into account local insights into the types and contents of documents that will be included in Mercy Corps collections, such as that each document will always have a readily distinguishable title—and so the Title metadata should logically be filled in first, with the cursor focus initialized to that slot in the Creator form. The Mercy Corps experience provides strong evidence for improved usability of digital librarian tools through a design process that includes as broad a range of digital library stakeholders as possible.

The Librarian Interface

The lessons from the Organizer and the Mercy Corps Metadata Creator are that the standard Greenstone mechanisms for collection design and metadata assignment were not meeting the needs of our users. This feedback from our user community prompted the development of an improved environment for these elements of collection creation with Greenstone DLs (Bainbridge, Thomson, & Witten, 2003).

The Librarian Interface is our latest endeavour to support the digital librarian, see *Figures 6* and *7*. It encompasses the culmination of what we have learnt developing and reviewing other tools. The Librarian Interface (whose internal project name had been The Gatherer, a term which appears in some previous published work) allows users to collect sets of documents, import or assign metadata, and build them into a Greenstone collection. It differs from the Collector in that its default behaviour is to work on the computer running the Greenstone digital library software rather than building collections on a remote

Figure 6. Assigning metadata using the Enrich view of The Gatherer

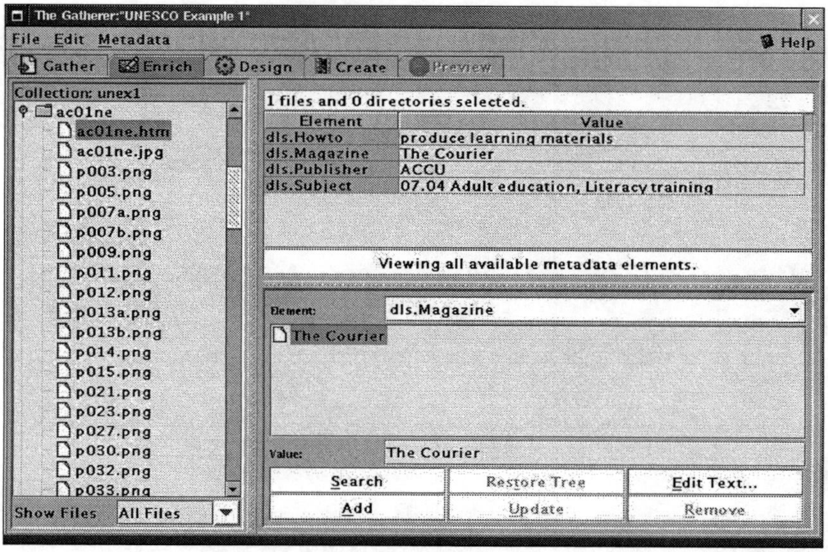

machine, and this permits a more flexible interface. It differs from the Organizer and the Metadata Creator in that it deals with unrestricted metadata sets, and can be tightly integrated with the Greenstone collection design and creation process.

The Librarian Interface shares the more supportive environment of these three tools, taking elements from all three to provide the digital librarian with an integrated tool. The change of technology to a Java application also enables The Gatherer to have a more responsive interface and a richer graphical environment. The Librarian Interface is written in Java to help promote cross-platform independence and, with all textual user interface fragments stored in a language-specific dictionary, support multilingual interfaces. It can be configured to run as standalone application, or through Signed Applets, over the Web.

Figure 6 shows the "Enrich" view of The Gatherer where a digital librarian can assign metadata to objects in the collection. In *Figure 7* the user has clicked the *Design* tab and is reviewing the general information about the collection, entered when the new collection was created. The panel replaces editing of the raw configuration file. On the left are listed the various facets that the user can configure: Indexes, Subcollections, Languages, Plug-ins, Classifiers, Format Settings, and Metadata Sets. Appearance and functionality varies between these components of the tool. For example, clicking the Plug-in button brings up a screen that allows you to add, remove or configure plug-ins, and change the order in which the plug-ins are applied to documents. Importantly it shows the user a

Figure 7. Designing a collection using The Gatherer

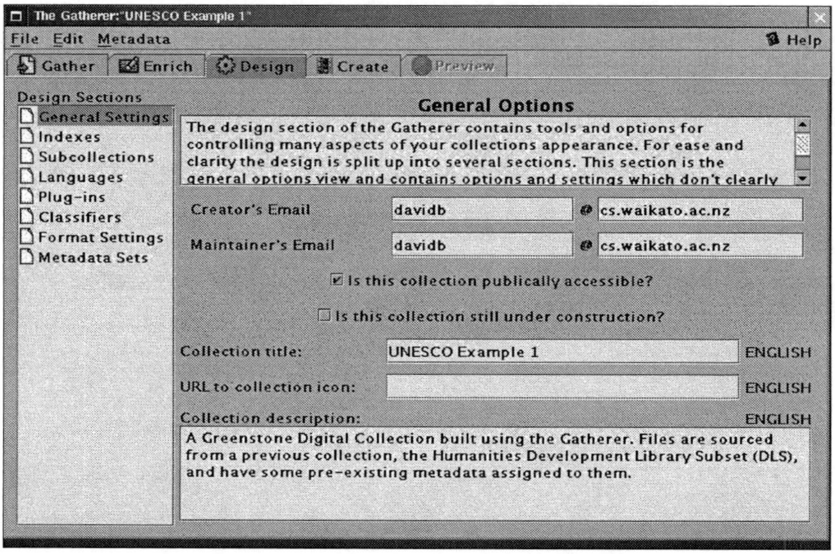

complete list of plug-ins that are available, and for each plug-in in the options that are supported. This differs from the environment of editing the raw configuration file where the user is simply expected to know what plug-ins and options exist. The same distinction occurs for classifiers and other features of the system.

Supporting Interface Design

Traditionally customizing Greenstone's user interface required librarians to be familiar with Greenstone's architecture and internal workings. To change the look and feel of Greenstone's user interface, librarians were required to manipulate a number of configuration files such as collection configuration files (see *Figure 2*), macro files and site configuration files. This required mastering the various commands and options that are available. In addition to this librarians were required to be competent Web designers with good HTML skills. While a number of librarians were able to take on the steep learning curve and acquire the necessary skills to create a multitude of creative digital library sites, the majority were unable to tap and exploit the true power of the Greenstone Software. This is especially true in developing nations, where the levels of computer literacy are low requiring an even greater effort to acquire the skills necessary to customize Greenstone.

It soon became obvious that if librarians were to harness the power of Greenstone software they would need to be able to tailor it to accommodate their individual needs and preferences. This view is consistent with a general consensus reached in 2002 at the CHI conference where the South African Development Consortium concluded that the best way to bridge the digital divide was to empower people with customizable software and not try to pre-empt the needs of particular users (Hugo, Marsden, & Walton, 2002). Customisation allows librarians to view information in a way that is relevant to a given collection, resulting in increased productivity and satisfaction.

However, empowering librarians in this manner would require a solution that provides a complete abstraction from Greenstone's low-level architecture. To support customisation, the solution would have to be flexible enough to cater for user needs and preferences. Furthermore, any functions, options or facilities offered by the solution would need to be visualised enabling the librarian to see what is customizable and where the boundaries and limits lie. In response to these needs, we embarked on a project to provide a tool that would provide this functionality.

One of the many unique features of Greenstone is its ability to publish collections on the Internet or on CD-ROM. Providing such information in a structured digital version makes it available to a wider audience and reduces costs incurred in printing and distribution (Witten et al., 2001). However, these collections can only have profound benefits if the people that need this information most are able to access it. Most people in developing countries are unable to access this information via the Internet. This is because gaining access to the Internet (and hence the collections) typically requires a PC and a land-based telecommunication infrastructure (or network), both of which are rarities in developing countries. A more viable alternative distribution mechanism involves exploiting the current mobile telecommunications infrastructure in many developing countries.

Countries such as South Africa have almost double the number of mobile subscribers compared to landline subscribers. In 2002, 92% of the South African population had access to a mobile network. Furthermore the end user devices (i.e., cell phones or GSM-enabled Pocket PC's) needed to provide wireless

Figure 8. Customizing the Food and Nutrition Collection for the Compaq iPAQ Pocket PC

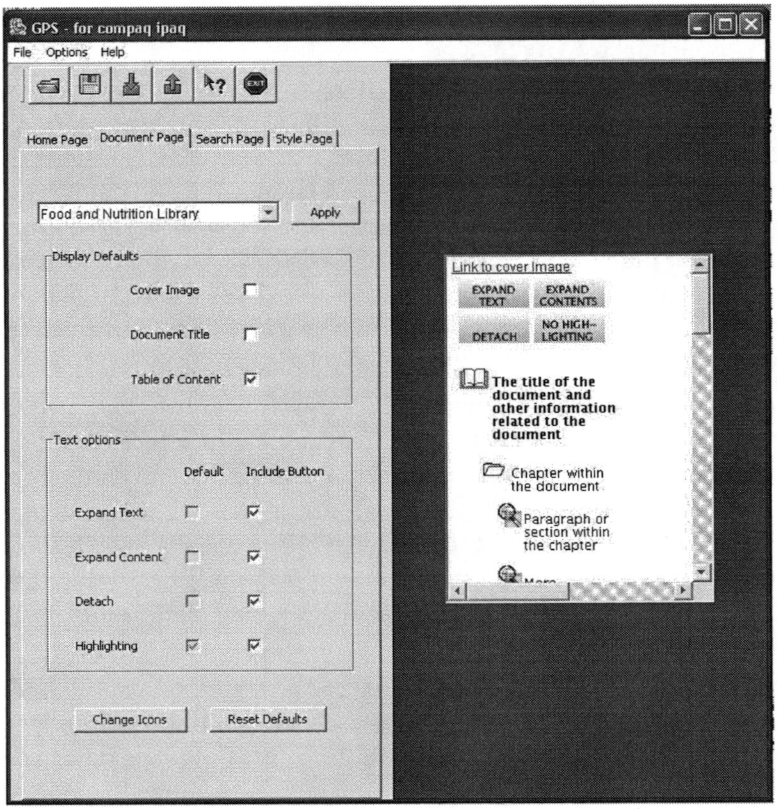

connectivity are becoming more affordable. Thus, providing wireless access to these libraries is an ideal solution for Africa as it has the potential to reach a wider audience, creating an opportunity for social and economic development.

With the notion of providing mobile access in mind, we developed a prototype system that performs two tasks. Firstly, as a high-level customisation tool that allows librarians to tailor the Greenstone site, and any available collections, using a graphical interface. Secondly, it allows librarians to create collections that can be accessed from a wireless PDA (personal digital assistant).

The resulting tool can be seen in *Figure 8*. The user can select the options they want to change and all user changes are visualised in a device window, providing dynamic feedback on the eventual appearance of the Greenstone site.

Figure 8 shows the options available under the "Document Page" tab, on the left of the display. Users can choose to customize the Greenstone site for a specific collection (as in *Figure 8*) or for all collections. In this case the librarian has decided they only wish to publish one collection, that is the "Food and Nutrition Library." Furthermore, on the document page they have specified that they wish to have no cover image or document title, however they do wish to include a Table of Contents and all four document buttons.

In terms of Greenstone configuration files, these options are selected or deselected by set generating the appropriate format statements. *Figure 9* shows an extract from the "Food and Nutrition Library" collection configuration file that corresponds to the settings in the *Figure 8*. Not only is it less intuitive to alter these values in a text editor, but to even find the correct file for editing would require considerable expertise on the user's part.

Similarly, the tool can be used to customize the look and feel of the home page of a document collection. Again the low level details are hidden from the users. For each page the librarian can set the default style by specifying document headers, footers, background colors, background images, text and link colors. For each available collection users are able to set a number of search preferences and can also customize how the search results are displayed. All user changes are visualised in the device window allowing the librarian to quickly prototype a desired design or solution. When the librarian wishes to apply the changes the tool generates configuration files that reflect user settings and are also optimized for the particular screen size setting. Once the configuration files have been generated, the Greenstone Digital Library is automatically restarted. The new configuration files are then processed to apply the changes and alter the DL's appearance.

Although this system is in its infancy, the power it provides has been recognized by several organisations. For example, HealthNet in Kenya are currently investigating its potential to provide medical information to doctors equipped with PDAs. Currently we are extending this system to provide customisation to future

Figure 9. An extract from the collection configuration file for the "Food and Nutrition Library"

```
format DocumentImages    false
format DocumentTitle     false
format DocumentContents  true
format DocumentButtons   "Expand Text|Expand Contents|Detach|Highlight"
```

versions of Greenstone and support templates for different types of access device.

Future Trends

Greenstone is open source software that is free to download and use (Witten et al., 2000); consequently the development team usually doesn't know who is using Greenstone unless they send a message to the mailing list. Typically these messages are requests for help or reports of possible errors with the software. As has been observed in other bug reporting systems (Nichols, Mckay, & Twidale, 2003) the precise nature of the problem often has to be clarified through a series of further messages between the developers and the user.

The distributed nature of Greenstone's usage and its non-expert users mean that it is difficult for the developers to obtain a clear idea of exactly how the software is used. One mechanism for addressing this developer-user gap is to simplify the reporting of problems while enhancing the contextual information of the report. We have developed a prototype system that adds user-driven error reporting to Greenstone (Nichols et al., 2003). The main features it provides:

- Integrating error reporting into the Greenstone system.

- Allowing end-users to efficiently contribute their experiences to the software development team.

- Producing error reports that include more of the information the developers need to understand the user's problem.

The deployment of this feature should widen the communication channel between the end-user, the digital librarians and the Greenstone development team. In turn, this increased participation will help to address the difficulties the developers face in obtaining usability information from a distributed user base.

In this chapter we have described how development efforts from third parties, Simple Words and Mercy Corps, have prompted the Greenstone developers to recognize limitations in the current system and suggested further enhancements to the software. The open source nature of Greenstone has facilitated this evolution for developers, but encouraging this feedback for typical end-users is a significant challenge for the future.

We anticipate further development of the existing Greenstone tools to provide a supportive environment for users to create DLs. In addition to improving existing tools we intend to add more tools to support other elements of the system. Greenstone can present DLs with many different interface languages (in addition to multi-lingual content) and maintaining consistency as the interface evolves is very complex. A new Web-based tool manages the changes in these language interfaces, incorporating version control and allowing authorized users to contribute new translations of the interface text (Bainbridge, Edgar, McPherson, & Witten, 2003).

The current suite of tools in Greenstone doesn't yet reflect all of the facets of the job of the digital librarian that were discussed earlier. For example, the maintenance of a collection should be guided by the usage patterns of the end-users, but the tools to report on usage are less well developed than the other tools described in this chapter. However, the development of Greenstone is driven by requests from its users, so predicting the next stage of tool development is sometimes difficult.

The combination of all these developments aims to fulfill Greenstone's goal, that everyone should "participate actively in our information society rather than observing it from outside. It will stimulate the creation of new industry. And it will help ensure that intellectual property remains where it belongs—in the hands of those who produce it" (Witten et al., 2001, p. 94).

Usability is key to achieving this goal of placing empowering DL technology in the hands of all computer users. In practical terms this means concealing irrelevant technical details, an increasing use of abstractions and the instantiation of those abstractions in easy-to-use tools.

Conclusion

Greenstone has developed several tools to enable non-technical users to access the power of DL technology. In this chapter we have reviewed some of the tools and described some of the usability issues we have encountered as the tools have evolved. A major challenge with software such as Greenstone is the global distribution of its users and the increasing variety of contexts in which it is used. We see increased interaction between developers and users, at all stages of the software development lifecycle, as the only way to maintain the utility and usability of Greenstone.

References

Bainbridge, D., Edgar, K.D., McPherson, J.R., & Witten, I.H. (2003). Managing change in a digital library system with many interface language, In *Proceedings of the 7th European Conference on Research and Advanced Technology for Digital Libraries (ECDL 2003)* (pp. 350-361). LNCS 2769. Berlin: Springer-Verlag.

Bainbridge, D., Thompson, J., & Witten, I.H. (2003). Assembling and enriching digital library collections. In *Proceedings of the 3rd ACM/IEEE-CS Joint Conference on Digital Libraries (JCDL 2003)* (pp. 323-334). New York: ACM Press.

Blandford, A., Stelmaszewska, H., & Bryan-Kinns, N. (2001). Use of multiple digital libraries: A case study. In *Proceedings of the First ACM/IEEE-CS Joint Conference on Digital Libraries (JCDL 2001)* (pp. 179-188). New York: ACM Press.

Borgman, C.L. (2003). Designing digital libraries for usability. In A.P. Bishop, N.A. Van House & B.P. Buttenfield (Eds.), *Digital library use: Social practice in design and evaluation* (pp. 85-118). Cambridge, MA: MIT Press.

Hastings, K., & Tennant, R. (1996, November). How to build a digital librarian. *D-Lib Magazine, 2* (11). Retrieved November 21, 2004 from the World Wide Web: *http://www.dlib.org/dlib/november96/ucb/11hastings.html*

Hugo, J., Marsden, G., & Walton, M. (2002). CHI 2002 Development consortium: A South African perspective. *SIGCHI Bulletin, 34* (5), 4-10.

Keith S., Blandford A., Fields B., & Theng Y.T. (2002). An investigation into the application of claims analysis to evaluate usability of a digital library interface. In A. Blandford & G. Buchanan (Eds.), *Proceedings of the Workshop on Usability of Digital Libraries, 3rd ACM/IEEE-CS Joint Conference on Digital Libraries* (JDCL 2003), Houston, TX.

Marion, L. (2001). Digital librarian, cybrarian, or librarian with specialized skills: Who will staff digital libraries? In H. Thompson (Ed.), *Crossing the divide: Proceedings of the 10th National Conference of the Association of College and Research Libraries* (pp. 143-149). March 15-18, 2001, Denver, CO. Chicago, IL: American Library Association.

Nichols, D.M., Mckay, D., & Twidale, M.B. (2003). Participatory usability: Supporting proactive users. In *Proceedings of the 4th Annual Conference of the ACM Special Interest Group on Computer Human Interaction - New Zealand Chapter (CHINZ'03)* (pp. 63-68). Dunedin, New Zealand: ACM SIGCHI New Zealand.

Nichols, D.M., Thomson, K., & Yeates, S.A. (2001). Usability and open source software development. In E. Kemp, C. Phillips, Kinshuck, & J. Haynes (Eds.), *Proceedings of the Symposium on Computer Human Interaction* (pp. 49-54). Palmerston North, New Zealand: ACM SIGCHI New Zealand.

Rice-Lively, M. L., & Racine, J.D. (1997). The role of academic librarians in the era of information technology. *Journal of Academic Librarianship, 23* (1), 31-41.

Sreenivasulu, V. (2000). The role of a digital librarian in the management of digital information systems (DIS). *The Electronic Library, 18* (1), 12-20.

Witten, I.H., & Bainbridge, D. (2003). *How to build a digital library*. San Francisco: Morgan Kaufmann.

Witten, I.H., Bainbridge, D., & Boddie, S.J. (2001). Power to the people: End-user building of digital library collections. In *Proceedings of the First ACM/IEEE-CS Joint Conference on Digital Libraries* (pp. 94-103). New York: ACM Press.

Witten, I.H., Boddie, S.J., Bainbridge, D., & McNab, R.J. (2000). Greenstone: A comprehensive open-source digital library software system. In *Proceedings of the Fifth ACM Conference on Digital Libraries (DL 2000)* (pp. 113-121). New York: ACM Press.

Witten, I. H., Loots, M., Trujillo, M. F., & Bainbridge, D. (2001). The promise of digital libraries in developing countries. *Communications of the ACM, 44* (5), 82-85.

Section IV

Use and Impact

Chapter XI

Digital Libraries and Society:
New Perspectives on Information Dissemination

Ian H. Witten
University of Waikato, New Zealand

Abstract

Digital libraries are large, organized collections of information objects. Well-designed digital library software has the potential to enable non-specialist people to conceive, assemble, build, and disseminate new information collections. This has great social import because, by democratizing information dissemination, it provides a counterbalance to disturbing commercialization initiatives in the information and entertainment industries. This chapter reviews trends in today's information environment, introduces digital library technology and explores the use of digital libraries for disseminating humanitarian information in developing countries, a context that is both innovative and socially motivated. We demonstrate how currently available technology empowers users to build and publish information collections. Conventional public libraries are founded on the principle of open access, and extending this to digital libraries presents a challenge to human-computer interaction—a challenge that is magnified if open access is extended to those who create library collections too.

Introduction

Digital libraries are large, organized collections of information objects. Whereas standard library automation systems provide a computerized version of the catalog—a gateway into the treasure house of information stored in the library—digital libraries incorporate the treasure itself, namely the information objects that constitute the library's collection. Whereas standard libraries are, of necessity, ponderous and substantial institutions, with large buildings and significant funding requirements, even large digital libraries can be lightweight. Whereas standard libraries, whose mandate includes preservation as well as access, are "conservative" by definition, with institutional infrastructure to match, digital libraries are nimble: they emphasize access and evolve rapidly.

The four chapters in this section provide an excellent illustration of the huge variety of interesting issues in digital library research that impacts the Asia Pacific region.

Libraries are pillars of education, and it is natural to expect that digital libraries will provide new opportunities for innovative educational practices. These will be particularly relevant to the Asia Pacific region because of the huge disparities in access to education between the different communities there. Peer-to-peer learning has always been a crucial factor in personal development, although it is frequently ignored in educational studies. Natalie Pang, from Monash University, Malaysia, in Chapter XIV describes her studies of how digital libraries can provide an innovative, perhaps revolutionary, environment for peer-to-peer learning amongst youths. She touches on many practical issues: gender differences, different learning styles, different levels of media and computer literacy, and age-related differences.

Many economies in the Asia Pacific region are agriculturally based. Modern agriculture is a knowledge-based activity that can benefit greatly from digital libraries. Mila Ramos, from the International Rice Research Institute in the Philippines, describes in Chapter XII a large-scale digital library system designed to support the growth, nurturing, harvesting, and distribution of that most Asian of staples, rice. This digital library supports an institute whose goal is to improve the well being of present and future generations of rice farmers and consumers, particularly those with low incomes. The institute's library houses the world's most comprehensive collection of technical literature on rice, and provides a widely used international reference service. As in many specialized libraries, digital library technology is seen to have special advantages in a world of shrinking library budgets.

Intellectual property issues are a central driving force behind the market in information of which libraries are a part. And the questions become more complex as the nature of today's information shifts from a primarily book-based culture to one that embraces all types of multimedia objects, and large, carefully curated collections of such objects. Chapter XIII on "Multimedia Digital Library as Intellectual Property" by Sasaki & Kiyoki at Keio University in Japan clarifies the copyright situation as it affects multimedia collections and compilations. They go on to discuss the patentability of particular retrieval mechanisms, an essential component of digital libraries.

The fourth chapter in this section on how digital library research impacts the Asia Pacific region is the present one, on digital libraries in society. Most existing digital library projects, being research-oriented, are predicated on state-of-the-art equipment and interfaces, academic and research institutions, and special collections. In contrast, this chapter argues for universal access: digital library technology can and should be available to everyone, on all platforms, in all countries; and it can and should enable ordinary people to exercise their creative powers to conceive, assemble, build, and disseminate new information collections that are designed not just for western academics but for a wide diversity of different audiences throughout the world. Though less glamorous, this may, in the end, be a more important goal for society. Digital libraries pose an inherent tension between the technologist's desire for advanced solutions that use the latest and greatest hardware and software, and the librarian's desire for wide, cross-platform availability and long-term preservation—as epitomized by the sustained success of paper as a delivery medium. To achieve universal access for both information consumers and collection-builders is really a problem for human-computer interaction (HCI).

In the next subsection we examine the social need for digital libraries, particularly in developing countries, by briefly sketching some trends in commercial publishing and contrasting them with a growing international perspective of information as a public good. We draw out the implications for the user interface, which is the principal bottleneck in allowing non-specialist people to make public information available in focused collections that are universally usable. Then we introduce digital library technology and illustrate it with a particular example, the Greenstone digital library software, which is designed for a broad user base and is in widespread use in many corners of the world—from Uganda to the U.S., Kazakhstan to Canada, Nepal to New Zealand. Following that, we review a project that is applying digital library technology to the distribution of humanitarian information in the developing world, a context that is both innovative and socially motivated. Next, we discuss issues of universal access and illustrate them with reference to the Greenstone software. We include a brief demonstration of a prototype system that is intended to allow anyone to build and disseminate information collections, and illustrates some human interface challenges that arise when providing necessarily complex functionality to a non-computer-oriented user base. We close with the hope that future digital libraries will find a new role to play in helping to reduce the social inequity that haunts today's world, both within our own countries and between nations.

Books, Libraries, and the Socially Disadvantaged

Today, the long-standing three-way tension between the commercial interests of publishers, the needs of society and information users, and the social mandate of public libraries is being pulled and stretched as never before.

First, the very notion of a "book" is evolving in many different directions: books become more interactive; publishers rent content; books are distributed under restrictive conditions that mechanically prohibit sharing. While it would be premature to make specific predictions, it seems likely that these trends will further disadvantage the disadvantaged—particularly those in poorer countries who have yet to benefit from ready access to ordinary books. Second, a huge body of information is becoming freely available on the Internet. Much is of questionable quality, but some is very good indeed. In many cases the information is provided for the "public good" rather than for commercial profit, and the redistribution of such information is likely to be encouraged, rather than prohibited, by those who make it available. Initiatives like UNESCO's "Information for all" program and the upcoming World Summit on the Information Society highlight the importance of public information; they are founded on the belief that information literacy will help alleviate many of the problems confronting human societies. Third, the implications for libraries are mixed. Whereas new controls by publishers over how the content they own may be used presents libraries with significant problems, the ready availability of "public good" information meshes well with library philosophy. A new role is emerging for information professionals who can select material, index it, add appropriate metadata, and redistribute it in added-value form for the good of society. Suitable technological infrastructure is being provided by the open source movement, which is making available high-quality software for repackaging and distribution of information (and not just on computer networks).

We expand on each of these points below, and then summarize the prospects of digital libraries and what we see as the implications for the field of HCI.

Books

What future has the book in the digital world? The question is a complex one that is being widely aired [see Lynch (2001) for a particularly thoughtful and comprehensive discussion]. Authors and publishers ask how many copies of a work will be sold if networked digital libraries enable worldwide access to an electronic copy of it. Their nightmare is that the answer is *one*: how many books will be published online if the entire market can be extinguished by the sale of one electronic copy to a public library (Samuelson & Davis, 2000)? To counter this threat, the entertainment industry is promoting new "digital rights management" (DRM) schemes that permit a degree of control over what users can do that goes far beyond the traditional legal bounds of copyright. Indeed, the acronym is more aptly expanded as "digital restrictions management" because it is concerned solely with content owner's rights and not at all with user's rights. It is, in effect, a "private governance system in which computer systems regulate which acts users are and are not authorized to perform" (Samuelson, 2003). Anti-circumvention rules are sanctioned by the Digital Millennium Copyright Act (DMCA) in the U.S. (similar legislation is being enacted in other countries). The DMCA has been used; for example, to prosecute a Norwegian teenager for writing software to play a DVD that he had purchased on a computer for which no commercial playback systems exist.

Can DRM be applied to books? The motion picture industry can compel manufacturers to incorporate encryption into their products because it holds key patents on DVD players. Commercial book publishers are promoting e-book readers that, if adopted on a wide scale, would allow the same kind of control to be exerted over reading material. Basic rights that we take for granted (and are legally enshrined in the concept of copyright)—such as the ability to lend a book to a friend, resell it on the second-hand market, keep it indefinitely, continue to use it when your e-book reader breaks down, donate it to charity, preserve it for your grandchildren, copy excerpts without resorting to a handwritten transcription—are in jeopardy. DRM allows such rights to be controlled, monitored, and withdrawn instantly, and DMCA legislation makes it illegal for users to seek redress by taking matters into their own hands. Fortunately, perhaps, lack of standardization and compatibility issues are delaying consumer adoption of e-books.

In the realm of scholarly publishing, digital rights management is more advanced. Academic libraries license access to content in electronic form, often in tandem with purchase of print versions too. They have been able to negotiate reasonable conditions with publishers—probably because they represent the lion's share of the scholarly market. However, the extent of libraries' power in the consumer book market is moot. One can envisage a scenario where publishers establish a system of commercial, pay-per-view, libraries for e-books and refuse public libraries access to books in a form that can be circulated [Roehl & Varian (2001) describe an interesting parallel between historical circulating libraries and video rental stores].

These new directions present our society with puzzling challenges, and it would be rash to predict what society's response will be. But one thing is certain: they will surely increase the degree of disenfranchisement of those who do not have access to the technology.

Public Information

In parallel with publishers' moves to reposition books as technological artifacts with refined and flexible control over how they can be used, an opposing trend has emerged: the ready availability of free information on the Internet. Of course, the World Wide Web is an unreliable source of enlightenment, and undiscriminating use is dangerous—and widespread. As early as 1996 complaints arose that the Web's contents are largely unattributed, undated, unannotated, and unreliable; information about author and publisher is unavailable or incomplete; far too many resource catalogues ("hubs") are chasing far too few original or non-trivial documents ("authorities") (Ciolek, 1996)—complaints that are very familiar today. But one thing has changed: search engines and other portals have enormously increased our ability to locate information that is at least ostensibly relevant to any given question. Teachers complain bitterly that students view the Web as a replacement for the library, harvesting information indiscriminately to provide answers to assignments that are at best shallow and at worst incoherent and incorrect. One consolation is that the very same search facilities can be used to detect plagiarism.

Nevertheless, the Web abounds with accessible, high-quality information. Many social groups, non-profit societies and charities make it their business to create sites and collect and organize information there. To take a single example at random, a Google search for *diabetes* returns three national diabetes associations (U.S., Canada, U.K.) in the top ten hits, and of course many more exist. Each of these sites offers a cornucopia of valuable information on the disease, which is not commercial and provided for the public good. Widespread use is strongly encouraged, and it seems likely that arrangements could be made for redistribution of the material presented there, particularly it was intended as a not-for-profit service and appropriate acknowledgement was made.

One of the key problems with information distribution via the Web is that it disenfranchises developing countries. Although the Web does not extend into the homes of the socially disadvantaged in developed countries either, various national programs are working to provide access (such as the Bill and Melinda Gates Foundation grants to public libraries). But network access varies enormously across the world. Whereas in 1998 more than a quarter of the U.S. population were surfing the Internet, the figures for Latin America and the Caribbean was 0.8%, for Sub-Saharan Africa 0.1%, and for South Asia 0.04% (UNDP, 1999). Schools and hospitals in developing countries are poorly connected. Even in South Africa, the best-connected African country, many hospitals and 75% of schools have no telephone line. Universities are better equipped, but even there up to 1,000 people can depend on just one terminal. The Internet "is failing the developing world" (Arunachalam, 1998).

Prompted by this inequity, the importance of information, and particularly public information, is today being highlighted by prominent international bodies. For example, UNESCO's "Information for all" programme was established in 2001 to foster debate on the political, ethical and societal challenges of the emerging global knowledge society and to carry out projects promoting equitable access to information. It reflects a growing awareness that information is playing an increasing role in generating wealth and human capital, and that participation in the "global knowledge society" is essential for social and individual development. Information literacy is described as "a new frontier" by the Director of UNESCO's Information Society Division (Quéau, 2001). The International Telecommunications Union has established a World Summit on the Information Society, held in Geneva in December 2003 and Tunis in 2005, to promote a global discussion of the fundamental changes that are being brought about in our lives by the transformation from an industrial to an information society, and to confront the extreme disparities of access to information between the industrialized countries and the developing world.

Libraries and Their Role

What is the librarian to make of all this? The mandate of today's public libraries, in sharp contrast to that of publishers, is to facilitate the open distribution of knowledge. Librarians strive to enable the free flow of information. Their traditions are liberal, founded on the belief that libraries should serve democracy. To help fulfill their mission as resource centers for citizens, public libraries maintain collections of records, policy statements, government documents, and so on. A recent promotional video from the American Librarian's Association exults that "the library is democracy's place of worship" (ALA, 2002).

Clearly, the impending redefinition of the book as a digital artifact that is licensed rather than sold, tied to a particular replay device, with restrictions that are clearly laid out and mechanically enforced, is an innovation that goes right to the heart of libraries. The changing nature of the book may make it hard, or even impossible, for libraries to fulfill their mandate by providing quality information to readers. And on the other hand, the emergence of a vast storehouse of information on the Internet poses a different kind of conundrum. Librarians, the traditional gatekeepers of knowledge, are in danger of being bypassed, their skills ignored, their advice unsought. Search engines send users straight to the information they require—or so users think—without any need for an intermediary to classify, catalogue, cross-reference, and advise on sources.

The ready availability of information on the Internet, and its widespread use, really presents librarians with an opportunity, not a threat. Savvy users realize they need help, which librarians can provide. A good example is Infomine, a cooperative project of the University of California and California State University (amongst others) (Mason et al., 2000). Infomine contains descriptions and links to a wealth of scholarly and educational Internet resources, each of which has been selected and described by a professional academic librarian who is a specialist in the subject and in resource description generally. Participating librarians see this as an important expenditure of effort for their users, a natural evolution of their traditional task of collecting and organizing information in print.

What kind of technical infrastructure is needed to support and promote this kind of work? Open source software is a powerful ally for librarians who wish to extend liberal traditions of information access. These systems make the source code freely available for others to view, modify, and adapt; and the very nature of the licensing agreement prevents the software from being appropriated by proprietary vendors. But the open-source movement is more than just a vehicle for librarians to use: its link with library traditions goes much deeper. Public libraries and open source software both enshrine the same philosophy: to promote learning and understanding through the dissemination of knowledge. Both are pervaded by a sense of community, on the one hand the kind of inter-institutional cooperation exemplified by inter-library loan and, on the other, teams of designers and programmers that frequently cross national boundaries.

New trends in information access present librarians in developed countries with difficult and conflicting challenges. Meanwhile, however, the situation in the developing world is dire. Here, traditional publishing and distribution mechanisms have failed tragically. For example, according to the 1999 UN Human Development Report (UNDP, 1999), whereas a U.S. medical library subscribes to about 5,000 journals, the Nairobi University Medical School Library, long regarded as a flagship center in East Africa, last year received just 20 journals (compared with 300 a decade before). In Brazzaville, Congo, the university has only 40 medical books and a dozen journals, all from before 1993, and the library in a large district hospital consisted of a single bookshelf filled mostly with novels.

Digital Libraries and the Challenge for HCI

Traditional libraries are substantial institutions that occupy physical space, present a physical appearance, and exhibit tangible physical organization. When standing on the threshold of a large bricks-and-mortar library you gain a sense of presence and permanence that reflects the care taken in building and maintaining the collection inside. Digital libraries, in contrast, are lightweight. But they provide potentially far greater accessibility, which means that they will have even greater social effects. Once created, they can, without significant institutional support, continue to serve users. They can be distributed throughout most of the developed world over the Internet. In developing countries and remote corners of the developed world they can be circulated on removable media—CD-ROM, DVD, or 100 Gb disk units the size of videocassettes—and updated over radio (or in Internet cafés). Issues of copyright pose difficult problems, but they are manageable. For example, there is plenty of non-copyright material, or material whose owners are prepared to donate copyright for socially useful purposes, and trends towards more open access to academic and humanitarian information are visible. Not everyone sees digital rights management and the DMCA as the way forward, and in the longer term publishers, to remain viable, will have to investigate alternative revenue models for the information they own. No wonder international organizations such as the United Nations, along with many smaller non-government organizations (NGOs), are keenly interested in digital library technology.

Advances in digital library technology are radically lowering the bar for the design and production of richly organized, coherent, focused collections of information. Now, anyone with access to sufficient source material can use public-domain software to build large, fully searchable collections the size of traditional personal or institutional libraries—in minutes. Let the minutes stretch to hours and the collection can be polished, organized, branded, and distributed. It can include fully illustrated text, images, video, and music. It can present attractively designed pages with consistent use of icons. Keywords, key phrases, even acronyms and their definitions, can be extracted—automatically—and used to underpin novel means of access. Let the hours stretch to days and metadata can be manually added that permits further levels of organization. Given access to programming skills, creative new facilities that stretch the imagination can be rapidly integrated into the system.

All this, one might say, can be done with ordinary Web sites: there is no need for digital library technology. However, bitter experience has shown that all but the most rudimentary sites do require significant institutional support—for organization and maintenance. The Web is littered with incomplete, unfinished, unmaintained, out-dated, inconsistently organized, useless information collections. Just as traditional library cataloging procedures integrate new works into existing collections with minimal overhead so that they immediately become first-class members of the collection, so digital libraries allow new documents to be added completely automatically. In the case of traditional libraries this is done through the small but non-negligible overhead of generating a new catalog entry (one to two hours per book). With ordinary Web sites it requires inserting links manually into index pages and the like, and may involve adding links not only into the new document but also into existing ones that ought to reference it—it's like rewriting the book, and maybe revising all other books in the library too! In contrast, digital libraries bring access structures instantly and effortlessly up-to-date whenever new documents are added.

The challenge for HCI is to design and build digital library systems that fulfill the potential of digital libraries as a "killer app" for computers in developing countries, which will bring concomitant benefits in almost every other sphere of application. For the information consumer we need access to information that is guaranteed across space, time, and culture. We need flexible distribution mechanisms for documents, and for information objects of all types, that can be accessed on all computer platforms—including the lowliest. We need a choice of distribution over the Web or on removable media such as CD-ROM or DVD. Digital libraries can incorporate flexible presentation that caters to individual differences, such as large-font displays or spoken output for the visually impaired. Libraries are places where information is preserved, not rendered obsolete, and digital libraries must instill confidence that information prepared today can be accessed next week, next decade, next century—regardless of technological changes. An important aspect of digital libraries is their ability to work in local languages, promoting pluralism and reducing the risks of homogeneity. Because language is the vehicle of thought, communication, and cultural identity, this will encourage diversity and strengthen individual cultures. But there is a long way to go: even Unicode is woefully incomplete in certain areas, such as African languages.

Naturally, today's digital library systems focus principally on the reader: the consumer of the material stored in the library's treasure house. But digital libraries make a more radical, and perhaps ultimately more important, contribution by empowering ordinary users to conceive, assemble, build, and disseminate new information collections themselves. In principle, modest computing resources are quite sufficient to enable users to build new collections by gathering together material in local files or on the Web (or both); augmenting it with appropriate metadata that supports convenient search and browsing operations; incorporating advanced features like key-phrase extraction, document summarization, and metadata extraction; designing an attractive and functional interface; and publishing the collection on a variety of different media that are suitable for the intended readership. The HCI challenge is to realize this potential for users—such as most librarians—who have a strong understanding of information and its organization, but no more interest in computers than they have in papermaking technology, last millennium's vehicle for information dissemination.

What are Digital Libraries?

A digital library is an organized collection of information:

> ... a focused collection of digital objects, including text, video, and audio, along with methods for access and retrieval, and for selection, organization, and maintenance of the collection. (Witten & Bainbridge, 2002)

This definition deliberately accords equal weight to user (access and retrieval) and librarian (selection, organization and maintenance). The latter functions are often overlooked by digital library proponents, who often work from a technology perspective rather than from the viewpoint of library or information science, but it is precisely these aspects that allow digital libraries to be used to democratize information dissemination.

As a concrete example, consider the Humanity Development Library, a collection of some 1,200 authoritative books and periodicals, produced by many disparate organizations—UN agencies and other international organizations— on various areas of human development, from agricultural practice to economic policies, from water and sanitation to society and culture, from education to manufacturing, from disaster mitigation to micro-enterprises. It contains 160,000 pages and 30,000 images, which if printed would weigh 340 kg, cost $20,000, and occupy a small library book stack. Instead, it takes the form of a digital library and is distributed on a CD-ROM throughout the developing world at essentially no cost. (It's also on the Web at nzdl.org.)

The Humanity Development Library is produced using the Greenstone software, a freely distributed open-source project whose aim is to create novel digital library technologies and make them available for others to use. Greenstone digital libraries are arranged in *collections*. A collection comprises several (typically several thousand, or several million) documents, and a library may include several collections, each organized differently. Collections built with Greenstone offer simple but effective searching and browsing facilities based on metadata and the full text of electronic documents. Each collection is individually

Figure 1. The Humanity Development Library: (a) searching for biogas; (b) browsing by subject; (c) reading a document

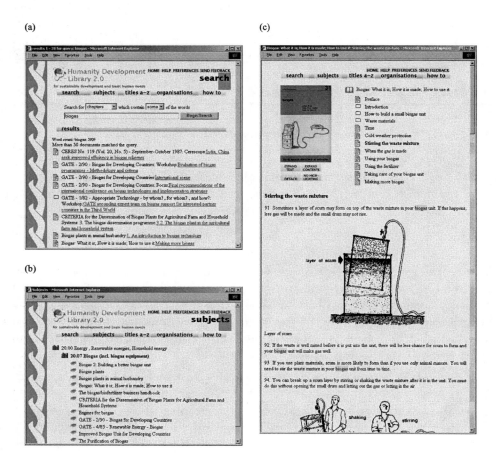

designed to take advantage of whatever metadata is available. All collections support full-text searching and most provide several different browsing options, although they differ depending on the collection design and the metadata available. Typically you can search for particular words that appear in the text, or within a section of a document, or within a title or section heading. A variety of interfaces exist for browsing collections by *title, subject, date,* or any other metadata chosen by the collection designer.

Figure 1 shows snapshots of the Humanity Development Library. In *Figure 1a* documents are being searched for chapters containing the word *biogas*. In *Figure 1b* the collection is being browsed by subject: by clicking on the bookshelf icons the user has discovered an item under *Section 20, Energy, Renewable energies, Household energy*. Pursuing an interest in energy from biogas, the user selects a book by clicking on its book icon (*Figure 1c*). All the icons in the screenshots of *Figure 1* are clickable. Those at the top of the page return to the library home page, provide help text, and allow you to set user interface and searching preferences. The navigation bar beneath gives access to the searching and browsing facilities, and they differ from one collection to another. This particular collection can be searched by book, chapter, or section, and browsed by subject, title, organization, and "how to" metadata as indicated by the navigation bar.

Documents are presented as Web pages generated by Greenstone from the source material. In *Figure 1c* the book's cover is displayed as a graphic on the left, and an automatically constructed table of contents appears at the start of the document. The current focus, *Stirring the waste mixture*, is written in bold in the table of contents; its text (including any illustrations) starts further down the page. Incidentally, the material in this collection on building household biogas plans is fascinating, though it is not directly relevant to this article.

Greenstone collections present documents as automatically generated Web pages. This allows documents in different source formats to be presented in a consistent manner, and lets users view the entire collection with a standard Web browser—no special viewing applications are required. However, the collection maintainer may choose to present the original source document (whether Word, PDF, PostScript, PowerPoint, Excel, a QuickTime movie, an audio file, or whatever) instead of, or as well as, the HTML version, and rely on the user's Web browser to select a suitable application to display the document. In general, Greenstone deals well with documents and metadata in a wide variety of different formats.

Using Digital Libraries to Disseminate Humanitarian Information

Digital libraries provide perhaps the first really compelling *raison d'être* for computing technology in the developing world. Priorities in these countries include health, agriculture, nutrition, hygiene, sanitation, and safe drinking water. Though computers *per se* are not a priority, simple, reliable access to practical information relevant to these basic needs certainly is. In an article entitled *The promise of digital libraries in developing countries*, Witten et al. (2002) mention 10 information collections, available on the Web (at nzdl.org) and CD-ROM, from organizations ranging from UN agencies to small NGOs, in which

Greenstone is being used to deliver humanitarian and related information in developing countries. For example, the Humanity Development Library described above is a compendium of practical information aimed at helping reduce poverty, increasing human potential, and giving a practical and useful education. Rather than recapitulating the brief summaries of collections that appear in the above-cited paper, we describe four new ones that have been created recently, and distributed in the same way (*Figure 2*).

The Researching Education Development library is a project of the Department for International Development (DFID), a British government department responsible for promoting development. Its central focus is a commitment to an internationally agreed target of halving the proportion of people living in extreme poverty by 2015. Associated targets include ensuring universal primary education, gender equality in schooling, and skills development. It works in partnership with other governments and multilateral institutions, with business and the private sector, with civil society and the research community. It has created a CD-ROM library containing many education research papers and other documents. Each one represents a study or piece of commissioned research on some aspects of education and training in developing countries.

The Energy for Sustainable Development library was initiated as part of the outreach phase of the World Energy Assessment, which was initiated jointly by the United Nations Development Programme (UNDP), the United Nations Department of Economic and Social Affairs (UNDESA), and the World Energy Council (WEC), along with funding from the United Nations Foundation. This library contains a broad and valuable collection of 350 documents (26,000 pages) from UNDP, UNDESA, WEC and many other organizations. It includes titles that all these organizations have published on the subjects of energy for sustainable development—technical guidelines, journals and newsletters, case studies, manuals, reports, and other training material. The documents are in English, Spanish and French, and one document has Arabic, Russian and Chinese translations as well.

The UNAIDS Library contains publications in the "Best Practice" collection (including key materials, case studies, technical updates, and points of view) which form a unique resource for those working in planning and practice. It is produced by the Joint United Nations Programme on HIV/AIDS, whose global mission is to lead, strengthen and support a response to the AIDS epidemic that will prevent the spread of HIV, provide care and support for those infected by the disease, reduce the vulnerability of individuals and communities to HIV/AIDS, and alleviate the socioeconomic and human impact of the epidemic.

The Health Library for Disasters is the result of a collaboration between the emergency and disaster programs of the World Health Organization (WHO) and the Pan American Health Organization (PAHO), with the participation of many other organizations: the United Nations High Commissioner for Refugees (UNHCR), the United Nations Children's Fund (UNICEF), the International Strategy for Disaster Reduction (EIRD); the Red Cross Movement (ICRC and IFRC); the SPHERE Project; non-governmental organizations such as OXFAM; and national organizations such as the National Emergency Commission of Costa Rica. It contains more than 300 technical and scientific documents on disaster reduction and public health issues related to emergencies and humanitarian assistance. A follow-up to the Spanish language Biblioteca Virtual de Desastres discussed by Witten et al. (2002), it includes technical guidelines, field guidelines, case studies, emergency kits, manuals, disaster reports, and other training materials.

Universal Access

Universal access to digital libraries presents huge challenges to software engineers and HCI practitioners. The Greenstone digital library software allows us to glimpse some of the issues, although it certainly does not yet effectively address them all. We summarize some technical details in the next subsection, before turning to more interesting questions of access for readers, collection builders, and international users.

Platforms and Distribution

Most digital libraries are accessed over the Web, using any Web browser. However, in many environments, particularly in developing countries, Web access is insufficient and the system must run locally. And if people are to build and control their own libraries, a centralized solution is inadequate: the software must run on their own computers. Thus digital library systems intended for broad access should run on a wide variety of computer systems, particularly low-end ones.

Developed under Linux, the Greenstone server runs on any Windows, Unix, or MacOS/X system. All versions of Windows are supported, from 3.1 up (including 3.1/3.11, 95/98/ME/, NT/2000 and XP). Supporting primitive platforms poses substantial challenges of a rather mundane nature: for example, Microsoft compilers no longer support Windows 3.1 and it is necessary to acquire obsolete versions (e.g., at software auctions). Under Windows, pre-built collections can be viewed on any system with at least 8 Mb RAM, but collections cannot be built under Windows 3.1/3.11—for this at least a Pentium processor is generally

Figure 2. A selection of recent humanitarian digital library collections on CD-ROM

required, except for very small collections. The fact that Greenstone does not run on early Macintosh systems is a serious drawback in certain environments (e.g., many schools).

In an international cooperative effort established in August 2000 with UNESCO and the Belgium-based Human Info NGO, Greenstone is being distributed widely in developing countries with the aim of empowering users, particularly in universities, libraries, and other public service institutions, to build their own digital libraries. UNESCO recognizes that digital libraries are radically reforming how information is acquired and disseminated in its partner communities and institutions in the fields of education, science and culture around the world, and particularly in developing countries. Their hope is that this software will encourage the effective deployment of digital libraries to share information and place it in the public domain.

The UNESCO distribution of Greenstone is a CD-ROM that contains the full source code and executable binaries for Windows and Linux, along with all necessary associated software (e.g., Perl for Windows). Full documentation (four PDF manuals) and five demonstration collections are included. The current CD-ROM is trilingual, with complete interfaces, instructions, and documentation in English, French and Spanish. For those with Web access, the same package is also available for download from the Greenstone Web site (greenstone.org), often in a form that is slightly ahead of the CD-ROM version—for example, many other language interfaces are included and full documentation is available in Russian and Kazakh too. Providing accessibility in different languages is more difficult than one might at first realize. As well as the manuals, installation instructions and installation prompts, the licensing agreement, and the readme files have to be translated too.

Access for Readers

Greenstone collections like the Humanity Development Library can be published as stand-alone collections on removable media such as CD-ROM, or presented on the Web. CD-ROM is a very practical format in developing countries. Any Greenstone collection can be converted into a self-contained Windows CD-ROM that includes the Greenstone server software itself (in a version that runs right down to Windows 3.1) and an integrated installation package. The installation procedure has been thoroughly honed to ensure that only the most basic of computer skills are needed to install and run a collection under Windows.

Even stand-alone Greenstone users interact through a Web browser: Netscape is supplied on each CD-ROM for those who do not already have a browser. In stand-alone mode the software runs locally but incorporates a Web server so that if the system happens to be connected to a network—say a hospital or school intranet—information is available to other machines that may not possess CD drives. This happens automatically: no special configuration is necessary. Another difficult engineering challenge is checking for the existence of a network. While installed network software is easily detected, it is hard to determine non-intrusively whether it is operational (sending oneself a message often results in the user being asked to dial their local Internet service provider). Incorrectly installed or configured software is endemic in developing countries, because computers there are often cast-offs whose software is inappropriate to their present environment, yet system support to rectify the problems is unavailable. It is essential for universal access that such problems are addressed properly and solved satisfactorily without involving the user, even though they are mundane and time-consuming.

Greenstone provides some support for the visually impaired by incorporating a "textual" mode of access that replaces all images by textual prompts. This output is suitable for users with speech synthesizers or other specialized access devices. However, the facility is not well advanced: in particular, we have not yet refined it through usability testing and interface improvement.

Building New Collections

Effective human development blossoms from empowerment rather than gifting. As the Chinese proverb says, "Give a man a fish and he will eat for a day; teach him to fish and he will eat for the rest of his days." Disseminating information originating in the developed world, like the Humanity Development Library, is a useful activity for developing countries. But a more effective strategy for sustained long-term human development is to disseminate the capability of creating information collections, rather than the collections themselves. This will allow developing countries to participate actively in our information society, rather than observing it from outside. It will stimulate the creation of new industry. And it will help ensure that intellectual property remains where it belongs, in the hands of those who produce it.

Users whose skills resemble those of librarians rather than computer specialists should be able to build and distribute their own digital library collections. As an initial step in this direction, Greenstone includes an interface called the "Collector" that is intended to help people build their own library collections (Witten et al., 2000). Collections may be built and served locally from the user's own Web server, or (given appropriate permissions) remotely on a shared digital library host. End users can build new collections styled after existing ones from material on the Web or from their local files—or both, and collections can be updated and new ones brought online at any time. The interface, which is intended for non-professional end users, is modeled after widely used commercial software installation packages (such as InstallShield[1]), frequently called software "wizards"—a term we deprecate because of its appeal to mysticism and connotations of utter inexplicability. We chose this interaction style because it simplifies the choices and presents them very clearly.

Figure 3 shows a new Greenstone librarian interface, currently undergoing beta testing by UNESCO at sites in Argentina, India, Kazakhstan, Mexico, and South Africa, which builds on lessons learned from the Collector. It incorporates a great deal of additional functionality, particularly the ability for users to associate metadata with any item or group of items, and to reuse metadata elements without retyping them. In *Figure 3* it is being used to collate a selection of images for a digital library collection, augment these source documents with textual metadata and then build and view the collection. From here, it is a matter of a few further clicks to produce a self-installing CD-ROM version of the collection.

In this illustration, the user is developing a digital library collection of historic paintings of New Zealand. The user creates a new collection using the file menu (*Figure 3a*), and a resulting pop-up window prompts for some general information about the collection. Once the user has filled out this form the main window becomes active. A series of panels guide the user through the processes required to build the collection. The left-hand pane of the *Gather* panel, shown in *Figure 3b*, shows the file system and the right-hand one represents the contents of the collection, initially empty, which the user populates by dragging and dropping files. In *Figure 3c* the user has moved to the *Enrich* panel and is adding textual metadata (the name of the artists) to the selected documents. The next two panels, *Design*, *Create*, help the user structure the collection, control its appearance, and build it. On completion the result is viewed in the *Preview* panel. *Figure 3d* shows a page from the newly built collection, in which source documents are alphabetically listed by artist. Shown alongside each thumbnail are the artist's name, its catalog number, image dimensions, and its download size. The full-size image is shown by clicking on the thumbnail. The user may skip backwards and forwards through the panels using them to augment and enhance the collection, perhaps adding further source documents, editing metadata values, and altering the collection's appearance.

Customization

An important component of access is allowing people to control the appearance of the collections they create. Many who build digital libraries want to brand them to ensure that they with an appropriate personal, institutional, or corporate image, and some can only contemplate software solutions that allow them to do so. Although Greenstone comes with the standard appearance shown in *Figure 1*— a distinctive bar down the side of all pages except those that show documents in the library, a green access bar with yellow buttons, etc.—the interface is highly configurable.

Figure 3. Building a collection with the Gatherer

(a)   (b)

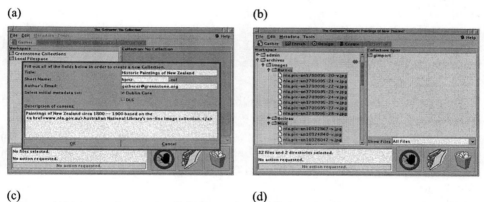

(c)   (d)

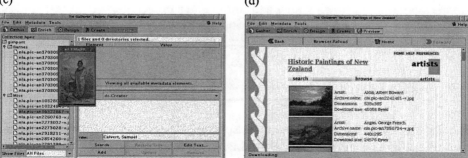

Greenstone creates all pages that appear on the screen on the fly: none are stored in advance. They are generated using macros, written in a simple language specially designed for the job, that perform textual replacement. One reason is that Greenstone accommodates a large number of different interface languages (see next subsection), and macros help cope with this. All text fragments are couched as macro definitions. To add a new language, just the macro contents need to be translated—no Web pages need be reworked. Every page displayed by the system is passed through a macro interpreter that expands all the macros on the page. The interpreter checks a language variable and uses the macro definitions pertaining to it, which loads the page in the appropriate language.

Macros can have parameters. In this case, the parameter is the language variable: it causes the appropriate text fragment to be used for the macro's expansion. If there is no Arabic version for a particular macro, the interpreter will automatically substitute the default version (English). This lets system developers experiment with the interface without having to worry about translating every little bit of new text immediately. Defaulting to English is not ideal—it reflects an Anglo-centric mindset—but it seems better than displaying nothing. (However, if "nothing" were preferred, it would be a simple matter to alter the software to default to the empty language!)

Macros are also used to deal with display variables. Whenever a Web page contains information that is not known in advance—like the number of documents returned by a search, or the value of a particular metadata item, or the content of a document page—a macro name is used in the page description. Unlike language macros, these macros are *dynamic*: their content is not stored in advance but generated by the system in accordance with the value of the variable in question.

Users can completely alter the form of the user interface by rewriting the macro files—or even by writing their own Web pages which embed the dynamic macros that generate bits of Greenstone output. *Figure 4* shows a Greenstone interface that has been heavily customized by Lehigh University Library, Pennsylvania (bridges.lib.lehigh.edu). The standard Greenstone appearance has been completely obliterated in favor of an in-house style, yet all the Greenstone functionality is available. *Figure 4* shows a thumbnail of a book cover on the left, and full bibliographic information on the right. Entering a book displays facsimile images of its pages.

Internationalization

The international Unicode character set is used throughout Greenstone, and documents in any Unicode-supported language and character encoding can be imported. (In fact, the software can automatically detect the language and encoding of most documents.) Collections of documents in Arabic, Chinese, Cyrillic, English, French, Spanish, German, Hindi, and Maori are publicly available. The New Zealand Digital Library Web site (nzdl.org) hosts many of these, and the Greenstone Web site (greenstone.org) links to sites that contain further examples.

It makes little sense to have a collection whose content is in Chinese or Russian, but whose supporting text—instructions, navigation buttons, labels, images, help text, and so on—are in English. Consequently, the entire Greenstone interface has been translated into a range of languages, and the interface language can be changed by the user as they browse from the *Preferences* page. As noted above, all the language fragments in the interface (and also the contents of language-dependent images) are stored in macro files. These have been translated by Greenstone users in other parts of the world and contributed back to the project. (The same mechanism provides text-only versions of the interface to accommodate visually impaired users.) *Figure 5* shows an example: a Russian collection. Currently, interfaces are available in Arabic, Czech, Chinese, Dutch, French, Galician, German, Hebrew, Indonesian, Italian, Kazakh, Maori, Portuguese, Russian, Spanish, Turkish, and English.

Managing the organizational and software complexity of any comprehensive and evolving open source software system presents a significant challenge. However, the challenge is greatly magnified when the interface is available in different languages, for enhancements to the software and changes to the interface must be faithfully reflected in each language version. No single person knows all interface languages; no single person knows about all modifications to the software—indeed there is likely no overlap at all between those who translate the interface and those who build the software. Currently, Greenstone has about twenty interface languages and there are around 600 linguistic fragments in each interface, ranging from single words like *search*, through short phrases like *search for, which contain, of the words*, to sentences like *More than ... documents matched the query*, to complete paragraphs like those in the online help text. Maintaining the interface in many different languages is a logistic nightmare. The solution adopted by Greenstone is to incorporate a language translation facility, which allows authorized people to update the interface in specified languages. A standard version control system is used to manage software change, and from this the system automatically determines which language fragments need updating and presents them to the human translator.

Figure 4. A customized interface to Greenstone

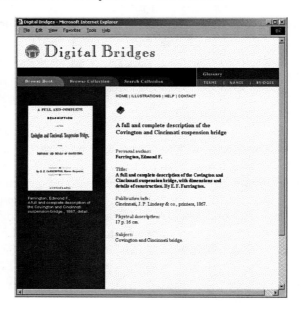

Figure 5. A Russian digital library collection

Conclusion

By allowing people to easily create and disseminate large information collections, digital libraries extend the applications of modern technology in socially responsible directions, and counter a possible threat towards the commercialization of information in line with practices developed by the entertainment industry. As far as the developing world is concerned, digital libraries may prove to be a "killer app" for computer technology—that is, an application that makes a sustained market for a promising but under-utilized technology. The World Wide Web is often described as the Internet's killer app. But the Internet does not really extend to developing countries, and the developing world is missing out on the prodigious amount of basic, everyday human information that the Web provides, and its enormous influence on promoting and internationalizing business opportunities. There is little incentive to make copies of the entire Web available locally because of its vast size, rapid change, and questionable information value per gigabyte. However, it is easy to provide focused information collections on both the Web and, in exactly the same form, on removable media such as CD-ROM, DVD, or bulk disk storage devices—indeed, the Greenstone software described above allows one to create a complete, runnable, self-installing CD-ROM image from a Web collection in just a few mouse clicks.

Public libraries are founded on the principle of universal access, and digital libraries should be too. This provides HCI with enormous practical challenges. Universal access means running on low-end devices, but one does not want to provide a lowest –common denominator solution that sacrifices high-end capability where it is available. Universal access means that interfaces should be available in the world's languages, but one does not want the burden of translation to stifle the development of new functionality and features. Universal access means educating users: UNESCO is mounting training courses on building collections with Greenstone in Bangalore, Almaty, Senegal, and Suva, and discussions are underway for Latin America; the Tulane Institute has run courses that use Greenstone collections as a resource in many locations in Africa (e.g., Burkina Faso, Cameroon, Cote d'Ivoire, Democratic Republic of Congo, Ghana, Rwanda, Senegal, Sierra Leone, Togo) and Latin America (e.g., Argentina, Bolivia, Colombia, Ecuador, Guatemala).

Universal access also means that non-textual material should enjoy first-class status in a digital library—perhaps first-class status in "the literature." This has important cultural ramifications. It should be possible to create digital library collections intended for use by people in oral cultures, who may be illiterate or semi-literate. Or people whom, though they can read and write their own language, cannot speak or read the language of the digital library. Imagine having access to collections that spring out of the rich cultures of China or Arabia, created by people who grew up in these cultures, without having to learn a new language. More practically—since you, the reader, being culturally privileged, can probably access this kind of information in translation—imagine giving someone in the highlands of Peru, fluent and literate in her native language of Quechua, first-hand access to the information in humanitarian collections such as the Humanity Development Library (currently available only in English and French) or the Biblioteca Virtual de Desastres (until recently available only in Spanish). Opening up digital libraries for the illiterate is a radical and potentially revolutionary benefit of new interface technology.

An important, and liberating, difference between digital libraries and conventional ones is that anyone should be able to create their own digital collections. This presents HCI challenges that are difficult yet more conventional: providing non-computer users with access to advanced and complex functionality. Users should be able to collect their own source material, provide their own metadata, design their own collections, and present it through their own interface.

Digital libraries give software engineers and HCI practitioners a golden opportunity to help reverse the negative impact of information technology on developing countries and reduce the various "digital divides" that cleave our world (Norris, 2001)—the "social divide" between the information rich and the information poor in our own nations, the "democratic divide" between those who do and do not use the panoply of digital resources to engage, mobilize and participate in public life, as well as the "global divide" that reflects the huge disparity in access to information between people in industrialized and developing societies.

Acknowledgments

I gratefully acknowledge all members of the New Zealand Digital Library project for their enthusiasm, ideas and commitment, particularly David Bainbridge and John Thompson who worked on the Greenstone librarian's interface. I have benefited enormously from cooperation with John Rose of UNESCO, and Michel Loots of Human Info NGO. Harold Thimbleby of University College London and Gary Marsden of the University of Cape Town made very useful comments on the draft of this chapter.

References

ALA. (2002). *Rediscover America @ your library.* Video produced by the American Library Association, Chicago, IL. Available from the World Wide Web: *www.ala.org/@yourlibrary/rediscoveramerica*

Arunachalam, S. (1998, June). *How the Internet is failing the developing world.* Presented at Science Communication in the Next Millennium, Egypt.

Ciolek, T. M. (1996). The six quests for the electronic grail: Current approaches to information quality in WWW resources. In *Review Informatique et Statistique dans les Sciences humaines (RISSH)* (No. 1-4) (pp. 45-71). Centre Informatique de Philosophie et Lettres, Universite de Liege, Belgium.

Lynch, C. (2001, June). The battle to define the future of the book in the digital world. *First Monday, 6* (5).

Mason, J., Mitchell, S., Mooney, M., Reasoner, L., & Rodriguez, C. (2000, June). INFOMINE: Promising directions in virtual library development. *First Monday, 5* (6).

Norris, P. (2001). *Digital divide? Civic engagement, information poverty and the Internet worldwide.* New York: Cambridge University Press.

Quéau, P. (2001). Information literacy: A new frontier. *UNISIST Newsletter, 29* (2), 3-4.

Roehl, R., & Varian, H.R. (2001, May). Circulating libraries and video rental stores. *First Monday, 6* (5).

Samuelson, P., & Davis, R. (2000, September). *The digital dilemma: A perspective on intellectual property in the information age.* Presented at the Telecommunications Policy Research Conference, Alexandria, Virginia.

UNDP. (1999). *Human development report 1999.* New York: UNDP/Oxford University Press.

Witten, I.H., & Bainbridge, D. (2002). *How to build a digital library.* San Francisco: Morgan Kaufmann.

Witten, I.H., Loots, M., Trujillo, M.F., & Bainbridge, D. (2002). The promise of digital libraries in developing countries. *The Electronic Library, 20* (1), 7-13.

Endnotes

[1]   *www.installshield.com*

Chapter XII

Sharing Digital Knowledge With End-Users:
Case Study of the International Rice Research Institute Library and Documentation Service in the Philippines

Mila Ramos
International Rice Research Institute, Philippines

Abstract

This chapter portrays how resources of the International Rice Research Institute Library and Documentation Service are harnessed to develop its collection of technical rice literature and other information sources by searching, selecting and organizing print and electronic resources for addition to its Web page or the online catalog. With the acquisition of an integrated library system in 1996, the creation of its home page, at http:// ricelib.irri.cgiar.org, became a major concern. Links to digital resources, like Web sites, databases, full-text electronic journals and newspapers, and reference materials are now available through this page. The Library operates on the principle that electronic resources must supplement rather than replace printed sources. The author intends to share the mechanics of linking digital knowledge with users, the problems embedded in this activity, and possible ways of dealing with them.

Introduction: Initial Steps Toward a Digital Library

This chapter describes work carried out by the International Rice Research Institute (IRRI) Library and Documentation Service (LDS) focusing on digital delivery of rice-related and other information. IRRI, established in 1960 and located in Los Baños, Laguna, Philippines, is one of the 15 international centers under the umbrella of the Consultative Group on International Agricultural Research (CGIAR). Its goal is to "improve the well-being of present and future generations of rice farmers and consumers, particularly those with low incomes" (IRRI, 1996). In pursuance of this mandate, a Library was established in 1961, which now houses the world's most comprehensive collection of rice technical literature. The Library and Documentation Service (LDS) has clients, which include rice scientists from more than 58 countries all over the world. It has a staff strength of 14 (five librarians and nine paraprofessionals), all equipped with computers. While utilizing advances in information technology, it is the responsibility of the LDS to link knowledge sources with potential users everywhere.

The changing information needs of IRRI staff and worldwide clients and the recent advances in information and communication technologies make digital delivery of information a necessity. The IRRI LDS management opted to take advantage of available technology and offered the convenience of digital access to its users.

Early attempts at computerization were focused on the rice bibliography, the library's flagship project, which is a compilation of the world's technical rice literature. In 1989, with the acquisition of additional personal computers, a field structure for the main catalog was devised using an early version of *Cardbox Plus* (Cardbox, 2003). The program was deemed to be sufficient at that time because exposure to more sophisticated systems was very limited. Searching and retrieval was faster than using the card catalog. However, the non-expandable fields did not lend themselves to efficient data entry.

This system was in use till migration to an integrated library system, the *Innopac* (Innovative, 2003), took place in 1996. The initial database consisted of 10,000 records imported from the Cardbox Plus database. From 1996 onwards, updating of the card catalog ceased. Retrospective conversion was finished in mid-2002 and this manual searching tool, which has been an effective instrument for many years, was relegated to the background.

The adequate computer facilities of IRRI enabled the staff to be adept with the use of computers and to avail of information sources which otherwise would be difficult to access. An upgrade from the character-based *Innopac* to the Web-based *Millennium* took place in 2003.

From here on, efficient linking of electronic resources to library users became a reality. This is one of the initiatives that qualified the IRRI LDS to be awarded as the Outstanding Academic/Research Library for 2001 by a major library association in the Philippines, the Philippine Association of Academic and Research Libraries, in January 2002.

Tools for Linking Users and Digital Resources

In this age of shrinking budgets, the IRRI Library is trying its best to develop its collection by searching, evaluating, selecting, and cataloging online information sources for addition to its Web page and online catalog. Byrne (2003) gives three elements that must be included in building a digital library. These are "integrated content provision, support and training, and library effectiveness." Careful evaluation and selection of content are vital in developing and maintaining a digital library. Materials for the Web site are included on the basis of relevance to IRRI's research program. Since the integrated library system being used, the Millennium, is user-friendly, there is no need for formal training. However, brief orientation is given to new staff, walk-in clients, and visitors to make them aware of what the library could offer and what digital resources are available through the library's Web site. Library effectiveness is a product of the extent to which digital resources are used by clients. In the IRRI Library, the digital tools being utilized are:

The Library's Home Page at *http://ricelib.irri.org*

As a consequence of computerization, the next step pursued was the creation of the Library's home page (http://ricelib.irri.org, retrieved May 28, 2004) in late 1996. Since then, the site has been available to users from any computer with Internet connection, 24 hours daily (Wallace, 1998). In designing the Web site, the major considerations are contents and usability, with due regard to artistic quality. Web sites of other libraries, particularly those that are appealing in terms of design and content, served as models. The best attributes of other Web sites are noted and adopted in planning the page. The earlier design of the LDS home page carried graphical icons. Based on users' feedback, this resulted in slow connection, especially in locations with low bandwidth. In view of this, the current design was made simpler and with minimal use of graphics.

Various access points to digital resources were included to enable users to have seamless connection to vital information sources. The evolution from a conventional to a digital library is currently under way. *Figure 1* is the third design since its creation. Through this Web site, users everywhere can avail of the following tools:

- The Main Catalog serves as a digital portal to the library's print and special collections (see *Figure 2*). It has 72,608 bibliographic records, 500+ of which carry links to full text electronic documents, Web sites, and databases on the WWW or the IRRI's local area network. The catalog has a user-friendly interface; hence no training for users is required. One big advantage of having an online catalog is that it is now very easy to update or edit large amounts of information. Also, ease of searching and flexibility in configuring search and result screens are added improvements (Cohen, 2003).

Figure 1. The IRRI Library Web site

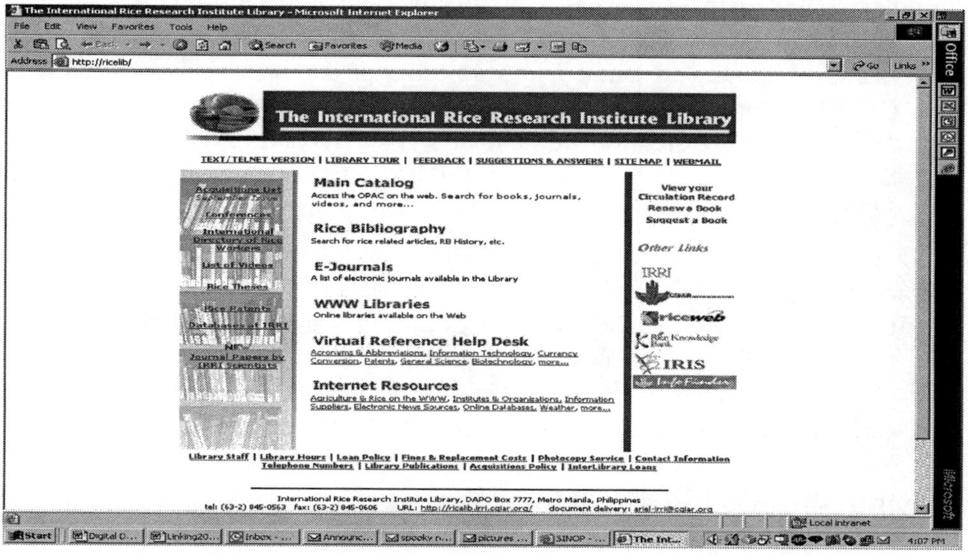

Figure 2.   The Online Public Access Catalog

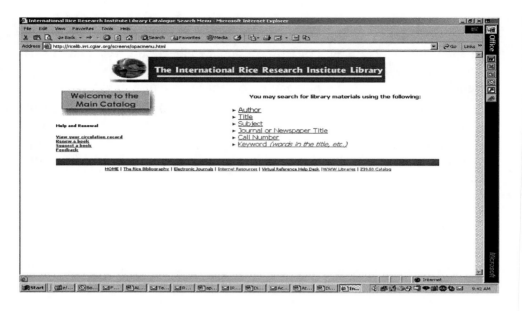

- The Rice Bibliography is an active, comprehensive database of the world's rice technical literature, published and unpublished, and written in more than 80 languages. There are 224,564 bibliographic entries covering the years 1968 up to the present. The full coverage of this bibliography is from 1951 up to present. Earlier entries are undergoing retrospective conversion. In addition to the print and Web versions, this database is also available in CD-ROM format. Each item in the database is backed up by full-text print or microforms or electronic documents. As in the main catalog, some items have electronic links to abstracts or full text articles. Updating and addition of bibliographic records are done on a daily basis.

- The link to Electronic Journals opens a table, which lists the titles and corresponding access modes (see *Figure 3*). Some of these connect to full text articles through the payment of stiff license fees. Many others are freely available on the Web. The rest link to Tables of Contents or abstracts only. Core collecting is followed in this Library, as the budget falls short of acquiring all the titles needed by Institute scientists. Brach (2001) cites the basic steps to follow in making e-journals available and these are exactly what the IRRI LDS follows:

Figure 3.   The Electronic Journals Page

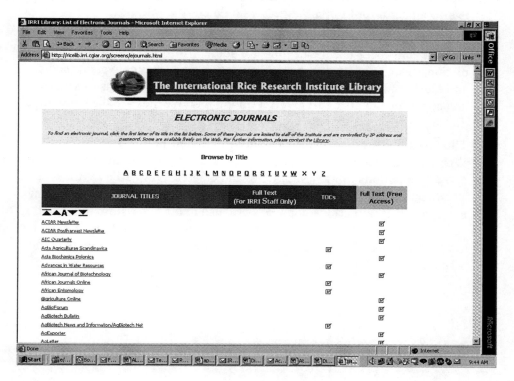

1. Careful selection of journal or package by evaluating its relevance to rice research.

2. Negotiation (individual or consortia) with publishers or with the aggregator, Swets Blackwell. Developing country rates are always taken advantage of.

3. Review of license agreements.

4. Cataloging of the journal title and creation of entries on the Web page and the online catalog.

5. Web loading or creation of links.

• The WWW Libraries button connects to catalogs of major libraries located in many parts of the world. In looking for obscure publications, which are not locally available, users may search the catalogs of major libraries, which are likely to have them. Foremost among these are the Library of Congress, the Ohiolink, the British Library, Bibliotheque Nationale, and others. This is also a useful tool for catalogers who do copy cataloging.

- The Virtual Reference Help Desk is a virtual library in itself (*Figure 4*). Remote and local users can look for factual information using full text dictionaries, encyclopedias, book of quotations, currency conversion sources, and etcetera. Local libraries with weak reference collections use this site, and so with students of all levels. Among the favorites are the encyclopedias and the currency conversion sources.

- The Internet Resources button carries links to agricultural and rice-related Web sites, databases, Web sites of international and national institutions and organizations, library suppliers, and etcetera from all over the world. This section serves as a digital directory. Electronic English language newspapers from various countries are also made accessible through this section. IRRI scholars, who come from different parts of the world, find this very interesting and useful as they are updated with current events in their respective countries (see *Figure 5*).

Figure 4.   The Virtual Reference Help Desk

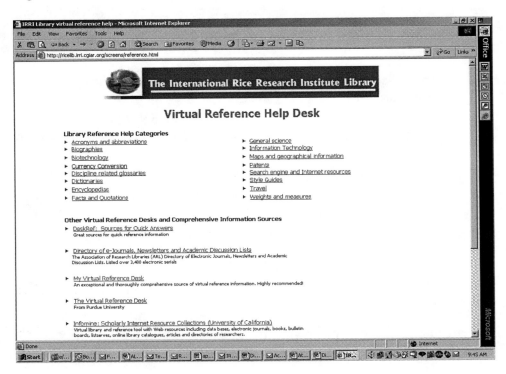

Figure 5.   Internet Resources

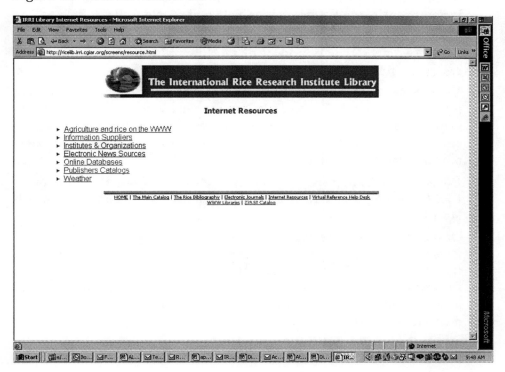

The other access points provided in the Web site are as follows:

- The Acquisitions List, updated every month, is a current awareness service. It covers all new materials added to the collection.

- The List of Conferences informs scientists of forthcoming events, which might be of interest.

- The International Directory of Rice Workers is an active database of rice scientists coming from all over the world.

- The List of videos links to a list of visual resources available for viewing at the Library's Audio Visual Learning Center.

- The Rice Theses link connects users to a list of rice dissertations acquired recently.

- Rice Patents is a database of rice patents, with abstracts, compiled by the Library from various sources.

- Journal Papers by IRRI Scientists is a listing of technical articles published in prominent journals. Some entries include abstracts. Full text links will be added soon.

- Databases at IRRI is a product of the Library's survey of knowledge resources in IRRI, conducted in 2001.

- View Your Circulation Record, Renew a Book, Suggest a Book are intended for IRRI staff, who wish to renew loans without going personally to the Library or to suggest new titles for purchase. While before, those who enjoy borrowing privileges had to come to the Library to renew their loans, now this can be done in the luxury of their desktops.

- Other links will bring visitors to the Web sites of the CGIAR, Riceweb, the Rice Knowledge Bank, IRIS, and the InfoFinder (Infofinder, 2002), which are all vital information sources.

- On the upper portion are links to the Telnet version, scheduling library tours, the suggestion box and answers given to suggestions, the site map, and a facility for e-mail contact. The IRRI Librarian answers all questions and suggestions posted here as soon as they appear on screen. There are positive and negative comments, but the positive ones outnumber the negative ones, which is a good sign of competence.

- The lower portion has links to vital information about the LDS and its policies.

The maintenance and improvement of this Web site is a continuing process and there is always room for improvement. Researchers and students within and outside the IRRI campus make use of this site as evidenced by feedback received in the suggestion box. Most of the users come from countries other than the Philippines.

Cataloging Electronic Resources

Organizing knowledge in the home page, however, was not enough because not every resource can be accommodated in this limited space. There was a felt need to go through the vast resources on the WWW and then to select and organize those that will meet the information needs of worldwide clients. Efforts to catalog Internet resources were being questioned by some sources but it has become common knowledge that there is a strong demand for the creation of bibliographic records for Internet resources and for these to be incorporated in online catalogs (Olson, 1997).

Kaplan (1993) cites an agreement among cataloging experts to divide remotely accessed information into two categories: (1) data resources (e.g., software, text and data files, and bibliographic databases); and (2) systems or services (e.g., campus-wide information systems, library catalog systems, and bulletin boards). In IRRI, we just make a distinction between Web sites, e-monographs, and databases on one end, and electronic journals on the other. It is possible to assign call numbers to electronic resources, as in the National Agricultural Library (http://www.nal.usda.gov/ag98/). Classification of digital resources   could be used in measuring the strengths and weaknesses of the collection. This practice, however, is found to be time-consuming. The practice is just to distinguish between the two categories through call numbers assigned. EJ is used for electronic journals and ER is used for the non-journals. Then a system of accession numbering is followed. Hence EJ2003-01 is the first e-journal cataloged in the year 2003 and so on.

Computerized Literature Searches

The Library is the starting point of any scientific inquiry. Researchers need to conduct a literature search and a review of the literature before initiating a research project. Very often, the LDS receives requests for listings of literature on specialized subject areas. The lists are generated using in-house (rice database) or commercial databases. More often than not, the lists are sent in electronic format to requestors with e-mail addresses. These lists serve as a selection tool for future document requests.

Electronic Document Delivery

Requests for documents are received from scientists working in more than 40 countries in different parts of the world. The libraries in the CGIAR system are regular users of IRRI's document delivery services. Ninety percent of these documents were delivered, free of charge, in digital format. The LDS has a policy of providing free documents to scientists from the less developed countries. Those from the developed countries are charged reasonably. Ariel, the software, enables digital delivery of documents (Infotrieve, 2003). There is a strong preference for documents in portable data file format sent as e-mail attachments for faster delivery. This results in instant access and savings in time and money. Print copies of documents are sent only when the scientist sending the request has no e-mail facility.

Current Awareness Initiatives

Clients are informed of what is new in their fields of interest. The Library's user-friendly computerized system and the robust Internet Connection are vital factors in achieving this. While the Web site is a good source of current awareness materials, digital tools are promptly brought to the attention of IRRI staff and others through other means.

An electronic newsletter published on the LAN, the *IRRI Bulletin* (IRRI Bulletin, 2000), features a *Library Corner*, where announcements about Internet resources, for example, Web sites, free access to databases or e-journals, full text documents and journals are announced regularly. Table of Contents (TOC) alerts for journals not included in the Library's subscriptions list are regularly posted here on a weekly basis.

Another current awareness tool is the Public Announcements folder of the Institute's e-mail facility. Occasional announcements regarding vital electronic information sources or free trial access to major databases are announced to staff promptly.

Electronic copies of significant news articles about rice are promptly brought to the attention of management and interested scientists. The Library subscribes to free alerting services for news about rice.

Dilemmas, Constraints, and Challenges Posed by Digital Delivery of Information

Maintaining a digital library and handling electronic resources are not easy tasks. While benefits accrue to users, the information providers are confronted with many issues, which should be dealt with daily or occasionally. Managing electronic resources does not stop in cataloging or creating links. There is a wide interplay of factors, which complicate this trend. Byrne (2003) presented the dilemma of digital libraries serving as barriers or gateways to scholarly communication. One outstanding factor emphasized is that access to digital resources is limited to those who are computer literate and to those who can afford to have Internet access. In addition to this and the time constraint, the following factors contribute to the complexity of dealing with digital resources:

- *Volume and Selection of Electronic Resources.* On account of the geometric increase in volume of Internet resources, locating specific information on the WWW has become a problem. Searching, selection, and evaluation consume a lot of time. The extensive number of records makes it impossible for one library to handle all single-handedly. The IRRI LDS framed a collection development policy for electronic resources. Relevance to rice research is the main criteria for selection.

Selection is anchored on the principle that electronic resources must supplement rather than replace printed sources. Currently, the selection tools being used are scientific and technical journals, e-mail alerts from prestigious publishers and organizations, listservs, colleagues in the information management field, recommendations from the IRRI scientists themselves, plus the various search engines. Some Web resources, however, present no evidence of scholarly research.

- *Intellectual Property Considerations*. Digital libraries disseminate content not owned by the parent institution but by other content owners. There are many information materials in the Web that can be made available freely but due respect to intellectual property needs to be exercised. It would be ideal to search a catalog and to have full text documents available with a single click of the mouse. However, for everyone to have universal access to this catalog and the full-text documents would mean a breach of intellectual property. For example, the rice bibliography is the flagship project of the IRRI Library. All items in this database with more than 200,000 entries are available, in print or in microfilm. It is possible to scan these papers, convert them to electronic format, and provide electronic links so that rice researchers the world over could read them through the Library's home page. However, this cannot be done because of copyright issues. To seek the permission of individual authors and/or publishers is beyond the capacity of any information provider. Besides, copyright laws vary from country to country (Online, 2004) and this makes matters more complicated. Before making a Web resource publicly available, there must be an assurance that no legal right is infringed upon.

- *Absence of or Incomplete Bibliographic Details*. A major constraint encountered by catalogers of electronic resources is the difficulty in creating a bibliographic record for something that has no physical form and location (Fecko, 1997). Not all bibliographic data are present in a Web site title page. For example, not all Web pages carry the date of creation or the person or entity responsible for creation. Normally, one has to do some research to complete the details.

- *To Catalog or not to Catalog*. A lot of decision-making has to be done once a library adopts a policy for cataloging electronic resources on the WWW. Aside from the strict selection process, several options are open to the cataloger and the Web site developer.   First, what kind of access can be offered to clients? Access may be provided through hyperlinks in the Web page or by cataloging every electronic resource selected and creating a bibliographic record in the OPAC. In the case of the IRRI Library, both are being practised. A main consideration here is not every resource can be lumped on a home page so it is better to have the more important ones on the home page and to catalog them as well and have their presence in the OPAC along with the others.

Once cataloged, the metadata should be checked occasionally. Cataloging electronic resources involves creating a permanent record that pertains to a dynamic document. Changes may be incorporated in electronic sources anytime. Once altered, the data provided by the cataloger, for example, subject analysis, will not be relevant anymore.

- *Evolving Standards*. Another problem with cataloging computer files is how to cope with the rapid changes or developments that metadata standards undergo. Cataloging guidelines are continuously evolving. The cataloger has to be on the lookout, lest the ones that he got used to are already obsolete. The Library of Congress is continually developing guidelines for dealing with digital resources, for example, the *Draft Interim Guidelines for Cataloging Electronic Resources* (Library of Congress, 1998), the *Guidelines for the Use of Field 856* (Library of Congress, 2003), and many others.

By the time one has selected the standard terminology to describe the characteristics of available technology, more innovations come in making the earlier one obsolete. An example given by Olson (1997) is the case of interactive multimedia, which is now available through the Internet. Moreover, strict adherence to local as well as international standards is a necessity in order to meet the retrieval needs of users. It is necessary to promote the wiser use of standard subject headings and classification systems for more effective discovery of obscure resources (Byrum, 2001).

As catalogers face many dilemmas in organizing resources that are remotely accessible, there is a Web resource that attempts to provide a solution to the problem. The *Internet Library For Librarians* (InfoWorks, 2002) is a very useful portal designed to enable librarians, especially catalogers, to find resources on the WWW that would facilitate the organization of electronic resources.

The IRRI LDS uses the U.S. Library of Congress List of Subject Headings and the MARC 21 format in cataloging and Tag 856 is used to create a link from the OPAC to the electronic resource. Simplified cataloging is used as much as possible.

- *Vanishing URLs.* The most difficult problem of all is monitoring URLs. A Web site may be there today and gone tomorrow. Tenopir (2003) calls the disappearing act of e-journals as a magician's trick. While the number of electronic resources incorporated in the IRRI Library's catalog is still manageable, manual checking can be done. To create a list of URLs and to check them regularly could help. The occasional presence of on-the-job trainees from neighboring colleges is a big help. These trainees are tasked to check whether URLs are still active or not.

  Weibel (2004) suggests a solution to this problem through the use of Uniform Resource Names, or URNs. The Online Computer Library Center (OCLC) has adopted a naming and resolution service for general Internet resources. The names are referred to as Persistent URLs (PURLs), which "points to an intermediate resolution service." More information about PURLS is available at http://www.oclc.org/purl/docs/download.html. This has yet to be tested in IRRI.

  Budgetary constraints prevent the IRRI LDS from purchasing efficient URL checking software, which can be added to its system to help in verifying links.

  Again, in the absence of a URL checker, this time-consuming activity needs to be addressed even at irregular intervals or whenever time permits. A URL checking facility has to be purchased in the future but this will definitely add to system maintenance costs.

- *To Download or to Retain the Virtual Format.* Ownership versus access is a dilemma being faced by many librarians. Whether to download a full text electronic source or to just leave it in its present format is a matter to be decided on. In IRRI, short documents are downloaded while voluminous ones are not. In some instances, it is better to download a copy, as the URLs are not permanent; they are constantly changing and even vanishing. In downloading, there are two options: to download a print or an electronic copy. Decision on this is determined by the computer infrastructure available. A personal computer or a server for storing electronic files should be at hand if the electronic format is preferred for storage. The main consideration in downloading is relevance to clients; format is only secondary. The IRRI LDS deals with this on a case-to-case basis.

- *Licensing and Costs.* The content of electronic resources are neither owned nor managed by libraries. Vendors control the storage, availability and life span of many digital resources. At present no standards exist for licenses to e-journals or to databases, so that each license requires close examination before acceptance and signature. The number of licenses or authorized users adds to the cost of electronic resources. Publishers tend to impose more restrictive use and access policies, while jacking up fees.

The CGIAR Libraries and Information Services Consortium (CGIARLISC), of which the IRRI LDS is a member, solves the cost constraint through joint subscriptions (Ramos, 2003). Currently, agreements for joint subscription with four publishers are in place. While content bundling may not be fully beneficial to all center libraries on account of their diverse mandates, this negative aspect has yet to make its impact. Sustained access is determined by the availability of financial resources. More often than not, information managers can deliver only a portion of what the clients really need.

The CGIARLIS consortium is slowly moving into electronic only formats. This gives rise to the continuing problem of access to archives or back issues. Some publishing firms may fold up, so perpetual access becomes impossible. In the Consortium, this problem of archival access was addressed by requiring at least one member to keep a print copy of each title subscribed to by the group.

- *IT Infrastructure and Levels of Access.* For some libraries, hardware and software as well as slow Internet connection or absence of connection may hinder clients from linking to valuable sources of information. The IRRI LDS is fortunate to have personal computers, servers, printers, scanners, and a robust Internet connection (bandwidth of 2 MBps), which enable quick access to the WWW. One problem being faced today is whether the access provided through the OPAC is equal to or better than the access provided by commercial search engines (Ward, 2000). Moreover, access to electronic resources should be at the same level as that provided for other materials in the collection.

- *Number of Staff and Expertise.* Staff expertise on Web page development and cataloging special materials is a primary requisite for maintaining a virtual library. Also, there must be enough people to go through and monitor URLs once they are included in the catalog. The IRRI LDS has very few staff members, but its trained staff enables the dissemination of electronic information.

These are the main challenges faced by the staff at IRRI Library in dealing with digital information sources. Some can be resolved in time, while others will be perennially present. As mentioned earlier, digital libraries demand more staff time. The process of dealing with these challenges presents a long and continuous journey that librarians will have to undertake.

Social Implications of Increased Access to Digital Resources

As users are better connected to digital resources, the value of the library as a venue where users go to find information and borrow books is diminishing (Falk, 2003). Electronic sources are now at their disposal and they have a choice on whether to stay where they are or to go to a library. More often than not, the former is preferred.

Less Face-to-Face Contact

The availability of digital resources has encouraged clients to do their research on their own desktops. Clients prefer to work in their homes or offices rather than spend time in the Library. Face-to-face interaction with the Library staff was lessened to a great degree. IRRI staff comes to the Library only when they need to see print publications. They would search online databases or read e-journals in their workstations, if these were possible. The people that fill up the Library's main reading room are students from neighboring and remote universities or researchers from other institutions.

While this happens, Ward (2000) suggests that clients need to be convinced that not all information can be obtained from the Internet. They also must be aware that access to electronic resources is enabled through the Library's budget and efforts.

A negative effect of decline in face-to-face contact with clients is that identification of user needs has become somewhat difficult. While advanced library systems can generate usage statistics, hearing or seeing the need personally is more real and convincing. What is missing in the current state of the digital world is the feeling of self-fulfillment in delivering information personally and seeing the facial expression of a satisfied client.

On the other hand, frustrations felt by the prospective users in failing to find the required resource could be remedied on the spot by suggesting alternative search techniques or sources. Generally, facing blank walls or disappearing resources might give the impression that library services are below standard, when the real reason is inappropriate searching techniques or wrong choice of search engines to use.

To identify user needs as far as e-journals are concerned, a survey of the top ten electronic journals preferred by IRRI scientists was conducted in February and March 2003. This was patterned, although on a small-scale, after Oregon State University Libraries survey for assigning journal title priorities (Christie & Kristick, 2001). Of the 15 titles on the top ten choices by IRRI scientists, only one was not accessible online through the LDS. The print edition of that sole title was available in print. The reason for this is the high cost of the license for online access. Immediate steps were taken to purchase a site license, thereafter. The survey results show that the selection process for acquiring e-journals is in the right track.

Need for Collaboration

One good effect of the advent of digital information is the increasing realization that no library can stand alone. Since it is not possible for one library to have and provide everything, the information professionals need to be proactive and to establish partnerships within and outside the parent institution. The need to connect, either personally or electronically, must be addressed. Linking with communities of practice enables a person to expand his horizons as new ideas are acquired, delivering more with less resources (Ramos, 2003). The IRRI Library is an active member of the Consultative Group on International Agricultural Research Libraries and Information Services Consortium (CGIARLISC), which was formed in 2001. Through the consortium, more electronic journals are available for use by IRRI staff through joint subscriptions. The first venture of the consortium started in 2002 with *Science Online.* Although not all members joined in the agreement, reasonable savings was achieved. The following year, more publishers became partners, for example, Kluwer, Marcel Dekker, National Research Council (Canada), Oxford University Press, and Cambridge University Press. Through the consortium, more access is being enjoyed by CGIAR Center staff while paying less (Ramos, 2003).

Linkage with Users

The librarian of today needs to be more proactive and to circulate with clients whenever possible in venues other than the library. Personal contacts, e-mails, and other vehicles for linkage must be resorted to. User satisfaction is the ultimate goal of every library and serious consideration must be devoted to it. As knowledge managers, emphasis should be placed not only on content management and better services, but on social impact as well (Chen, 2003). Continuing communication between scientists and information specialists is a must.

The IRRI Library's home page has a provision for interactive communication with overseas and local clients. Staff on campus may renew their loans through the Web site provided that the item is not requested by someone else and it is not overdue. There is also a link to a suggestion box, where users may type in their suggestions. Answers to these suggestions are also posted online. Fortunately, most of the comments are positive. There is also a facility for users to suggest books for purchase.

There are many opportunities for librarians of today to establish links with clients whom they do not see physically. All these need to be explored and used to the fullest. While digital libraries lessen physical contact to a large extent, access to knowledge is widened.

Conclusion: The Future Scenario

Digital libraries are currently envisioned to become effective repositories of global knowledge resources, encompassing "all aspects of human activities, from industries to governments, and from education to research" (Chen, 2003a, p.1).

The future of digital libraries is influenced by two schools of thought. Information may be viewed as a commodity (Arms, 1997), produced by commercial entities with a corresponding price, normally unaffordable to many. Optimistic minds, on the other hand, look positively towards open access publishing as a solution to the exorbitant costs of access to electronic information. As open access to information gains ground, and as more and more scientists and researchers are convinced that it is indeed the most practical venue for sharing knowledge, the future for digital libraries appear to be very bright.

The creation of digital portals results in dramatic increase in usage of databases and other electronic information sources (Hamblin, 2003). Digital libraries are now making a major impact in the fields of molecular biology, earth sciences, astronomy, and medicine (Lesk, 2003). Researchers in all fields of endeavor are relying more and more on the Internet. The demand for desktop access to scholarly information is on the rise and this is expected to go on as technology comes up with new products and new sources. As more and more printed publications and even art objects are being digitized for preservation and for easy access, organization and efficient retrieval pose a big challenge to digital libraries.

While it is recognized that libraries can bridge the digital divide, librarians and other information providers have to struggle to sustain access (Bill, 2004). Scholarly access to information is clearly a function of finances, technology, the volume of knowledge sources, IT infrastructure, the library's physical and human resources, as well as dynamic user needs. Hence, more time is needed on the part of knowledge organizers for searching as well as evaluating virtual resources and for seeking ways to improve access to knowledge. At IRRI LDS, the project of cataloging electronic resources is a continuing endeavor and efforts are being exerted towards its improvement. Based on IRRI's experience, the critical factors in linking electronic resources to users are (Ramos, 2001):

- Strategic planning with IRRI's mission and goals plus users' needs in mind.

- Adequate hardware and a library software with an efficient Web interface.

- Trained human resources with writing, editing and Web development skills.

- An active collection development policy, wherein virtual sources of information are given as much importance as printed publications.

- Active commitment for Web site development and maintenance.

- Collaboration with IT experts and other Web masters in the Institute.

- Strong and continuing support from management.

It is not possible to capture and organize every relevant materials on the Internet, but the most one can do is to select carefully and to catalog as much as time permits. Through this, users can easily link to the electronic publication or Web site of their choices instead of using a search engine or going through the maze of electronic resources available on the Internet. It is preferable to start small and then build up its collection of virtual materials slowly.

There is an ongoing project in IRRI, wherein its publications are digitized and links are provided on the Institute's Web site. As this goes on, links to the full text are also created on the online catalog and the Library's Web site. This is a continuing project that the Library will pursue as long as staff time permits. In addition, the plan is to digitize all publications listed in the Library's rice bibliography. The main objective here is to preserve this comprehensive collection of technical rice literature for posterity. In addition, retrieval of documents will be faster and easier than dealing with the print editions. However, it is not possible to have them all accessible as full-text electronic publications from remote sites due to copyright considerations.

Through strategic planning and adoption of innovations, the IRRI Library will align her vision spelt out by Marcum (2003). One thing that stands out, though, is that while automation has made the life of information seekers a lot easier, the people behind the scene, those who work to organize and to place information within the reach of clients, have to exert more effort in linking the two. As long as there is an attempt to bridge the gap between knowledge and users, then electronic sources are not left to waste. The big challenge is how to deal with the exponential increase in knowledge, continue to keep the collection up-to-date, and sustain access. Information providers should add value to their institutions by rethinking and assuming their altered roles in the digital world.

References

Albanese, A.R. (2003). Special librarians: Opportunity in the air. *Library Journal, 128* (12), 36-38.

Arms, W.Y. (1997, April). Relaxing assumptions about the future of digital libraries: The hare and the tortoise. *D-Lib Magazine*. Retrieved February 26, 2003, from the World Wide Web: *http://www.dlib.org/dlib/april97/04arms.html*

Bill & Melinda Gates Foundation. (2004). Toward equality of access: The role of public libraries in addressing the digital divide. Seattle, Wash. Retrieved March 4, 2004, from the World Wide Web: *http://www.gatesfoundation.org/nr/Downloads/libraries/uslibraries/reports/TowardEqualityofAccess.pdf*

Brach, C.A. (2001). Electronic collections – Evolution and strategies: Past, present and future. In M. C. Schlembach (Ed.), *Information practice in science and technology: Evolving challenges and new directions* (pp. 17-27). New York: Haworth Press.

Byrne, A. (2003). Digital libraries: Barriers or gateways to scholarly information? *The Electronic Library, 21* (5), 414-421.

Byrum, J.D. (2001). Challenges of electronic resources: State of the art and unresolved issues. [English version presented at the International Conference]. In *Proceedings International Conference Electronic Resources: Definition, Selection and Cataloguing*, Rome. Retrieved October 10, 2003 from the World Wide Web: *http://eprints.rclis.org/archive/00000341/*

Caplan, P. (1993). Cataloging Internet resources. *The Public-Access Computer Systems Review, 4* (2), 61-66. Retrieved September 4, 2003, from the World Wide Web: *http://www.ifla.org/documents/libraries/cataloging/caplan.txt*

Cardbox Softwares Ltd., UK. (n.d.). CardboxPlus. Retrieved October 11, 2003, from the World Wide Web: *http://www.cardbox.co.uk/index.htm*

Chen, H. (2003). Achieving information resources empowerment: A digital library and knowledge management experience. In *Information resources empowerment*. Papers presented at the 12th Congress of Southeast Asian Librarians (Vol. 1, pp. 1-12). Bandar Seri Begawan, Brunei: Dewan Bahasa dan Pustaka.

Chen, H. (2003a). *Towards building digital library as an institution of knowledge*. Paper presented at Wave of the Future: NSF Post Digital Libraries Futures Workshop, June 15-17, Chatham, Massachusetts. Retrieved from the World Wide Web: *http://www.sis.pitt.edu/%7Edlwkshop/ paper_chen.html*

Christie, A., & Kristick, L. (2001, Spring). Developing an online science journal collection: A quick tool for assigning priorities. *Issues in Science and Technology Librarianship*. Retrieved February 2, 2003, from the World Wide Web: *http://www.istl.org/01-spring/article2.html*

Cohen, L.B., & Calsada, M.M. (2003). Web accessible databases for electronic resource collections: A case study and its implications. *The Electronic Library, 21* (1), 31-38.

Falk, H. (2003). Developing digital libraries. *The Electronic Library, 21* (3), 258-261.

Fecko, M. B. (1997). *Electronic resources: Access and issues*. West Sussex, UK: Bowker-Saur.

Hamblin, Y., & Stubbings, R. (2003). The implementation of Metalib and SFX at Loughborough University Library: A case study. Retrieved March 4, 2003, from the World Wide Web: *www.jisc.ac.uk/uploaded_documents/ Metalibcasestudy.pdf*

Infofinder. (2002). Retrieved November 11, 2003, from the World Wide Web: *http://infofinder.cgiar.org/*

Infotrieve. (2003). *Ariel*. Retrieved November 11, 2003, from the World Wide Web: *http://www4.infotrieve.com/ariel/sfserver.html*

InfoWorks Technology Company. (2002). Internet library for librarians. Retrieved February 26, 2004 from the World Wide Web: *http:// www.itcompany.com/inforetriever/catinet2.htm*

Innovative Interfaces. (2004). Retrieved November 11, 2003, from the World Wide Web: *http://www.iii.com/*

IRRI Bulletin (weekly). (2000). Los Baños, Laguna: IRRI. Retrieved March 15, 2004, from the World Wide Web: *http://Bulletin.irri.cgiar.org*

Kebede, G. (2002). The changing information needs of users in electronic information environments. *The Electronic Library, 20* (1), 14-21.

IRRI toward 2020. (1996). Los Baños, Laguna: IRRI.

Lesk, M. (2003). *The future of digital libraries*. Paper presented at Wave of the Future: NSF Post Digital Library Futures Workshop, Chatham, Mass., June 15-17, 2003. Retrieved February 26, 2004, from the World Wide Web: *http://www.sis.pitt.edu/~dlwkshop/paper_lesk.html*

Library of Congress. (1998). Draft interim guidelines for cataloging electronic resources. Retrieved December 15, 2003, from the World Wide Web: *http://lcweb.loc.gov/catdir/cpso/dcmb19_4.html*

Library of Congress. Network Development and MARC Standards Office. (2003). Guidelines for the Use of Field 856. Retrieved February 26, 2004, from the World Wide Web: *http://www.loc.gov/marc/856guide.html*

Marcum, D. (2003). *Requirements for the future digital library*. An Address before the Eksevier Digital Libraries Symposium, Philadelphia, Pa., January 25, 2003. Retrieved October 10, 2003, from the World Wide Web: *http://www.clir.org/pubs/archives/dbm_elsevier2003.html*

National Agricultural Library [Web site]. (n.d.). Retrieved March 3, 2004, from the World Wide Web: *http://www.nal.usda.gov/ag98/*

Ockerbloom, J. M. (2004). The Online books page. Retrieved March 3, 2003, from the World Wide Web: *http://onlinebooks.library.upenn.edu/okbooks.html*

Olson, N.B. (1997). *Cataloging Internet resources: A manual and practical guide* (2nd ed.). Dublin, OH: OCLC Online Computer Library Center. Retrieved September 4, 2003, from the World Wide Web: *http://www.oclc.org/oclc/man/9256cat/toc.htm*

Ramos, M.M. (2001). *The International Rice Research Institute Library and Documentation Service: Sharing knowledge globally in a Web-based environment*. Poster paper presented at the IAALD International Conference on the Development of Agricultural Information, Technology, and Market in the 21st Century, Beijing, China.

Ramos, M.M. (2003). Cultivating communities of practice: The CGIAR information management professionals' experience. In *Information resources empowerment*. Papers presented at the 12th Congress of Southeast Asian Librarians (Vol. 1, pp. 27-37). Bandar Seri Begawan, Brunei: Dewan Bahasa dan Pustaka.

Tenopir, C. (2003). The art of conjuring e-content. *Library Journal, 128* (9), 38-41.

Tenopir, C. (2003a). Use and users of electronic library resources: An overview and analysis of recent research studies. Washington, D.C.: Council on Library and Information Resources. Retrieved September 4, 2003, from the World Wide Web: *http://www.clir.org/pubs/reports/pub120/pub120.pdf*

Wallace, I. (1998). Delivering information to rice scientists around the world. *Information Development, 14* (4), 198-201.

Ward, D., & Vander Pol, D. (2000). Librarian, catalog thy work! Getting started integrating Internet resources into OPACs. *Journal of Internet Cataloging, 3* (4), 51-61.

Weibel, S., Jul, E., & Shafer, K. (2004). PURLs: Persistent Uniform Resource Locators. Retrieved March 10, 2004, from the World Wide Web: *http://purl.oclc.org/docs/new_purl_summary.html*

Chapter XIII

Multimedia Digital Library as Intellectual Property

Hideyasu Sasaki
Keio University, Japan

Yasushi Kiyoki
Keio University, Japan

Abstract

The principal concern of this chapter is to provide those in the digital library community with the fundamental knowledge on the intellectual property rights and copyrights regarding multimedia digital libraries. The main objects of our discussion are the multimedia digital libraries with content-based retrieval mechanisms. Intellectual property rights are the only means for database designers to acquire their incentive of content collection and system implementation in database assembling. We outline the legal issues on multimedia digital libraries and retrieval mechanisms. As the protection of intellectual property rights is a critical issue in the digital library community, the authors present legal schemes for protecting multimedia digital libraries and retrieval mechanisms in a systematic, engineering manner.

Introduction

Digital library is the global information infrastructure in the networked society (Borgman, 2000). The rights protection of multimedia digital libraries and retrieval mechanisms is a critical issue in the digital library community that demands intellectual property schemes for recouping their investment in database design and system implementation. In this chapter, we describe the technical and legal issues on multimedia digital libraries and retrieval mechanisms as intellectual properties.

The purpose of this chapter is to discuss copyright and intellectual property rights on digital libraries from the designer/architecture perspective, which has not been discussed with sufficient attention at the present. The end-user perspective has been discussed as an important element for users of information services, including librarians, in the context of copyright law on multimedia digital libraries. Its typical case is the public use of copyright for educational or academic service. Content creators of digital libraries have definitely enjoyed copyright enforcement over their works under that current legal scheme. However, the designers or architectures of multimedia digital libraries do not have proper foundations for their rights protection that is to be equivalent to the copyright protection. Under this designer/architecture perspective, we especially focus on content-based retrieval and its application to multimedia digital libraries. Content-based retrieval is a promising technique for networked multimedia digital libraries whose tremendous volume demands automatic indexing rather than manual indexing for retrieval operations.

The scope of this chapter is also restricted within the current standard of laws and cases for transnational transaction and licensing of digital copyright and intellectual property rights regarding multimedia digital libraries. Cultural diversity in the Asia-Pacific region allows a number of legislative differences in copyright and intellectual property laws. Meanwhile, digital content is the object of its worldwide transaction. The harmonization of its related rights is inevitable because a number of countries have joined international trade agreements on intellectual property rights. We need a clear and uniform standard with which the Asian-Pacific countries are able to keep up with the foregoing countries.

In this chapter, we discuss three current issues on multimedia digital libraries and intellectual property laws, and then present three types of intellectual property schemes, respectively. The first issue is copyright protection of indexed digital contents that are stored in digital libraries. Its corresponding scheme is for copyrighting multimedia digital libraries that are associated with keyword-based retrieval operations. The second issue is patentability of retrieval mechanisms. Its corresponding scheme is for patenting content-based retrieval processes in multimedia digital libraries. Finally, the last issue is the limitations of copyright in the advent of content-based retrieval. Its corresponding scheme is a promising direction, which leverages the *de facto* protection of multimedia digital libraries that are associated with content-based retrieval operations.

Background

Intellectual property law gives incentive to advance appropriate investment in database design and implementation (Jakes & Yoches, 1989). However, present legal studies are not satisfactory as the source of technical interpretation of the intellectual properties regarding multimedia digital libraries and retrieval mechanisms. With the advent of content-based image retrieval (CBIR), we face novel issues on the right protection of multimedia digital libraries and retrieval mechanisms.

Multimedia digital libraries consist of digital contents and retrieval systems. The digital contents are copyrightable materials whose stakeholders are content creators. The retrieval systems are patentable processes of database designers.

The principal problem discussed in this chapter is restricted into the conflicting interests between content creators and database designers. Intellectual property lawyers in the area of digital libraries have somehow neglected this designer/architecture perspective. The issues related to the problem are found in three stages. First, copyright does not always solve conflicting interests between content creators and database designers. Content creators create copyrightable individual contents, for example, pictures and images. Database designers integrate the entire content of each multimedia digital library with indexes or metadata. The problem is deciding which component differentiates the entire content of each digital library as an independent object of right protection from its copyrightable individual contents. Second, CBIR mechanisms need the specific examination of patentability. The computer-implemented processes in CBIR consist of the combinations of means, some of which are prior disclosed inventions. Those processes consist of the means for parameter setting that is adjusted to retrieve specific kinds of images in certain narrow domains. The problem is determining which process is of technical advancement (non-obviousness) based on its combinations of the prior arts and parameter setting. Finally, the dynamically indexed content of multimedia digital libraries goes beyond the scope of conventional copyright protection. CBIR mechanisms generate indexes to individual contents every time queries are requested for retrieval. The problem is selecting which component leverages the protection of each multimedia digital library, as the entire content is independent of its individual contents.

Indexes and Copyright Protection

U.S. Copyright Act (1976) defines that a compilation or assembling of individual contents, that is, preexisting materials or data, is a copyrightable entity as an original work of authorship. Typical examples of copyrightable multimedia materials stored in digital libraries take a variety of forms like text or images, photos or video streams. *Figure 1* outlines that the collection of static indexes and individual contents forms a component of contents-plus-indexes. That component identifies the entire content of each database, as is a static and copyrightable compilation. Indexes including metadata must be *statically* assigned to individual contents that are restored in databases for keyword-based retrieval operations.

Gorman & Ginsburg (1993) and Nimmer et al. (1991) state that a compilation is copyrightable as far as it is an "original work of authorship that is fixed in tangible form." A database is copyrightable in the form of a component of contents-plus-indexes while static indexes or metadata are fixed in a tangible medium of repository, database. In keyword-based retrieval, static indexes or metadata represent a certain kind of categorization of the entire content of each database. The originality on the categorization makes each database copyrightable as is different from the mere collection of its individual contents. What kind of categorization should be *original* to constitute a copyrightable compilation? The case of *American*

Figure 1. Digital library of visual content associated with keyword-based retrieval

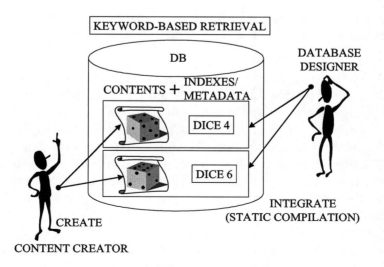

Dental Association v. Delta Dental Plan Association (1997) determined that minimal creativity in compilation sufficed this requirement of originality on databases. A uniform scheme on the categorization regarding indexes or metadata must be formulated in an engineering manner.

Copyrighting Multimedia Digital Libraries with Keyword-Based Retrieval

We technically interpret a scheme for copyrighting the multimedia digital libraries with keyword-based retrieval as a set of conditions that determine which type of database should be copyrightable in the form of a component of contents-plus-indexes.

Copyrightable compilation is said to be of sufficient creativity, that is, originality in the form of a component of contents-plus-indexes. Its original way of categorization is represented in the selection of the type of index or metadata that is assigned to individual contents, or the type of taxonomy regarding indexes or metadata that integrate the individual contents into the entire content of each database.

The set of conditions on the original categorization regarding indexes or metadata is formulated as shown below: A categorization regarding indexes or metadata is original only when:

(1)   the type of index or metadata accepts discretionary selection in the domain of a problem database; otherwise,

(2)   the type of taxonomy regarding indexes or metadata accepts discretionary selection in the domain of a problem database.

We describe five typical cases of original or non-original categorization regarding indexes or metadata for keyword-based retrieval. Typical cases of non-original categorization include photo film cartridge database and white pages. Those cases do not accept any discretion in the selection of the type of index or metadata, or the type of taxonomy. The photo film cartridge database uses its respective film numbers as indexes for its retrieval operations. The taxonomy of the indexes is only based on page numbering. This kind of database does not have any other discretion in its selection of the type of index or taxonomy. The white pages extract metadata from telephone numbers and names of subscribers. The case of *Feist Publications, Inc. v. Rural Telephone Service* (1991) judged that its selection of the type of taxonomy was not discretionary because its alphabetical ordering of the metadata was a single alternative in that field of practice.

Meanwhile, the discretionary selection of the type of index or metadata, or taxonomy, constitutes copyrightable compilation of minimal creativity, that is, originality on the categorization regarding indexes or metadata. Typical cases of discretionary selection of the type of index or metadata include the Web document encyclopedia and the other types of telephone directory, such as yellow pages. The latter yellow pages satisfy minimal creativity as a copyrightable compilation. The white pages list telephone numbers of subscribers in alphabetical order, while the yellow pages list business phone numbers by a variety of categories and feature-classified advertisements of various sizes. In the case of discretionary selection of the type of taxonomy, even numerical indexing, such as page numbering, could form an original compilation, when page indexes work as categorization identifiers of a specific type of taxonomy in the domain of the problem database. For example, lawyers often identify individual cases by citing their page numbers without any reference to case titles or parties. Mere page numbers work as categorization identifiers as far as the selection of page numbers is based on a specific type of taxonomy and still allows other discretionary selection of the type of index, in this case, different ranges in paging or indexing of case numbers. The component of contents-plus-indexes, in particular, cases-plus-pages, constitutes an original work of authorship as a copyrightable compilation as affirmed by the case of *West Publishing Co. v. Mead Data Central, Inc.* (1986/1987).

Let us suppose that a database restores pictures of starfish that are manually and numerically numbered by day/hour-chronicle interval based on their significant life stages from birth to death. That database is to be an original work of authorship as a copyrightable compilation in the form of a component of contents-plus-indexes, that is, pictures-plus-numbers.

We have formulated the set of conditions that determine which type of database is copyrightable as a multimedia digital library by assessing its original categorization regarding indexes or metadata whose collection identifies the entire content of the database as the referent of copyright protection. That condition set is effective in protecting the multimedia digital libraries that are associated with keyword-based retrieval approach for image retrieval.

Patentability of CBIR Mechanisms

CBIR realizes its retrieval operations by performing a number of "processes," that is, methods or means for data processing that constitute computer-related inventions in the form of computer programs. The computer-related inventions often combine means for data processing, some of which are prior disclosed inventions as computer programs. Meanwhile, the processes comprise the components for parameter setting that is adjusted to retrieve specific kinds of images in certain domains, particularly in the case of domain-specific approach of CBIR.

In CBIR, parametric values determine as thresholds which candidate image is similar to an exemplary requested image by computation of similarity of visual features (Rui et al., 1999; Smeulders et al., 2000; Yoshitaka & Ichikawa, 1999). A component for parameter setting realizes the thresholding operations in the form of a computer program with a set of ranges of parametric values. The parameter-setting component is familiar in mechanic inventions. Its typical example is a patented invention of an automatic temperature controller that adjusts body temperature of raw fish in cargo within certain range as fish are not frozen but kept chilled during the course of transportation. Inventors and practitioners demand a detailed set of the conditions for patenting the data-processing processes for CBIR in multimedia digital libraries.

Patenting CBIR Mechanisms

In this section, we technically interpret the scheme for patenting CBIR mechanisms in the form of the conditions on patentability. We focus on combinations of prior disclosed processes and parameter setting components. The formulated conditions consist of the following three requirements for patentability: "patentable subject matter" (entrance to patent protection), "non-obviousness" (technical advancement), and "enablement" (specification) (Merges, 1997).

For satisfying the requirement for patentable subject matter, the processes for performing CBIR functions must be claimed as the means for parameter setting, which perform certain retrieval functions. Otherwise, the discussed processes are considered not as specific inventions of the data-processing processes for performing CBIR functions but as the inventions that are peripheral or just related to general retrieval functions.

A data-processing process or method is patentable subject matter in the form of a computer-related invention, that is, a computer program (U.S. Patent Act, 2003; Jakes & Yoches, 1989) as far as the "specific machine ...... produce(s) a useful, concrete, and tangible result ... for transforming ... " physical data ("*physical transformation*") (in *re Alappat*, 1994). A process must "perform independent physical acts (post-computer process activities)," otherwise, "manipulate data representing physical objects or activities to achieve a practical application (pre-computer process activities)." CBIR operations automatically generate indexes as physical results on a computer and a memory, which require pre-and post-computer process activities as indispensable procedure through data processing between feature extraction and indexing, also between indexing and classification. Inventions should be of "technological arts." That requirement does not limit patentability of computer-related inventions because technological arts are equivalent to, in broad sense, the concept of useful or practical arts (Merges, 1997).

The requirement for non-obviousness on the combinations of the processes for data processing is listed as below:

(1)   The processes for performing CBIR functions must comprise the combinations of prior disclosed means to perform certain functions that are not predicated from any combination of the prior arts; in addition.

(2)   The processes for performing CBIR functions must realize quantitative and/or qualitative advancement.

Otherwise, the discussed processes are obvious so that they are not patentable as the processes for performing CBIR functions.

First, a combination of prior disclosed means should not be "suggested" from any disclosed means "with the reasonable expectation of success" (in *re Dow Chemical Co.*, 1988). Second, its asserted function must be superior to the conventional functions that are realized in the prior disclosed or patented means. On the latter issue, several solutions for performance evaluation are proposed and applicable. Müller et al. (2001) and Manchester Visualization Center (2000) proposed benchmarking of CBIR functions. Another general strategy is restriction of the scope of problem claims into a certain narrow field to which no prior arts have been applied. This claiming strategy is local optimization of application scope.

The requirement for enablement on the parameter setting components is listed as below:

(1-a)   the descriptions of the processes for performing CBIR functions must specify the formulas for parameter setting, otherwise,

(1-b)   the disclosed invention of the processes should have its co-pending application that describes the formulas in detail. In addition,

(2-a)   the processes must perform a new function as domain-general approach by a combination of the prior disclosed means; otherwise,

(2-b)   the processes as domain-specific approach should have improved formulas for parameter setting based on the prior disclosed means for performing CBIR functions and also examples of parametric values on parameter setting in descriptions.

For 2-b, the processes must specify the means for parameter setting by "giving a specific example of preparing an" application to enable those skilled in the arts to implement their best mode of the processes without undue experiment (*Autogiro Co. of America v. United States*, 1967; *Unique Concepts, Inc. v. Brown*, 1991). U.S. Patent and Trademark Office (1996a, 1996b) suggested that the processes comprising the means, that is, the components for parameter setting must disclose at least one of the following examples of parametric values on parameter setting:

(1)   Working or prophetic examples of initial values or weights on parameter setting.

(2)   Working examples of the ranges of parametric values on parameter setting.

The "working examples" are parametric values that are confirmed to work at actual laboratory or as prototype testing results. The "prophetic examples" are given without actual work by one skilled in the art.

It is a critical problem to define the scope of equivalent modification of process patents because parametric values in parameter setting are easy to modify and adjust at application. The scope of patent enforcement extends to what is equivalent to a claimed invention, as far as it is predictable from claims and descriptions (*Graver Tank & Mfg. Co. v. Linde Air Products Co.*, 1950; *Laitran Corp. v. Rexnord, Inc.*, 1991). Especially, domain-specific approach for performing CBIR functions must distinguish its claimed invention with its examples of parametric values from other improved formulas for parameter setting that are based on prior disclosed means. The scope of the equivalent modification of a patented process is defined within a certain specified scope as suggested from the exemplary parametric values.

Limitations of Copyright in the Advent of CBIR

Two limitations on copyright are to be identified in its application to image databases as multimedia digital libraries:

(1)   a component of contents-plus-indexes does not identify the entire content of any database that is associated with CBIR operations; and,

(2)   any copyrightable compilation in that database does not identify its entire content.

Figure 2 outlines the first limitation that the component of contents-plus-indexes, which is a collection of individual contents with *dynamic* indexes but does not identify the entire content of any database that is associated with CBIR operations. In the application of CBIR operations to a database, its component of contents-plus-indexes is just a collection of respectively rated and displayed individual contents whose similarity rating order changes every time new sample images are requested as queries.

The second limitation is to be discovered in two phases. The discussed mere collection of individual contents in an image database is a static compilation without any minimal creativity in its categorization. That database is not copyrightable but so are its individual contents. Any proposed scheme does not offer the remedy for that problem at the present. The European Union legislated and executed a scheme for protecting databases, known as the *sui generis* right of database protection (Reinbothe, 1999; Samuelson, 1996). Its fundamental concept is based on the property of copyrightable compilation so that it does not protect the image databases with CBIR operations under the same reasons of the discussed limitation of the copyright protection. An only resort for a new scheme must be discovered in retrieval mechanisms that are to identify the entire content of each image database, multimedia digital library, as the referent of its protection.

Promising Direction for Protecting Multimedia Digital Libraries with CBIR

Another new scheme must realize that the protection of multimedia digital libraries is to be leveraged by using the intellectual property of their retrieval mechanisms or data processing methodologies but not the copyright of their referents, that is, databases.

The practice in the field of bioinformatics offers a typical case of that kind of protection.

The methodologies for identifying genetic codes have been yielded with process patent in the form of computer programs, even before the admission of the patentability of genomic DNA sequences per se as material patent. A kind of exclusive protection over its referents, the gene per se, is leveraged by patenting the component of the data processing methodology that identifies a certain genetic code that is to represent the common and unique elements of genomic DNA sequences encoding a certain protein. Without such that patentable invention, any other means neither identifies the genetic code that corresponds to a specific gene nor represents the single and unique collection of genomic DNA sequences encoding a protein.

If certain conditions let a component in retrieval mechanisms identify a classification of the entire content of an image database as a single and unique collection in a specific domain, patenting that component realizes the same *de facto* protection of its referent, that is, the database with CBIR, as patenting the discussed component in bioinformatics does. It is based on a logic that CBIR is optimized in that specific domain of the image database as far as the patented component of the methodology integrates or identifies the classification of its referents (individual contents) into the single and unique collection (the entire content) (Sasaki & Kiyoki, 2003, 2002a).

That component must be discovered from consulting the technical properties of CBIR mechanisms, especially, domain-specific approach whose application focuses on the narrower or specific domains for image retrieval. In those domains, the feature extraction and index classification of the referent images are realized by optimizing the components for thresholding operations that evaluate structural similarity of extracted visual features of the images to identify a classification of the entire content of an image database. The component for

Figure 2. A digital library of visual content associated with CBIR

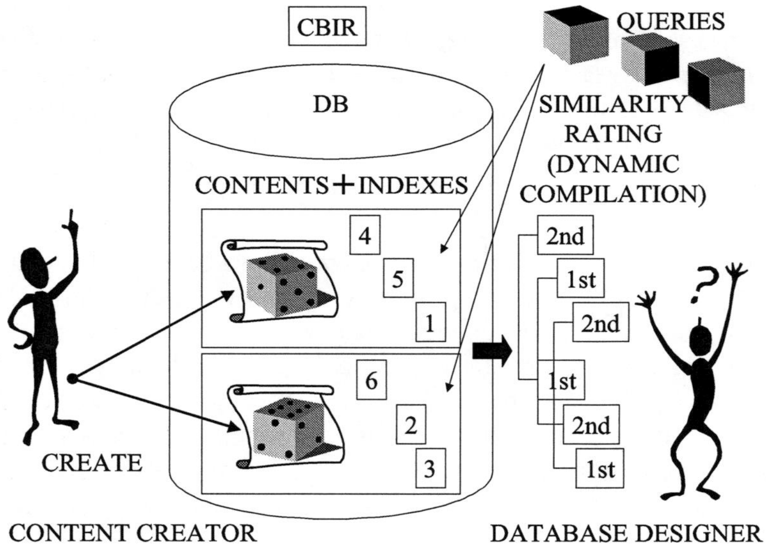

thresholding operations consists of the means for selecting and/or adjusting parametric values. The parameter-setting component identifies a classification of the entire content of its referent image database by optimizing the parametric values on feature extraction and index classification in each specific domain (Sasaki & Kiyoki, 2003). That parameter setting component is to be a computer-related invention in the form of computer programs (U.S. Patent and Trademark Office, 1996a, 1996b; Sasaki &Kiyoki, 2002b, 2002c, 2005).

A specific domain has a *sign* that is a set of visual features, for example, shape, color, texture, region, and etcetera that are extracted out of mutually similar images (Smeulders et al., 2000). Signs bridge the gaps between the sets of sample images requested as queries and the classes of mutually similar candidate images in each specific domain. When the pre-defined ranges of parametric values identify the signs and a classification of an image database as a single and unique collection, the patentable parameter-setting component leverages the de facto protection of the entire content of an image database in its referent specific domain. *Figure 3* outlines the scheme that leverages the de facto protection of an image database as a multimedia digital library in a certain specific domain:

(1) Identify a specific narrow domain of an authentic image database, and assure its parameter setting component of the patented methodology to identify a classification of the entire content of an image database as a single and unique collection in a specific domain.

(2) Assemble another forgery image database in the same or equivalent domain by duplicating, otherwise, restoring images that are similar or equivalent to the images of the authentic image database.

(3) Discover that forgery image database to implement a circumventing methodology that classifies and identifies the same or equivalent classes of mutually similar images as the authentic patented methodology does.

(4) Verify that the circumventing methodology is the equivalents to the patented methodology and infringes that methodology under the logic that without the methodology for identification no other method for retrieval is optimized in the discussed domain.

(5) Realize the de facto protection of the authentic image database as is leveraged by the protection of the patented methodology for domain-specific approach of CBIR in the specific domain.

An advantage of the above patent-based protection is to use the registered right for leveraging its de facto protection of its referent, database. Another merit is to restrict its exclusive protection leveraged by patent protection in the modest scope of specific domain. It is a well-known fact that parametric values are easy to modify and adjust in the application. Exemplary parametric values must be

Figure 3. The patent-based protection scheme

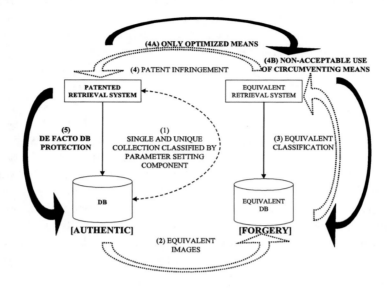

specified to define a clear boundary of the scope of equivalent modification of the claimed methodologies. As suggested from exemplary parametric values, the scope of modification is restricted within respective specific domains. The most significant problem in the protection of digital libraries is the preemption of application fields by the foregoing that are often the western countries. Reinbothe (1999) mentioned that any prospective protection of digital libraries should be fair to both the developers and the followers. The proposed scheme is not to have any excessive protection over a number of image databases as multimedia digital libraries in general domains.

Conclusion

In this chapter, we have discussed the legal issues on multimedia digital libraries and retrieval mechanisms, and technically interpreted the legal schemes for protecting multimedia digital libraries and retrieval mechanisms. The protection of its intellectual property right is a critical issue in the digital library community.

We have presented the schemes for copyrighting the multimedia digital libraries with keyword-based retrieval, patenting the CBIR mechanisms, and protecting the multimedia digital libraries with CBIR.

References

American Dental Association v. Delta Dental Plan Association, 126 F.3d 977 (7th Cir. 1997).

Autogiro Co. of America v. United States, 384 F.2d 391, 155 U.S.P.Q. 697 (Ct. Cl. 1967).

Borgman, C.L. (2000). *From Gutenberg to the global information infrastructure: Access to information in the networked worl*d. Digital Libraries and Electronic Publishing. Cambridge, MA: MIT Press.

Feist Publications, Inc. v. Rural Telephone Service, 499 U.S. 340, 111 S.Ct. 1282, 113 L.Ed.2d 358 (1991).

Gorman, R.A., & Ginsburg, J.C. (1993). *Copyright for the nineties: Cases and materials* (4th ed.). Contemporary legal education series. Charlottesville, NC: The Michie Company.

Graver Tank & Mfg. Co. v. Linde Air Products Co., 339 U.S. 605 (1950).

In *re Alappat*, 33 F.3d 1526, 31 U.S.P.Q.2d 1545 (Fed. Cir. 1994) (en banc).

In *re Dow Chemical Co.*, 837 F.2d 469, 473, 5 U.S.P.Q.2d 1529, 1531 (Fed. Cir. 1988).

Jakes, J.M., & Yoches, E.R. (1989). Legally speaking: Basic principles of patent protection for computer science. *Communications of the ACM, 32* (8), 922–924.

Laitran Corp. v. Rexnord, Inc., 939 F.2d 1533, 19 U.S.P.Q.2d (BNA) 1367 (Fed. Cir. 1991).

Manchester Visualization Center. (2000). CBIR evaluation. Retrieved from the World Wide Web: *http://www.man.ac.uk/MVC/research/CBIR/*

Merges, R.P. (1997). *Patent law and policy: Cases and materials* (2nd ed.). Contemporary legal education series. Charlottesville, NC: The Michie Company.

Müller, H., Müller, W., Squire, D.M., Marchand-Maillet, S., & Pun, T. (2001). Automated benchmarking in content-based image retrieval. In *Proceedings of the 2001 IEEE International Conference on Multimedia and Expo (ICME 2001)*, (pp. 321–324). Tokyo, Japan.

Nimmer, M., Marcus, P., Myers, D., & Nimmer, D. (1991). *Cases and materials on copyright* (4th ed.). St. Paul, MN: West Publishing.

Reinbothe, J. (1999). The legal protection of non-creative databases. In *Proceedings of the Database Workshop of the International Conference of Electronic Commerce and Intellectual Property*, (WIPO/EC/CONF/99/SPK/22-A). Geneva, Switzerland, September 14-16. WIPO.

Rui, Y., Huang, T.S., & Chang, S.F. (1999). Image retrieval: Current techniques, promising directions and open issues. *Journal of Visual Communication and Image Representation, 10* (4), 39–62.

Samuelson, P. (1996). Legally speaking: Legal protection for database content. *Communications of the ACM, 39* (12), 17–23.

Sasaki, H., & Kiyoki, Y. (2002a). Media kensaku enzin no tokkyo shutoku niyoru maruchimedia-detabesu no kenri hogo hoshiki [A methodology to protect a multi-media database by a patentable program of indexing and retrieval based-on semantic similarity]. *IPS of Japan Transactions on Databases, 43* (13), 108–127.

Sasaki, H., & Kiyoki, Y. (2002b). Patenting advanced search engines of multimedia databases. In S. Lesavich (ed.), *Proceedings of the 3rd International Conference on Law and Technology* (pp. 34–39). Cambridge, MA, November 6–7. International Society of Law and Technology (ISLAT). Anaheim, Calgary, Zurich: Acta Press.

Sasaki, H., & Kiyoki, Y. (2002c). Patenting the processes for content-based retrieval in digital libraries. In E.P. Lim, S. Foo, C. Khoo, H. Chen, E. Fox, S. Urs, & T. Costantino (eds.), *Proceedings of the 5th International Conference on Asian Digital Libraries (ICADL) – Digital Libraries: People, Knowledge, and Technology, Lecture Notes in Computer Science,* 2555 (pp. 471–482). Singapore, December 11–14. Berlin: Springer-Verlag.

Sasaki, H., & Kiyoki, Y. (2003). A proposal for digital library protection. In *Proceedings of the 3rd ACM/IEEE-CS Joint Conference on Digital Libraries* (p. 392). Houston, TX, May 27–31. Los Alamitos, CA: IEEE Computer Society Press.

Sasaki, H., & Kiyoki, Y. (2005). A formulation for patenting content-based retrieval processes in digital libraries. *Information Processing and Management, 41*(1), 57-74.

Smeulders, A.W.M., Worring, M., Santini, S., Gupta, A., & Jain, R. (2000). Content-based image retrieval at the end of the early years. *IEEE Transactions on Pattern Analysis and Machine Intelligence, 22* (12), 1349–1380.

Unique Concepts, Inc. v. Brown, 939 F.2d 1558, 19 U.S.P.Q.2d 1500 (Fed. Cir. 1991).

U.S. Copyright Act, 17 U.S.C. Sec. 101, & 103 (1976).

U.S. Patent Act, Title 35 U.S.C. Sec. 101, 103, & 112 (2003).

U.S. Patent and Trademark Office (1996a). *Examination guidelines for computer-related inventions*, 61 Fed. Reg. 7478 (Feb. 28, 1996) (*"Guidelines"*). Retrieved from the World Wide Web: *http://www.uspto.gov/web/offices/pac/dapp/oppd/patoc.htm*.

U.S. Patent and Trademark Office. (1996b). *Examination guidelines for computer-related inventions training materials directed to business, artificial intelligence, and mathematical processing applications ("Training Materials")*. Retrieved from the World Wide Web: *http://www.uspto.gov/web/offices/pac/compexam/examcomp.htm*.

West Publishing Co. v. Mead Data Central, Inc., 799 F.2d 1219 (8th Cir. 1986), cert. denied, 479 U.S. 1070 (1987).

Yoshitaka, A., & Ichikawa, T. (1999). A survey on content-based retrieval for multimedia databases. *IEEE Transactions on Knowledge and Data Engineering, 11* (1), 81–93.

Chapter XIV

Digital Libraries as Learning Environments for Youths

Natalie Lee-San Pang
Monash University, Malaysia

Abstract

Students have long been associated to learn in groups in physical environments. As more and more digital libraries emerge, and libraries take a greater role in education together with academic institutions, there is a need to address digital libraries as learning environments. This chapter looks specifically at the process of learning between peers in a group and how digital libraries can lend themselves as a learning environment towards this purpose. Using a participatory process involving two groups of youths, observations were made to suggest design features for digital libraries used for electronic learning. This is a pilot study to investigate how youths collaborate with one another in a simulated learning environment. It is hoped that with a good understanding of the peer learning process, researchers can be assisted in future studies looking into digital libraries for educational purposes amongst learning groups.

Introduction

"Because we enjoy each other's company, we generally learn best from each other."– Mark Stefik

The traditional classroom has a long history of children teaching younger ones (Briggs, 1998). Like Stefik, many researchers have found evidence of students learning better, or reinforcing key concepts when they do it in a peer group (Briggs, 1998; Chen, 2002; Kilby, 2001; Druin, 2001). The environment in which they conduct such peer learning has evolved over the years – from the same bench in the library or cafeteria, to the virtual community accessible through a computer. In the latter scenario, they do not see each other, but interact with each other by means of communication tools (Khoo et al., 2002). The role of libraries in providing instructional support has changed to one of a more dynamic nature in recent years – developing new digital resources and services for the purposes of distance learning, teaching aids, or support for the academic faculties in students' research and coursework (Logue, 2003). Libraries are not just passive repositories of resources, but provide immense support in education.

In Viggiano et al.'s (2001) study, libraries have taken on the role of the direct educator, not only providing students with remote access to online materials, but also support services like technical help and research advice. Going further, how can digital libraries lend themselves as an environment for peer learning? Digital libraries are not just as a service to information seekers – they are potential learning environments. This chapter seeks to examine group learning dynamics and how digital libraries may lend themselves to support the peer learning process. Like Theng et al. (2001), Druin et al.'s (2001) work on the children's digital library began using prototypes of learning by children. Druin et al. (2001) involved children and teachers as design partners and used prototypes developed through such participatory design as design contributions, the result of which is the International Children Digital Library (Druin, 2003), an educational digital library that also supports collaborative learning between children.

In Singapore, many digital libraries have evolved in education. One of the most significant implementations is IVLE (Integrated Virtual Learning Environment); developed initially by the National University of Singapore (Microsoft, 2003). At the time of writing, it is supporting more than 24,000 users in universities and schools. In a simulated learning environment here, characteristics of collaborated learning using a model of peer learning are observed. Preliminary observations could be used as a basis for future studies on how digital libraries may be used as learning environments for peer-learning groups.

Related Work

According to Kearsley (2000), online education goes back about four decades with computer-assisted instruction. The initial concept for involving computers was to provide programs to allow students to interact with and learn specific content. Over time, it became more apparent that computers used for the purposes of communication, sharing information, and database searching became more valuable (Fisher et al., 1996; see also, Kearsley, 2000). One of the fundamental influences on online learning had also been the increased tendency towards collaboration among students and teachers, largely due to the ease of online interaction brought about by online computing tools (Kilby, 2001; Lim, 2003). Cowie et al. (2000) provide reasons for this phenomenon in their discussion of peer support in youths. Besides fulfilling their emotional needs, youths can gain a supportive learning community, providing them with educational opportunities. Briggs (1998) also found crucial support between young people who have befriended each other through a peer group. They will usually be motivated to help one another.

According to Cowie et al. (2000) and Briggs et al. (1998), there are two broad types of peer support: the first gives emotional support like befriending and conflict resolution; the second emphasizes education and information-giving like peer tutoring, peer education and mentoring. *Table 1* shows the types of peer support activities and the effective age groups to be trained.

While recognizing different peer support, it should be noted that peer activities should not be seen as mutually exclusive from each other in a peer group. As seen from *Table 1*, the optimal training age for most peer activities lies between 11-18 years. As such, the experimental study shall be based on subjects from this group.

Table 1. Age-groups that can most effectively be trained in different types of peer support (Cowie et al., 2000)

	7-9 years	9-11 years	11-18+ years
Co-operative group work	Yes	Yes	Yes
Circle Time	Yes	Yes	Yes
Befriending	Yes	Yes	Yes
Circles of Friends	Yes	Yes	Yes
Conflict resolution/Mediation	No	Yes	Yes
Peer tutoring	No	Yes	Yes
Counselling-based interventions	No	No	Yes
Peer education	No	No	Yes
Peer mentoring	No	No	Yes

Jose et al. (2002) argued that a digital library enabling collaboration between peers needs to be equipped with a common workspace as well as communication tools for the sharing of resources and comments. They began with a system design, refined later through their discussion. In contrast, Druin et al. (2003), while developing a digital library for children, explored collaborative actions in a physical setting between children in order to suggest collaborative technologies for learning between children. Theng et al. (2001), when examining digital libraries for children, embarked on a similar observational study between children in a physical setting – with findings used as refinements to a prototype of a digital library. Such approaches bring benefits of bridging discrepancies between actual tasks required and the eventual technologies supporting such tasks (Robertson, 2000). Inspired by the rationale for this approach, this study aims to examine, in particular, actual peer-learning behavior between youths and uses these results as preliminary recommendations for digital libraries.

Objectives

Borgman (2002) said that digital libraries mean different things to different groups of people. While digital libraries can be seen as "a set of electronic resources and associated technical capabilities for creating, searching, and using information," they can also be defined as an organized construction for a specific community of users, containing functionalities to support the informational needs of its users (Borgman, 2002).

With the proliferation of digital libraries in education, institutions and schools are realizing the benefits of digital libraries to provide new opportunities for learning activities – which were otherwise not feasible in traditional libraries (Jose et al., 2002; Kearsley, 2000). Peer learning contains many benefits. Cowie et al. (2000) has found that peers not only reinforce and correct their knowledge; they also gain confidence and a sense of belonging to a group. While many studies have examined the use of digital libraries in education, it is the intent of this chapter to study, in particular, peer learning and how digital libraries may support such learning activities.

Cowie et al. (2000) defines peer learning by their peer support activities: peer tutoring, peer education, and mentoring. In peer tutoring, one person is the tutor while the other takes on the role of the learner. In many situations one can take on both roles. Finn (1981) defines peer education as "the sharing of information, attitudes or behaviors by people who are not professionally trained educators but whose goal is to educate." It has been acknowledged in earlier context that the availability of online computing tools has made the sharing of information easier.

In the context of peer education, not only can information be shared, attitudes and behaviors can also be communicated between peers.

In both definitions, peer learning is a process requiring time and commitment to achieve. As such, this study cannot be conclusive on its own and must be followed up by future studies involving subjects in the same age group. Recognizing also that peer groups require time to build, subjects have not been randomly selected and only already-established peer groups are chosen to participate in this study. In a systematic manner, the processes by which subjects learn from each other in a peer learning session are then captured. Through recording these observations, the process of peer learning in both groups are surmised for youths, which then provide suggestions on how digital libraries may lend themselves as learning environments to these youths. As this is a pilot study, these impressions must be followed up and tested by later experimental studies.

Methodology

To examine peer-learning behaviour amongst youths, it is necessary to establish first an analogy of peer learning to serve as the basis for the experimental study. Heron (see also, Tosey, 1999) saw peer learning in its context of the community it is in. It is a process, a dynamic environment and cannot be easily expressed as an entity or a product. Riding on the theory of peer learning developed by Heron (see also, Tosey, 1999), Tosey et al. (1998) identified five characteristics, providing a contextual design for peer learning.

- *Personal Development:* According to Heron (1992), for effective learning to occur, personal emotional competence must be present – awareness and management of emotions in terms of control, expression, catharsis, and transmutation. The Oasis School of Human Relations (2003) reinforces the importance of the self in peer learning and states that peer learning begins when an individual begins to make sensible choices taking into account impacts on the self and other people. Notable inputs come from responses to questions on the individual's goal of being in the peer group and expressions of emotions and control.

- *Community Interaction:* Peer learning occurs when two or more participants come together to learn. Community interaction is therefore inevitable when peers participate in experiential learning together (Tosey, 1999), through peer tutoring, peer education, and mentoring (Cowie et al., 2000). An extent of this aspect of the model is the dependence of face-to-face interaction for community interaction to occur. While Tosey (1999) did not seek to undermine the value of interaction in a virtual community through a digital library, he found limitations in community interaction when peers were not able to sense the physical and energetic presence of each other. In Vygotsky's theory of human development, the zone of proximal development is said to be of primary importance, as this will also influence the tools and styles used in interaction (O'Donnell et al., 1999). This is an important aspect to evaluate for in the digital environment, as peers enshrined in the virtual community do not normally experience face-to-face interactions. Actions to be transcribed for are related to the verbal and nonverbal communication within each group.

- *Facilitation:* Tosey et al. (1998) argued that facilitation is mandatory for effective manifestation of peer learning – when individuals achieve optimal sense of personal development and share useful knowledge and resources through community interaction. Heron (1992) saw the facilitator as an educationalist, thus participants have in themselves the right to be potential facilitators, whether or not they were formally appointed. Facilitation may include directives in education and space, deciding the start and end of learning sessions, and mediation where appropriate.

- *Formal Interdependence:* In Tosey's (1999) study of peer learning in higher education, formal structural conditions were found mandatory to support the development of peer learning. This is known as formal interdependence (Thompson, 1967), where participants are expected to rely and work with each other in order to meet learning needs, rather than doing it only if they choose to. Bearing in mind that the study was based on peer learning communities enshrined in higher learning, this aspect may not be applicable to youths. In the context of this study, formal interdependence is regarded as formal membership to the peer group and how students regard their membership as mandatory for them to collaborate with each other. This is noted by students' reliance on their belonging in the group to help one another.

- *Boundary Management:* Boundary management refers to the isolation of a community, in our context the peer group, in a private space for peer learning to take place (Tosey, 1999). Miller (1993) argued that boundary management is a vital component in any organization or system. To the relevance of our discussion, once a peer group has been formed, there must be an appropriate boundary to be formed in order for the peer group to function. To test this characteristic, the students will be brought to a common study area and observed for their tolerance for boundaries.

Two groups of students were selected from a secondary school in Singapore and asked to collaborate in learning. As peer groups cannot be built up overnight, random selection of participants is not ideal in order to study the interactions within a real peer-learning group. Peer groups that had already been formed for at least six months were asked to participate for this study. Coincidentally, the students were divided according to their genders. Four boys formed one group, while four girls formed the second group. The boys and girls were placed in the same community library and given a mathematical assignment to complete with the group. Observations were carried out at two different timings to minimize influences on one another. Seated at the same table, they were each given a common notepad in the middle of the table. They were also asked to think aloud their thoughts, whenever possible. The study session lasting 30 minutes was captured using a video camera and observations were transcribed according to the five characteristics of peer learning (Heron, 1992; see also, Tosey, 1999). For ease of analysis, observations were captured according to blocks of ten minutes. The method of transcription was inspired by the work of Theng et al. (2001), which examined how children collaborated with each other using a children's digital library. Each characteristic of the peer-learning model was given a symbol and transcribed accordingly. Table 2 shows the basis used for transcribing results.

The study being qualitative, only impressions could be noted at this point. The next section discusses observational results and suggests preliminary recommendations for digital libraries supporting learning activities. As this is a pilot study, any further conclusive derivations on these recommendations must only be supported by future studies.

Table 2. Transcription table

Characteristic	Symbol	Criteria
Personal Development	Ж	Goal of being in the peer group Expressions of emotions and control.
Community Interaction	B	Verbal and non-verbal communication (1 symbol represents 2 units of interaction)
Facilitation	Ω	Ability to give directions to the group Mediation when necessary
Formal Interdependence	¥	Reliance on their belonging in the group to collaborate
Boundary Management	Φ	Relative tolerance of boundaries (1 symbol most tolerant, 4 symbols least tolerant)

Learning on the Same Bench:
Results and Discussions

At the start of the observational study, subjects were asked to describe, explicitly, goals of being in the peer group. *Figure 1* shows a summarized overview of the results transcribed.

- *Personal Development:* All girls were able to express their thoughts and emotions, though the youngest subject G3, experiences occasional difficulties. Out of the four subjects, G1, G2 and G4 expressed that although their goal of forming a peer study group was to educate "oneself," one other motivation also lies in desires to belong to a social group. This latter motivation is more apparent in G3. Goals of being in the group were clear in all girls, although they differ. Boys, on the other hand, had different results. Although subject B3 was able to express his emotions and control as observed with his peers, he had little notions on his goal of being in the peer group – whether for learning or to belong to a social group. From both groups, it was observed that the stronger their notions of goals, emotional expressions and control, tendencies to collaborate were also higher. Subjects who had a stronger sense of personal development were also observed to have a seemingly positive correlation with their study materials – subjects B1, B2, B4, G1, G2 and G4 had came prepared with good

Figure 1. Overview of transcribed results

Boys/Girls			
B1	Ж Ж Ж β β β β β β Ω ф ф ф ф	Β β β β β β β β β ¥ ¥ ¥ ¥ Ω Ω Ω Ж Ж Ж Ж Ж Ж	Ω Ω Ω Ω Ω β β β β β β β β β β β β β ¥ ¥ ¥ Ж Ж Ж
B2	Ж Ж Ж Ж β β β β β ф	β β β β Ж Ж Ж	Ω β β β β β β β ¥ Ж Ж Ж Ж Ж Ж Ж
B3	Ж Ж β β β β β ф	β β β β β Ω Ж Ж Ж Ж	Ω β β β ¥ ¥ Ж Ж Ж Ж
B4	Ж Ж Ж Ж β β ф ф ф	β β β β β β Ω Ω Ж Ж Ж Ж Ж	Ω Ω Ω β β β β β β β β ¥ ¥ Ж Ж Ж
G1	Ж Ж Ж Ж β β β β β ф Ж Ж	Ж Ж Ж Ж β β β β β β β β ¥ ¥ Ω Ω	Ω β β β β β β β β β β ¥ ¥ ¥ Ж Ж Ж Ж
G2	Ж Ж Ж Ж β β β β β β Ω ф ф ф ф	Ж Ж Ж β β β β β β β β β β β ¥ ¥ ¥ ¥ ¥ Ω Ω Ω Ω	Ω Ω Ω Ω Ω β β β β β β β β β β β β β β β β ¥ ¥ ¥ Ж Ж Ж
G3	Ж Ж β β β β β β β β β ф	β β β β β β β β ¥ Ω Ж Ж Ж	β β β β β β β β Ж Ж Ж
G4	Ж Ж Ж Ж Ж β β β β Ω ф ф ф	β β β β β β β β β β ¥ ¥ Ω Ω Ω Ω Ж Ж Ж Ж Ж Ж Ж	Ω Ω β β β β β β β β β β β ¥ ¥ ¥ ¥ β β Ж Ж Ж Ж Ж Ж
Minutes	0 10	11 20	21 30

knowledge and a more comprehensive study materials such as textbooks, supplementary assessments to share, even stationery. A consistent observation is that students without the same amounts of materials had lesser involvements.

Though varying degrees of expressions were observed for different individuals, they all had consistent needs for communication for learning and interaction to occur. In the context of the digital library, tools that allow users to display expressions may be useful. The availability of study materials and resources such as stationery also seemed to be critical to both groups. With a digital library, there is also a potential vast amount of informational resources to be shared amongst a learning community. Digital whiteboards allowing free expressions by users, and public folders enabling the sharing of resources within the learning group may be useful too.

- *Community Interaction:* It was observed that in the first block of ten minutes, face-to-face interaction was stronger where socializing is concerned. In both groups, interaction concerning the subject matter at hand only occurred in the next subsequent time blocks – although the second group of girls got down to it sooner than the boys. This may appear that the girls had more intense socializing-type of interaction in the first time block. Kochenderfer et al. (1997; see also, Cowie et al., 2000) supports this impression, when they observed more socialized techniques by girls in communication. Diverse learning and communication styles were also observed – G2 and G4 interacted much more through words, while B1 and B4 were more tactile, many times working out problems by scribbling and demonstrating the solution to the group. Considering this observation, to support various learning styles, it may be useful for digital libraries to provide a variety of communication methods, such as voice, digital drawings, and text messaging.

Both groups were observed to require continuity in discussions – when one loses track of the discussion at hand, he will be briefed again or risk being left out completely. It was observed also that both groups used different terminologies to refer to the same materials and concepts. In the digital library, tracked discussions allowing users to refer to previous interactions may seem to support this observation of peer-learning groups. Group taxonomies unique to the community may also help users identify with the context of their discussions with their peer group.

- *Facilitation:* All girls participated in facilitating the entire discussion, although G2 came across stronger throughout the study as the facilitator in her group, giving signals to start and end the learning sessions. While she dominated decisions in terms of formal cooperation and learning, subject G4 was also heavily involved in facilitating the discussion, although her role differed somewhat from G2. G4 was more involved as a mediator between the girls in the group. Interestingly, both G2 and G4 whose facilitating characteristics were the strongest also fared well in terms of their counts for community interaction. This may mean that where interaction is frequent, subjects may also take up roles in facilitation more often. The same observation was found for the boys – with B1 and B4 being stronger in community interaction and facilitation. They also played an important role in bringing discussions to the next level in their own groups. While it is not possible at this point to define the relevance of roles to different individuals, it is observed from the study that each individual does take up differing roles to allow group learning to take place. In a digital library community, this could translate into the manifestation of roles, such as a moderator in a forum (Kearsley, 2000).

- *Formal Interdependence:* As there was no formal authority coercing formations of the peer groups, subjects were instead evaluated for commitments to collaborate based on their membership to the peer group. In order to study this, subjects were asked to think aloud their motivation for helping each other. Throughout the study, collaborations were observed for both groups of boys and girls, although there were variations in motivations. For the first group of boys, motivations to collaborate were spurred by a strong sense of friendship and belonging, lesser reasons based on formal membership. For the second group, motivations to collaborate were comparatively more inspired by their formal membership to the peer group, and subject G2 (being also the stronger facilitator) expressed keener motivations to collaborate due to her perceived belonging to the group and role as a "coordinator and motivator." For the rest of the girls, formal interdependence was observed to be somewhat consistent. This appears to correlate with Thompson's (1967) studies of formal membership to a group. In terms of learning in the digital library, user groups, which specify memberships of users to their study communities, may help to establish such formal interdependence within a group.

- *Boundary Management:* For all subjects, principles applied to boundary management seem to occur in the first time block. After subjects were inducted into their chosen time and space, they kept very much to it until the end of the whole learning session. It seems to suggest that, for a peer group to collaborate effectively, a defined workspace that belongs only to any given peer learning groups is imperative. Jose et al. (2002), in the development of virtual tutor, mentioned a digital workspace – like a piece of paper where tutors can share information and conduct teaching to a group of learners. Having a defined workspace for a learning group to work in could also define a digital boundary to collaborate in learning in the digital library.

Conclusion

Unlike the traditional classroom where students follow instructions of an adult teacher, digital libraries open up new opportunities for students to learn from peers. It is easier to interact with each other online, unlike the traditional classroom setting, where a class is isolated from other classes. The study had a consistent observation – expressions and face-to-face interactions seem to play an important part in assisting the progress of group learning. Online interaction, however, has a distinct lack of face-to-face interaction. To help overcome this obstacle, it is suggested that tools include interactive emoticons to help students interact with each other. Learning materials also appeared to be of primary importance – without which peer learning comes to halt. With the resource-rich digital library, students could be aided to overcome a lack of resources – in contrast to a physical setting where each student is dependent on themselves and others to share or bring learning resources. With higher rates of interaction, peer learning was observed to advance further. When studying online communities, Khoo et al. (2002) found that online communication tools can be used to stimulate threaded discussions. It is important to also support diverse communication styles – some youths interact better with text, and others communicate better tactilely, like drawing or demonstrating a solution on a "working pad." Jose et al. (2002) suggested having annotations and tracks to help students in a peer group to keep track of where the last discussion ended. This is consistent with observations from this study; students participate more when they were kept up with discussions while others were eventually left out.

Also observed from the study were the different terminologies and context the two groups used to refer to similar terms and concepts. Allowing peer groups to build up their own taxonomies and terminologies in the digital library may be useful. The work of Bontcheva et al. (2002) is relevant towards this requirement, where they used robust human language for automatic annotation and indexing. With this technique, it would also be possible to document learning between students in a tangible manner, unlike a physical environment where it is difficult to record tangibly, progress of learning. Along with indexing discussions between peers, it would also be possible for students to search for "last lessons learnt" and pick up quickly where they had last left off. What is useful to note was also the implication facilitation brings to the student – greater interaction with all members of the group. To help students be more involved in a peer group, it is suggested that digital libraries incorporate role-assignments for its users to enhance its value as a learning environment. For example, students may have options to assign each other as the facilitator, and rotate these tasks. Ismail et al. (2003) proposed a metadata scheme for educational digital libraries based on assigned roles. In their study, such a role-based metadata scheme helps to make the contributions of users visible within the community.

While formal interdependence was found not to be mandatory, it serves as a reminder on the importance of forming a proper learning group – whether or not youths collaborate eventually because of due memberships to the group, or out of a perceived bonding with other members. In the digital library, this can be translated into the formation of user communities coming together to collaborate in learning. Having friends that peers are comfortable with seem to form the basis for the coming together of the peer group, as observed from the study. This is congruent with Theng's (2001) study, where abilities of children to select their own friends to engage in collaborative learning were of significance. As observed, having a defined boundary that belonged only to the peer group was important for any interactions to occur. Both groups could only start work after everyone was satisfied with the physical boundary they have selected. In the digital library, such physical boundaries may be translated into stipulated virtual workspaces. Jose et al. (2002) proposed an example of one such workspace implemented in a digital library.

In raising design issues that perpetrates peer learning between youths, the chapter also attempted to highlight potential impacts of digital libraries on peer groups through visualizing the process of peer learning. As today's technology advent towards one recording high rates of interaction, digital libraries can be implemented as learning environments – involving resources, services, tools, and a profiled community of users. Digital libraries are potentially highly interactive environments encouraging electronic learning between its users. Online learning is different from the way students learn traditionally – yet should not compromise the benefits peers can gain from one another in the conventional classroom.

Future Work

More studies are required to investigate the validity of features in digital libraries to support peer learning. Some predicaments of peer learning exist, which may impose themselves as limitations. Kochenderfer & Ladd (1997; see also, Cowie et al., 2000) noted gender differences in youths when responding to other peers.

The study had not been set up to measure the impacts of such gender differences. Diverse learning styles can also have significant impacts on manner of peer learning within a group (Briggs, 1998). Together with the potential of gender variance, this variable suggests an exciting avenue of collaborative learning research. With digital libraries, there is an issue of differing levels of user literacy. Chowdhury (2002) suggests that differing levels of information literacy result in eventual disparities in exploiting benefits from digital libraries. Researchers such as Kearsley (2000) and Kilby (2001) have also found that increased online peer learning had brought with it increased computer literacy amongst members of the peer group. Within a digital library, such differing levels of literacy may actually be bridged with a peer group. This provides yet another valuable area of research.

References

Bontcheva, K., Maynard, D., Cunningham, H., & Saggion, H. (2002). Using human language technology for automatic annotation and indexing of digital library content. In M. Agosti & C. Thanos (Eds.), *Proceedings of 6th European Conference on Research and Advanced Technology for Digital Libraries* (pp. 613-625). Germany: Springer.

Borgman, C. (2002). Challenges in building digital libraries for the 21st century. In E.P. Lim, S. Foo, C. Khoo, H. Chen, E. Fox, S. Urs, & T. Costantino (Eds.), *Proceedings of 5th International Conference on Asian Digital Libraries* (pp. 1-13). Germany: Springer.

Briggs, D. (1998). *A class of their own*. Westport: Bergin & Garvey.

Chen, C.S. (2002). Self-regulated learning strategies & achievement in an information systems course. *Information Technology, Learning, and Performance Journal, 20* (1), 11-26.

Cowie, H., & Wallace, P. (2000). *Peer support in action*. London: SAGE Publications.

Druin, A. (2001). *Digital libraries for children*. Retrieved October 1, 2003, from the World Wide Web: *http://www.cs.umd.edu/hcil/kiddesign/searchkids.shtml*

Druin, A., Bederson, B., & Hourcade, J.P. (2001). Designing a digital library for young children: An intergenerational partnership. In E. Fox, & C. Borgman (Eds.), *Proceedings of ACM/IEEE Joint Conference on Digital Libraries* (pp. 398-405). Roanoke, VA: ACM Press.

Finn, D. (2000). *What is peer education?* Retrieved September 27, 2003, from the World Wide Web: *http://www.nceta.flinders.edu.au/pdf/peer-education/chapter2-what.pdf*

Gleason, A.L. (1987). Peers learning from peers. *Association Management, 39* (9), 64-71.

Ismail, D.M.M., Yin, M., Theng, Y.L., Goh, D.H.L., & Lim, E.P. (2003). Towards a role-based metadata scheme for educational digital libraries: A case study in Singapore. In T. Koch & I.T. Solvberg (Eds.), *Proceedings of 7ᵗʰ European Conference on Research and Advanced Technology for Digital Libraries* (pp. 41-51). Germany: Springer.

Jose, J.M., Braddick, H., Martin, I., Robertson, B., Walker, C., & MacPherson, G. (2002). Virtual Tutor: A system for deploying digital libraries in classrooms. In E.P. Lim, S. Foo, C. Khoo, H. Chen, E. Fox, S. Urs & T. Costantino (Eds.), *Proceedings of 5ᵗʰ International Conference on Asian Digital Libraries* (pp. 275-286). Germany: Springer.

Kearsley, G. (2000). *Learning and teaching in cyberspace.* Canada: Wadsworth.

Khoo, M., Devaul, H., & Summer, T. (2002). Functional requirements for online tools to support community-led collections building. In M. Agosti & C. Thanos (Eds.), *Proceedings of 6ᵗʰ European Conference on Research and Advanced Technology for Digital Libraries* (pp. 190-203). Germany: Springer.

Kilby, T. (2001). The direction of web-based training: A practitioner's view. *The Learning Organisation, 8* (5), 194-199.

Lim, A. (2003). Collaborative digitisation projects: Opportunities to enhance teaching and learning. *Information Technology and Libraries, 22* (2), 75-78.

Logue, S. (2003). The changing role of libraries in instructional support. *Information Technology and Libraries, 22* (2), 52.

Microsoft. (2003). *Microsoft's case study on IVLE.* Retrieved October 2, 2003, from Microsoft in Education on the World Wide Web: *http://www.bpghs.wizlearn.net/public/case_study.htm*

O'Donnell, A.M., & King, A. (1999). *Cognitive perspectives on peer learning.* NJ: Lawrence Erlbaum Associates.

Oasis School of Human Relations. (2003). *Peer principle: Ideology, knowledge and research.* Retrieved September 20, 2003, from the World Wide Web: *http://www.oasis-centre.demon.co.uk/ideol/peer.html*

Robertson, T. (2000). Building bridges: Negotiating the gap between work practice and technology design. *International Journal of Human-Computer Studies, 53,* 121–146.

Theng, Y.L. (2002). Information therapy in digital libraries. In E.P. Lim, S. Foo, C. Khoo, H. Chen, E. Fox, S. Urs & T. Costantino (Eds.), *Proceedings of 5th International Conference on Asian Digital Libraries* (pp. 452-464). Germany: Springer.

Theng, Y.L., Mohd-Nasir, N., Buchanan, G., Fields, B., & Thimbleby, H. (2001). Dynamic digital libraries for children. In E. Fox & C. Borgman (Eds.), *Proceedings of ACM/IEEE Joint Conference on Digital Libraries* (pp. 406-415). Roanoke, VA: ACM Press.

Thompson, J.D. (1967). *Organisations in action.* New York: McGraw-Hill.

Tosey, P., & Gregory, J. (1998). The peer learning community in higher education: Reflections on practice. *Innovations in Education and Training International, 35* (1), 74-81.

Viggiano, R., & Ault, M. (2001). Online library instruction for online students. *Information Technology and Libraries, 20* (3), 135-138.

Section V

Users and Usability

Chapter XV

Usability of Digital Libraries in a Multicultural Environment

Christine L. Borgman
University of California Los Angeles, USA

Edie Rasmussen
University of British Columbia, Canada

Abstract

Usability is a critical issue for digital libraries, complicated by the fact that users have varying levels of knowledge of library systems and subject knowledge and may be novices or experts and frequent or occasional users of specific digital libraries. Usability is further complicated by multicultural issues, as digital library users may come from many cultures and nations, or it may be necessary to orient a digital library toward the needs of users from one or more specific localities or cultures. Usability evaluation may be formative, summative, iterative or comparative and is usually specific to a particular digital library context. The four papers in this section, illustrating formative, iterative and summative approaches, cover a variety of contexts—education, music, cultural heritage and a national digital library.

Introduction

Interest in research and practice for digital libraries (DLs) is growing around the world, and the Asia Pacific region is no exception. The International Conferences on Asian DLs have attracted a broad array of researchers and practitioners from around the region and around the world. Over the five years of this conference series, papers and panels on usability have increased from minor to major parts of the program. Many usability issues are global, given the user communities for DLs. Others are local, given the varying languages and cultures within and between regions.

This chapter provides a brief summary of usability, multicultural, and evaluation issues for DLs in the Asia Pacific and serves as an introduction and overview of the four contributed chapters in the section on "Users and Usability."

Usability and Digital Libraries

Usability can be defined as "the ease with which a user can learn to operate, prepare inputs for, and interpret outputs of a system or component" (IEEE, 1990). Nielsen (2003), a well-known usability expert, defines it as "a quality attribute that assesses how easy user interfaces are to use." Other authors point out that reference to the "ease of use" of a system is best seen as shorthand for a set of characteristics that determine "the extent to which a product can be used by specified users to achieve specified goals with effectiveness, efficiency, and satisfaction in a specified context of use," per the ISO 9241 standard. Quesenbery (2001) further deconstructs this definition into five characteristics: the effectiveness of the system in allowing the user to meet his or her goals in a comprehensive and accurate manner; the efficiency or speed with which users can achieve those goals; the degree to which the system engages the user by providing a pleasant and satisfying interaction; the error tolerance of the system in preventing and responding to errors; and the extent to which the system is easy to learn initially and over time.

Identification of attributes that contribute to usability is a necessary first step to evaluation and measurement. In their study of user acceptance of DLs, Thong et al. (2002) summarize attempts to operationalize usability and conclude that ease of use and usefulness are component attributes. Usefulness is a measure of the performance of the system, its ability to deliver relevant material to the user, and therefore is determined not only by how the user interacts with the system, but also by the mechanisms for interacting with DL content. The quality of the metadata, the nature of the search engine, and the ability of the system to create meaningful summaries are all "behind the interface" characteristics that determine the success of the system in providing relevant material to the user.

Usability has proven to be remarkably difficult to achieve in the library environment, as Borgman (1996) illustrated in a study asking "Why are online catalogs *still* hard to use?," despite many years of research and experience in designing these systems. DLs are yet more complex than online catalogs or information retrieval systems. DLs usually contain documents in multiple media, rather than just text or bibliographic records, and they provide a wider array of services, supporting the seeking, use, and creation of information resources (Borgman, 2000, 2003). DLs often must facilitate the retrieval of information by users whose patterns of information-seeking behavior are based on their "ongoing effort to understand and act in the world" (Marchionini, 1995). Users may want to search for known information or browse for what is not known. They demonstrate varying levels of knowledge of library systems and subject knowledge and may be novices or experts and frequent or occasional users of specific DLs.

Organizational usability also plays a role in the acceptance of DLs (Kling & Elliott, 1994). This concept recognizes that the development of a DL is influenced by a variety of stakeholders, including librarians, vendors, software engineers, and end-users. These stakeholders often lack an understanding of each other's expectations and culture (Davies, 1997). Organizational usability reflects the extent to which a system matches structure and practice within an institution, so that the system is used rather than being ignored or overlooked (Elliott & Kling, 1997). The organizational approach has led to studies in specific environments such as the university (Davies, 1997) and civil and criminal courts (Elliott & Kling, 1997) to identify ways in which the usability of DLs can be improved by adapting systems for the context of a community's work habits and information needs.

Multicultural Issues

DLs exist in a technological environment in which the World Wide Web has had a tremendous influence. Many DLs are accessed via the Web or use a Web browser interface. Users' expectations of DLs have been shaped by their use of the Web for information seeking, e-commerce, and entertainment. Web designers are on the leading edge of design for international, multicultural user communities. These designers usually make a choice between globalization, in which their sites are intended for an audience that is multicultural and international, and localization, in which sites are intended to meet the needs of a particular audience (Main, 2002). In comparing the tradeoffs between these approaches, a number of usability factors arise.

The most obvious issue related to multicultural use of DLs is language, and by extension, systems of writing. At a basic level, this might involve making the interface available in more than one language or dialect, and incorporating an encoding system such as Unicode that can display text in many languages. However, the language issues for DLs are more complex than simple display because of the need to search or browse the collection. If multilingual access is provided via a thesaurus or other controlled vocabulary, the thesaurus must be available in the languages of the user communities, or else some form of switching vocabulary should be provided to translate between languages. Multilingual thesauri are difficult to produce and are not widely available. Those that do exist are usually intended to serve a specific topic area and well-defined community, such as the EUROVOC Thesaurus,[1] which covers the 11 official languages of the European Community and the fields in which the Community is active.

Alternatives to controlled, multilingual vocabularies are keyword searching in individual languages. In an ideal system, users would be able to submit queries in their own language, which could then be searched against digital records in multiple languages (Oard, 1997). Multilingual searching is a non-trivial problem and one that has generated considerable interest in the information retrieval, natural language processing, and DLs research communities. This research area, known as cross-language information retrieval, has focused primarily on bilingual approaches, such as querying Chinese text using English terms or querying English text using Spanish terms, though occasionally a third language is used as an intermediary. Cross-language information retrieval has been an active track in the TREC (Text REtrieval Conference)[2] experiments sponsored by NIST, where experiments in English, German, French, Italian, Chinese, and Arabic have been considered. Research on cross-language retrieval is a growing part of DL conference papers (see, for example, Lim et al., 2002).

Many other DL usability issues are related to what Main (2002) refers to as "objective culture," such as varying representations for dates, calendars, time, currency, numbers, units of measurement, addresses, and phone numbers around the world. These seemingly trivial differences cause confusion and inconvenience. Does 10/09/2003 refer to September 10 or October 9? Is 30 degrees hot (Celsius) or cold (Fahrenheit)? The user who cannot force a six-character Canadian postal code into a form designed with a five-digit U.S. postal code in mind, or an international phone number into a form designed for a North American one, is effectively prohibited from proceeding with his or her registration or other operation. Many of these objective factors are well documented for Web design and can be applied to DL design (Nielson, 2000).

More difficult to identify and address are usability issues related to cultural identity at a subjective level (Main, 2002). Cultural usability is a complex issue because cultural identity is complex. An individual's cultural identity may be formed by a specific culture and subculture but is also influenced by a set of relationships and experiences that are unique to that individual. This complexity is illustrated by Duncker et al. (2000), who show that seemingly simple color preferences are influenced by factors such as race, country of birth, parents' culture, and immigrant experience. The impact of color goes well beyond a preference for one color over another; through cultural associations, colors carry meanings, both readily recognized and unconscious, which differ from culture to culture. Similarly, certain shapes, symbols or gestures that may be acceptable in one culture are seen as offensive or absurd in another.

While reaction to color and symbolism in the DL interface are manifestations of cultural differences, resolution of these issues offers only a partial, and relatively high level, solution to cultural adaptation of a Web site or DL. Researchers exploring the dimensions of cultural identity have identified factors, such as attitudes to authority, degree of individualism, adaptation of traditions to modern times, sense of time, and avoidance of uncertainty, that differ between cultures (Main, 2002). These differences have been explored and proposed for consideration in Web design and DLs (Thong et al., 2002; Zahedi et al., 2001), but it is far from simple to determine how to operationalize these cultural traits for specific audiences.

Content is also a significant factor in cross-cultural usability. DLs by their nature contain materials that are culturally significant, such as digitized texts of historic importance, images of paintings, sculpture, and artifacts. These materials may also be culturally sensitive, so that what has artistic merit in one environment may be offensive in another, or a document which has historical significance to one group may be heretical to another. In fact, the very idea of general access to some cultural heritage materials may be counter to the traditions of that culture, as Duncker (2002) points out in the context of public access to certain Maori records in public libraries. Further, she suggests that the very concept of the DL, based as it is on a library metaphor that is not culturally relevant for the Maori, leads to a lack of usability. Her study, based on an ethnographic analysis and an experimental study of the usability of a DL by Maori and non-Maori students, is one of the few that looks at usability of a DL from the perspective of the users' culture.

DLs have made tremendous progress in making information available across borders and cultures, but the usability of these systems in multicultural and cross-cultural environments is only beginning to be examined. Crane (2003) makes a case for the importance of cultural communication:

Increased cross-cultural understanding/exchange can increase communication, reduce the impulse to violence and expand socio-eco-
nomic connections. Thus, potential benefits include enhanced global
peace and prosperity. (n.p.)

The potential of DLs to contribute to this cross-cultural understanding will
depend on their ability to inform rather than disappoint, offend, confuse, or amuse
their users. A positive step toward engaging a broader community in multicultural design principles is through workshops on cross-cultural usability at Joint
Conferences on Digital Libraries (JCDL). The central goal of the most recent
workshop, held at JCDL '03, was to bring together researchers and practitioners
who would contribute to a collaborative research agenda. Outcomes included a
list of research issues and directions related to DLs, culture and usability (Caidi
& Komlodi, 2003).

Evaluating Usability

It is one thing to state that the design of DLs should address usability and
sensitivity to cultural differences and quite another to measure whether a given
system meets a specific set of criteria for usability, cultural relevance, or other
factors. To determine whether DLs meet such criteria, some form of evaluation
must be done. Yet research on DL evaluation is in relatively early stages. The
concern for DL evaluation is growing, as evidenced by workshops on this topic
funded by the United States and the European Union (Borgman, 2002; Borgman
& Larsen, 2003) and by the attendance at the tutorials and workshops on DL
evaluation at the ICADL in Singapore and the China DL Conference in Beijing,
both held in 2002.

DLs should be evaluated in the context of specific applications. DLs are not ends
in themselves; rather, they are enabling technologies for digital asset management, electronic commerce, electronic publishing, teaching and learning, and
other activities. The methods and metrics for evaluating DLs will vary by
whether they are viewed as institutions, as information systems, as new
technologies, or as new services. They also will vary by local culture, language,
and intended user community.

Results of evaluation studies can provide strategic guidance for the design and
deployment of future systems, can assist in determining whether DLs address
the appropriate social, cultural, and economic problems, and whether they are as
maintainable as possible. Consistent evaluation methods also will enable comparison between systems and services.

Evaluation research can be a highly applied form of investigation, or it can test theory. It is particularly useful for studying aspects of communication technologies such as interactivity, adoption, use, implementation, and social impacts. Evaluation itself can be cost effective, particularly in areas of usability. Even a small amount of usability evaluation in the development of information systems can pay for itself several times over in cost savings from avoiding lost productivity (Computer Science and Telecommunications Board, 1997).

Evaluation is a general term that includes various aspects of performance measurement and assessment. Activities include laboratory experiments, regional, national, and international surveys or quasi-experiments, time-series analyses, online monitoring of user-system interactions, observation of use, and other forms of data collection. Evaluation has a long history in fields such as computer science, education, communication, health, and criminal justice. In human-computer interaction, measures include time to learn, error rates, efficiency, memorability, and satisfaction (Nielsen, 1993; Shneiderman, 1998). Systems can be benchmarked for aspects of performance, using quantitative measures specific to applications, such as recall and precision measures of information retrieval. Evaluation of cross-language aspects of DLs is a particular emphasis of European Union activities.[3]

At least four types of evaluation are relevant to DLs (Borgman, 2002):

•   *Formative evaluation* begins at the initial stages of a development project to establish baselines on current operations, set goals, and determine desired outcomes. Such evaluation is usually driven by context and project-specific goals.

•   *Summative evaluation* takes place at the end of a project to determine if the intended goals were met. Goals and outcomes must be compared to initial states, so formative evaluation generally precedes summative evaluation.

•   *Iterative evaluation* takes place throughout a project, beginning in the earliest design and development stages. Interim stages of design are assessed in comparison to design goals and desired outcomes, and the results inform the next stages of design. Iterative approaches encourage designers to set measurable goals at the beginning of a project and provide opportunities to re-assess goals throughout the development process.

•   *Comparative evaluation* requires standardized measures that can be compared across systems. Communities can identify and validate measures. If such measures are implemented in a consistent manner, they enable comparisons between systems. Test beds are another way to compare measures and to compare performance of different functions and algorithms.

A particular concern of this book is the usability of DLs in Asia Pacific contexts. DLs are a new technology that is just beginning to move from research to practice and from prototypes to operational systems and services. As DLs are implemented, people gradually adopt and adapt them as part of their information practices. These behaviors are evolving rapidly, along with the implementation of systems. The papers in this section, and others in recent ICADL and other Asia Pacific regional DL conferences, are early efforts at understanding local contexts.

Context has a variety of aspects, including goals and tasks, socio-cultural milieu, and environment, as identified by the breakout group on Evaluation in Context at the EU-US Workshop on Evaluation of Digital Libraries[4] (Borgman, 2002). The breakout group on Users and Interfaces at the same workshop identified a complementary set of research questions and methods for studying DLs in context. These include criteria for determining the "best" research questions and methods, such as the cost of evaluation, cost-benefit ratios of evaluation, adaptability of methods, sharability of methods, instruments, and test beds, and validity and reliability. Both groups concluded that evaluation can serve many different goals, and that the effectiveness of evaluation metrics and methods must be goal-specific. Methods and metrics to evaluate usability are unlikely to yield cost-benefit data and vice versa, for example.

Because DLs serve a rich variety of content to a wide array of user populations, most DL evaluation to date has been specific to a context. Methods are often handcrafted and are time-consuming to develop and deploy. We need more experience with context-specific evaluation methods to produce methods that can be applied more easily in new contexts. We also need to conduct evaluation in a wide variety of contexts to determine the commonalities and differences among DLs along various dimensions. Thus, research on DLs in specific contexts will lead to better metrics and methods that can be applied across DL systems and services. A new book on the use and evaluation of DLs includes case studies in many contexts (Bishop, Van House, & Buttenfield, 2003). Although none of the chapters in that book are specific to the Asia Pacific region, the variety of cases and the innovative choices of research methods should be of interest to readers of the present book.

Introduction to Contributed Papers

The four contributed chapters in the "Users and Usability" section cover a variety of contexts and employ either formative, iterative or summative evaluation approaches, as shown in *Table 1*. The table is a matrix with Content and

Table 1. Overview of contributed chapters on usability of digital libraries

Usability assessment	Educ- geography	General- national	General- music	Cultural heritage
Initial requirements for evaluation				Liew
Formative evaluation	Goh		Bainbridge	
Iterative evaluation	Goh	Theng	Bainbridge	
Summative evaluation		Theng		
Comparative evaluation				

Context across the top (columns) and Types of Usability Assessment down the side (rows).

Three of these chapters address one or more systems in progress, and one reports on a summative evaluation of a deployed system. Although several of the chapters report on multiple systems, they tend to be complementary rather than comparative evaluations. One of the chapters was classified as "initial requirements" because the authors identify the requirements for empirical research, as determined by the designers, but do not report any data from studies that involve prospective users. The contexts in which DLs are used include a music database for general users, secondary school geography education, Maori cultural heritage and a national DL. Because the four contexts do not overlap, it is more constructive to analyze the chapters by the approaches to usability evaluation.

Initial Requirements

Liew's Chapter XVI is an essay about the potential for a DL to support Maori cultural heritage. This chapter identifies some of the same issues regarding Maori use of libraries and attitudes toward documentation of culture that were reported by Duncker (2002), mentioned earlier. Among the most problematic issues in the digitization of cultural heritage is how to capture content and make it available in ways that respect the wishes of the originators of the resources and of their descendants. Some communities, including the Maori, are reluctant to make their resources widely available due to concerns that the content may be misinterpreted or that the materials may be used out of context. Yet at the same time, such communities desire greater recognition of their cultural heritage.

Liew's chapter begins to identify potential subjects for a formative evaluation of a DL of Maori culture, but does not directly address the inherent dilemma in digitizing such content.

Formative Evaluation

Bainbridge, Cunningham, Downie, McPherson, & Reeves' Chapter XVIII is an excellent example of formative evaluation. The context is music information retrieval, a topic of wide interest yet one where relatively little is known about user behavior or usability. The paper draws upon multiple studies in three countries (New Zealand, United States, United Kingdom) performed by this multinational group of authors. The formative evaluation consists of baseline studies of music searching in multiple contexts, using multiple methods. They analyze the transaction logs of a music information retrieval system, perform a content analysis of music queries to determine the content and structure of queries, and they observe browsing behavior while shopping for music recordings in a store. By studying people searching by keyword, browsing, and humming, they began to build a model of music searching behavior that would form the basis for system design.

The research goal of Goh, Theng, & Lim in Chapter XVII is to construct a DL application to assist secondary school students (aged 13-14) in studying for "O" level exams in geography. The context is specific to the Singapore educational system. While similar to the education systems of the U.K. and those of other countries that remained British colonies into the 20th century, the educational context is much different than that of the U.S., for example (the education systems have diverged considerably in the two centuries since the U.S. was a British colony). The study is specific to the type of testing and the particular format of the O-level exams, although the randomized and categorized approach presumably could be applied to other topic areas in this series of exams. In this case, they observed a small sample of students intensively, followed by a focus group with all of the subjects. Results of this formative evaluation provided input to the design of a more sophisticated DL-based tutoring system for the exams.

Iterative Evaluation

The Bainbridge et al. study is also classified here as iterative evaluation because they have conducted a series of studies, albeit often on different systems in different countries, toward the common goal of understanding music information retrieval behavior and developing design models to support that behavior. Out of the series of formative studies came the design and development of MELDEX, which they have continued to evaluate. Each usability study provides input to the design of the system, which is continually improved. The authors report on their plans for further research and development.

Results from Goh, Theng, & Lim's research on how students study for exams led to the design of a tutoring system, which was then evaluated with student subjects to improve the design.

Summative Evaluation

Theng, Chan, Khoo & Buddharaju report on the *eLibraryHub* of the Singapore National Library Board in Chapter XIX. This DL offers a wide range of content to its four million potential users, who may act as individuals or as members of a corporate, professional or community group. Theng et al. describe two studies of the system, one quantitative, the other qualitative, which were conducted in 2003. The quantitative study used a questionnaire to evaluate the perceived value of the library and the effect on the intention of use. The qualitative study explored usability of the navigation structure and layout using a modified version of Carroll's Claims Analysis (2000). The data derived from the study lead to suggestions for refinement for *eLibraryHub,* so that although this is nominally a summative evaluation, it has elements of iterative evaluation as well.

Summary and Conclusion

DL research and development, which initially focused on issues related to technology, architecture, and standards, has matured to encompass a holistic approach to DLs and their users. Marchionini et al. (2003) state as a principle of DL design that "all efforts to design, implement, and evaluate DLs must be rooted in the information needs, characteristics, and contexts of the people who will or may use those libraries," while noting that "the devil is in the details." Many DLs are global and distributed, accessible to users around the world and far from their original context; many are culture-specific and/or contain culturally significant and sensitive materials. Designing DLs that can be used in specific cultures or across cultures is a difficult task. Fortunately perhaps, many of the issues of multicultural access and usability evaluation are common to other information systems, notably the World Wide Web, and research and methods from these environments are available to enrich DL design and development, as demonstrated in the papers in this section.

Recognizing that the problem exists is only a first step to solving it, and much research will be needed on the nature of users of DLs, their behavior as information seekers, and how their use and behavior is impacted by culture, before DLs can be built which are culture-appropriate and/or offer cross-cultural usability. The nature of culture and cultural heritage, the implications of digitizing representations of a culture, the impact of culture on user behavior, definitions of usability for multi-cultural environments, and methods to study it, are all important questions to address in advancing DL research and development.

References

Bainbridge, D., Cunningham, S.J., Downie, J.S., McPherson, J., & Reeves, N. (2004). Designing a music digital library: Discovering what people really want. In Y.L. Theng & S. Foo (Eds.), *Design and usability of digital libraries: Case studies in the Asia Pacific*. Hershey, PA: Idea Group Publishing.

Bishop, A.P., Van House, N., & Buttenfield, B.P. (eds.) (2003). *Digital library use: Social practice in design and evaluation*. Cambridge, MA: The MIT Press.

Borgman, C.L. (1996). Why are online catalogs still hard to use? *Journal of the American Society for Information Science, 47*(7), 493-503.

Borgman, C.L. (2000). *From Gutenberg to the global information infrastructure: Access to information in the networked world*. Cambridge, MA: The MIT Press.

Borgman, C.L. (2002). *Final report to the National Science Foundation. Fourth DELOS Workshop. Evaluation of digital libraries: Testbeds, measurements, and metrics*. Hungarian Academy of Sciences, Computer and Automation Research Institute (MTA SZTAKI), Budapest, Hungary, 6-7 June 2002. Grant IIS-0225626. Retrieved from the World Wide Web: *http://www.sztaki.hu/conferences/deval/presentations/ final_report.html*

Borgman, C.L. (2003). Uses, users, and usability of digital libraries. In A.P. Bishop, B.P. Buttenfield, & N. Van House (Eds.), *Digital library use: Social practice in design and evaluation* (pp. 85-118). Cambridge, MA: The MIT Press.

Borgman, C.L., & Larsen, R. (2003). ECDL 2003 workshop report: Digital library evaluation - Metrics, testbeds and processes. *D-Lib Magazine, 9*

(9). Retrieved from the World Wide Web: *http://www.dlib.org/dlib/ september03/09inbrief.html#BORGMAN*

Caidi, N., & Komlodi, A. (2003). Digital libraries across cultures: Design and usability issues. Outcomes of the "Cross-Cultural Usability for Digital Libraries" workshop at JCDL '03. *SIGIR Forum, 37*(2), 62-64.

Carroll, J.M. (2000). *Making use: Scenario-based design of human computer interaction.* Cambridge, MA: MIT Press.

Computer Science and Telecommunications Board. Commission on Physical Sciences, Mathematics, and Applications. National Research Council. (1997). *More than screen deep: Toward every-citizen interfaces to the nation's information infrastructure.* Washington, DC: National Academy Press.

Crane, G. (2003). *Culture and cyberinfrastructure: The need for a cultural informatics.* Paper presented at Wave of the Future: NSF Post Digital Library Futures Workshop. Chatham, MA, June 15-17, 2003. Retrieved from the World Wide Web: *http://www.sis.pitt.edu/~dlwkshop/ paper_crane.html*

Davies, C. (1997). Organizational influences on the university electronic library. *Information Processing & Management, 33*(3), 377-392.

Duncker, E. (2002). Cross-cultural usability of the library metaphor. In *JCDL '02: Proceedings of the Joint Conference on Digital Libraries* Portland, Oregon, July 13-17 (pp. 223-230). New York: ACM.

Duncker, E., Theng, Y.L., & Mohd-Nasir, N. (2000). Cultural usability in digital libraries. *Bulletin of the American Society for Information Science, 26*(4), 21-22.

Elliott, M., & Kling, R. (1997). Organizational usability of digital libraries: Case study of legal research in civil and criminal courts. *Journal of the American Society for Information Science, 48*(11), 1023-1035.

Goh, D.H.L., Theng, Y.L., & Lim, E.P. (2004). From GeogDL to PAPER: The evolution of an educational digital library. In Y.L. Theng & S. Foo (Eds.), *Design and usability of digital libraries: Case studies in the Asia Pacific.* Hershey, PA: Idea Group Publishing.

Institute of Electrical and Electronics Engineers. (1990). *IEEE standard computer dictionary: A compilation of IEEE standard computer glossaries.* New York: IEEE.

Kling, R., & Elliott, M. (1994). Digital library design for organizational usability. *SIGOIS Bulletin, 15*(2), 56-69.

Liew, C.L. (2004). Cross-cultural design and usability of a digital library supporting access to Mäori cultural heritage resources. In Y.L. Theng &

S. Foo (Eds.), *Design and usability of digital libraries: Case studies in the Asia Pacific*. Hershey, PA: Idea Group Publishing.

Lim, E.P., Foo, S., Khoo, C., Chen, H., Fox, E., Urs, S., & Costantino, T. (eds.) (2002). Digital libraries: People, knowledge, and technology. *Proceedings of the 5th International Conference on Asian Digital Libraries, ICADL 2002*. Lecture Notes in Computer Science 2555/2002. Singapore, December 11-14. Heidelberg: Springer-Verlag.

Main, L. (2002). *Building Websites for a multinational audience*. Lanham, MD: Scarecrow Press.

Marchionini, G. (1995). *Information seeking in electronic environments*. Cambridge, UK: Cambridge University Press.

Marchionini, G., Plaisant, C., & Komlodi, A. (2003). The people in digital libraries: Multifaceted approaches to assessing needs and impact. In A. Bishop, N. Van House, & B. Buttenfield (Eds.), *Digital library use: Social practice in design and evaluation*. Cambridge, MA: MIT Press.

Nielsen, J. (1993). *Usability engineering*. Boston: Academic Press.

Nielsen, J. (2000). *Designing Web usability*. Indianapolis, IN: New Riders Publishing.

Nielsen, J. (2003, August 25). Usability 101. *Jakob Nielsen's Alertbox*. Retrieved from the World Wide Web: *http://www.useit.com/alertbox/20030825.html*

Oard, D. (1997, December). Serving users in many languages: Cross-language retrieval for digital libraries. *D-Lib Magazine*. Retrieved from the World Wide Web: *http://www.dlib.org/dlib/december97/oard/12oard.html*

Quesenbery, W. (2001). What does usability mean: Looking beyond 'ease of use.' In *Proceedings of the 48th Annual Conference of the Society for Technical Communication*. Retrieved from the World Wide Web: *http://www.wqusability.com/articles/more-than-ease-of-use.html*

Shneiderman, B. (1998). *Designing the user interface: Strategies for effective human-computer interaction* (3rd ed). Reading, MA: Addison-Wesley.

Theng, Y.L, Chan, M.Y., Khoo, A.L., & Buddharaju, R. (2004). Quantitative and qualitative evaluations of the Singapore National Library Board's Digital Library. In Y.L. Theng & S. Foo (Eds.), *Design and usability of digital libraries: Case studies in the Asia Pacific*. Hershey, PA: Idea Group Publishing.

Thong, J.Y.L, Hong, W., & Tam, K.Y. (2002). Understanding user acceptance of digital libraries: What are the roles of interface characteristics, organizational context, and individual differences. *International Journal of Human-Computer Studies*, *57*, 215-242.

Zahedi, F.M., Van Pelt, W.V., & Song, J. (2001). A conceptual framework for international Web design. *IEEE Transactions on Professional Communication*, *44*(2), 83-103.

Endnotes

1   *http://europa.eu.int/celex/eurovoc/*

2   *http://trec.nist.gov/*

3   *http://clef.iei.pi.cnr.it/*

4   *http://www.sztaki.hu/conferences/deval/presentations.html*

Chapter XVI

Cross-Cultural Design and Usability of a Digital Library Supporting Access to Maori Cultural Heritage Resources

Chern Li Liew
Victoria University of Wellington, New Zealand

Abstract

Part of the worldwide appeal for digital libraries (DLs) lies in their potential to preserve cultural heritage resources, to expand access to indigenous resources, and to promote deeper understanding among user communities. As cultural heritage resources are being made into a shared worldwide collection of information resources, cross-cultural design and usability issues of DLs supporting access to such resources become critical concerns. This chapter looks specifically at issues concerning supporting access to Mâori heritage materials available in New Zealand through DL technologies. The chapter commences with an examination of the Mâori culture, the nature and forms of Mâori heritage resources and their specific requirements for representation, organisation and retrieval. It then proceeds to identify a set of critical research issues crucial to the success of such DLs. For these research issues, challenges are identified and potential strategies to meet these challenges are proposed.

Introduction

Part of the worldwide appeal for digital libraries (DLs) lies in their potential to open up new dimension of reaching traditional and new audiences by providing access to cultural heritage resources in ways undreamt of a decade ago, and to promote better understanding of indigenous knowledge. Over the last three decades, cultural heritage institutions including libraries, archives and museums have started to integrate technology in one way or another into various aspects of their mission and services. As cultural and heritage resources are being made into a shared worldwide collection of information resources, the implications of information representation and organisation, and usability practices for the conduct of scholarship and indigenous knowledge sharing will need to be explored and addressed appropriately.

Digital Libraries and Mâori Cultural Heritage Resources

This chapter looks specifically at issues concerning supporting access to Mâori indigenous resources through DL technologies. The chapter commences with an examination of the Mâori culture, the nature and forms of Mâori heritage resources and their specific requirements for representation, storage, organisation and retrieval in a DL environment. The chapter then proceeds to identify a set of critical research issues crucial to the success of a DL aimed at promoting worldwide access and for the appropriate use of Mâori cultural heritage resources.

Mâori Cultural Heritage Resources: Forms and Nature

In designing DLs of Mâori indigenous resources, it is important to consider the forms and nature of traditional Mâori heritage resources and to examine the digitisation needs of the material types involved. Traditional Mâori knowledge and skills have been transferred in the forms of waiata (songs), môteatea (folk songs), whakaahua (paintings), whakairo (carvings) and stories or legends (kôrero, pûrâkau). It makes an interesting case, therefore, to examine the transfer of these various forms of Mâori heritage materials to DLs, and to look into the use and usability of such resources in the electronic environment. While indigenous resources are being made available to international community, it is important to remember that DLs of such collections will be important to the Mâori community as well. Hence, the issue of Mâori culture as user context will need to be addressed.

Since the signing of the Treaty of Waitangi (Waitangi Tribunal, 2004) on February 6, 1840, Mâori culture has been greatly influenced by the settlement of tauiwi (immigrants), colonization and involvement in international conflicts. Against this backdrop, the need to preserve Mâori cultural and heritage resources in all forms becomes an urgent matter. Many institutions in New Zealand (NZ) find themselves in a position where they have to take note of developments relating to practices surrounding the rediscovery and preservation of the Mâori culture and to practices of making available previously largely inaccessible Mâori indigenous materials. There is a wealth of Mâori heritage materials in NZ, and DLs have been explored as a potential platform to support these practices. Collections of Mâori manuscripts, letters, early printed materials, such as the 1908 Southern Mâori electoral roll, as well as collections of pictures, photographs, maps, sound and oral history recordings are held in various institutions in the country. The sheer volume of these materials together with the firmness with which the Mâori communities are now asserting their rights in respect of their cultural resources (Diesch, 2003) make the case an important, timely and interesting study.

The Ranfurly Collection (NLNZ, 2003) is an example of a project taking advantage of digital technologies to make publicly available a major heritage collection of NZ. The Ranfurlys were enthusiastic chroniclers and the collection provides a unique record of the private lives of the family and their entourage The collection includes letters, diaries, scrapbooks, sketchbooks, paintings and photographs, and the collection forms a rich source of information about NZ and New Zealanders. The Niupepa Collection (NZDL, 2004; Apperly et al., 2001) is another heritage collection that has recently been made available. Niupepa is an electronic Mâori newspaper collection based on "Niupepa 1842 – 1933," a microfiche collection produced by Alexander Turnbull Library. This collection is now publicly available from NZDL, with full-text search and browse capability. It is the largest digital collection of heritage Mâori language documents to-date.

Mâori Culture and the Library Metaphor

Metaphors convey meaning in an unknown domain using terms of a familiar domain. Metaphors have recently become an integral part of the graphical user interface design (UID) process. While this has become common practice, it has also been a controversial subject. While Neale & Carroll (1997), for instance, argue that metaphors are inherent in designs; Norman (1998) disapproves of their use. Whether one disapproves of metaphors in UID or not, it is hardly controversial that metaphors and metaphorical thinking are deeply rooted in culture (Hudson, 2000; Mac Cormac, 1988). Significant conflicts are rooted in culturally different cognitive, behavioural, emotional and social processes and structures. Cultural differences in the comprehension of metaphors, hence, need to be addressed. An effective metaphor has to match the community's mental model of related objects and this principle applies to the design of a DL for Mâori indigenous resources.

Cross-cultural usability of the library metaphor seems at first, a straightforward case. Libraries are a widespread phenomenon and are, therefore, conformed to metaphorical use. It is important to note, however, that cultures that traditionally transfer knowledge mostly in an oral fashion often embed their knowledge in songs, stories, legends, artefacts and rituals, and knowledge is often handed down from person to person. Mâori are such a culture. Duncker (2002) has carried out a study examining why and when the DL metaphor does not fit well with the information needs of Mâori and other indigenous users. The study has pointed out that Mâori find DLs difficult to use because there is a lack of culturally specific representation and classification of Mâori concepts on the DLs. There is also a lack of knowledge on the users' side on how materials are organised and presented in existing DLs that are heavily based on Anglo-American culture. An earlier study has also pointed out that genealogies were core to the Mâori traditional knowledge - even today, Mâori trace their ancestors back to a particular passenger of one of the canoes with which they came to NZ and this knowledge is considered tapu (sacred) by many and, as such, should not be made publicly available (Hakiwai, 1996). As such, the Mâori communities are particularly sensitive about the repositories that hold their knowledge and to whom the knowledge is transmitted. According to the Repositories of Rôpû Tku Iho (Whatarangi Winiata, 2002), among the whânau (family, extended family), hapû (sub-tribe) and iwi (tribes) are people trained to be repositories of their knowledge, and Mâori records in libraries and public domains have created ambiguous response. On the one side, part of the Mâori community is glad that these materials have been gathered and preserved. Some, however, feel strongly that these resources should be protected from the public. This conflict translates to an important issue that needs to be addressed in the design of a DL for Mâori cultural heritage materials. A DL that acts as a repository for Mâori indigenous resources has to fulfil — amongst other functions — storing the resources with integrity beyond doubt and applying appropriate judgement in the description and representation, rights management, use and dissemination of the indigenous resources and knowledge. Some forms of ethnographical study will be required to look at Mâori cultural resources and their forms of knowledge transfer. This knowledge can contribute to the successful design and usability of the DL, and to acceptable use of the indigenous resources.

Future Trends and a Research Agenda

User Requirements

The design of DLs should be informed by knowledge of user requirements (Bates, 1996). One needs to know the potential users, for what purposes they wish to use the resources and how they wish to use the resources — for instance, what kinds of search criteria or access points would prove useful to them and what specific subject descriptors they would need? Specific data on the use of materials by different user groups and communities will need to be collected and analysed. The design of DLs will need to take into consideration the needs and requirements of all user communities – including the different cultural representative groups amongst the Mâori community and non-Mâori community in NZ, the international audience, and users who use these materials for specific purposes. Different groups of users may approach a DL with different needs. Historians, anthropologists, sociologists, genealogists and map researchers are likely, for instance, to have very high domain knowledge and their search for heritage resources may involve very specific concepts. These users would likely require advanced search capabilities that would help them zoom into the target information quickly. On the other hand, there may be teachers and students, documentary producers, and users from different cultures who are simply curious about the Mâori and may like to use the DL. These users are likely to have only medium or low domain knowledge and they may not be certain or confident of what concepts or search terms to use while searching the DL. Hence, more browsing support and capability to search in Mâori and English or other languages may be essential for these users. It is, therefore, important to study what Mâori indigenous resources would be required by the different user and potential user groups, how exactly they will seek the information, and on what basis they are likely to make relevance judgements. A better understanding of these issues will help the DL to more effectively meet the needs of its end-users.

Knowledge Representation and Organization Requirements

Classification of Mâori Resources

Classification of Mâori resources with Anglo-American classification system, such as Dewey Decimal Classification (DDC) and Library of Congress Subject Headings (LCSH), has long been deemed inappropriate. Anglo-American classification systems have been criticized for making Mâori resources and contents inaccessible (Sudweeks & Ess, 2000). Mâori knowledge, when divided into subject areas based upon an Anglo-American system, becomes scattered across the libraries in a seemingly random manner. Terms and concepts belonging together are separated and undergo an artificial discussion and end up in different subject fields, to the point that sometimes terms and concepts become barely recognizable to its native speakers. The Anglo-American systems are not capable of, for instance, accommodating inter-related Mâori concepts such as whànau, hapû and iwi. Tribal groupings are fundamental to the identification and relationship of Mâori to their ancestors. Consistency in representation and classification of Mâori concepts is, hence, important if it is to reflect understanding. This issue has long been debated and discussed in NZ (Salmond, 1991) and in October 1998, LIANZA (Library and Information Association of New Zealand Aotearoa) and Te Ropu Whakahau (TRW – Mâori Library and Information Workers Association) formed a Mâori Subject Headings Working Party (MSHWP). The working party came up with formats and conventions regarding the production of Mâori subject headings (MSH) (MSHWP, 2001). The project has become a national concern, and is currently in its Phase 3 that includes the establishment of the core MSH list and the Mâori Name Authority File (MNAF) as cataloguing tools (LIANZA, 2004). The MSH list, which is a list of subject headings in the Mâori language that follows the conventions of LCSH is yet to be completed and released, but it is anticipated that these subject headings would better meet the requirements of Mâori resources, and subsequently better support the access and use of these resources.

Before a document or an artefact can be classified, an analysis of the overall structure of the document may also be necessary. A document segmentation and analysis process will be needed to analyse the overall structure of the document or artefact, segment it into appropriate sections and perhaps, identify and remove unnecessary elements. Document analysis tools unfortunately, are generally not available for documents in rare indigenous languages such as the Mâori language. The lack of tools specifically targeted at these types of documents is not likely to change in the near future because of the limited market for them.

There are, nevertheless, several academic projects that explore the connection between cultural heritage materials and technology. The Digital Atheneum Project (2003), for instance, focuses on the development of algorithms and techniques to allow humanists to restore severely damaged manuscripts, to search manuscripts as images, and to present electronic editions for a widely distributed DL of restored, edited, and previously inaccessible manuscripts. There are also projects that examine cursive and semi-cursive optical character recognition (OCR) technology for recognition and indexing of handwritten documents (Vinciarelli, 2002; Manmatha et al., 1996). Though with somewhat different *foci*, the Gamera (Droettboom et al., 2002) is an open-source system developed as part of an international, multidisciplinary project to build a data capture framework and test bed for cultural heritage materials. The system is currently being explored to develop applications for the recognition of documents in a number of diverse collections, including manuscripts, handwritten text, paintings and diagrams. Mâori and other indigenous resources could benefit from these technologies.

A related issue is designing the DL user interface to assist end-users with formulating a good query. Several tools for query elicitation could be explored. One could display for instance, a query frame with certain categories of criteria (concrete subjects or concepts, abstract themes) to assist the user in thinking through all aspects of a query. Descriptor-based searching could be another option, supporting user query by mapping free-text entry vocabulary and bilingual vocabularies to suggest thesaurus term, using cataloguing data for training and providing a browseable thesaurus hierarchy to be used by itself, or after descriptor candidates are identified through the earlier mapping stage. The DL interfaces need to include tools that do not require users to have the knowledge of the internal organisation of documents. One approach to achieve this is by providing search and browsing tools that process local Mâori natural language or phrase, such as the phrase browser of the NZDL (Paynter et al., 2000), which enables users to zoom into a selection of documents that contain a particular phrase without requiring any knowledge on how these documents are organised. The interface would also need to be usable by non-Mâori users. Culturally adaptable intelligent agents (Guye-Vuillème & Thalmann, 2001) for some form of semantic mappings might be another venue of improvement in this area.

Metadata Standards

In 2000, NLNZ in conjunction with its Millennium Project in providing an archival collection of drawings, photographs, illustrated reports, letters and manuscripts, developed a metadata standard (NLNZ, 2000). This particular experience has shown that the provision of optimum resource discovery in a DL environment must be considered at organizational, community and global levels, and tools and techniques, standards and metadata framework for the management and preservation of digital Mâori cultural heritage resources must reflect the cultural needs of the Mâori community and the various forms of Mâori heritage materials. One particular area that needs careful consideration is the use of metadata to govern rights management. Sullivan (2002) examined some of the ways in which Mâori are now placing cultural information in the digital environment, and discussed the issues in indigenous cultural and intellectual property management. Mâori cultural protocols need to be documented and followed prior to the creation of digital content, and the relevant communities must be consulted with regard to the digitisation of content including those already gathered by institutions of social memory. Digitizing material that has its origins with indigenous cultures such as Mâori has implications beyond strict intellectual property law. According to Sullivan (2002), a cornerstone of an indigenous DL is that the control of rights management of cultural intellectual property remains with the appropriate indigenous communities themselves. Seadle (2002) suggested three factors that could affect how one deals with intellectual property issues across a wide range of indigenous and Western cultures – *law* (includes both the copyright law of the country in which the results will be published, and the ethics of the researcher's profession), *technology* (includes the kind of technology used to capture information, as well as the technology to publish it) and *permission* (includes both the explicit permission of the informants and any unspoken rules that might limit how the information is used).

International Usability

Classic literature on usability (Dray, 1996; Nielsen, 1996) generally neglects to detail the appropriateness and success of usability assessment techniques, which are predominantly originated in Anglo-American culture, when used in a different cultural context. It is generally assumed that such techniques can be applied successfully in any target communities of users. This assumption has been proven incorrect in some instances. Herman (1996), for instance, found that subjects from the Far East nations positively evaluated a product that later led to poor performance, and noted that it was culturally unacceptable for the subjects to criticize too openly or directly. The same could be referred to the Mâori communities. Special care must, therefore, be taken when testing usability in Mâori communities. Herman (1996) suggested that objective tests be conducted to augment subjective evaluations. Local authorities such as ERMA New Zealand could also be consulted in dealing with Mâori issues. ERMA has a range of resources that provides guidelines for working with Mâori and for dealing with specific Mâori issues (ERMA New Zealand, 2004). Such local experts can assist, for instance, in devising tests to ensure that they are designed with the target culture in mind.

Practice and Policies

Practices, policies and attitudes in respect of the information and resources of indigenous community have attracted much attention in recent years and research that looks into how cultural resources should be stored, presented and used are emerging (CHIN, 2002; NINCH, 2002). It is generally thought that there have been serious shortcomings in how heritage resources have been collected from one culture group in the past. Makoare (1999) has raised the issues of how such resources have been misrepresented and inappropriately used by another, and that general assumptions about the ownership, collection and use of such resources are mainly based on the culture of the collector and not the creator or donor. Ngaa Rauru and Ngati Toa, for instance, are listed in LCSH as iwi, which are in fact, regarded as hapû rather than iwi. Such misrepresentation could lead to clashes of issues concerning the collection and guardianship of Mâori heritage resources. Hence, it is critical for policies and practices of a DL to be based on the cultural norms and perspectives of the Mâori communities concerned. Cultural resources in all forms, which in one way or another have a crucial part in the identification of the Mâori communities in NZ, must be treated thoughtfully, whether it is a physical artefact or a body of knowledge. In this context, a number of questions need to be considered:

- From which particular Mâori culture group does it originate? Who are the key representatives that need to be consulted regarding the collection, care and use of these resources?

- What are the expectations of the Mâori communities? What are the expectations of the associated institutions in terms of professional standards and practices?

- What is the best means of implementation, and who are the appropriate persons to be involved in facilitating the DL project?

A potential strategy is to set up a working process building on consultation and communication between different groups of stakeholders to assist the incorporation of appropriate Mâori perspectives into custodial practice and service delivery decisions. It can be employed to ensure that institutional practices and various parties remain abreast of political and cultural differences in the environment of information and property rights, and to help resolve intellectual and cultural property issues.

Conclusion

Access to cultural heritage resources depends upon services "to unlock cultural resources by offering personalised, highly interactive, stimulating, hybrid environments and shared spaces" (DigiCULT Report, 2002). This chapter has identified and discussed a set of critical research issues that need to be addressed appropriately when designing a DL to provide access to Mâori cultural heritage resources. Such a DL needs to provide a platform for the indigenous information and knowledge to be appropriately represented, organised, linked, packaged, retrieved and personalised to meet the needs of various user communities. The effectiveness of the DL in meeting the needs of its end-users must also be continually evaluated, and the evaluation and usability techniques and tools must be appropriate to the context of use. Potential strategies to meet the challenges identified and outlined have also been proposed in the chapter.

Acknowledgments

Special thanks to reviewers, especially Sally Jo Cunningham from the University of Waikato (NZ), for their feedback in making the paper more situated in the work carried out on the Mâori DL and cultural heritage resources.

References

Apperley, M., Cunningham, S.J., Keegan, Te Taka, & Witten, I.H. (2001). Niupepa: An historical newspaper collection. *Communications of the ACM, 44* (5), 86-87.

Bates, M.J. (1996, November). The Getty end-user online searching project in the humanities. Report No.6: Overview and conclusions. *College and Research Libraries, 57,* 514-523.

CHIN (Canadian Heritage Information Network). (2002). *Digital content development and heritage resources.* Retrieved March 16, 2004, from the World Wide Web: *http://www.chin.gc.ca/English/index.html*

Diesch, F. (2003, December). Protection of Mâori intellectual and cultural property. *Library Life, 285,* 16.

DigiCULT Report. (2002). *Technological landscapes for tomorrow's cultural economy: Unlocking the value of the cultural heritage.* Luxemborg: Office of the Official Publications of the European Communities.

Digital Atheneum Project. (2003). Retrieved February 12, 2004, from the World Wide Web: *http://www.digitalatheneum.org/*

Dray, S. (1996). Designing for the rest of the world: A consultant's observations. *Interactions, 3* (2), 15-18.

Droettboom, M., Fujinaga, I., MacMillan, K., Chouhury, G.S., DiLauro, T., Patton, M., & Anderson, T. (2002). Using the Gamera framework for the recognition of cultural heritage materials. In *Proceedings of 2nd ACM/ IEEE-CS Joint Conference on Digital Libraries* (pp. 11-17).

Duncker, E. (2002). Cross-cultural usability of the library metaphor. In *Proceedings of 2nd ACM/IEEE-CS Joint Conference on Digital Libraries* (pp. 223-230).

ERMA New Zealand. (2004). *Mâori Issues Resources.* Retrieved March 16, 2004, from the World Wide Web: *http://www.ermanz.govt.nz/resources/ maori-pubs.asp*

Guye-Vuillème, A., & Thalmann, D. (2001). A high-level architecture for believable social agents. *VR Journal, 5,* 95-106.

Hakiwai, A. T. (1996). Mâori society today: Welcome to our world. In J. Davidson, A.T. Hakiwai, R. Jahnke, et al. (Eds.), *Mâori art and culture* (pp. 50-68). London: British Museum Press.

Herman, L. (1996). Towards effective usability evaluation in Asia. In J. Grundy & M. Apperly (eds.), *Proceedings of OZCHI 96* (pp. 135-136).

Hudson, W. (2000). Metaphor: A double-edged sword. *ACM Interactions, 7* (3), 11-15.

LIANZA. (2003). *LIANZA Bicultural Plan.* Retrieved October 16, 2003, from the World Wide Web: *http://www.lianza.org.nz/profile/bi- cultural_plan.shtml*

LIANZA. (2004). *Mâori Subject Headings Working Party Phase 3 Project Plan.* Retrieved March 16, 2004, from the World Wide Web: *http:// www.lianza.org.nz/mshwp/mshw_projplan.shtml*

Mac Cormac, E. (1988). *A cognitive theory of metaphor.* Cambridge, MA: The MIT Press.

Makoare, B. (1999, October). Katiakitanga I roto I nga whare pukapuka: Appropriate care for Mâori materials in libraries and archives. *Archifacts*, 18-26.

Manmatha, R., Han, C., Riseman, E.M., & Croft, W.B. (1996). Indexing handwriting using word matching. In *Proceedings of the First ACM International Conference on Digital Libraries* (pp. 151-159).

MSHWP (Mâori Subject Headings Working Party). (2001, August). *Report to LIANZA/Te Rau Herenga O Aotearoa and to Te Ropu Whakanau Phase 2.* Unpublished manuscript.

Neale, D.C., & Carroll, J.M. (1997). The role of metaphors in user interface design. In M.G. Helander, T.K. Landauer, & P. Prabhu (Eds.), *Handbook of Human-Computer Interaction* (2nd ed.). Amsterdam: Elsevier Science.

Nielsen, J. (1996). International usability engineering. In E. Del Galdo & J. Nielsen (eds.), *International User Interfaces*. New York: John Wiley & Sons.

NINCH (National Initiative for a Networked Cultural Heritage). (2002). *The NINCH Guide to Good Practice in the Digital Representation and Management of Cultural Heritage Materials.* Retrieved March 16, 2004, from the World Wide Web: *http://www.nyu.edu/its/humanities/ninchguide/*

NLNZ (National Library of New Zealand). (2003). *Ranfurly Collection.* Retrieved from October 16, 2003, from the World Wide Web: *http://ranfurly.natlib.govt.nz/about.htm*

NLNZ (National Library of New Zealand). (2000). *Metadata standards framework for NLNZ.* Retrieved October 16, 2003, from the World Wide Web: *http://www.natlib.govt.nz/mi/whatsnew/framework.pdf*

Norman, D. (1998). *The invisible computer.* Cambridge, MA: MIT Press.

NZDL (New Zealand DL). (2004). *Niupepa: Mâori Newspapers.* Retrieved March 16, 2004, from the World Wide Web: *http://www.nzdl.org/niupepa*

Paynter, G.W., Witten, I.H., Cunningham, S.J., & Buchanan, G. (2000). Scalable browsing for large collections: A case study. In *Proceedings of ACM Conference on Digital Libraries* (pp. 215-223).

Salmond, A. (1991). *Two Worlds: First meetings between Mâori and Europeans 1642-1772.* Auckland: Viking.

Seadle, M. (2002). Whose rules? Intellectual property, culture, and indigenous communities, *D-Lib Magazine, 8* (3). Retrieved March 16, 2004, from the World Wide Web: *http://www.dlib.org/dlib/march02/seadle/03seadle.html*

Sudweeks, F., & Ess, C. (eds.). (2002). Cultural attitudes towards technology and communication. In *Proceedings of 2nd International Conference on Cultural Attitudes towards Technology and Communication.*

Sullivan, R. (2002). Indigenous cultural and intellectual property rights: A digital library context. *D-Lib Magazine, 8* (5). Retrieved March 15, 2004, from the World Wide Web: *http://www.dlib.org/dlib/may02/sullivan/05sullivan.html*

Vinciarelli, A. (2002). A survey on off-line cursive script recognition. *Pattern Recognition, 35* (7), 1433-1446.

Waitangi Tribunal. (2004). *Introduction to the Treaty of Waitangi.* Retrieved October 16, 2004, from the World Wide Web: *http://www.waitangi-tribunal.govt.nz/about/treatyofwaitangi/*

Whatarangi Winiata. (2002). Repositories of Röpü Tku Iho: A contribution to the survival of Mâori as a people. In *LIANZA Annual Conference* November 17-20, 2002. Retrieved October 16, 2003, from the World Wide Web: *http://www.confer.co.nz/lianza2002/PDFs/What arangi%20Winiata.pdf*

298 Goh, Theng & Lim

From GeogDL
to PAPER:
The Evolution of an
Educational Digital Library

Dion Hoe-Lian Goh
Nanyang Technological University, Singapore

Yin-Leng Theng
Nanyang Technological University, Singapore

Ee-Peng Lim
Nanyang Technological University, Singapore

Abstract

*This chapter traces the evolution of GeogDL, a digital library of geography
examination resources. The initial version of the system was evaluated with
a group of secondary school student design partners through the use of
scenario-based design and claims analysis to identify areas of refinement.
The findings from this study led to the development of a second-generation
system with a redesigned user interface and a new module named PAPER
(Personalized Adaptive Pathways for Examination Resources) that provides
mock exams and personalized recommendations of examination questions.
A second study involving teacher design partners generated positive
feedback that generally concurred with the goals and features of PAPER.
Implications for the future development of GeogDL are also discussed in
the context of these studies.*

Copyright © 2005, Idea Group Inc. Copying or distributing in print or electronic forms without written
permission of Idea Group Inc. is prohibited.

Introduction

Students in Singapore undergo four or five years of secondary-level education after which they take the Singapore-Cambridge General Certificate of Education "Ordinary" (GCE "O") Level examination. This is an annual national examination covering a variety of subjects such as mathematics, the sciences, and humanities, among others. Students are then admitted to various higher-level educational institutions, such as junior colleges and polytechnics, depending on the results obtained.

The learning of geography at the secondary-level is predominantly textbook-based supplemented with resources such as Web sites, CD-ROMs, and physical models. In addition, a popular approach to examination revision involves students working on past-year GCE "O" level geography examination questions and perusing their solutions. With these, students are able to see examples of the types of questions typically covered in the geography examination, look at possible solutions, judge the relative importance of certain topics, and even spot "trends" in the types of questions asked.

Though pedagogically debatable, past-year examination solutions when properly used with existing teaching materials can be a useful educational resource. For example, teachers could first author acceptable solutions and supplement them with related topics for students to explore. The GeogDL project (Chua, Goh, Lim, Liu, & Ang, 2002) adopts this approach to geography education through a Web-based digital library application containing past-year examination questions and solutions supplemented with additional geographical content.

This chapter describes GeogDL, its usage, architecture and evolution through two studies involving system developers, design partners and usability-trained evaluators. The chapter concludes with findings and implications for education-oriented digital libraries.

GeogDL: Initial Design

The first version of GeogDL was built above G-Portal (Lim et al., 2002), a digital library providing services over geospatial Web content. Past-year examination questions are created as separate G-Portal projects. Each project consists of Web resources such as solutions and related supplementary material for further exploration. Resources may be further organized into layers depending on the needs of the teacher.

Figure 1 shows the sequence of steps for accessing examination questions in GeogDL. The user first selects a question using GeogDL's classification interface, causing the system to display metadata associated with it on the Resource Information Window. This includes information such as year in which the question appears, type of question, and its URL. The user then selects the URL and the question appears in a separate Web browser window. Viewing the solution and supplementary resources follow a similar process.

While GeogDL shares similar objectives with existing education-oriented geography digital libraries, its design philosophy differs due to the importance of examinations in the Singapore education system. For example, the Alexandria Digital Earth Prototype System (Smith, Janee, Frew, & Coleman, 2001) provides students with "learning spaces" (Coleman, Smith, Buchel, & Mayer, 2001), personalized collections of geospatial resources relevant to one or more concepts. Through the process of exploring, manipulating and interacting with the resources in these learning spaces, students' scientific reasoning skills in geography may be cultivated. In contrast, GeogDL adopts a "bottom-up" approach in which students are first assisted with examination preparation. As students explore examination questions and solutions, GeogDL provides related higher-level concepts for them to investigate, allowing them to draw associations

Figure 1. Viewing an examination question

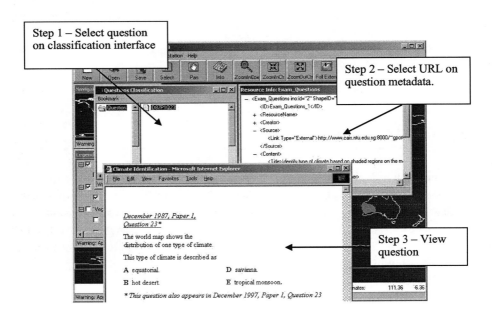

between various geographical issues and developing their reasoning skills. GeogDL is thus unique in that it not only provides an environment for active learning (Lebow, 1993); it also adopts a pragmatic approach that recognizes the importance and usefulness of examinations especially in the Singapore education system

The Initial Study

Having completed the first phase of development, a study was conducted to engage a group of intergenerational partners involving secondary school students and usability-trained evaluators for the purposes of reinforcing and refining the initial design of GeogDL. The study was inspired by Carroll's (2000) work on the task-artifact cycle, user-centered strategies such as scenario-based design and claims analysis.

Participants

Participants (four boys and four girls) came from a local secondary school in Singapore and they formed a representative sample of prospective users. The boys were between 13 to 14 years old, and were generally more confident Web users compared to the girls. They rated themselves as novice to intermediate in terms of library searching/browsing skills. The girls rated themselves as novice or intermediate users of the Web. Similar to the boys, library searching/browsing skills were not good, ranging from novice to intermediate.

Objectives of the Study

Four usability-trained evaluators were involved in the study. Two of the evaluators were Masters of Information Studies graduates while the other two were lecturers. All had a working knowledge of scenario-based design and claims analysis.

The following sub-goals were brainstormed with the student participants, system designers and evaluators to provide the possible scenarios of use. These were in accordance with established success factors for implementing interactive learning environments [see, for example, Ellington, Percival & Race (1995), Lennon (1997), and Boyle (1997)]:

- *Goal #1: Practice/revision on multiple-choice and essay-type questions*. Model answers and hints to answer these questions should be provided.

- *Goal #2: Trends analysis*. Provide information on when and what questions are being asked over the years. This would help students identify trends in the types of questions asked and the topics covered, increasing their motivation to want to learn.

- *Goal #3: Mock exam*. This helps students better manage their time in answering questions. To make it fun, a scoring system could be incorporated for multiple-choice questions, while hints/model answers could be provided for essay questions.

- *Goal #4: Related links and resources*. This could include related topics, teachers' recommendations, and etcetera, thus showing relationships between concepts and linking concepts to the real world.

At the time of the study, only Goals #1 and #2 were implemented. Therefore, GeogDL was only examined in terms of these goals.

Experimental Protocol

Sessions with the student participants involved each student being assigned to an evaluator. They were asked to carry out claims analysis on either Goals #1 or #2. Each session lasted approximately two hours and was divided into three parts. Part 1 began with getting to know the students in terms of their experience with Web-based interfaces, searching skills and study habits. The session ended with a discussion on the possible scenarios of use for students preparing for the GCE "O" Level geography examination. The students performed iterative walkthroughs of the system together with the respective evaluators in Part 2 of the session. This was done by questioning stages of actions in Norman's (1988) execution-evaluation model of task completion. They were asked to identify the positive outcomes as well as negative consequences of the features provided in GeogDL in supporting either Goals #1 or #2. In Part 3, the students together with the evaluators congregated for a focus group discussion. The purpose was to confirm and/or refine the four goals identified by the evaluators described earlier, and brainstorm other goals, if any, that students might have when preparing for the geography examination.

Findings and Analyses

We made the following assumptions: students' comments with positive consequences suggest compliance with the design heuristics while comments with negative consequences indicate violation of design heuristics. By categorizing all eight students' comments in this manner, a list of claims with positive and negative outcomes in relation to design heuristics was derived (Theng et al., 2002). We then identified areas for refinement grouped according to violations detected in established design heuristics (Newman & Lamming, 1995; Preece et al., 1994). Some of these were:

1. *Match between system and real world.* Make information appear in a natural and logical order. Instead of a map-based interface only, a list of questions, possibly organized by topics, could be created also as a point of access to GeogDL.

2. *Consistency and standards.* Users should not have to wonder whether different words, situations, or actions mean the same thing. GeogDL should be designed using the standards of the Web (Nielsen, 1999) – as it is perceived by users as a Web-based system.

3. *Recognition rather than recall.* Instructions for use of the system should be visible or easily retrievable whenever appropriate. This is important because students were unable to identify with the newness of the geospatial-like interface in GeogDL.

4. *Minimalist design.* Dialogs should not contain information that is irrelevant or rarely needed. GeogDL could be improved by integrating certain functions together in one window instead of displaying multiple overlapping windows.

5. *Help and documentation.* These should be easy to search, focused on the user's task, and list concrete steps to be carried out. A "help mascot", suggested by the students, could monitor and guide users' actions.

PAPER: A Second Generation Design

In response to the first study, GeogDL's interface was redesigned to sport a familiar look-and-feel closer to desktop applications as highlighted by the student designer partners. Criteria for selection of features to incorporate into the next iteration of GeogDL were based on Nielsen's (n.d.) severity ratings. Specifically, all design violations were ranked according to their level of severity and priority was given to those problems that our design partners felt were most critical. At the same time, features for Goals #3 and #4, not ready at the time of the initial study (see above), were also implemented. The result was a new assessment and coaching module named PAPER – Personalized Adaptive Pathways for Examination Resources. PAPER is built using the generic services of GeogDL and draws content from GeogDL's repository of examination questions and solutions. PAPER consists of two major components: mock exam and personal coach.

Mock Exam

The mock exam provides a timed and scored test that reflects the structure and content of the actual geography examination. *Figure 2* shows the mock exam interface for multiple-choice questions. It has a deliberate minimalist design to focus users on the content. Upon reading a question, users select an answer and proceed to the next question. Upon completion of the mock exam, PAPER grades it and displays a performance report which contains a summary of the results and includes the total score and total time taken to complete the exam. Performance data for individual questions are also provided. This includes the correct answer, time taken, question topic and difficulty level. Students and teachers may use the performance report to gauge mastery of geography concepts as well as areas for further improvement. Students may also review the solutions and explore supplementary resources from the report's interface.

The content of a mock exam is defined by a *mock exam paper* – a virtual collection of examination questions. The paper is virtual because questions are not predefined. Instead, a teacher indicates the characteristics of questions that should appear including question type, topic area, number of questions and level of difficulty. When a mock exam session is initiated, PAPER selects questions using the characteristics set in the paper. Students are thus presented with a unique exam each time a session is run, allowing them to attempt a wider variety of questions. Authors may also create static mock exam papers so that each session results in the same set of questions.

Personal Coach

Upon completion of one or more mock exams, students may wish to attempt more questions for further practice. With print, teachers would typically help students identify such questions – a time-consuming, manual task. PAPER assists in this process through the personal coach, which analyzes a student's performance in previous mock exams and then recommends questions pitched at appropriate levels of difficulty. Questions are thus tailored to individual abilities. Although the

Figure 2. PAPER's mock exam interface

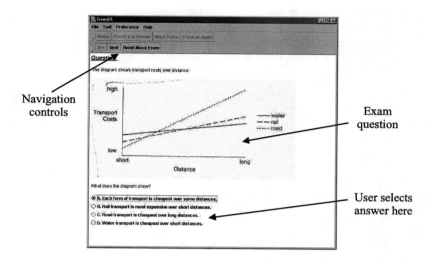

Navigation controls

Exam question

User selects answer here

personal coach and the mock exam are intertwined, students access them separately depending on their learning needs.

The personal coach's interface consists of two major sections as shown in *Figure 3*. The left panel provides a list of recommended questions organized into topics as described in the geography syllabus (Ministry of Education, 1998). The panel on the right presents a question selected by the user and also allows users to attempt it. The solution may also be viewed and users may explore any related supplementary resources found there.

Questions are recommended based on a user's past performance in the mock exams. Specifically, each question in a mock exam is associated with one or more topics in the geography syllabus. A competency level is calculated for each topic based on a user's performance for that topic in previous mock exam sessions. This is a weighted score involving the most recent mock exam and a cumulative score from previous sessions.

Using this approach, the personal coach adapts to the student as he or she interacts with PAPER. For example, if a student consistently answers questions correctly in a topic such as "agricultural systems," the personal coach will recommend questions with a higher level of difficulty. Conversely, if a student performs poorly in a topic such as "elements of weather and climate," easier questions will be recommended. Recommendations may change each time a mock exam is completed, and is dependent on the student's topic scores. Difficulty levels range from 1 (easiest) to 5 (most difficult) and are stored in each

Figure 3. The personal coach

Recommended questions   Question selected from the
classified by topics   recommended list

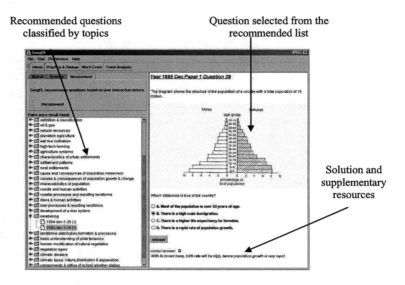

Solution and
supplementary
resources

question's metadata. These are assigned by geography teachers to ensure validity. We term this approach *personalized adaptive pathways*, to refer to the ability of the personal coach to adapt to the changing needs of students by recommending learning paths in the form of examination questions, solutions and supplementary resources. It is hoped that this approach will better cater to the learning needs of individuals by providing challenging questions for familiar areas in geography while asking easier, confidence-boosting questions for more problematic areas.

PAPER's Architecture

The major components of PAPER are shown in *Figure 4*. Note that other GeogDL components are not shown for clarity. A detailed discussion of the technical aspects of the system is beyond the scope of this chapter, and more information can be found in Lim et al. (2002) and Melati, Ming, Theng, Goh & Lim (2003).

The collection of the digital library is maintained in the question database and contains examination resources (questions, solutions, supplementary content and mock exam papers) as well as their associated metadata.

The mock exam module extracts questions from the question database given a mock exam paper, and displays them to the user. Upon completion of a paper, the module grades it, generates the performance report and updates the user's profile through the profile manager. All profiles are maintained in the user profile database, which keeps track of users' competencies in the various geography topics.

When the user requests the personal coach to recommend suitable questions for further practice, the question recommender will be invoked. This component retrieves the user's profile from the user profile database, determines the competency level of each geography topic and then consults the recommendation database for a list of questions matching each competency level. The question recommender then extracts the questions from the question database and delivers it to the personal coach for formatting and presentation.

Figure 4. Architectural diagram of PAPER

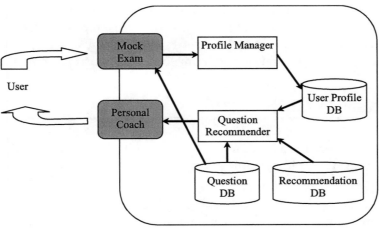

Second Study: Evaluation of PAPER

PAPER was developed using the participatory design (PD) methodology (Druin et al., 1999). In contrast with the first study employing student design partners, the second study used teacher design partners to carry out PD to further refine PAPER.

Participants

Two design partners (P1 and P2) in the education field were recruited. P1 is a secondary school geography teacher with over 30 years of experience teaching the subject. P2 is a school psychologist involved in teacher training. Both are well versed in pedagogical theories and methods, and familiar with Singapore's education system.

Protocol

A facilitator involved in the initial study worked with each design partner in separate sessions to elicit opinions on PAPER. Each session lasted approximately 1.5 hours and was divided into four parts. Part 1 was a familiarization segment that provided an overview of PAPER's features. In Part 2, a guided tour of the mock exam was given and opinions elicited on four areas: (1) positive aspects of the mock exam; (2) areas of improvement; (3) usefulness in helping students learn and prepare for the geography exam; and (4) usefulness in helping teachers meet their educational objectives. Part 3 was a repeat of Part 2 except that the focus was on the personal coach. Finally, Part 4 was an open-ended interview used to identify, refine and brainstorm ideas for improving PAPER.

Mock Exam Findings

Design partners were introduced to the three major tasks afforded by the mock exam: selecting static and dynamic papers; attempting questions; and viewing mock exam reports.

Responses to the mock exam were generally positive. P1 liked the dynamic paper concept since it lessened the work required for creating new exam papers. P2 also liked the fact that students explore supplementary resources after the exam, as this would help reinforce concepts learnt, or elucidate areas of weakness. Both P1 and P2 also felt that the mock exam report was useful for identifying strengths and areas for further revision.

In terms of usefulness, P1 thought that PAPER would be a good alternative to print versions of past-year exam questions. For example, after completion of a lesson, teachers could ask students to attempt related questions to assess mastery of the topic. Further, being Web-based, students could access the system both at school and at home. P2 also felt that the mock exam would also be a useful tool for teachers in that "differentiated teaching" can occur, catering to individual differences and abilities. Through the dynamic paper, a teacher could create exams with varying levels of difficulty, and then instruct students to attempt a particular exam given his/her ability level.

However, P2 felt that there should be greater use of color and multimedia to take advantage of the digital medium, and differentiate the system from print. The use of such elements would not only help the learning process (for example, animation depicting ox-bow lake formation) but also maintain the interest level of students. P1 also pointed out that content was an integral part of the system and its acceptance by students and teachers would depend very much on the quality of the solutions and supplementary resources.

Personal Coach Findings

While PAPER's mock exam was relatively straightforward to describe since it had a print counterpart, the personal coach required more explanation as there was no physical parallel. For example, an overview of the recommendation algorithms used was provided to assure the design partners that the questions were not haphazardly selected.

Both design partners felt that the personal coach had good potential to facilitate exam preparation. They liked the fact students would be provided with questions that met their ability levels. Both P1 and P2 agreed that this would be something that teachers would not have time to do in a typical classroom with large numbers of students, each requiring individual attention. Further, P1 felt that students would benefit from the personal coach because they will be able to determine whether they have grasped the presented concepts, and will be able to find a level of question difficulty they are comfortable with. P2 added that this would be motivating factor since weaker students will not be discouraged and better performing students will be challenged by the more difficult questions.

Both design partners agreed that the personal coach would be useful from the teacher's point of view as well. Specifically, P1 felt that since students can be left on their own with PAPER, teachers would have more time to devote to individual students who are academically weaker or simply have trouble with certain topics or questions. P2 concurred and noted that since the personal coach (and the mock exam) runs without the need for intervention by teachers, there will be less resistance to adopting PAPER in the classroom.

P2 argued that one weakness of the personal coach is that it lacks comprehensiveness in terms of question coverage. In the long run, students cannot focus only on recommended questions but need to attempt as many questions as possible since the actual examination contains both easy and difficult questions. P2 also felt that the personal coach should be extended to become a recommender system for teachers by providing them with an average difficulty level for each topic. This serves as an overall performance indicator for the class, hence allowing teachers to pitch lessons or exams at an appropriate level.

Conclusion

Given the feedback from both studies involving students and teachers as design partners, several lessons were learnt that will be used to guide future development of GeogDL:

1. *The importance of differentiation.* GeogDL should take advantage of the digital medium and differentiate itself from print versions of exam questions. The personal coach is one such example. An area of improvement is the use of color, animation and other multimedia elements to maintain the interest level of students.

2. *The importance of content.* An attractively designed system will still fail if users do not find the content useful or of sufficient quality. This is especially so in GeogDL where students depend on it for exam preparation. Future development of the system should focus on features and usability as well as geography content.

3. *Ease of use.* Teachers and students have only a fixed number of hours at school and a variety of activities to perform. To facilitate adoption, a new system such as GeogDL should be intuitive, reliable and easy to use.

4. *Consultation with actual users.* Teachers will not adopt an educational tool simply because it is available. Instead, the system must demonstrate that it is able to help meet learning objectives, and be easily integrated into the existing curriculum. Consequently, system developers need to work with target users to determine how best to design and deploy GeogDL.

The development of GeogDL is ongoing. We plan to further refine GeogDL by incorporating the suggestions elicited from our design partners, conducting training programs on the use of GeogDL, and running trials of the system in schools. Nevertheless, we anticipate that this richer, personalized, interactive experience offered by GeogDL will better fulfill our goal of developing a digital library that meets the educational needs of students.

References

Boyle, T. (1997). *Design for multimedia learning*. Hertfordshire, UK: Prentice Hall.

Carroll, J. (2000). *Making use: Scenario-based design of human-computer interactions*. Cambridge, MA: MIT Press.

Chua, L. H., Goh, D. H., Lim, E. P., Liu, Z., & Ang, R. P. (2002). A digital library for geography examination resources. In W. Hersh & G. Marchionini (Eds.), *Proceedings of the Second ACM+IEEE Joint Conference on Digital Libraries* (pp. 115-116). New York: ACM Press.

Coleman, A., Smith, T., Buchel, O., & Mayer, R. (2001). Learning spaces in digital libraries. In P. Constantopoulos & I.T. Sølvberg (Eds.), *Research and Advanced Technology for Digital Libraries, ECDL 2001: Lecture Notes in Computer Science 2163* (pp. 251-262). Berlin: Springer-Verlag.

Druin, A., Bederson, B., Boltman, A., Miura, A., Knotts-Callahan, D., & Platt, M. (1999). Children as our technology design partners. In A. Druin (Ed.), *The design of children's technology* (pp. 51-72). San Francisco: Morgan Kaufmann Publishers.

Ellington, H., Percival, F., & Race, P. (1995). *Handbook of educational technology* (3rd ed.). London: Kogan Page.

Lebow, D. (1993). Constructivist values for instructional systems design: Five principles toward a new mindset. *Educational Technology Research and Development, 41*, 4-16.

Lennon, J.A. (1997). *Hypermedia systems and applications: World Wide Web and beyond*. Berlin: Springer-Verlag.

Lim, E. P., Goh, D. H., Liu, Z., Ng, W. K., Khoo, S. K., & Higgins, S. E. (2002). G-Portal: A map-based digital library for distributed geospatial and georeferenced resources. In W. Hersh & G. Marchionini (Eds.), *Proceedings of the Second ACM+IEEE Joint Conference on Digital Libraries* (pp. 351-358). New York: ACM Press.

Melati, D., Ming, Y., Theng, Y.L., Goh, D.H, & Lim, E.P. (2003). Towards a role-based metadata scheme for educational digital libraries: A case study in Singapore. In T. Koch & I. Sølvberg (Eds.), *Proceedings of the Seventh European Conference on Research and Advanced Technology for Digital Libraries, ECDL 2003, 2769* (pp. 41-51). Berlin: Springer-Verlag.

Ministry of Education. (1998). Geography: Singapore-Cambridge GCE Ordinary Level. Retrieved October 2, 2003, from the World Wide Web: *http://www.moe.edu.sg/exams/syllabus/2232.pdf*

Newman, W., & Lamming, M. (1995). *Interactive system design.* Wokingham, UK: Addison-Wesley.

Nielsen, J. (1999). *Designing Web usability.* Indianapolis, IN: New Riders.

Nielsen, J. (n.d.). Severity ratings for usability problems. Retrieved March 4, 2004, from the World Wide Web: *http://www.useit.com/papers/heuristic/severityrating.html*

Norman, D. (1988). *The psychology of everyday things.* New York: Basic Books.

Preece, J., Rogers, Y., Sharp, H., Benyon, D., Holland, S., & Carey, T. (1994). *Human-computer interaction.* Wokingham, UK: Addison-Wesley.

Smith, T., Janee, G., Frew, J., & Coleman, A. (2001). The Alexandria Digital Earth ProtoType system. In E. Fox & C. Borgman (Eds.), *Proceedings of the First ACM+IEEE Joint Conference on Digital Libraries* (pp. 118-119). New York: ACM Press.

Theng, Y.L., Goh, H.L., Lim, E.P., Liu, Z., Pang, L.S., Wong, B.B., & Chua, L.H. (2002). Intergenerational partnerships in the design of a digital library of geography examination resources. In E. P. Lim, S. Foo, C. Khoo, H. Chen, E. Fox, S. Urs, & T. Constantino (Eds.), *Proceedings of the 5th International Conference on Asian Digital Libraries, ICADL2002, 2555* (pp. 427-439). Berlin: Springer-Verlag.

Chapter XVIII

Designing a Music Digital Library:
Discovering What People Really Want

David Bainbridge
University of Waikato, New Zealand

Sally Jo Cunningham
University of Waikato, New Zealand

John McPherson
University of Waikato, New Zealand

Stephen Downie
University of Illinois, USA

Nina Reeves
University of Gloucestershire, UK

Abstract

This chapter describes a set of techniques that have been successfully employed in eliciting user needs for a music digital library. Our focus has been on discovering the types of music information that users would hope to find in a music digital library, the browsing and searching strategies that users "natively" employ, the attributes that are used to describe music information needs, and the purpose for which the music information is sought. We concentrate on studying authentic music information needs— that is, we analyze the information seeking behavior of real people engaged in attempting to satisfy real music-related questions, outside of a lab. Once a rich understanding is reached of what people really want, then the lessons learned can be applied to designing the contents, interface, and search interactions for a music digital library.

Introduction

The development of Music Digital Library (MDL) and Music Information Retrieval (MIR) systems represents an intriguingly multi-national, multi-disciplinary and interconnected area of scientific research. MDL/MIR research teams, situated in locations as diverse as New Zealand, Taiwan, Japan, and Australia (not to mention Europe and North America also) strive to develop innovative music-centric content-based searching schemes, novel interfaces, and evolving networked delivery mechanisms. Good overviews of MDL/MIR's interdisciplinary research areas can be found in Downie (2003a), Byrd & Crawford (2002), and Futrelle & Downie (2002). Despite the technological, geographical and cultural diversity manifest across the MDL/MIR research teams, each shares the common goal of making the world's vast store of music accessible to all.

Currently there is an acute shortage of research on how people *really* prefer to search for music (Futrelle & Downie, 2002)—the types of music-related information needs that a MDL should be prepared to support, the attributes that users of a music retrieval system could supply to describe what they want, and the strategies that are employed in searching or browsing music collections. In the absence of a rich understanding of user needs and music-seeking behavior, the MDL/MIR community runs the risk of developing systems ill-suited to their intended users (Futrelle & Downie, 2002; Cunningham, 2002). It is the purpose of this chapter to inspire future research in the fundamental questions concerning what people *really* do, or *want* to do (if only the ability were there) with a MDL system.

All of the work represented in this chapter is motivated by one thing: to add real-world empirical grounding for design decisions when constructing the music retrieval systems that will play such important roles in future MDLs. To this end, we begin with a presentation of the various user-centered research methods we have employed. We next describe MELDEX, one of the longer-lived MDL systems, because examining how people use existing music retrieval systems can provide essential clues for designing improved systems. The section following this discusses transaction log analysis techniques for summarizing user behavior in a MDL (i.e., describes the results of a log analysis of real-world MELDEX usage). However, such usage studies of current MDLs cannot tell us what additional facilities might be useful, nor give us insight into the motivations behind a user's search. To address these questions, we next present an overview of our analyses of real-world music-related questions posted to Usenet newsgroups and the Google Answers "ask an expert" service. To further enhance our understanding of real-world user behaviour, we follow on with a presentation of our use of ethnographic techniques to examine searching and browsing behavior in a widely used source of music documents—CD shops. We conclude with an overview of the work being done to create a scientifically grounded music query analytic model.

To summarize, this chapter has three primary goals. First, we wish to acquaint other researchers with a range of techniques that they themselves should explore as they design their MDL/MIR systems. Second, we want to acquaint the reader with a brief synopsis of some of the interesting findings we have made over the course of our investigations. Third, and finally, we want to provide an overview of some recently launched larger-scale projects designed to place the future of MDL/MIR research on a more secure and scientifically solid foundation.

Background

Our efforts in understanding user requirements for a music digital library system have been based on three basic research techniques: transaction log analysis, content analysis, and participant observation.

Transaction log analysis is just that: the quantitative analysis and summarization of user actions, as they appear in the transaction or Web logs for a system. Log analysis can potentially allow the researcher to examine the activities of vast numbers of users, over extensive periods of time—a scope not possible with other types of study. However, this data tends to be as shallow as it is broad: while we can know, for example, what percentage of users performed a text-based search over music metadata rather than a QBH (Query by Humming or 'sung') search, we cannot know what underlying information need motivated the search, why they chose text input over hummed input, or even whether their information need was eventually satisfied. Few log analysis studies have been conducted of music digital libraries (see McPherson & Bainbridge, 2001; Olsen & Downie 2003), perhaps because few working music digital library systems exist that have both attained the usage levels appropriate for log analysis, and whose usage is not too commercially sensitive to be reported in the research literature.

In content analysis, a set of documents (usually textual) are analyzed to quantify the extent to which a concept is present in the corpus (Weber, 1990). Focus is generally on the occurrence of selected terms representing that concept, although the concept may also occur implicitly in the text (e.g., the concept "food" may be implied by a description of "eating"). The key is to create as algorithmic as possible a set of "coding" rules—that is, an objective description of how to identify whether or not the concept occurs in a given text. We use content analysis of textual music queries to develop an understanding of three facets of music information seeking: the types of documents or music information that people want an MDL to return as a result of their query; the sorts of details that people can provide when specifying their music information need; and the intended uses for the results obtained from a successful music-related query (Bainbridge, Cunningham, & Downie, 2003; Downie & Cunningham, 2002).

Participant observation is a technique in which the researcher participates in real-life examples of the social interactions or events under study, while at the same time maintaining enough distance to permit the researcher to record and analyze the observed behavior. The observations may occur in the physical world [for example, Dunker (2002) studied Maori patrons in a university library] and in the virtual world [for example, Kibby (2000) examined social interactions in a Web-based community of music lovers]. Observations are generally supported by additional information gathering techniques such as interviews, think-aloud protocol sessions, or examinations of physical artifacts associated with the subject of study. Insights gained through these techniques flesh out the results of the observations, and also suggest directions for further observations. In the context of music digital libraries, participant observations can be most useful in gaining a sense of the strategies employed in information seeking and the "flow" of a set of music information seeking actions, as perceived by the individual.

MEDLEX: An Example MDL System

To convey a flavor of the facilities offered in a music digital library and the "feel" of an interaction, we describe MELDEX: a Web-based system that supports searching through text and sung queries, and browsing through automatically compiled lists of metadata, such a titles. Sample collections include 1,000 popular tunes derived from sheet music using Optical Music Recognition (OMR) software, 10,000 folksongs donated by two other computer music projects, and 100,000 MIDI files gathered from the Web at large.

Figure 1. Entering a text and sung query

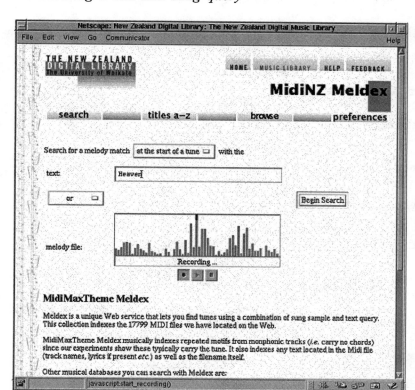

Figure 1 shows a typical interaction with the service, which is part way through recording a sung query. Through the home page (*www.nzdl.org/musiclib*) the user has selected the MIDITHEME collection to arrive at the search page (shown). The user has entered the text "Heaven", pressed the record button, and started to sing the remembered fragment of a tune (a Led Zeppelin song) by sing "ta" for each note sung. Once the singing is complete, the user presses the stop button and submits the query by pressing "Begin Search."

After a short delay, the query results page is displayed (the main window to the right-hand side of *Figure 2*) listing possible matches, best to worst. By clicking on the [icon] icon to the left of a matching entry an audio rendition of the tune can be heard, an automatically generated score is displayed by clicking on [icon], and any text extracted from the file is displayed by clicking [icon]. In our example, the user has chosen the first two options. Alternatively a user may wish to browse the collection by textual metadata, such as title or composer. In the MIDITHEME

Figure 2. The result of entering a query

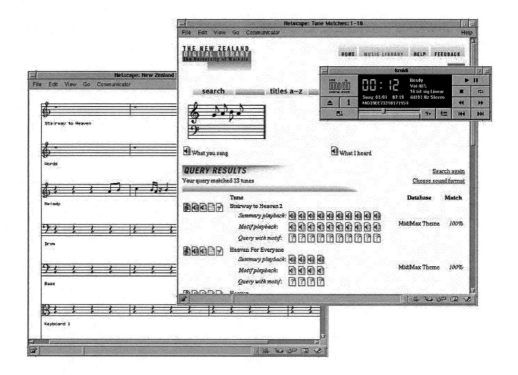

collection only alphabetically listed titles are available, accessed through the Titles A-Z button that forms part of the navigation bar at the top of the page.

A preferences page is also available for controlling search parameters for both text and sung queries (for example ignore case of text, and ignore duration of notes), how many hits to show per results page, the form of audio input (live recording, pre-recorded file) and so on. Audio support covers a variety of popular formats including Wav, AIFF and Au for input and output, with the service storing the user's preferred output format for subsequent playback.

Matching is monophonic to monophonic — more specifically monophonic query to monophonic track. Collections are permitted to include polyphonic tracks, however no matching against these tracks occurs at present. The software, written in C++ and Perl, implements a distributed architecture making it possible to serve different indexes (text or music) to the same collection, even different parts of the same index, on different computers if so desired.

LOG Analysis: What Current Users Do

Log file analysis can help system implementors see how their digital library is used. A sampling of the discoverable trends that are applicable to digital libraries are listed below:

- "Obvious" statistics including the popularity of individual items in the collection and frequency of words used in searches. The results of commonly occurring queries can be cached for faster retrieval, and a profile of popular items can be useful in collection development.

- Popularity of various methods for finding items: for example, searching, browsing, or link (from external Web sites), and how many people use more than a single method to find content. If a searching or browsing facility is under-utilized, then its implementation may suffer from usability problems, or perhaps that facility is simply ill-suited to the focus of this particular digital library.

- Number of interactions with the digital library before either a document is retrieved, or the user gives up. Are users quickly satisfying their information needs, or does a session seem to require endless clicks?

- The number of unique visitors there are, and how frequently visitors come back. Is the digital library attracting a core of ongoing users—who may desire an advanced feature set, as they become familiar the library's contents and interface—or is library usage generally "one-off"?

As digital libraries of all descriptions—text, music, or multimedia—are generally served over the Web, the transaction logs are generally produced by the Web server for the digital library, rather than by the digital library software itself. Web servers can log a variety of information for every request for a page or page component, including date and time of the request, the name of the requested component (including any arguments in the case of a dynamically generated page), the Internet Protocol (IP) address of the remote user, the link followed to generate the request, any details stored in a "cookie," and the version string of the user's Web browser. All of this information is sent by the remote user's Web browser for every request.

There are many programs available that parse log files and automatically generate graphs and tables, displaying statistics such as page access counts, accesses by time of day and day of week, referring page, and visitor's network name. The Open Source Webalizer (*www.mrunix.net/webalizer*) is a popular log fine analysis program.

By logging the referring address, it is possible to determine how a user traverses a Web site, which can be valuable in discovering usage trends that page access statistics can not show. The information is not usually enough to identify the individual making the request, but it is easy to determine which particular organisation or Internet Service Provider an IP address is assigned to, and the organisation (or ISP) is often able to combine an IP address together with a date and time to identify the user/customer assigned that address. If log transcripts are made available to outsiders of the organisation running the Web server, anonymising the IP address of requests is the "generally accepted" method for protecting individuals' privacy.

The following are some discoveries made after performing some transaction analysis on the log files for the MELDEX system described in the previous section (McPherson & Bainbridge, 2001). The results can be broken down by country (although often IP addresses could not be resolved to determine the country of origin).

- Different genres of music were accessed disproportionately by users from different countries, although this is probably influenced by the content of the MELDEX sub-collections, containing folk songs of different nationalities.

- Observed differences between expected behaviour and end user behaviour highlighted potential problems with the presented user interface. As an example, for a significant number of text-only queries the user had selected "search anywhere," although that option only affects the audio component of the search. The user interface needed to be changed to make this more clear. A second example is that a number of users submitted "empty" queries containing neither text terms nor an audio file for searching; the log files alone cannot tell us why these searches were submitted, but their presence suggests some problem with the interface.

- A significant proportion (44%) of the queries involved text search alone, without including the QBH facility. This usage pattern contradicts one of the MELDEX design hypotheses, which was that most searches would involve QBH. QBH is only suitable for "known item" searches, and so perhaps the majority of MELDEX searches are not of that type. We also speculate that the current interface to the QBH system may require too high an overhead for many users.

- Retrieved items tended to appear near the top of the first page when browsing, suggesting that many users were trying to retrieve any item of out curiosity, rather than looking for a particular song. (The browsing structure was a set of pages, one for each letter of the alphabet, and many of these items returned were near the top of the page for song titles beginning with "A.") It seems likely that the users are simply trying to explore the system, or understand the facilities, rather than attempting to satisfy a specific music information need.

Further insights into current music digital library usage are given by Olson & Downie (2003) in a log analysis of the University of Chicago Library's Chopin MDL. The significant findings with regard to how users found information include: browsing by song title was the most frequently used method, followed by browsing by genre, then metadata searching; and browsing by genre resulted in the highest ratio of items being viewed. For queries, searching by title was by far the most frequently used metadata field.

In summary, transaction log analysis can provide valuable insight into how a musical digital library is being used, as well as highlighting potential usability issues in the interface presented to the end users. Log analysis does, however, tend to raise new questions rather than to provide definitive answers. Do the MELDEX users prefer to use text-based searching rather than QBH because the QBH interface is difficult to use, or because their information needs can't be answered by a QBH style query? Why do users submit queries with no text or audio content—is it just to see what happens, or are they confused by some aspect of the interface? Are there additional search or browsing features whose inclusion would benefit MELDEX users? Perhaps the greatest contribution of a log analysis is to uncover further questions about music digital library usage that must be addressed by other research methods.

Finding Out What People Want: Ethnographic Analyses of Real-World Music Queries

Transaction log analysis tells us how people currently use a particular MDL system, but cannot reveal what additional interaction features users would prefer, or provide insight into "why" (motivations for using an MDL system) or "how" (searching/browsing strategies employed) an MDL is used. Employing ethnographic techniques can provide deeper insights into user activities by capturing real-world information need descriptions representing a wide variety of music information seeking behaviors. Interface and system designers can—and increasingly, do—use ethnographically derived rich descriptions of behaviour to inform system design and development (Crabtree et al., 2000). For digital library development, ethnographic studies can suggest desirable searching/browsing features, potentially useful content and document formats, potential sources of confusion for users, or even identify users whose needs might not be satisfiable with the current design (Cunningham et al., 2001).

The three ethnographic studies described next were undertaken with an eye toward the development of user requirements for an MDL system designed for personal use, as would be the case for a public digital library attempting to serve a broad range of users. We do not examine information seeking behavior and information needs of specialized users such as musicologists, music historians, and performers. Instead, we have focused our analyses on two everyday searching and browsing domains: 1) the Internet (specifically, Usenet and Google Answers); and, 2) music CD shops and the CD sections of public libraries. The ethnographic data gathering techniques employed in our studies were content analyses (i.e., of the Internet data) and participant observations (i.e., of people searching for CDs). The participant observations were followed up with unstructured or semi-structured interviews, and focus group discussions. Data was analysed using grounded theory (Glaser, 1967) a method whereby researchers attempt to approach the data without prior assumptions, and generate theory from it. The emergent theory can then be tested for validity through further qualitative or quantitative studies. We triangulated our work by using the above variety of data gathering techniques, and by conducting our observations and interviews in two countries (the United Kingdom and New Zealand).

Ethnographic Analyses: Content Analyses

The first content analysis study considered 161 music queries posted to the *rec.music.country.old-time* Usenet newsgroup during the period July 2001–Jan 2002 (Downie & Cunningham, 2002). During this period, approximately 760 "threads" were represented. Each thread was manually examined, and only the 161 postings which began a thread and which contained a music-related request were retained. This newsgroup was selected as a source of queries for several reasons: it is an active newsgroup (by February 2002, the group's archive contained over 32,800 discussion threads); the group focuses tightly on discussions of music and music events; and the discussions are relatively serious—that is, the participants focus on the genre, rather than on personalities or gossip. Satisfying an information need related to old-time music is not a simple matter of browsing in a CD shop or running a quick search on a peer-to-peer file-sharing service.

Why analyze postings to a newsgroup? Given the acute shortage of real-world query data available for analysis from formal MDL systems, we sought a source of authentic music information requests. This newsgroup provides such a source of queries, and in practice functions as a human-based MDL system: it is effectively an old-time music reference desk, run by volunteers keen to share their expertise in and passion for old-time music. We argue this adds up to a "Wizard of Oz" system for music information retrieval—that is, the newsgroup participants (and the Google Answers experts discussed later) simulate the processing of an MDL system. The Wizard of Oz technique is commonly used in computer application design to evaluate an approach before it is implemented, in an attempt to gain insights that can help evolve the design before irrecoverable coding decisions are made (see, for example, an overview in Dahlback et al., 1993). We use the approach here to see what sort of capabilities an MDL needs to serve a diverse group of users.

The "interface" to this people-powered system is flexible and usable: the users can post natural language requests, expressing their information needs in their own words and unrestricted by the artificial constraints of a search syntax. These requests contain rich contextual details and background information, permitting the researcher a greater insight into search motivations than is generally available in, for example, a transaction log from a computer-based IR system. Further, information requests to a formal IR system are often constrained by the user's pre-conception of what types of information or document formats are available—the user tailors requests (consciously or unconsciously) to what s/he thinks could be retrieved from that system. In contrast, newsgroup readers recognize that posted requests to a newsgroup could literally retrieve anything: a desired fact, an opportunity to purchase a much-desired album, a pointer to an MP3 file, and so forth.

The text-based format of newsgroup postings limits this study to primarily text-based queries, and so we cannot examine in any depth the audio or symbolic techniques that people may wish to use when describing a music information need. Nonetheless, even in this ASCII-constrained medium, we found newsgroup posters including transcriptions and links to audio files in their queries.

Four principal analytic categories emerged from our reading of the queries: Information need (*Table 1*); Desired outcomes (*Table 2*); Intended uses of information (*Table 3*); and Social and contextual elements.

The data from the first three analytic categories are easily quantified and are presented in a relatively self-evident summary form below (unfortunately, space precludes more detailed explication of the categories). The fourth category, however, defies prima facie quantitative summarization as it involves the qualitative description of extra-musical information that users presented to better

Table 1. Features used to describe the information need

Information need description	Percentage	Occurrences
BIBLIOGRAPHIC	75.2%	121
LYRICS	14.3%	23
GENRE	9.9%	16
SIMILAR WORKS	9.9%	16
AFFECT	7.5%	12
LYRIC STORY	6.8%	11
TEMPO	2.5%	4
EXAMPLE	1.8%	3

Table 2. Characterizations of desired information

Outcome type	Percentage	Occurrences
BIBLIOGRAPHIC	35.4%	57
LYRICS	29.8%	48
RECORDING	16.8%	27
NOTATION	13.0%	21
BACKGROUND	13.0%	21
RESOURCE	5.0%	8
OTHER	2.5%	4

Table 3. Intended uses for requested music information

Category	Percentage	Occurrences
LOCATE	49.7%	80
RESEARCH	19.3%	31
PERFORM	18.6%	30
COLLECTION BUILDING	18.0%	29
LISTEN	6.8%	11

contextualize their queries. For example, an associative or environmental context of the desired music-related information was mentioned in 18% (30) of the postings analyzed. By this, we mean that the posting mentioned a social connection that brought the music to the requestor's attention, or an emotional/ social memory associated with the music, or that the music is associated with an event other than simply listening to a CD or LP ("I've heard it at a couple of jam sessions," "ex-friend of mine ... used to sing a song when bowling," "a mandolin class").

In some cases, this associative context may be helpful in satisfying the information need; for example, the detail that a song was heard by the requestor "Last week at the Fraley festival" is potentially useful to responders, as the responders may have also attended the festival, may have access to the festival programme, or may use background knowledge about the type of music included in that festival to identify the song in question.

The second content analysis study focused upon Google Answers (Bainbridge, Cunningham, & Downie, 2003). Google Answers made an interesting case study since it has a sizable number of users and experts, has been running a reasonable length of time (over one year at the time of the study) and music questions in particular seem a popular preoccupation: music is a large sub-category within Arts and Entertainment. 626 postings were retrieved from the music sub-category, spanning April 10, 2002-April 1, 2003. Note that it is the poster who determines the subject category associated with the question, so it is the users themselves who have decided that these are fitting music queries. However, five postings in our analysis were discarded as being off-topic (for example, "How do you find investors?"). An additional 119 postings were related to the music industry rather than to music itself, and so these postings were not further analyzed.

Of the 502 remaining queries analysed, the majority of these (slightly over 80%), contained some form of bibliographic metadata to describe the information request. By far the most common bibliographic attributes supplied were the name of the performer(s) and the title of a work. This finding reinforces the notion that an MDL system should always include these metadata fields, as a bare minimum. A small proportion of queries included a URL link to a Web page providing additional bibliographic metadata. Orchestration might include instrument, vocal range of singers, or (most commonly) the gender of the singers. The assumed default language for lyrics appeared to be English, as language was only mentioned in the query if the desired work(s) had non-English lyrics. Similarly, the nationality of the performer was primarily mentioned when that person was not from the U.S. or the U.K. These categories suggest that quality bibliographic metadata is crucial for use in music searching, although there is a caveat to this.

Users experienced difficulty in coming up with crisp descriptions for several of the categories, indicating a need to support fuzzy or imprecise metadata values for searches. For example, the date of composition or recording for the desired musical items is rarely specified precisely by year. More typically, the decade will be given, or other somewhat nebulous date indications such as "recent" or "old." The user may be uncertain as to the accuracy of the lyrics that they recall ("the chorus went something like..."). Some lyric elements may not be dictionary words ("bling bling"), which poses problems for the user in trying to come up with an acceptable spelling; it is also not clear how to transcribe repetitions ("Money money money mooooooooneeeeeeyy..... MO-NEY!"). Sometimes users were uncertain as to the accuracy of their descriptions: "female singer, African-American likely (but i could be wrong..heck it might just be a male with a female-sounding voice)."

Genre descriptions ranged from standard (but not crisply defined) characterizations ("jazz," "pop") to the highly idiosyncratic ("Sort of that teenie bop bitter angst genre"). The lack of consensus over genre categories and descriptions suggests that it may be appropriate to support (or replace) a genre label with examples of music falling within the genre; perhaps a more productive way of locating new pieces within a genre is to allow the user to ask for "more things like this" by providing music query-by-example facilities

Few queries included an audio example, yet it would be premature to conclude that query-by-humming systems have no potential user-base. Analysis of some queries suggested that users would have liked to include a musical representation but were stymied by the form-based interface to Google Answers: "The only other information that I have is what the song sounds like, but it is hard to express that via the Web."

Ethnography: Participant Observations

Despite the advent of Internet-based music sharing systems and music services, CD shops and libraries are still popular resources for people when they search for music. While descriptions of music information needs found in sources such as Google Answers or Usenet postings can provide a richer picture of what people want—how they describe their information need, and sometimes even why they want the information—they cannot reveal the information seeking strategies that are employed when trying to satisfy music information needs. Observing and analyzing music information behavior in CD shops and CD sections of public libraries offers an opportunity to elicit some of the common music information seeking strategies (Cunningham, Reeves, & Britland, 2003).

From a practical point of view, these locations are well suited to "public space" participant observations, allowing—in our case—the researchers to mingle unobtrusively with shoppers. One can literally step back and take a broad view of relatively large numbers of music searchers/browsers. The shopping population is drawn across the spectrum of society—including both the elderly and the young, men and women (music shopping is one of the very few past-times indulged in to the same extent by men and women), and every imaginable ethnic group.

Anonymous participant observations allow us to see what people do when they search for music, but gives only limited insight into overall music information seeking strategies. We gained a deeper understanding of searching/browsing strategies and goals through a second type of participant observations: accompanying shoppers who agreed to use a think-aloud protocol to describe their actions during a CD shopping expedition. Additional contextual information was obtained from interviews and focus group sessions; these included discussions of music shopping strategies, preferred music sources, recreational and social aspects of music shopping, and the types of music metadata or additional information that may be required to confirm interest in a particular CD or song.

Perhaps the most striking result of this study was the realization of the importance of browsing in music information behaviour. Browsing can occur to locate potentially interesting music within a genre known to be of interest, to serendipitously bringing unexpected songs or types of music to the shopper's attention (for example, by flipping through a jumble of on-sale CDs), to bring the shopper up to date on the latest musical offerings (for example, by looking through a display of current chart-toppers), or simply as a pleasant way to pass time. Browsing tends to be interleaved with searching: the shopper easily moves from casually flipping through the Jazz CDs to searching for the latest Britney Spears CD as a gift for a niece, then back to browsing the half-off sale bin. Current MIR research is largely predicated on the model of a user searching for a specific song, using either textual metadata or employing query-by-humming; the observed behavior suggests that relatively undirected browsing for "interesting music" or "something that sounds like this" occur at least as frequently, indeed if not more often, than known-item searches. Browsing is generally ill-supported in MIR systems, and it is difficult to move easily between the two activities. In MELDEX, for example, the browse and search screens are functionally separated, so that it is not possible to locate an interesting song and then directly switch to browsing other songs in that genre.

Another observation with implications for MIR interface design is that music shopping has a strong visual aspect. Shoppers can recognize items within a genre of interest by the style of CD cover art, and frequently use cover art to gain clues about how a CD is likely to sound. Specific CDs may be identified and retrieved from a pile by the remembered cover art, and the covers are useful in communicating with wandering shopping companions ("hey, have you seen this one?"). Currently MIR systems may include some cover art or other graphics, but they fail to systematically exploit the potential of images in searching and browsing.

Researchers engaged in refining QBH algorithms will be reassured to learn that our study uncovered evidence that QBH interfaces may indeed be welcomed by MIR system users. Shoppers generally avoided asking questions of CD shop sales staff or public library reference librarians, for fear of embarrassment or because they felt intimidated about revealing their personal tastes in music—and humming or singing remembered snatches of a tune for many of us in public would be particularly humiliating. The opportunity to privately and anonymously use QBH to search for a song seems likely to be popular!

Future Research Directions

To help us better understand the nature of real-world MDL queries, Downie (2003b) is leading a large-scale research project designed to create a scientifically grounded music query analytic model. The Human Use of Music Information Retrieval Systems (HUMIRS) is a co-operative undertaking involving researchers from the UIUC Graduate School of Library and Information Science, the National Center for Supercomputing Applications (NCSA), the UIUC Faculty of Music, the UIUC Music Library, UIUC Electrical Engineering and the Computer Science departments both of UIUC and the University of Waikato, New Zealand.

The MIR/MDL communities have long recognized the need for a scientific evaluation paradigm. A formal resolution expressing this need was passed on October 2001 by the attendees of the Second International Symposium on Music Information Retrieval (ISMIR 2001). The resolution highlights the fact that MIR/MDL research requires access to music materials consisting of inter-connected collections of symbolic (e.g., scores, MIDI, MusicXML, etc.), textual (e.g., lyrics, libretti, reviews, analyses, etc.), audio (e.g., MP3, WAV, etc.) and metadata (e.g., bibliographic records, etc.) information. In conjunction with the requirements for the material infrastructure, the resolution emphasizes the need for a common set of formal and standardized tasks that each team can use to evaluate its system(s). This notion of standardized collections and tasks is derived from the Text Retrieval Conference (TREC) paradigm. TREC, developed over a decade ago by the National Institute of Standards and Technology (NIST), is a highly regarded evaluation paradigm for those in the traditional Information Retrieval (IR) community (see *http://trec.nist.gov/overview.html*). Under this paradigm, each IR team is given access to: (1) a standardized, large-scale test collection of text; (2) a standardized set of test queries; and (3) a standardized evaluation of the results each team generates.

Item #2, the creation of the set of test queries specifically designed to address the needs of MDL researchers, is the HUMIRS project's central concern.

Before proceeding further, we must emphasize here the distinction between "queries" and "search statements." "Queries" are the verbalized expressions of a user's information need, whereas, "search statements" are the expression(s) of the queries in the syntax of particular retrieval engines (Tague-Sutcliffe, 1992). This distinction is important for it highlights the facts brought out in our early work, described in the sections above, that music queries, the objects of interest in the HUMIRS project, are: semantically-rich; syntactically-undetermined; structurally independent of any particular search system(s); and content variable (i.e., can contain singing, text, recorded examples, notation, etc.). Understanding the semantic richness, the possible syntactic options, the structural implications and the kinds of information contained in real-world music queries is the sine qua non of the project.

As we iteratively create the TREC-like evaluation programme for the MIR/MDL communities, it is very important that our TREC-like evaluation tasks be grounded in real-world requirements. That is, we must ensure that the test tasks developed are realistic proxies for the kinds of uses that MIR/MDL systems might expect to encounter. A synthesis of the observations made by the experts who participated in the preceding "MIR/MDL Evaluation Frameworks Project" (see http://music-ir.org/evaluation) suggests that a minimal TREC-like query record needs to include the following basic elements: high quality audio representation(s); verbose metadata (about the "user," the "need," and the "use"); and symbolic representation(s) of the music presented.

One is struck by how these requirements are less like a traditional TREC query or "topic statement" (see *Figure 3*) and more like the kind of information garnered in a traditional, well-conducted, reference interview (Dewdney &

Figure 3. A TREC "topic statement" as found in Vorhees (2002)

```
<num> Number: 409
<title> legal, Pan Am, 103
<desc>Description: What legal actions have resulted from the
destruction of Pan
Am Flight 102 over Lockerbie, Scotland, on December 21, 1988?
<narr> Narrative: Documents describing any charges, claims, or fines
presented
to or imposed by any court or tribunal are relevant, but documents that
discuss
charges made in diplomatic jousting are not relevant.
```

Michell, 1997; Bopp & Smith, 2001). This suggests that the involvement of professional music librarians in the development of the TREC-like music query records is important—perhaps even critical. Thus, the UIUC Music Library and its staff will be playing a pivotal role in the project, as will other members of the international music library world.

Over the course of the project we will be setting up, and running, the first TREC-like evaluation "contests" whereby each MIR/MDL research team will be given the opportunity to test their system(s) using the set of standardized test queries and results that we will be developing. This will be an iterative process as feedback from the research community and the project's advisory panel will be solicited to ensure that the test queries and the evaluation measures used are truly reflective of system performance (i.e., the evaluations give us a true picture of the strengths and weaknesses of each participating system). Based upon the data collected, we will develop a database of well-formed, standardized query record prototype(s). These records will be developed to reflect both the complexity of music queries and the principle of retrieval neutrality (i.e., will not favor one retrieval approach over another). They will incorporate, in some form, textual metadata, audio, and symbolic information.

Conclusion

At present, music digital library systems reported in the research literature are largely prototypes, developed as proof-of-concept demonstrations for a given tool, or are focused around providing access to an available set of documents (Futrelle & Downie, 2002). We argue in this chapter that the time is ripe to focus research efforts on improving the efficacy of music-specific searching and browsing facilities, as based on a deep understanding of music information behaviour. Such studies can provide supportive evidence for (or, alas, against) the potential usefulness of experimental MDL features, and can suggest additional searching/browsing facilities or output types that users may desire.

Acknowledgements

Downie acknowledges project support from the Andrew W. Mellon Foundation and the National Science Foundation (NSF) under Grant Nos. NSF IIS-0340597 and NSF IIS-0327371.

References

Bainbridge, D., Cunningham, S.J., & Downie, J.S. (2003). How people describe their music information needs: A grounded theory analysis of music queries. In *Proceedings of the 4th International Conference on Music Information Retrieval (ISMIR)* (pp. 221-222). Baltimore, MD: Johns Hopkins University.

Bainbridge, D., Nevill-Manning, C.G., Witten, I.H., & Smith, L.A. (1999). Towards a digital library of popular music. In *Proceedings of the 4th ACM Conference on Digital Libraries (ISMIR)* (pp. 161-169). New York: ACM Press.

Bopp, R.E., & Smith, L.C. (Eds.). (2001). The reference interview. In *Reference and Information Services: An Introduction* (pp. 47-68). Englewood, CO: Libraries Unlimited.

Byrd, D., & Crawford, T.C. (2002). Problems of music information retrieval in the real world. *Information Processing and Management, 38*, 249-272.

Cooper, M., & Foote, J. (2002). Automatic music summarization via similarity analysis. In *Proceedings of the 3rd International Conference on Music Information Retrieval (ISMIR)* (pp. 81-85). Paris: IRCAM-Centre Pompidou.

Crabtree, A., Nichols, D.M., O'Brien, J., Rouncefield, M., & Twidale, M.B. (2002). Ethnomethodologically-informed ethnography and information system design. *Journal of the American Society for Information Science, 51 (7)*, 666-682.

Cunningham, S.J., Knowles, C., & Reeves, N. (2001). An ethnographic study of technical support workers: Why we *didn't* build a tech support digital library. In *Proceedings of the Joint Conference on Digital Libraries* (pp. 189-198). New York: ACM Press.

Cunningham, S.J., Reeves, N., & Britland, M. (2003) An ethnographic study of music information seeking: Implications for the design of a music digital library. In *Proceedings of the ACM/IEEE Joint Conference on Digital Libraries* (pp. 5-16). New York, NY: ACM Press.

Dahlback, N., Jonsson, A., & Ahrenberg, L. (1993). Wizard of OZ studies— Why and how. In *Proceedings Intelligent User Interfaces '93* (pp. 193-200). New York: ACM Press.

Dewdney, P., & Michell, G. (1997). Asking "why" questions in the reference interview: A theoretical justification. *Library Quarterly, 67*, 50-71.

Downie, J.S. (2003a). Music information retrieval. *Annual Review of Information Science and Technology, 37*, 295-340.

Downie, J.S. (2003b). Toward the scientific evaluation of music information retrieval systems. In *Proceedings of the 4th International Conference on Music Information Retrieval (ISMIR)* (pp. 25-32). Baltimore, MD: Johns Hopkins University.

Downie, J.S., & Cunningham, S.J. (2002). Toward a theory of music information retrieval queries: system design implications. In *Proceedings of the Third International Conference on Music Information Retrieval (ISMIR)* (pp. 299-300). Paris: IRCAM-Centre Pompidou.

Dovey, M.J. (2002). A collaborative virtual organization for music information retrieval collaborateion and evaluation. In J.S. Downie (Ed.), *The MIR/ MDL Evaluation Project White Paper Collection* (2nd ed.) (pp. 50-52). Champaign, IL: GSLIS.

Duncker, E. (2002). Cross-cultural usability of the library metaphor. In *Proceedings of the 2nd ACM/IEEE-CS Joint Conference on Digital Libraries* (pp. 223-230). New York: ACM Press.

Futrelle, J., & Downie, J.S. (2002). Interdisciplinary communities and research issues in music information retrieval. In *Proceedings of the 3rd International Conference on Music Information Retrieval (ISMIR)* (pp. 215-221). Paris: IRCAM-Centre Pompidou.

Glaser, B., & Strauss, A. (1967). *The discovery of grounded theory: Strategies for qualitative research.* Chicago.

Itoh, M. (2000). Subject search for music: Quantitative analysis of access point selection. In *Proceedings of the 1st International Symposium on Music Information Retrieval (ISMIR)*. Plymouth, MA: University of Massachusetts at Amherst.

Kibby, M.D. (2000). Home on the page: A virtual place of music community. *Popular Music, 19* (1), 91-100.

Kim, J.Y., & Belkin, N.J. (2002). Categories of music description and search terms and phrases used by non-music experts. In *Proceedings of the Third International Conference on Music Information Retrieval (ISMIR)* (pp. 209-214). Paris: IRCAM-Centre Pompidou.

McPherson, J.R., & Bainbridge, D. (2001). Usage of the MELDEX digital music library. In *Proceedings of the Second International Symposium on Music Information Retrieval (ISMIR)* (pp. 19-20). Bloomington, IN: Indiana University.

Olson, T., & Downie, J.S. (2003). Chopin early editions: The construction and usage of a collection of digital scores. In *Proceedings of the Fourth International Conference on Music Information Retrieval (ISMIR)* (pp. 247-248). Baltimore, MD: Johns Hopkins University.

Tague-Sutcliffe, J. (1992). The pragmatics of information retrieval experimentation, revisited. *Information Processing & Management, 28*, 467-490.

Voorhees, E.M. (2002). Whither music IR evaluation infrastructure: Lessons to be learned from TREC. In J.S. Downie (Ed.), *The MIR/MDL Evaluation Project White Paper Collection* (pp. 7-13). Champaign, IL: GSLIS.

Weber, R.P. (1990). *Basic content analysis.* Newbury Park, CA: Sage Publications.

Chapter XIX

Quantitative and Qualitative Evaluations of the Singapore National Library Board's Digital Library

Yin-Leng Theng
Nanyang Technological University, Singapore

Mei-Yee Chan
Singapore Polytechnic, Singapore

Ai-Ling Khoo
Singapore Polytechnic, Singapore

Raju Buddharaju
National Library Board, Singapore

Abstract

As part of the Singapore National Library Board's (NLB) on-going efforts to improve the usefulness and usability of the eLibraryHub in meeting users' needs, this chapter reports two empirical studies – a quantitative and a qualitative study – conducted on the eLibraryHub, the NLB Digital Library. In the quantitative study, we evaluated the effectiveness of the eLibraryHub from users' perspectives. Results show that users rated favorably their satisfaction of the overall effectiveness, usefulness and ease of use of the eLibraryHub. They also perceived it as generally quite useful and easy to use. In the qualitative study, we made use of Scenario-Based Design and Claims Analysis, to determine the usability of the eLibraryHub. Findings indicate that most usability problems occurred during the interpretation and evaluation stages of navigational actions. It concludes with recommendations on design refinement of the eLibraryHub. The chapter illustrates the rich interplay of quantitative and qualitative data crucial in helping designers/developers to better understand users, uses and usability of deployed systems, to address the dilemma of Carroll's task-artifact cycle of changing user needs and design possibilities.

Introduction

Designers often design for themselves unless they are trained to realize that people are diverse, and that users are unlikely to be like them. The more errors that can be avoided "up front" by the right method, the less work both test-users and designers will have to put in to refine prototypes to improve their usability. Landauer (1995) points out that it is not good enough to design interactive system without subjecting it to some form of evaluation, because it is impossible to design an optimal user interface in the first attempt. Dix et al. (1998) argue that even if one has used the best methodology and model in the design of usable interactive system, one still needs to assess the design and test the system to ensure that it behaves as expected and meets users' requirements. Nielsen's (1993) advice with respect to interface evaluation is that designers should simply conduct some form of testing.

As digital libraries (DLs), interactive systems with organized collections of information, become more complex, the number of facilities provided by them will increase and the difficulty of learning to use these facilities will also increase correspondingly. Like the Web, DLs also provide non-linear information spaces in which chunks of information are inter-connected via links. However, they are different in character from the Web in several important respects: a DL represents a collection for a specific purpose containing text-based and/or geospatial content, and has search strategies that are clearly defined and more powerful.

After a decade of DL research and development, DLs are moving from research to practice, from prototypes to operational systems (Borgman, 2002). In the digital world, real world cues such as face-to-face interactions with human librarians and thumbing through hardcopy books have been replaced by drop-down menus, search screens and Web page browsing. In DLs, users must map their goals onto DLs' capability without the assistance of a human librarian. As a result, wide acceptance of DLs will only be achieved if they are easy to learn and use relative to the perceived benefit (Borgman, 2000).

This chapter reports two empirical studies – a qualitative and a quantitative study – conducted on the *eLibraryHub*. It is hoped that the two studies of the *eLibraryHub*, Singapore National Library Board's (NLB) Digital Library, would contribute to the under-studied usability research on DLs constructed by community organizations such as public libraries and hospitals, as highlighted by Borgman (2002).

The Singapore National Library Board Digital Library

The *eLibraryHub* (see *http://www.elibraryhub.com*; retrieved April 3, 2004), launched on September 7, 2001, aims to provide its four million individual users access to information resources and services anytime, anywhere (Chan, 2002). In 1997, TIARA, which stands for Timely Information for All, Relevant and Affordable, was launched as a national effort to bring affordable and timely information to users in Singapore. TIARA was later evolved to the *eLibraryHub* from April 1, 2002. The *eLibraryHub* was launched in September 2001 as an enhancement of TIARA. It is also a one-stop integrated DL for immediate access to vast amount of information and resources. It is both a content and community portal (Chia, 2002) and caters to users from multiple environments, from individuals, businesses, professionals, corporate to community groups (Abu Bakar, 2002).

On the content side, the library resources in the *eLibraryHub* include some 13,000 electronic magazines, journals, and online databases; 10,000 electronic books and more than 700 CD-ROM and 900 video-on-demand titles. In the "Reference Library," links to resources selected by NLB's information specialists are provided. In a bid to target the information needs of niche markets, NLB has plans to create specialized libraries within the *eLibraryHub*. Its first offering launched in end-2002 is the "China Resource Library" that provides business-related information about China. Another two specialized libraries that are being planned will cater to children and teenagers. *Figure 1* shows the default login page of the *eLibraryHub*.

Figure 1. Screenshot of default login page for the eLibraryHub

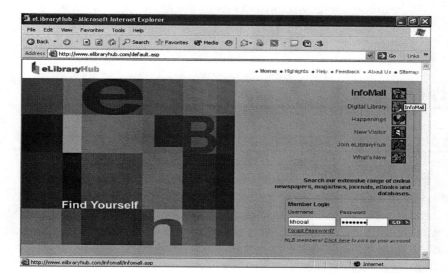

Two Studies

As part of NLB's on-going efforts to improve the usefulness and usability of the *eLibraryHub* in meeting users' needs, two studies were conducted in the first half of 2003:

- *Quantitative Study*. This study evaluated the effectiveness of the *eLibraryHub*. The study, conducted in early 2003, considered the users, uses, usefulness and ease of use of the digital library. It attempted to employ a quantitative approach based on questionnaire survey to evaluate the perceived value of the digital library and the effect on the intention of use by users.

- *Qualitative Study*. This study examined the navigation structure and information layout of the *eLibraryHub*. Therefore, the objectives of this study, conducted over a two-week period from February 24, 2003, to March 6, 2003, are to:

  - investigate the usability of the *eLibraryHub* by using established usability techniques to identify positive and negative consequences of the design features; and

- propose refinement to alleviate negative consequences of design features, thereby improving usability of the *eLibraryHub*, especially in relation to the navigational structure and information layout.

First Study: Quantitative

Experimental Protocol and Sample Subjects

A quantitative approach based on questionnaires was employed for this study. The questionnaires were disseminated in two modes – hardcopy via person-to-person and softcopy via email attachment. They were collected over a period of six weeks from March/April 2003, out of which 40 of them were returned via email. The completed questionnaires were checked to ensure there were no missing or ambiguous answers. A minor problem occurred for three respondents who were Macintosh users. The Microsoft Word format for the softcopy version of the questionnaire was incompatible and their replies could not be read properly. The respondents were thus requested to resend their answers as part of the text message and not as an email attachment.

The target respondents of this study were library users, namely students (tertiary level and above) and working adults, spanning the age group of 18-44. This group accounts from almost 60% of the resident library book borrowers (Yeo, 2002) and constitutes more than 63% of home Internet users (Infocomm Development Authority of Singapore, 2001). They would usually need to search and find information in the course of their schoolwork and jobs. A total of 107 respondents completed the questionnaire used in this study. The respondents were recruited from fellow course mates and friends and were chosen on the only condition that they belonged to the age group mentioned earlier.

Questionnaire Development

The development of the questionnaire involved an iterative process of formulation and evaluation by five peers who were taking the Masters in Information Studies course at the Nanyang Technological University, a means of obtaining feedback from a small, convenient sample of potential respondents. The purpose was to determine the relevance of the questions and the extent to which there may be problems in obtaining responses.

The final refined questionnaire was structured such that all respondents, regardless of whether they are users of the *eLibraryHub*, could answer the first part comprising demographic questions.

Users of the *eLibraryHub* were then asked in the second part about their usage of the DL. For *user satisfaction*, the users assessed the resources and services of the *eLibraryHub* as well as the overall effectiveness. The questions asked were:

- How satisfied are you of the resources used?

- How satisfied are you of the services used?

- Overall, how would you assess the effectiveness of *eLibraryHub*?

They were asked to rate their satisfaction of the resources and services from 1 (most satisfied) to 5 (least satisfied) in terms of four factors: availability, accessibility, quality, and effort. The factors were based on the second major class (Class B: "Interaction") of the taxonomy derived by Saracevic & Kantor (1997). They were also asked to rate the effectiveness of the *eLibraryHub* from 1 (most useful/usable) to 5 (least useful/usable). The purpose is to find out if the *eLibraryHub* fulfils users' needs, if there is a difference in satisfaction level for different factors, and if users find the *eLibraryHub* equally useful and usable or more useful/usable.

To study *user intent and user perception*, six statements were presented and the users were then asked whether they agree of disagree with it. They were:

- I can obtain the resources and services I need when using *eLibraryHub*.

- Using *eLibraryHub* would enable me to accomplish my task or project more effectively.

- I find *eLibraryHub* easy to use.

- My interaction with *eLibraryHub* is clear and understandable.

- Assuming I currently use *eLibraryHub*, I intend to continue my use in future.

- I intend to increase my use of *eLibraryHub* in future.

The statements were adapted from the study by Hong et al. (2002) to determine user acceptance of the Open University of Hong Kong's e-Library. Likert scales (1-5) with anchors ranging from "strongly agree" to "strongly disagree" were used for all statements. Respondents were requested to select the category that corresponds most closely to their responses. The statements were to serve as an initial stimulus, and the response categories could be used to measure reactions and assess respondents' attitudes or opinions. Five response categories were used to allow for sufficient information without exaggerating the decision-making abilities of the respondents (Gray & Guppy, 1994).

For *user intent*, the following question was also asked:

•   How often do you access *eLibraryHub*?

The purpose is to determine if the *eLibraryHub* is used on a regular basis, if users will keep using it, and even increase their usage. For the area of user perception, the purpose is to examine users' perceived usefulness and ease of use of the *eLibraryHub*.

Second Study: Qualitative

Experimental Protocol

This qualitative evaluation carried out in this study was based on Carroll's work on the task-artefact cycle, user-centred strategies such as the Scenario-based Design and Claims Analysis (Carroll, 2000). As usability is relative and must be evaluated on the basis of intended goals (Borgman, 2000), Scenario-based Design allows for usability to be inspected in the context of different goals. However, the underlying casual relationship among the entities within a situation of use is left implicit. Claims Analysis was later developed by Carroll (2000) to enlarge the scope and goal of the Scenario-Based Design approach to provide more comprehensive and focused reasoning. Claims provide a schema that articulates the desirable as well as the less desirable consequences of an artefact or design feature in the context of a particular usage situation (Carroll & Rosson, 1992). It helps to surface the inconsistencies and conflicts among scenarios and enable designers to make decisions regarding design trade-offs and consequences. Norman's (1988) model of interaction was used as a framework in Claims Analysis for "questioning the user's stages of action" when interacting with a system in terms of goals, planning, execution, interpretation and evaluation.

Carroll's original Claims Analysis consists of nineteen questions to step through the interaction cycle of goal formulation, planning, execution, interpretation and evaluation. The questions in this study were modified, built upon work by Theng et al. (2002), to be more relevant to its goals. For example, the original question "How does the artefact encourage the use of background knowledge (concepts, metaphors, skills) in planning a task?" was modified to reflect the goal of browsing for e-Books in the *eLibraryHub*, and was changed to "How does the system (screen) encourage you to make use of your computer skills, prior knowledge about the Web, or your previous experience with other e-Books services to browse for e-Books?"

The actual evaluation sessions were divided into three parts. Part 1 began with the subjects completing an information gathering questionnaire on their demographic details, educational qualifications, current employment status, Internet usage patterns, personal preferences on the usage and features of DLs as well as their prior experiences using the *eLibraryHub*, if any. In Part 2 of the session, subjects were given a pre-evaluation briefing, covering details of the evaluation. The facilitator then gave out the Claims Analysis questions to the subjects during Part 3 of the session to solicit comments on the positive and negative consequences of the *eLibraryHub*'s features as they tried to complete the task goal. Subjects were told to think aloud throughout the entire session. All the interactions were voice-recorded as the source of data. On the average, Part 3 lasted about 50 minutes per subject.

Sample Subjects

The subjects, denoted by S1, S2 (Students 1 and 2), W1, W2 (Working Adults 1 and 2), P1 and P2 (Pilot Studies 1 and 2), were university graduates with considerable experience in using the Web. They were also confident Web surfers and searchers, rating themselves as intermediate users. Five out of six subjects (excluding subject W1) surfed the Web daily. Only subjects P1, P2 and S2 had experience using the *eLibraryHub*. All were infrequent users with usage rate of less than once per week.

The subjects performed iterative walkthroughs of the *eLibraryHub* together with the facilitator to achieve the goal of browsing for e-Books. This was done by questioning stages of action in Norman's execution-evaluation model of task completion, broadly divided into three phases (Carroll, 2000): (1) before executing an action; (2) when executing an action; and (3) after performing an action.

Findings and Analyses

Although many usability evaluation techniques are available to help designers (Dix et al., 1998), there is generally considerable controversy about the relative effectiveness of different methodologies (Wixton, 2003), creating great chasm between staunch proponents of quantitative and qualitative approaches. For example, Wixton (2003) argues for the practicality of a qualitative, broad-based "case study" approach to usability methods as they are applied in industry. He went on to suggest that making methods effective is by and large ignored in the formal literature, such as rigorous experimental procedure advocated by Gray & Salzman (1998), which "treats [quantitative] usability studies as if they were experiments, when in reality they are more like organizational interventions."

There is, however, a growing emphasis on triangulation of data gathered from both quantitative and qualitative approaches to gain better insights in design and usability problems. For instance, in evaluating the *eLibaryHub*, findings from the quantitative First Study provided us with statistically-based numbers on users' intent, satisfaction and perception on the effectiveness of the *eLibaryHub* while findings from the qualitative Second Study helped us understand the reasons for users' intent, satisfaction and perception with regard to occurrence of usability problems, and hence recommendations for improvement to the *eLibaryHub* to address usability problems were proposed.

Findings from First Study: Quantitative Approach

Demographic Characteristics of Respondents

A total of 107 respondents completed the questionnaire used in this study. The sample population was almost split in half by gender, with males constituting 49.6%. 75.7% of the respondents were between 25-34 years of age and 89.7% held degree qualifications and above. The high proportion of respondents in these categories could be due to the fact that they were recruited from fellow course mates and friends who shared similar backgrounds. A majority of the respondents (65.4% of the sample) were working persons. The occupations of the working persons varied from professional, administrative and managerial, technical, and sales, marketing and service-related. The percentage of the *eLibraryHub* users was 36.4%. Below are findings on user intent, user satisfaction and user perception. More detailed analyses are found in Khoo et al. (2004).

User Intent

Almost 95% of the *eLibraryHub* users accessed it less than once a week. 66.7% of the users agreed or strongly agreed with the statement that indicates their intention to continue using the *eLibraryHub*. However, only 35.9% agreed or strongly agreed with the statement that indicates the intention to increase their usage. This could mean that existing users are generally satisfied with the *eLibraryHub*, but more could be done to increase their usage level.

User Satisfaction

Users rated favorably their satisfaction of the availability, accessibility, quality and effort of use of the *eLibraryHub*'s resources and services as well as its overall effectiveness. On a scale of 1 (most satisfied) to 5 (least satisfied), the *eLibraryHub*'s services received marginally higher mean ratings (2.71 to 2.87) than the resources (2.97 to 3.03) for the four factors. Overall, users rated the *eLibraryHub* to be slightly more useful (mean=2.82) than usable (mean=2.95), where usefulness was defined as "providing useful information and services," and usable was defined as "easy to use" in the questionnaire. This could mean that users are generally satisfied with the usefulness of the *eLibraryHub* but more could be done to improve its ease of use.

Correlation analysis was done to see which user satisfaction factors are related to overall effectiveness of the *eLibraryHub*. The Pearson r was calculated for each pair of variables. Statistical tests were also carried out to determine whether the calculated value of r is significantly greater than 0. The t-statistic was used for the test and p-values of 0.05 and below were considered statistically significant. From the correlation results, it can be observed that almost all but four correlation pairs were found to be statistically significant. For overall usefulness, the strongest positive correlations were with the *accessibility* (r=0.503, p=0.002), *availability* (r=0.490, p=0.002) and *effort of use* (r=0.462, p=0.004) of resources. For overall ease of use, the strongest positive correlations were with *effort of use* (r=0.701, p=0.000), *accessibility* (r=0.550, p=0.000) and *quality* (r=0.448, p=0.005) of the resources.

User Perception

From the results, it can be gathered that users perceived the *eLibraryHub* as generally quite useful and easy to use. In terms of perceived ease of use, 61.5% of the *eLibraryHub* users agreed that it is easy to use and 46.2% agreed that their interactions are clear and understandable. In terms of perceived usefulness, 51.3% agreed that they can obtain the resources and services they need when using the *eLibraryHub*. However, only 33.3% agreed that using the *eLibraryHub* would enable them to accomplish their task or project more effectively. This seems that users perceived the *eLibraryHub* as more easy to use than useful. Yet, from their satisfaction ratings, they seemed less satisfied with this perceived level of ease of use compared to the level of usefulness. This reinforces the idea that more could be done to improve the ease of use of the *eLibraryHub* for its users.

Findings from Second Study: Qualitative Approach

A total of nine well-accepted usability heuristics (Nielsen, 1994) and seven design guidelines (e.g., Shneiderman, 1998; etc.) were used to categorize the subjects' comments. It was assumed that comments with positive consequences suggested compliance with the usability heuristics and design guidelines, while comments with negative consequences indicated violation of the usability heuristics and design guidelines (Theng et al., 2002).

In this study, subjects went through three iterations of Norman's execution-evaluation model. Summaries of positive and negative consequences respectively from subjects S1, S2, W1 and W2 were drawn for the following five stages: (1) before execution (stages 1a & 1b); (2) during execution (stage 2); and (3) after execution (stages 3a & 3b). *Table 1* shows a summary of negative consequences detected.

Table 1.   Summary of negative consequences

Stage	Negative Consequences in Violation of Design Heuristics	Subjects			
		S1	S2	W1	W2
First Iteration – From Homepage to InfoMall					
1a & 1b	1. Access barrier		√	√	√
	2. Match between system & real world	√		√	
	3. Simplicity of task structure	√		√	
	4. User Model versus Design Model	√		√	
	5. Visibility of system status	√	√	√	√
3a & 3b	6. Aesthetics & minimalist design	√	√		
	7. Consistency & standards	√	√	√	
	8. Match between system & real world	√	√		√
	9. Recognition rather than recall	√	√		√
Second Iteration – From InfoMall to e-Books					
3a & 3b	10. Access barrier	√	√	√	
	11. Aesthetics & minimalist design			√	√
	12. Consistency & standards	√			√
	13. Flexibility & efficiency of use	√	√		√
	14. Match between system & real world	√			√
	15. Recognition rather than recall	√			√
Third Iteration – From e-Books to netLibrary					
1a	16. Flexibility & efficiency of use	√			
3a	17. Working across boundaries	√	√	√	√
	18. Recognition rather than recall	√	√	√	√
	19. Blind alleys	√	√	√	√

Recommendations for Improvement

Findings from the first study suggest that ensuring users' satisfaction with the ease of use of the *eLibraryHub* could secure their continued usage of it. Additionally, getting users to perceive the *eLibraryHub* as being useful in terms of enabling them to accomplish their tasks more effectively could help secure their continued usage, and potentially to increase their usage. User satisfaction in the first study could be likened to the *"hygienic factors"* and user perception to the *"motivators,"* as described in the "two-factor" theory of work motivation proposed by Herzberg (as cited in Evans, Ward, & Rugaas, 2000). Improvements to the *"hygienic factors"* (user satisfaction) could maintain users' use of a digital library, but improvements need to be made to the *"motivators"* (user perception) to improve usage levels. Specifically for the *eLibraryHub*, user satisfaction of ease of use seemed to be the significant *"hygienic factor,"* while user perception of usefulness was the significant *"motivator."* Hence, evaluators of DLs could try to elucidate the significant factors influencing behaviour intention of their users. Subsequently, appropriate recommendations and improvements to the DLs could be made based on these factors.

The second study showed that usability problems could be detected by analyzing claims made by subjects as they stepped through the various stages in Norman's execution-evaluation cycle model in pursuit of their task goal, as proposed in Carroll's Claims Analysis. Although only six subjects participated in the usability evaluation sessions, a rich set of data could be derived. Areas of refinement are proposed and grouped according to the violations against established usability heuristics and design guidelines (see *Table 1*), more details found in Chan et al. (2004):

- *Access Barriers and Blind Alleys*. Subjects viewed log-in requirement as a form of barrier. They also did not know that if they did not register as a member in both the *eLibraryHub* and *netLibrary*, they would not be able to download e-Books for reading (see Table 1, Stages 1a and b, Item 1; Stages 3a and b, Item 10; Stage 3a, Item 19). The *eLibraryHub* could explore a tie-up with the netLibrary to provide direct access to all registered users of the *eLibraryHub* to minimize the need to sign-up for multiple accounts.

- *Match between System and Real World*. Wordings or icons used must reflect the match between system and real world (see Table 1, Stages 1a and b, Item 2; Stages 3a and b, Items 8 and 14). Sufficient information should be given to provide context to headings and icons. Alternatively, it would be more challenging to design more meaningful icons that facilitate easy recognition and retention.

- *User Model versus Design Model.* There was a mismatch between what the subjects viewed (User Model) and what the system offers (Design Model) under the InfoMall and Digital Library function (see Table 1, Stages 1a and b, Item 4). To help users understand the resources available in InfoMall, more descriptive and scan-friendly text could be provided. Alternatively, consideration could be given to merge the two functions, as there seemed to be some overlaps in the resources provided.

- *Visibility of System Status.* Subjects S1, S2 and W1 did not pay much attention to the mouse-over text provided and jumped straight into action (see Table 1, Stages 1a and b, Item 5). The subjects suggested that the mouse-over text could be repositioned next to the respective headings and font size increased for ease of reading.

- *Simplicity of Task Structure.* Tasks should be made simple such that planning efforts could be minimized. In this study, subjects had to deliberate over their subsequent mouse-clicks (see Table 1, Stages 1a and b, Item 3).

- *Consistency and Standards, Aesthetics and Minimalist Design.* Consistency and standards should be adopted to ensure that users need not wonder whether the different words, situation or actions mean the same thing (see Table 1, Stages 3a and b, Items 6, 7, 11 and 12).

- *Recognition Rather than Recall.* It was interesting to note that although the subjects felt that the mouse-over text and navigational icons were adequate, they would not make use of them (see Table 1, Stages 3a and b, Items 9 and 15; Stage 3a, Item 18). It would be beneficial to design more meaningful icons that facilitate easy recognition and retention, especially for infrequent users and when there is no mouse-over text to provide context.

- *Flexibility and Efficiency of Use.* It was found that registered account holders had to click on the *netLibrary* account hyperlink (meant for non-account holders) to gain access to *netLibrary* homepage (see Table 1, Stages 3a and b, Item 13; Stage 1a, Item 16). It is recommended that a shortcut be provided for registered account holders to gain access to the netLibrary homepage.

- *Working across Boundaries.* In this study, the subjects were not prepared to see a new *netLibrary* interface and had to re-learn the navigational features (see Table 1, Stage 3a, Item 17). The transition from the *eLibraryHub* and *netLibrary* was necessary as the latter provides outsourcing services to digital libraries worldwide. It could only be hoped that with frequent usage, users would be more familiar with the new navigational features.

Conclusions and Future Work

The above two summative evaluations using quantitative and qualitative approaches to triangulate data across different strategies yield rich data to gain different insights about the effectiveness of the *eLibraryHub*, and hence recommendations for further improvement to the *eLibraryHub* are proposed.

This chapter illustrates the rich interplay of quantitative and qualitative data crucial in helping designers/developers to better understand users, uses and usability of deployed systems, to address the dilemma of the task-artifact cycle of changing user needs and design possibilities by Carroll (2000).

It is recommended that future work from the first study could expand the size of the sample and obtain responses from participants of more diversified backgrounds. Interviews, focus group discussions, or further qualitative studies could be done to obtain more in-depth information and to further examine user perceptions. The first study could also be further developed to connect the perceived value of DLs with appropriate economic indicators. This could then help to provide a more tangible means of prioritizing the development and improvement of usable and useful DLs.

However, due to the small sample size, the results in the second study could not be generalized to a larger group of users with different demographic characteristics. Nevertheless, the findings of the second study provide useful insights on the potential usability problems when users navigate the *eLibraryHub*. Several possibilities exist for future studies. These include replicating the study with different scenarios of use or work with another group of target users. More can also be done to make Scenario-Based Design and Claims Analysis intuitive to use.

Acknowledgments

We would like to thank the National Library Board for their support, and the subjects who gave us valuable feedback.

References

Abu Bakar, H. (2002). Use of information technology in library services: The Singapore experience. In *Proceedings of the 9th National PLA Conference, 2002*. March 12-16, 2002, Phoenix, Arizona, USA. Retrieved Jan 14,

2003, from the World Wide Web: *http://www.pla.org/conference/conf02/singapore.pdf*

Borgman, C.L. (2000). *From Gutenberg to the global information infrastructure. Access to information in the networked world.* Cambridge, MA: The MIT Press.

Borgman, C.L. (2002). Challenges in building digital libraries for the 21st century. Keynote address. In E.P. Lim et al. (Eds.), *Proceedings of the 5th International Conference on Asian Digital Libraries* (pp. 1-13). Berlin: Springer-Verlag.

Carroll, J., & Rosson, M.B. (1992). Getting around the task-artifact cycle: How to make claims and design by scenario. *ACM Transactions on Information Systems, 10*, 181-212.

Carroll, J.M. (2000). *Making use: Scenario-based design of human computer interaction.* Cambridge, MA: MIT Press.

Chan, M.Y., Khoo, A.L., Theng, Y.L., & Buddharaju, R. (2004). Applying scenario-based design and claims analysis to evaluate usability of the National Library Board Digital Library. Accepted to *7th International Conference on Work With Computing Systems, WWCS 2004*, June 29 - July 2, Kuala Lumpur, Malaysia.

Chan, P.W. (2002, July 22). Gaining more business opportunities at libraries. Retrieved January 8, 2003, from the World Wide Web: *http://www.it.asia1.com.sg/thisisit/sayit_20020722.html*

Chia, C. (2002). Creating an inclusive information future through Singapore's libraries. In *Proceedings of VALA2002 Conference.* Retrieved March 7, 2003, from the World Wide Web: *http://www.vala.org.au/vala2002/2002pdf/32Chia.pdf*

Dix, A., Finlay, J., Abowd, G., & Beale, R. (1998). *Human-computer interaction.* Prentice-Hall.

Evans, G.E., Ward, P.L., & Rugaas, B. (2000). *Management basics for information professionals.* New York: Neal-Schumann.

Gray, G., & Guppy, N. (1994). *Successful surveys: Research methods and practice.* Toronto: Harcourt Brace.

Gray, W., & Saltzman, M. (1998). Damaged merchandise? A review of experiments that compare usability evaluation methods. *Human Computer Interaction, 13* (3), 203-261.

Hong, W., Thong, J.Y.L., Wong, W., & Tam, K. (2002). Determinants of user acceptance of digital libraries: An empirical examination of individual differences and system characteristics [Electronic version]. *Journal of Management Information Systems, 18* (3), 97-124.

Infocomm Development Authority of Singapore. (2001, August 29). *Survey on Infocomm Usage in Households 2000.* Retrieved January 8, 2003, from Infocomm Development Authority of Singapore Web site on the World Wide Web: *http://www.ida.gov.sg*

Khoo, A.L., Chan, M.Y., Theng, Y.L., & Buddharaju, R. (2004). Quantitative evaluation of effectiveness of the National Library Board digital library – eLibraryHub. Accepted to *7th International Conference on Work With Computing Systems, WWCS 2004*, June 29- July 2, Kuala Lumpur, Malaysia.

Landauer, T. (1995), *The trouble with computers: Usefulness, usability and productivity.* Cambridge, MA: MIT Press.

Nielsen, J. (1993). *Usability engineering.* AP Professional.

Nielsen, J. (1994). Heuristic evaluation. In J. Nielsen & R.L. Mack (Eds.), *Usability inspection methods.* New York: John Wiley & Sons.

Norman, D (1988). *The design of everyday things.* New York: Basic Books.

Saracevic, T., & Kantor, P.B. (1997). Studying the value of library and information services. Part II. Methodology and taxonomy [Electronic version]. *Journal of the American Society for Information Science, 48* (6), 543-563.

Shneiderman, B. (1998). *Designing the user interface: Strategies for effective human-computer interaction* (3rd ed.). Addison Wesley Longman.

Theng, Y.L., Goh, H.L., Lim E.P., Liu, Z., Pang, L.S., Wong, B.B., & Chua, L.H. (2002). Intergenerational partnerships in the design of a digital library of geography examination resources. In E.P. Lim et al. (Eds.), *Proceedings of the 5th International Conference on Asian Digital Libraries* (pp. 427-439). Berlin: Springer-Verlag.

Wixton, D. (2003). Evaluating usability methods: Why the current literature fails the practitioner. *Interactions, 10* (4), 29-33.

Yeo, S.L. (2002, September). Library utilisation and reading patterns [Electronic version]. *Statistics Singapore Newsletter,* pp. 7-10.

Section VI

Future Trends of Digital Libraries

Chapter XX

A Snapshot of Digital Library Development:
The Way Forward in the Asia Pacific

Schubert Foo
Nanyang Technological University, Singapore

Yin-Leng Theng
Nanyang Technological University, Singapore

Abstract

This chapter highlights selective key issues and assesses the current situation of digital library development in the Asia Pacific under the broad categories of design architecture and systems, implementation issues and challenges, use and impact, and users and usability. Emphasis on cross-cultural and cross-lingual research would especially be beneficial to address the diversity and richness of the heritage, cultures and languages of this region. Nonetheless, a fundamental digital divide problem poses the greatest challenge as almost 70% of the population of the countries of Asia Pacific has little or no connectivity to the digital world. Concerted international collaborative efforts are much needed, not only to push ahead with the various aspects of the digital library research agenda and realize the global digital library vision of the future, but to derive novel solutions to eliminate or close the gap of digital divide across various parts of the world.

Introduction

The emergence of digital libraries in the 1990s, coupled with the take-off of the World Wide Web, has resulted in a phenomenal growth of online information that is produced and consumed by all facets of the information society, especially in academia, heritage, government, business and industry. The pervasiveness of online information can only increase over time, fuelling a future of more research, design, development, deployment, use, and evaluation activities in digital libraries. The different definitions of digital libraries culled by researchers and institutions over time attest to the growing importance and scope of digital libraries, and the recognition and emphasis of the role of people, knowledge and technology as key to deliver successful digital libraries (Lim, Foo, Khoo, Chen, Fox, & Costantino, 2002).

There is an increasing reliance on digital collections at the expense of traditional print collections. The first wave of digitization efforts afforded by digital libraries resulted in wider and more universal accesses to rare and special collections of cultural institutions and national heritage of various countries (Falk, 2003). There is a growing emphasis to increase substantially the level of collaboration in terms of both disciplines and geographical boundaries to create global digital libraries to reflect the intrinsic nature of digital libraries that are multi-disciplinary and geographically unbounded (Schäuble & Smeaton, 1998). Along with this, the "e" (electronic) wave in e-government, e-learning, e-commerce, e-communities, and other e-initiatives are sound indicators for future digital library options, which are fast becoming infused with the requirements of the knowledge economy, where the advent of the knowledge management discipline has created new forms of information and knowledge portals utilizing digital library technologies.

Digital library potentials, trends and challenges have been previously outlined by various institutions, such as The International Federation of Library Associations and Institutions (IFLA, Cleveland, 1998), and Digital Library Federation (DLF, 2004), corporations such as Sun Microsystems, Inc. (2002), the working groups such as Joint NSF-EU Working Groups (Schäuble and Smeaton, 1998), and authors such as Pope (1998), Fox & Marchionini (1998), Borgman (2002), and Shiri (2003). Chen & Zhou in Chapter I also provided an assessment of digital library development in Asia Pacific while Fox, Suleman, Gaur, & Madalli in Chapter II reviewed key issues and case studies of digital library design architectures. Lim & Hwang in Chapter VI outlined implementation challenges facing digital library researchers and Witten in Chapter XI examined digital library trends from the society point of view. As such, it is not the intention of this chapter to be exhaustive in identifying and documenting trends and developments but rather to highlight research ideas and works that are particularly worth noting. Although this chapter can be organized in more traditional forms of developing, deploying, operating and using digital libraries, or examining it from the viewpoint of technical, political, social and economic issues, we have adopted the main sections of the book to structure these developments and discussions.

Design Architecture and Systems

Digital libraries are indeed very complex and advanced forms of information systems. As a result, they give rise to many challenging problems and issues for research. These include collaboration support, digital document preservation, distributed database management, hypertext, information retrieval, information filtering, instructional modules, intellectual property rights management, multimedia information services, question answering and reference services, resource discovery, selective dissemination of information, and others (Fox & Marchionini, 1998).

In terms of design architecture and systems, a major aspect concerns the integration of technologies and the level or extent with which the integration continues to evolve. The resulting system and data architecture will impact the level of success to discover and retrieve networked resources across different systems (Pope, 1998). Open systems utilizing a multi-layer architecture separating applications, interface and databases into different tiers and layers appears to be the preferred means to develop future digital libraries. While single vendor solutions cannot be ignored, their main limitation lies in the availability of resources (documents) that can only be supported by the proprietary architectures. In this respect, we begin to see the development of "convertors" or "connectors" or APIs grounded by some standards to support flexibility and continued expandability (in both number and format types of documents) by providing connectivity and access to such resources by other applications.

A good example would be the recent development of the JSR 168 and WSRP standards in the knowledge portal industry. JSR 168 is a specification for portlet interoperability to allow users access enterprise applications through various portals without relying on connectors or proprietary APIs, while WSRP focuses on interoperability of portlet services developed in the Java and Microsoft .NET environments to support the plug and play paradigm to develop portal applications (*http://sourceforge.net/projects/portlet-opensrc/*).

Digital library design architecture and systems have also benefited from the proposals of frameworks and other design topologies. Goncalves & Fox (2002) proposed a 5S model (Stream, Structural, Spatial, Scenarios, Societies) that can be used in conjunction with the 5SL declarative language to specify and generate digital libraries. The practical feasibility of the approach is demonstrated for the MARIAN digital library system. At a higher level, the idea of developing Open Digital Libraries (ODL) was proposed with the aim to eliminate reinventing the wheel and developing system from scratch (Suleman & Fox, 2002). The focus is on simplicity and the model relies on the concepts of interconnecting components and lightweight protocols. This was followed by a later initiative, Open Community Knowledge Hypermedia Applications & Metadata (OCKHAM) that extended the ideas of ODL to incorporate the use of open reference models and the involvement of the community perspective and effort to build more complete and usable digital libraries for specific communities.

A globally distributed federated digital library provides great potential and scope for collaboration and resource discovery. Lagoze, Fielding, & Payette (1998) proposed a service architecture and server topology to make this possible by creating connectivity regions (groups of sites with good networked connectivity), collection services (metadata to support a group of servers to interoperate as a collection) and collection views (to represent the configuration of the collection).

Another interesting architecture is one based on a social setting where a digital library is created through the concepts of collaboration, multimodality and plurality (Hedman, 1999). The Universal Simulator system, set in an education context, allows users to create their own parts of the digital library by authoring content, assessing multimedia content on the Internet with the system acting as a meta-library. The system also supports parallel publishing to make several different versions of the same learning materials to be stored or referenced and made available to different user groups that can be based on age or learning abilities. The authored content or links are defined and organized using a hierarchical structure (book, chapter and section) for access and use.

As the contents in a digital library are scaled up manifold over time, the existing information organization techniques can become inadequate leading to a diminished quality of retrieval. In this instance, a two-layered architecture may be useful to support different levels of cognition support. The model proposed by Feng, Jeusfeld, & Hoppenbrouwers (2001) view an information space to be made up of a document and knowledge space. The low-level cognition support is accomplished through information searching and browsing based on traditional indexing and keyword-based searching. The high-level cognition support is accomplished through knowledge inquiry by adding knowledge to the documents in the information space to support knowledge-based searching.

Implementation Issues and Challenges

Metadata is a very important element of digital documents, offering a means to describe the information contained in the document, facilitating harvesting, access and enabling resource sharing. Metadata standards play an important role in this development. Metadata representation, metadata storage, metadata harvesting and dissemination are now better understood and adapted by digital libraries amidst ongoing metadata research. The developments of Dublin Core hold promises of better-standardized metadata management (Sugimoto, Baker and Weibel, 2002). Additionally, the quality control and consistency in metadata creation needs to be maintained to maximize the usefulness of these retrievable surrogates.

As with the growth of documents in the digital library, the growth of metadata records also warrants study. Collection-wide metadata can be developed to aid user navigate through large distributed and heterogeneous collections and aid user resource discovery and institutional collection management. This draws upon the concept of functional granularity whereby collections are viewed as varying sizes to create relationship between sub-collections, collections and super-collections (Macgregor, 2003). Granularity is extremely useful in the context of digital information as a document is viewed from the different perspective of a complete document, constituent sections, paragraphs, sentences and words. This will in turn have an impact on the way users can interact and use digital information in future (Liew & Foo, 1999; Liew, Foo, & Chennupati, 2000).

Integration problems across various metadata systems can be expected. A recent proposal to address the problem comes in the form of a multi-XML schema to construct an XML framework represented in the form of a complete hierarchical tree structure (Yu, Lu, & Chen, 2003). The system comprising components of schema constructor, catalogue, metadata import/export, and enquiry would interface to multiple XML schemas from different systems to support multiple different types of metadata, import and export, thereby permitting metadata schemes to be used by compatible systems. This is an example of a metadata interoperability issue. In fact, digital libraries are very disparate systems with a multiplicity of other interoperability challenges. These can include multiple and disparate operating and IR systems, data formats, languages and character sets, vocabularies, ontologies, and disciplines (Moen, 2001). More loosely, these can be classified as technical, informational and social interoperability problems, which become further exacerbated when we move towards the development of global digital libraries (Fox & Marchionini, 1998).

Information search and retrieval techniques using boolean and non-boolean models are established, matured and utilized in digital libraries and Web search engines. The well-established branch of information retrieval (IR) research utilizing the "black-box" model associated with data recall and data precision measurements of earlier text-based tracks in TREC experiments has given way to new tracks over the years, but notably from TREC2001 to TREC2004 (*http://trec.nist.gov/*). These developments in the latter TREC experiments articulate the type of information retrieval challenges that are currently receiving much attention from IR researchers. These latest tracks include those for cross-language, filtering, genomics, HARD (High Accuracy Retrieval from Documents), interactive (studying user interaction with text retrieval systems), novelty (system ability to locate new non-redundant information), question answering (moving towards information retrieval rather than document retrieval), robust retrieval (focusing on topic effectiveness rather than average effectiveness), terabyte (scalability of retrieval systems to large document collections), video and Web (search tasks on a document set that is a snapshot of the Web) experiments (*http://trec.nist.gov/tracks.html*). Other technical trends, including those of automated summarization, annotations, multi-cultural and multi-lingual support, recommender systems and personalization, are earlier outlined by Lim & Hwang (Chapter VI).

Aside from technology issues, the implementation success of digital libraries also hinges upon the resolution of legal, organizational, economic and social issues. Digital rights management, digital access management, intellectual property and copyright issues are legal issues that continue to pose challenges as digital libraries strives to promote knowledge sharing through connectivity and free access to information.

The JSTOR (*http://www.jstor.org/*) and ARTSTOR (*http://www.artstor.org/*) projects sponsored by the Andrew W. Mellon Foundation are examples of non-profit initiatives to promote the use of digital libraries to enhance scholarship, teaching and learning. The main components are a repository of digital documents, accompanying tools to support access and use, and more importantly, the creation of a restricted usage environment that aims to balance the rights of content providers with the needs and interests of content users. As of April 2004, JSTOR houses a comprehensive archive of important scholarly journal literature in the order of 14 million pages, with almost 400 journals from 230 publishers; while ARTSOR contains 300,000 images that are drawn from museums, archaeological teams, photo archives, slide collections, and art reference publishers. It would be interesting to monitor if the terms and conditions set for usage and compensation are appropriate and adequate in such settings. In order to do this, rights management software providing usage tracking, user identification and authentication, providing copyright status of documents, and handling user transactions becomes essential to ascertain if access and downloads are adhered to by users.

From an economic standpoint, the sustainability and survivability of digital libraries remains an important issue. Although the cost of digitization has somewhat reduced as a result of technological advances and cheaper hardware costs, long-term digital preservation, maintenance, library operations and value-added costs when accumulated together warrant the essential need to find alternative business models and marketing strategies. Although the funding possibilities include those coming from the organization (paying the full cost and providing free information), the reader via subscription or transaction, the author via page charges, or the advertisers; a theoretical analysis carried out in the context of academic libraries suggested a need to move towards the user access (transaction) funding model (Roberts, 2001). This topic of e-commerce and digital libraries was addressed by Hawamdeh & Foo (2003) where they identified the prepaid subscription model, pay-later subscription model and pay-now-as-you-use model as potential models that can be used in digital libraries. A theory and practice of intellectual property cost management was advocated by Sistla, Wolfson, Yesha, & Sloan (1998). Finally, the role of institutions in providing sustainable digital library systems and services was also addressed by Borgman (2000).

Use and Impact

An important aspect of use and impact relates to the ability of digital libraries to transform society. Three different types of digital libraries are emerging in parallel with the distinguishing feature of how it manages intellectual property (Lyman, 1999). The first is the research library model (copyright model) where online documents are provided by libraries, individually and in consortia, and by digitization efforts. They are often materials where the institution owns the intellectual property rights, or materials out of copyright. In this instance, inter-institutional co-operation seems critical to maintain these collections, which are largely funded by membership dues or subscriptions. National and global coordination appears lacking at this time in terms of common technical standards and collection policies and priorities (Lyman, 1999).

The second type of digital library is the gift-exchange society (gift exchange model), notably the Web, where content is largely built directly by authors. The millions of writers/authors on the Web form the largest gift exchange community ever created. They are giving away intellectual property that is indexed by search engines for everyone with Internet connectivity to search, retrieve and use. However, the severe downsides of this model are the potential poor quality of documents, problems with misinformation and disinformation, and the lack of the ability to be 'keep documents indefinitely" as Web pages and servers are dynamically created and removed. The concept of authoring has also changed. There is evidence to suggest that a document can be collectively authored by many. For example, Lyman (1999) noted that Cohen (1998) reported a biotechnology paper on DNA authored by 133 authors from 85 institutions raising questions about authorship and knowledge creation, and its implication to libraries of the future.

The third type of digital library is the e-commerce (contract model). Increasingly publishers do not sell digital content but use contracts to license the use of the information content. There is potential for contracts replacing copyright policies of first sale doctrine and fair use. On the downside, there is problem with digital preservation funding (who pays?) and how the Internet economy would shape the universal access principle while balancing the cost to sustain such accesses. As such, these three different digital libraries, each having a different intellectual property policy, have surfaced new problems that need resolution in future.

Chien (n.d.) outlined a number of digital challenges facing the information society in future and noted that while much progress has been accomplished in the technology aspect of digital library development, relatively little progress has been achieved from the perspective of economic and social benefits, so that the impact of digital libraries on the economy and society is limited at this point in time. In this respect, he envisaged challenges in the areas of digital literacy, digital divide, e-initiatives (such as e-government, e-education, e-commerce, and e-community), networking health care and global reach. For example, the digital divide problem, which is very real and evident in various parts of the world, can benefit from solutions of content and connectivity via multi-channel distribution of resources and multi-modality communication media and enable these deprived population groups to get access to information resources to support varying needs (Chien, n.d.). Other suggestions include the building and linking of local digital libraries, digital outsourcing, better organization of digital information sources and services, using freely available digital library software and support, improving information use, and improving information and digital literacy skills (Chowdhury, 2002).

In terms of success, it seems that most progress has been made in the area of educational digital libraries. Prey & Zia (2002) noted achievements in science, technology, engineering and mathematics (STEM) education through the NSDL (National STEM education DL) program that was initiated in 2000. Non-STEM areas of focus are expected in future through the next NSDL program in 2004 and in DLI-2 (U.S. Digital Libraries Initiative - Phase 2). Also notable are the large number of digital libraries created in the last decade by various institutions and government bodies across the world in the areas of history, arts, museum, culture, and archives, as well as subject-specific contents (e.g., sciences, technology, business, humanities, religion) and specialized content and media types (e.g., images, maps, digital video, journals, theses, dissertations). The obvious challenge is to provide the connectivity and a model of access and use between these disparate digital libraries to create a global digital library.

A number of these developments have benefited from early digital library initiatives that made available free software to build and distribute digital collections. An example is the Greenstone Digital Library Software produced by the New Zealand Digital Library Project (NZDL). Although some collections were created within NZDL as demonstration collections, the use of Greenstone has grown internationally and resulted in the emergence of various public digital library sites. Examples include the Peking University DL (China), Archives of Indian Labour (India), Kids' DL (UK), Project Gutenberg (US), New Zealand DL (New Zealand), and the UNESCO project, among others (Witten, 2002). Some of these sites have extended the basic facilities of Greenstone to meet specific requirements.

Users and Usability

The concept of usability and its associated problems and challenges have been iterated by Borgman & Rasmussen in Chapter XV. The complexity of digital libraries has certainly made usability very difficult to achieve. Nonetheless, we see evidence in a number of research areas that attempts to make digital libraries more useful and easy to use through the use of user-centered design, development of better and more friendly user interfaces, improved query construction/ guidance, visualization/presentation, user task understanding, user evaluation, and improved interaction mechanisms to facilitate users seeking and using information to complete tasks.

The first important aspect of usability pertains to the digital library collection that is deemed to be of the highest quality. This does not happen by chance but involves the inputs of competent library and information professionals to select, acquire, organize, conserve, and preserve content for access. To achieve usability, a well-designed user-needs assessment should first be carried out. The problem surfaces and becomes apparent once we address the question of "Who does the digital library serve?" Such a problem only touches upon the tip of the iceberg when we think about achieving usability of digital libraries for various groups of users. A study set in an institutional setting found that users who are familiar with electronic access to external sources (i.e., quality information) will very often expect similar access to internal sources (Preston & Allmand, 2001) so that a participative action research methodology was needed for user expectation management and service provision.

The OPAC or other equivalent bibliographic search system, which users often use as the first step in information seeking, has progressively achieved better usability through the inclusion of URLs and hypertext functionality. Ranking of retrieved results and the provision of direct links to the resources are useful advances in this respect (Pope, 1998).

Searching and browsing are important forms of interaction support for information seekers. User interfaces can be endowed with value-added browsing capability in addition to showing list of retrieved results from searches. In order to do so, the retrieved results go through a process of classification and clustering. Text classification classifies documents into predefined categories, while text clustering groups documents into categories dynamically defined based on their similarities. Techniques used include the Bayesian method, k-nearest neighbor method, neural networks and support vector machine. Examples of clustering applications can be found in Web search engines such as Vivisimo (*http://vivisimo.com/*) and Wisenut (*http://www.wisenut.com/*) that cluster retrieved results into hierarchical folders and categories respectively. In relation to the neural network approach, Kohonen's self-organizing map that produces a 2-D grid representation for *n*-dimensional features have also been used in information retrieval systems (Kohonen et al., 2000).

Another example of the use of browsing cum searching is the Deja Vu system where users interact with the digital library by browsing through subject terms used to catalog the documents shown in the form of a thesaurus (Gordan & Domeshek, 1998). The standard relationships provided by the thesaurus that include broader (BT), narrower (NT), and related term (RT) links, are supplemented with links to Expectation Packages which group together sets of relevant related terms. By using different organizational theories for different thesauri, different sub-lists can be created to categorize the terms via the roles they play such as *events*, *places*, *people* and *things*.

Information visualization for search results is also an important part of usability and HCI (human-computer interaction) design. Future user interfaces would continue to explore different and new types of visualization techniques to display search results. Examples of previously proposed visualization techniques can be found in Rao et al. (1995) and Liew, Foo, & Chennupati (2000).

Future user interfaces are likely to be more interactive – moving towards the creation of personal workspaces that are endowed with rich features to create more integrated environments to support various user information seeking and use tasks. A useful study is PROPIE - a mock-up novel environment developed to evaluate users' perception to enhanced interaction and value adding of electronic documents (Liew, Foo, Chennupati, 2000, 2001a, 2001b). The environment contains workspaces that operate independently but yet in a closely coordinated manner with each other to allow users to interact with document collections through various forms of interaction and visualization. The system allows documents to be manipulated at various levels of granularity through various value-added tools and functions.

Other aspects of usability issues have surfaced through the design and implementation of information and knowledge portals. The delivery of relevant quality information and personalized access to resources and library services in these portals are now coupled with offerings of various content delivery options, including open URL citation linking, and electronic and physical document delivery (Murray, 2003). The mechanisms of document check-in, check-in and versioning found in content management systems (CMS) can also add to the usability of digital libraries as different versions of documents are created over its life (Wu & Liu, 2001). The concept of the "living" document (that goes through a cyclic loop of comments and annotations by users and reviewers, followed by review and updates by the author) in future will add on to the complexity of managing contents in digital libraries.

Closely associated with usability is the issue of evaluation that appears to have received less attention in comparison with the many aspects of digital library research. Nonetheless, we are beginning to see some activities in the development of evaluation matrices for digital libraries, such as the initiatives of the ARL Statistics and Measurement Program and projects such as the EQUINOX, COUNTER, ARL's LIBQUAL+initiative, JUBILEE and eVALUEd projects (Barton, 2004), as well as those of the Library and Information Statistics Unit (LISU, 2003) and IFLA Statistics and Evaluation Section (IFLA, 2003). Library concerns and practices in terms of usage and usability assessment were recently addressed in a Digital Library Federation report with particular emphasis on transaction log analysis (Covey, 2002).

Digital Libraries Development in the Asia Pacific: What's Next?

The region of Asia Pacific spans across half the globe, with 58 countries stretching from Afghanistan to India to Singapore to Australia and to Tuvalu on the Pacific Ocean. In order to get an idea of digital library developments, a query was posted to the United Nations Economic and Social Commission for Asia and the Pacific (UNESCAP) Web site (*http://www.unescap.org/stat/data/apif/ index.asp*) to ascertain the level of Internet connectivity of countries in the region. *Table 1* shows the results (retrieved May 25, 2004) for all countries from the Asia Pacific from 1995.

The highest number of Internet users as of 2002 comes from Singapore (59 per 100 people), Korea (55.2), New Zealand (48.4), Japan (44.9), Hong Kong (China) (43.1) and Australia (42.7). A total of only 17 countries (or 29.3%), including those above, achieved a number of at least 10 Internet users per 100 people. Unfortunately, a large 70.7% of the proportion of people in the Asia Pacific countries has very little or no connectivity to access the vast resources offered by public digital libraries and the Web. When another query was carried out on the telephone mainlines and mobile phone subscribers at UNESCAP, a similar pattern emerged. This can be seen as an indication of the poor state of Information and Communication Technologies (ICT) infrastructure in many Asia Pacific countries. These statistics are dire and point to the large digital divide problem faced in the Asia Pacific, since ICT and Web access are pre-

Table 1.   Asia Pacific Internet users (per 100 people)

	1995	1999	2000	2001	2002
Afghanistan	...	...	...	...	...
American Samoa	...	...	...	...	...
Armenia	0.0	0.8	1.3	1.8	...
Australia	2.8	29.6	34.4	37.1	42.7
Azerbaijan	-	0.1	0.2	0.3	3.7
Bangladesh	...	0.0	0.1	0.1	0.2
Bhutan	...	0.1	0.3	0.7	1.4
Brunei Darussalam	1.0	...	9.0	10.2	...
Cambodia	...	0.0	0.0	0.1	0.2
China	-	0.7	1.7	2.6	4.6
Cook Islands	1.2	11.9	14.2	16.0	...
Democratic People's Republic of Korea	...	...	...	-	...
Fiji	0.0	0.9	1.5	1.8	2.6
French Polynesia	...	3.5	6.4	8.5	10.4
Georgia	0.0	0.4	0.5	0.9	1.5
Guam	0.7	8.5	16.2	30.5	...
Hong Kong, China	3.2	21.2	27.8	38.7	43.1
India	0.0	0.3	0.5	0.7	1.6
Indonesia	0.0	0.4	1.0	1.9	...
Iran (Islamic Republic of)	-	0.4	1.0	1.6	...
Japan	1.6	21.4	29.9	38.4	44.9
Kazakhstan	0.0	0.4	0.6	0.9	...
Kiribati	...	1.2	1.8	2.3	...
Kyrgyzstan	...	...	0.4	0.5	3.0

Table 1. Asia Pacific Internet users (per 100 people) (cont.)

Lao People's Democratic Republic	...	0.0	0.1	0.2	0.3
Macao, China	0.3	9.1	13.6	22.5	26.3
Malaysia	0.2	12.8	17.2	27.3	...
Maldives	-	1.1	2.2	3.6	5.4
Marshall Islands	-	1.0	1.5	1.6	...
Micronesia (Federated States of)	...	2.6	3.5	4.3	...
Mongolia	0.0	0.5	1.3	1.7	...
Myanmar	...	-	0.0	0.0	...
Nauru	...	...	...	...	...
Nepal	-	0.2	0.2	0.3	...
New Caledonia	0.0	5.7	9.3	11.4	...
New Zealand	4.9	29.7	40.1	46.1	48.4
Niue	...	15.7	26.0	30.9	...
Northern Mariana Islands	...	...	...	...	...
Pakistan	-	0.0	0.2	0.2	1.3
Palau	...	...	...	...	...
Papua New Guinea	...	0.7	0.9	0.9	...
Philippines	0.0	1.5	2.0	2.6	...
Republic of Korea	0.8	...	41.4	52.1	55.2
Russian Federation	0.2	1.0	2.1	2.9	4.1
Samoa	...	0.3	0.6	1.7	2.2
Singapore	1.0	18.0	59.0	58.0	59.0
Solomon Islands	0.0	0.5	0.5	0.5	0.5
Sri Lanka	0.0	0.4	0.7	0.8	1.1
Tajikistan	...	0.0	0.0	0.0	0.0
Thailand	0.1	2.2	3.8	5.8	7.8
Timor-Leste	...	...	...	...	...
Tonga	0.1	1.0	2.4	2.8	2.9
Turkey	0.1	2.3	3.1	6.0	7.3
Turkmenistan	...	0.0	0.1	0.2	...
Tuvalu	...	...	4.3	10.0	...
Uzbekistan	-	0.0	0.5	0.6	1.1
Vanuatu	...	0.5	2.0	2.7	...
Viet Nam	...	0.1	0.2	1.2	1.8

Source: UNESCAP Statistics Division based on United Nations Millennium Indicators Database; National sources (Data reported on May 18, 2004. Database updated on March 11, 2004)

Note: Data are based on reported estimates, derivations based on reported Internet Access Provider subscriber counts, or calculated by multiplying the number of hosts by an estimated multiplier. However, comparisons of user data can be misleading because there is no standard definition of frequency (e.g., daily, weekly, monthly) or services used (e.g., e-mail, World Wide Web). Retrieved May 25, 2004.

requisites to support digital library functionality. While a few countries are enjoying good infrastructures and actively engaged in developing and using digital libraries, many have far more basic problems to resolve. Digital divide is caused by many factors including lack or inadequate infrastructure, hardware, manpower, maintenance, information and digital literacy competencies.

According to the Digital Divide Basic Fact Sheet (Digital Divide Network, 2004), there are only 429 million people (or 6% of the world's entire population) that are engaged online globally, so that digital divide is not only prevalent in Asia Pacific but in many other parts of the world. Digital divide actually occurs in every country at varying levels of severity as the result of the rich and poor divide, with the latter unable to afford Internet connectivity. In addition, a study of ICT skills and knowledge among information professionals working in academic and public libraries in Malaysia found that even a digital divide can exist between these professionals as a result of rapid emerging technologies (Abu Baker, 2003). A call for government funding was made for further e-training and e-retraining to close the gap of digital divide among these professionals, without which might lead to a bigger gap that may never be closed forever.

CONSAL (Congress of Southeast Asian Librarians) was founded in 1970 in response to a growing sense of Southeast Asian identity, which was fostered by the earlier formation of the Association of Southeast Asian Nations (ASEAN) partnership. The ten members include the library associations and librarians of Brunei, Cambodia, Indonesia, Lao, Malaysia, Myanmar, Philippines, Singapore, Thailand and Vietnam. A review of the country updates of the CONSAL member countries (*http://www.consal.org/*) provides some insights into the state of library development in some of these ten countries:

- With the non-existence of a National Library in Brunei, the libraries of Dewan Bahasa dan Pustaka (DBP) have become the main sources of information for the public and researchers. DBP collection focus is on Malay books along with a heavily used unique Brueniana collection.

- The National Library of Indonesia houses a collection of rare books and manuscripts. The IndonesiaDLN initiative reported by Fahmi in Chapter III represents the development of the country's national libraries network.

- The National Library of Malaysia (Perpustakaan Negara Malaysia) over-sees the establishment of the PERDANA integrated National DL system and is active in a number of ASEAN initiatives.

- The National Library of Philippines (NLP) houses a set of rare books and manuscripts written in the major Philippines dialects, and maintains a Web site providing access to databases containing Filipiniana and foreign library materials.

- Singapore National Library Board maintains the NLB Digital Library, *eLibraryHub*, that is interfaced with a host of electronic services as well as a Singapore Pages section comprising a digitized collection of cultural and heritage materials.

- The National Library of Thailand is the National Information System Secretariat connecting many other information network centers around the country. It also houses a collection of Thai traditional rare manuscripts.

Taking this scenario as representative of other regions within the Asia Pacific along with the figures of Internet connectivity in *Table 1*, it may be postulated that most countries are still very much print-based at this point, with each country having her own rich heritage of rare books, manuscripts and other materials. Few countries have national digital library initiatives. Many cannot afford one now. When the opportunity for digital library development arises, the logical path would be the adoption of best practices, the use of freeware and open source codes to build digital libraries, and to develop appropriate solutions culled from documentation of past experiences shared by early digital library development initiatives.

On a brighter note, we witness emerging individuals and groups of digital library researchers in a number of Asia Pacific countries who are well plugged into the global digital library community, collaborating with established researchers, fostering new initiatives, making good research progress, reporting findings in scholarly journals and conferences, and making significant contributions to the digital library research agenda (see Chapter I). The collection of chapters in this book also attests to the new and exciting areas of research undertaken by researchers in the Asia Pacific.

Conclusion

Significant progress was made in the first decade of the digital library evolution especially in areas of technological achievement. Significant challenges remain in collection development, information organization, content management, search and retrieval, system and user evaluation, and building more usable systems for all groups of digital library users. Cost and sustainability to realize self-supporting systems in conjunction with intellectual property issues require novel solutions that will eventually shape the digital economy.

The diversity and richness in heritage, culture and language across Asia Pacific and the rest of the world poses real challenges and opportunities for digital library development in future, especially in the areas of cross-cultural and cross-lingual research. Digital libraries research will continue to span across a range of subjects, disciplines, context and communities.

While good progress and momentum are achieved along many fronts, there is a race against time and resources to resolve the plight of information divide in many countries. The importance to transform digital libraries into effective social institutions and the realization of a truly global digital library require world-wide efforts and effective collaboration by the many groups of constituents across national boundaries.

References

Abu Baker, A.B. (2003). So near and yet so far: The digital divide among the information professionals. In *Proceedings of the 6ᵗʰ International Conference on Asian Digital Libraries (ICADL2003)* (pp. 310-316). Kuala Lumpur, Malaysia.

Barton, J. (2004). Measurement, management and the digital library. *Library Review, 53* (3), 138-141.

Borgman, C. L. (2000). *From Guntenberg to the global information infrastructure: Acess to information in the networked world.* Cambridge, MA: The MIT Press.

Borgman, C. L. (2002). Challenges in building digital libraries for the 21ˢᵗ century. In *Proceedings of the 5ᵗʰ International Conference on Asian Digital Libraries (ICADL2002)* (pp. 1-13). Singapore.

Chien, Y.T. (n.d.). *The role of digital libraries in the transformation of society: A perspective from the United States.* Retrieved, May 20, 2004, from the World Wide Web: *http://www.dl.ulis.ac.jp/DLjournal/No_23/1-ytchien/1-ytchien.html*

Chowdhury, G.C. (2002). Digital divide: How can digital libraries bridge the gap? In *Proceedings of the 5ᵗʰ International Conference on Asian Digital Libraries (ICADL2002)* (pp. 379-391). Singapore.

Cleveland, G. (1998). Digital libraries: Definitions, issues and challenges. IFLANET UDT Occasional Paper #8, Retrieved May 20, 2004, from the World Wide Web: *http://www.ifla.org/VI/5/op/udtop8/udtop8.htm*

Cohen, D. (1998). Toward a knowledge context: Report on the first annual U.C. Berkeley Forum on Knowledge and the Firm. *California Management Review, 40* (3), 228-240.

Covey, D.T. (2002) *Usage and usability assessment: Library practices and concerns*. Digital Library Federation, Council on Library and Information Resources, NW, Washington: Digital Library Federation.

Digital Divide Network. (2004). Digital divide basic fact sheet. Retrieved May 20, 2004, from the World Wide Web: *http://www.digitaldividenetwork.org/content/stories/index.cfm?key=168*

Digital Library Federation (DLF). (2004). Digital library standards and practices. Retrieved May 20, 2004, from the World Wide Web: *http://www.diglib.org/standards.htm*

Falk, H. (2003). Developing digital libraries. *The Electronic Library, 21* (3), 258-261.

Feng, L., Jeusfeld, M.A., & Hoppenbrouwers, J. (2001). Towards knowledge-based digital libraries. *SIGMOD Record, 30* (1), 41-46.

Fox, E.A., & Marchionini, G. (1998). Towards a worldwide digital library. *Communications of the ACM, 41* (4), 29-32.

Goncalves, M.A., & Fox, E.A. (2002). 5SL: A language for declarative specification and generation of digital libraries. In *Proceedings of the second ACM/IEEE-CS joint conference on digital libraries (JCDL'02)* (pp. 263-271). Oregon.

Gordan, A.S., & Domeshek, E.A. (1998). Deja Vu: A knowledge-rich interface for retrieval in digital libraries. In *Proceedings the 3rd international conference on Intelligent user interfaces (IUI'98)* (pp. 127-134). San Francisco.

Hawamdeh, S., & Foo, S. (2003). E-Commerce and digital libraries. In S. Nansi (ed.), *Architectural Issues of Web-enabled Electronic Business* (pp. 377-390). Hershey, PA: Idea Group Publishing.

Hedman, A. (1999). Creating digital libraries together: Collaboration, multimodality, and plurality. *In Proceedings of the 4th annual SIGCSE/SIGCUE ITiCSE conference on Innovation and technology in computer science education* (pp. 147-150). Cracow, Poland.

IFLA Statistics and Evaluation Section. (2003). Retrieved, May 20, 2004, from the World Wide Web: *http://www.ifla.org/VII/s22/ss.htm*

Kohonen, T., Kaski, S., Lagus, K., Salojärvi, J., Honkela, J., Paatero, V., & Saarela, A. (2000). Self organization of a massive document collection. *IEEE Transactions on Neural Networks* (Special Issue on Neural Networks for Data Mining and Knowledge Discovery), *11* (3), 574-585.

Lagoze, C., Fielding, D., & Payette, S. (1998). Making global digital libraries work: Collection services, connectivity regions, and collection views. In

Proceedings of the 3rd ACM International Conference on Digital Libraries 1998 (pp. 134-143). Pittsburgh, PA.

The Library & Information Statistics Unit (LISU). (2004). Retrieved, May 20, 2004 from the World Wide Web: *http://www.lboro.ac.uk/departments/dils/lisu/lisuhp.html*

Liew, C.L., & Foo, S. (1999). Derivation of interaction environment and information object properties for enhanced integrated access and value-adding to electronic documents. *Aslib Proceedings, 51* (8), 256-268.

Liew, C.L., Foo, S., & Chennupati, K.R. (2000). A proposed information environment for enhanced integrated access and value-adding to electronic documents. *Aslib Proceedings, 52* (2), 58-75.

Liew, C. L., Foo, S., & Chennupati, K. R. (2001a). A proposed integrated environment for enhanced user interaction and value-adding of electronic documents: An empirical evaluation. *Journal of the American Society for Information Science and Technology* (Special Topic Issue: Still the Frontier: Information Science at the Millennium), *52* (1), 22-35.

Liew, C. L., Foo, S., & Chennupati, K. R. (2001b). A user study of the design issues of PROPIE: A novel environment for enhanced interaction and value adding of electronic documents. *Journal of Documentation, 57* (3), 377-426.

Lim, E.P., Foo, S., Khoo, C., Chen, H., Fox, E., Urs, S., & Costantino T. (Eds.). (2002). *Digital libraries: People, knowledge, and technology: Proceedings of the 5th International Conference on Asian Digital Libraries, ICADL 2002.* (Lecture Notes in Computer Science 2555/2002). Singapore, December 11-14, 2002. Heidellberg: Springer-Verlag.

Lyman, P. (1999). The social functions of digital libraries: Designing information resources for virtual communities. In *Proceedings of the Ninth Australasian Information Online & On Disc Conference and Exhibition*, Sydney, Australia. Retrieved May 20, 2004, from the World Wide Web: *http://www.csu.edu.au/special/online99/proceedings99/300b.htm*

Macgregor, G. (2003). Collection-level descriptions: Metadata of the future? *Library Review, 52* (6), 247-250.

Moen, W.E. (2001). Mapping the interoperability landscape for networked information retrieval. In *Proceedings of the first ACM/IEEE-CS joint conference on digital libraries (JCDL'01)* (pp. 50-51). Virginia.

Murray, R. (2003). Information portals: Casting a new light on learning for universities. *Campus-Wide Information Systems, 20* (4), 146-151.

Pope, N.F. (1998). Digital libraries: Future potentials and challenges. Digital Libraries, *63* (3-4), 147-155.

Preston, H., & Allmand, M. (2001) Discovering the information professional: Organisational culture in a digital world. *Online Information Review, 25* (6), 388-395.

Prey, J.C., & Zia, L. L. (2002). Progress on educational digital libraries: Current developments in the National Science Foundation's (NSF) National Science, Technology, Engineering, and Mathematics Education Digital Library (NSDL) Program. In *Proceedings of the 5ᵗʰ International Conference on Asian Digital Libraries (ICADL 2002)* (pp. 53-66). Singapore.

Rao, R., Pedersen, J.O., Hearst, M.A., Mackinlay, J.D., Card, K.C., Masinter, L., et al. (1995). Rich interaction in the digital library. *Communications of the ACM, 38* (4), 29-39.

Roberts, S.A. (2001). Trends and developments in financial management of collections in academic and research libraries. *The Bottom Line: Managing Library Finances, 14* (3), 152-163.

Schäuble, P., & Smeaton, A.F. (1998). *An international research agenda for digital libraries: Summary report of the series of joint NSF-EU working groups on future directions for digital libraries research.* Retrieved May 20, 2004, from the World Wide Web: *http:// www.dli2.nsf.gov/internationalprojects/workgroups.html*

Shiri, A. (2003). Digital library research: Current developments and trends. *Library Review, 52* (5), 198-202.

Sistla, A.P, Wolfson, O., Yesha, Y., & Sloan, R.H. (1998). Towards a theory of cost management for digital libraries and electronic commerce. *ACM Transactions on Database Systems, 23* (4), 411-452.

Sugimoto, S., Baker, T., & Weibel, S.L. (2002). Dubin Core: Process and principles. In *Proceedings of the 5ᵗʰ International Conference on Asian Digital Libraries (ICADL2002)* (pp. 25-35). Singapore.

Suleman, H., & Fox, E. (2002). A framework for building open digital libraries. *D-Lib Magazine, 7* (12). Retrieved May 20, 2004, from the World Wide Web: *http://www.dlib.org/dlib/december01/suleman/12suleman.html*

Sun Microsystems, Inc. (2002). *Digital library technology trends.* Retrieved May 20, 2004, from the World Wide Web: *www.sun.com/products-n-solutions/edu/whitepapers/pdf/digital_library_trends.pdf*

Witten, I. H. (2002). Examples of practical digital libraries: Collections built internationally using Greenstone. In *Proceedings of the 5ᵗʰ International Conference on Asian Digital Libraries (ICADL2002)* (pp. 67-74). Singapore.

Wu, Y.D., & Liu, M. (2001). Content management and the future of academic libraries. *The Electronic Library, 19* (6), 432-439.

Yu, S.C., Lu, K.Y., & Chen, R.S. (2003). Metadata management system: Design and Implementation. *The Electronic Library*, *21* (2), 154-164.

Appendix:
Sources of
Further Information

This Appendix is a compilation of selected resources in the form of journal special issues, digital library journals, conference/proceedings and portals/online databases where advances in digital library research and development are reported. Although by no means exhaustive, the listing aims to surface the multidisciplinary nature of digital libraries and to serve as a starting point to locate important sources for the digital library researcher.

Journal Special Issues on Digital Libraries and Related Fields

- *Communications of the ACM* (CACM). Special Issue on Digital Libraries, April 1995, *38* (5).

- *ACM SIGLINK Newsletter*. Special Issue on Digital Libraries, September 1995, *4* (2).

- *Journal of the American Society for Information Science and Technology (JASIST)*. Special Topic Issue on Evaluation of Information Retrieval Systems, January 1996, *47* (1).

- *IEEE Computer*. Special Issue on the U.S. Digital Library Initiative, May 1996.

- *Journal of the American Society for Information Science and Technology* (JASIST), Special Topic Issue on Current Research in Online Public Access Systems, July 1996, *47* (7).

- *D-Lib Magazine*. Special Issue on Digital Libraries and Education, September 1996.

- *Journal of the American Society for Information Science and Technology* (JASIST). Special Topic Issue on Electronic Publishing, September 1996, *47* (9).

- ERCIM (European Research Council for Informatics and Mathematics) News. A Special Issue on Digital Libraries, October 1996.

- *Communications of the ACM* (CACM). Special Issue on Digital Libraries: Global Scope, Unlimited Access, April 1998, *41* (4).

- *Journal of the American Society for Information Science and Technology* (JASIST). Special Topic Issue on Full-Text Retrieval, April 1998, *47* (4).

- *Journal of the American Society for Information Science and Technology* (JASIST). Special Topic Issue on Artificial Intelligence Techniques for Emerging Information Systems, January 1999, *49* (7).

- *IEEE Computer*. Special Issue on the U.S. Digital Library Challenges, February 1999.

- *Journal of the American Society for Information Science and Technology* (JASIST). Special Topic Issue on The National Information Infrastructure, March 1999, *50* (4).

- *International Journal on Digital Libraries*. Special Issue on User Interfaces for Digital Libraries, September 1999, *2* (2-3).

- *Journal of Digital Information* (JoDI). Special Issue on Performance Issues in Digital Information Systems, January 2000, *1* (5).

- *Information Processing & Management* (IP&M). Special issue on Web-Based Information Retrieval Research, March 2000.

- *D-Lib Magazine*. Special Issue on Collection-Level Description, September 2000, *6* (9).

- *Communications of the ACM* (CACM). Special Issue on Digital Libraries, May 2001, *44* (5).

- *Journal of the American Society for Information Science and Technology* (JASIST). Special Topic Issue on Visual Based Retrieval Systems and Web Mining, June 2001, *52* (10).

- *ERCIM (European Research Council for Informatics and Mathematics) News*. A Special Issue on Human Computer Interaction, July 2001, *46*.

- *Journal of the American Society for Information Science and Technology* (JASIST). Special Topic Issue on Web Research, December 2001, *53* (2).

- *Journal of the American Society for Information Science and Technology* (JASIST). Special Topic Issue on XML and Information Retrieval, February 2002, *53* (6).

- *Information Technology and Libraries* (ITAL). Special Issue on Open Source Software, March 2002, *21* (1).

- *D-Lib Magazine*. Special Issue on Digital Technology and Indigenous Communities, March 2002, *8* (3).

- *Journal of the American Society for Information Science and Technology* (JASIST). Special Topic Issue on Digital Libraries: Parts 1 & 2, March 2000, *51* (3-4).

- *ERCIM (European Research Council for Informatics and Mathematics) News*. A Special Issue on Information Security, April 2002, *49*.

- *Journal of Digital Information* (JoDI). Special Issue on Interactivity in Digital Libraries, June 2002, *2* (4).

- *Communications of the ACM* (CACM). Special Issue on The Consumer Side Of Search, September 2002, *45* (9).

- *Information Processing & Management* (IP&M). Special Issue of Context In Information Retrieval (IR), September 2002.

- *ERCIM (European Research Council for Informatics and Mathematics) News*. A Special Issue on Semantic Web, October 2002, *51*.

- *Journal of Interactive Media in Education* (JIME). Special Issue on Reusing Online Resources, 2003, (1).

- *D-Lib Magazine*. Special Issue on Digital Reference, February 2003, *9* (2).

- *Information Processing & Management* (IP&M). Special Issue on Handling vagueness, subjectivity, and imprecision in information access, March 2003.

- *Communications of the ACM* (CACM). Special Issue on Digital Rights Management and Fair Use, April 2003, *46* (4).

- *Journal of Digital Information* (JoDI). Special Issue on Economic Factors of Digital Libraries, June 2003, *4* (2).

- *IEEE TCDL (Technical Committee on Digital Libraries) Bulletin.* Special Issue on User Interface, Summer 2003.

- *Information Technology and Libraries* (ITAL). Special Issue on Bibliomining Process, December 2003, *22* (4).

- *Information Research.* Special Issue: Papers from Conference, Towards User-Centered Approach To Digital Libraries (DIGILIB 2003), Espoo, Finland, January 2004, *9* (2),

- *Journal of Digital Information* (JoDI). Special Issue on New Applications Of Knowledge Organization Systems, March 2004, *4* (4).

- *Information Processing & Management* (IP&M). Special Issue on Best Works from the International Conference on Asian Digital Libraries, 2002 (ICADL2002), May 2004.

- *D-Lib Magazine.* Special Issue on Georeferencing And Geospatial Data, May 2004, *10* (5).

- *Journal of the American Society for Information Science and Technology* (JASIST). Special Topic Issue on Information Seeking Research, Part I, June 2004, *55* (8).

- *Journal of the American Society for Information Science and Technology* (JASIST). Special Topic Issue on Information Seeking Research, Part II, July 2004, *55* (9).

- *Journal of Digital Libraries* (JDL). Special Issue on Multimedia Contents and Management in Digital Libraries, forthcoming May 2004.

- *Journal of Digital Libraries* (JDL). Special Issue on Digital Museum, forthcoming, September 2004.

- *Journal of Digital Libraries* (JDL). Special Issue on Asian Digital Libraries, forthcoming September 2004.

- *Journal of Computer-Mediated Communication.* Special Issue on Computer-Mediated Collaborative Practices and Systems, forthcoming, Spring/ Summer 2005.

Digital Library Journals

- *Ariadne Magazine.* Reports on information service developments, information networking issues worldwide, and current digital library initiatives, January 1996 – Present. *http://www.ariadne.ac.uk/.*

- *D-Lib Magazine*. E-publication with primary focus on "digital library research and development, including but not limited to new technologies, applications, and contextual social and economic issues." July 1995- Present. *http://www.dlib.org.*

- *First Monday*. E-journal on the Internet, solely devoted to the Internet, 1996 – Present. *http://www.firstmonday.org/.*

- *International Journal on Digital Libraries*. Springer-Verlag: Berlin, Germany, 1996-Present.

- *Journal of Digital Libraries*. Springer-Verlag: Berlin, Germany and Center for Information Management, Integration and Connectivity (CIMIC - Rutgers University, U.S.). *http://www.dljournal.org/.*

- *Journal of Digital Information* (JoDI). Supported by British Computer Society and Oxford University Press (UK), 1997 - Present, *http://jodi.ecs.soton.ac.uk/.*

- *Journal of Digital Information Management* (JDIM). Supported by Digital Information Research Foundation (India), 2003 – Present. *http://www.dirf.org/jdim/.*

- *Library and Information Science Research Electronic Journal* (LIBRES). E-journal devoted to new research in Library and Information Science, 1996 – Present. *http://libres.curtin.edu.au/.*

- *Russian Digital Libraries Journal*. E-journal to present up-to-date reflection of research on and use of digital libraries, 1998 – Present. *http://www.elbib.ru/index.phtml?page=elbib/eng/journal.*

Digital Library Web Sites/Gateways

- *Digital Library Federation* (DLF). Operating under the administration umbrella of the Council on Library and Information Resources (CLIR), DLF is a consortium of libraries and related agencies that are pioneering in the use of electronic-information technologies to extend their collections and services. *http://www.dlf.org.*

- *RLG*. An international, not-for-profit membership organization of over 150 universities, libraries, archives, historical societies and other institutions with collections for research and learning. *http://www.rlg.org/.*

- *The European Research Consortium for Informatics and Mathematics* (ERCIM). Consortium that aims to foster collaborative work within the European research community and to increase co-operation with European industry. *http://www.ercim.org/.*

- *Academic Info: Digital Library Subject Gateway. http:// www.academicinfo.net/digital.html.*
- *BUBL Information Service.* Selected Internet Resources covering all subject areas but with a focus on Library and Information Science. *http://bubl.ac.uk/.*
- *D-Lib Magazine Ready Reference. http://www.dlib.org/reference.html.*
- *PADI* (Preserving Access to Digital Information). Subject Gateway to international digital preservation. *http://www.nla.gov.au/padi/.*

Conference/Proceedings

- ACM International Conference on Digital libraries (superceded by JCDL)
- IEEE Advances in Digital (ADL) Conference (superceded by JCDL)
- ACM/IEEE-CS Joint Conference on Digital libraries (JCDL)
- European Conference on Research and Advanced Technology for Digital Libraries (ECDL)
- International Conference on Asian Digital Libraries (ICADL)
- Organising the Global Digital Library (OGDL): Theory and Practice of Digital Libraries
- The International Symposium on Research, Development, & Practice of Digital Libraries
- The International Symposium on Digital Libraries (ISDL) (Japan)
- International Conference on Conceptions of Library and Information Science (CoLIS)
- International Conference on Digital Libraries (India)
- International Digital Library Conference (China)
- DELOS Series of Workshop Proceedings

Other Related Conferences

- ACM Conference on Hypertext
- ACM International Conference on Multimedia
- ACM Conference on Hypertext and Hypermedia
- ACM Symposium on Document Engineering

- ACM SIGUCCS Conference on User Services
- ACM SIGIR Conference on Research and Development in Information Retrieval
- ACRL (Association of College & Research Libraries) National Conference
- American Library Association (ALA) Annual Conference
- Canadian Association for Information Science/L'association canadienne des sciences d l'information (CAIS/ACSI) Annual Conference
- Canadian Library Association (CLA) Annual Conference
- CODATA (Committee on Data for Science and Technology) International Conference.
- Communications of the ACM
- Conference on Human factors in Computing Systems
- ELPUB (Electronic Publishing) Conference
- IEEE International Conference on Data Mining
- IEEE International Conference on Multimedia & Expo (ICME)
- International Symposium on Technology and Society (ISTAS)
- Joint International Conference of the Association for Literary and Linguistic Computing and the Association for Computers and the Humanities
- International Conference on Dublin Core and Metadata Applications
- International Conference on Formal Ontology in Information Systems (FOIS)
- International Conference on Information and Knowledge Management
- International Conference on Machine Learning and Application.
- International Conference on New Information Technology (NIT)
- International Conference on World Wide Web
- International Symposium on Music Information Retrieval (ISMIR)
- Museums and the Web
- RIAO (Recheche d'Information Assiste par Ordinateur – Computer Assisted Information Retrieval) Conference
- Russian Conference on Digital Libraries (RCDL)
- SLA (Special Libraries Association) Annual Conference

- WSEAS International Conference on Multimedia, Internet and Video Technologies

Online Databases/Portals

There are many individual journals where various aspects of digital library research and development are reported. The following are some portals and databases that provide a good coverage and access to such journals:

- ABI/Inform Global
- ACM Digital Library
- ACM Guide to Computing Literature
- Computer Source
- Ei Engineering Village 2 (includes Compendex & Inspec databases)
- EBSCOhost
- Emerald Fulltext
- Emerald Management Reviews
- IEEE Xplore
- Internet and Personal Computing Abstracts
- IRWI (Information Research Watch International)
- ISI Web of Science (SCI & SSCI)
- JSTOR, http://www.jstor.org/
- Kluwer Online
- LexisNexis
- Library Literature
- LISA (Library & Information Science Abstracts)
- NTIS (National Technical Information Service) Database
- OCLC FirstSearch
- CiteSeer.IST (Citations only), http://citeseer.ist.psu.edu/cs
- ScienceDirect Online
- SpringerLink

About the Authors

Yin-Leng Theng completed her PhD in 1997 on addressing the "lost in hyperspace" problem in hypertext. She then joined Middlesex University (London) as a lecturer (1998-2001). Currently, she is an assistant professor at the School of Communication and Information, Nanyang Technological University (NTU, Singapore). She teaches on Information Studies Master's Programme: Human-Computer Interaction and Digital Libraries. She was awarded two research grants from EPSRC (UK) during her four years of teaching at Middlesex University. Recently, she was also awarded a NTU grant to work on usability techniques on the Web and mobile environments.

Schubert Foo is professor and vice dean of the School of Communication and Information at Nanyang Technological University, Singapore. He received a BSc, MBA and PhD from the University of Strathclyde, UK. He is a chartered engineer, chartered IT professional, fellow of the British Computer Society and fellow of The Institution of Mechanical Engineers, UK. He is the author of more than 120 publications in the fields of Internet technology, multimedia technology, multilingual information retrieval, digital libraries, information and knowledge management. He is an editorial board member of the *Journal of Information Science, Journal of Information & Knowledge Management, International Yearbook of Library and Information Management* and *International Journal of Cases on Electronic Commerce.*

* * *

David Bainbridge is a senior lecturer in computer science at the University of Waikato, New Zealand. He holds a PhD in computer science from the University of Canterbury where he studied as a Commonwealth Scholar. Since moving to Waikato in 1996, he has developed his interest in digital media, with an emphasis on music. He is co-author with Ian Witten of the book, *How to Build a Digital Library*, and has published in the areas of image processing, music information retrieval, digital libraries, data compression, and text mining. David has also worked as a research engineer for Thorn EMI and graduated from the University of Edinburgh in 1991 as the class medalist in computer science.

Stefan J. Boddie joined the New Zealand Digital Library research project at the University of Waikato as a research programmer (1997). He developed several of the tools described in this chapter and has provided core programming skills and technical support for Greenstone over several years. Recently he founded DL Consulting Ltd. to provide commercial support for digital library activities around the world.

Christine L. Borgman is professor and presidential chair in Information Studies at the University of California Los Angeles (UCLA). She is a co-principal investigator for the Center for Embedded Networked Systems (CENS) and for the Alexandria Digital Earth Prototype (ADEPT) project, both funded by the National Science Foundation. She is the author of more than 150 publications in the fields of information studies, computer science, and communication. Her book, *From Gutenberg to the Global Information Infrastructure: Access to Information in a Networked World* (MIT Press, 2000), won the Best Information Science book of the year award from the American Society for Information Science and Technology.

Raju Buddharaju is chief information/technical officer of the National Library Board (Singapore) that operates public libraries, reference libraries, and academic libraries and provides Library services to various organizations. He specializes in information management and information technology areas, focusing specifically on return on IT investment and architectures, development of IT investment strategies and IT portfolio management. He holds a Bachelor of Engineering degree in electronics and communications (1971) from Andhra University, and Master of Technology degree in electrical engineering with computer sciences (1974) from Indian Institute of Technology, Kanpur, India. He is a member of ACM, IEEE, PMI, ITMA, IKMS and SCS.

Mei-Yee Chan is a recent graduate of the MSc (information studies) programme from Nanyang Technological University. She received her BBus from Nanyang Technological University in 1995. She is currently working in the Knowledge Management Office of the Department of Computer and Information Systems at Singapore Polytechnic.

Chao-chen Chen is a professor of the Graduate Institute of Library and Information Studies, National Taiwan Normal University. She received a PhD in Department of Library and Information Science from National Taiwan University (December 1994), and an MA from the same university. Currently, she is the secretary-general of the Library Association of China (in Taiwan), and consultant of the Council for Cultural Affairs. Dr. Chen has conducted many research projects and is interested in several research areas, including digital libraries, library automation, information organization and metadata, multimedia, electronic publishing, and electronic learning.

Hsinchun Chen (hchen@eller.arizona.edu), McClelland Professor of MIS at the Eller College of the University of Arizona (USA) and Andersen Consulting Professor of the Year (1999), received a PhD in information systems from New York University (1989), an MBA in finance from SUNY-Buffalo (1985), and a BS in management science from the National Chiao-Tung University in Taiwan. He is the author of more than 120 articles covering medical informatics, homeland security, semantic retrieval, search algorithms, knowledge management, and Web computing in leading information technology publications.

Hsueh-hua Chen is a professor in the Department of Library and Information Science at the National Taiwan University. She received an EdD in higher education and an MEd in educational media and librarianship from University of Georgia, and a BA in library science from the National Taiwan University. She is the author of more than 40 articles covering digital libraries, metadata, information organization and knowledge management. She has also served on the editorial board of many library and information science related journals. Currently, Dr. Chen is heavily involved in fostering digital library and knowledge management research and education in Taiwan. She was a PI of the National Science Council-funded Digital Museum Initiative project (1998-2001) and has continued to receive research grant from NSC for National Digital Archives Program (2002-2006) and many research projects.

Sally Jo Cunningham is a senior lecturer in computer science at the University of Waikato (New Zealand). Her research focuses on user studies through quantitative transaction log analysis of digital library usage and qualitative studies of information behavior; her particular interest is in user needs and user behavior analysis for music digital libraries. She received her PhD in computer science, with minors in library science and Asian studies, from Louisiana State University.

Stephen Downie is an assistant professor at the Graduate School of Library and Information Science, University of Illinois (USA) (UIUC). He is director of the Mellon and NSF-funded International Music Information Retrieval Systems Evaluation Laboratory (IMIRSEL), also at UIUC. Professor Downie is also principal investigator on the Human Use of Music Information Retrieval Systems (HUMIRS) project. He is also project leader on the Music Information Retrieval Bibliography Project (MIRBIB) (available at *http://music-ir.org/research_home.html*). Information about Professor Downie's Mellon-funded MIR/MDL Evaluation Frameworks Project can be found at *http://music-ir.org/evaluation/*. Dr. Downie holds a B.A. (music theory and composition), a Masters of Library and Information Science and a Ph.D. in library and information science, all earned at the University of Western Ontario, London, Ontario, Canada.

Ismail Fahmi is a PhD student in Alfa-Informatica at the University of Groningen, The Netherlands. He received his master's degree from the same department in 2004, and his bachelor's degree in electrical engineering from the Institut Teknologi Bandung, Indonesia in 1997. He was the principal investigator of the research project that developed the Ganesha Digital Library (GDL) software and was the chairman of the IndonesiaDLN (2000-2002). His main research interests include digital libraries, machine learning and knowledge extraction. He is currently working on automatic term recognition using linguistic knowledge.

Edward A. Fox, Director of NDLTD, is a professor of computer science at Virginia Tech (USA). There, he also directs the Internet Technology Innovation Center and Digital Library Research Laboratory. He is a member and former chairman of the NSDL Policy Committee, and serves on the OAI Steering Committee. He is chair of the IEEE Technical Committee on Digital Libraries.

Eibe Frank is a senior lecturer in Computer Science at the University of Waikato, New Zealand. He obtained a diploma from the University of Karlsruhe and a PhD from the University of Waikato. His main research interest is machine learning and he has published widely on this topic. He is also one of the main contributors to the Weka machine learning workbench and co-author of a well-known textbook on machine learning techniques for data mining. He has served on various program committees and is currently a member of the editorial boards for the *Machine Learning Journal* and the *Journal of Artificial Intelligence Research*.

Ramesh C. Gaur is a librarian at the Tata Institute of Fundamental Research (TIFR), Mumbai, India. A science graduate, he holds a PhD in library and information science. Recently he had visited Virginia Tech (USA) under Fulbright Fellowship in Information Science & Technology for the year 2003-2004. During the 14 years of his professional career he has contributed two books and more than 30 papers to various national and international publications. He is a member of all major Indian Library Associations and some important ones abroad. His major professional achievements include the formation of Ranganathan Research Circle (RRC). He is life trustee and joint secretary of Ranganathan Research Trust (RRT), New Delhi.

Dion Hoe-Lian Goh is an assistant professor in the Division of Information Studies, School of Communication and Information, Nanyang Technological University (Singapore). He received his Doctor of Philosophy degree in computer science from Texas A&M University. He has previously worked as a Web site developer and a software engineer Dion currently teaches a variety of subjects in the Master of Science in Information Studies programme offered by the Division of Information Studies. This includes data mining, Web development, programming, and networking. His research interests are in digital library applications, Web mining, information retrieval, Internet applications, and the use of information technology in education.

Carl Gutwin is associate professor of computer science and director of the Human-Computer Interaction Lab at the University of Saskatchewan, Canada. His research covers a variety of topics in HCI and CSCW, including information visualization, interfaces for information retrieval, the usability of distortion-oriented visualizations, groupware architectures, and groupware performance.

San-Yih Hwang is an associate professor at Information Management Department, National Sun Yat Sen University in Taiwan. He was the head of the Systems and Information Division of the university library (1999-2003) and developed numerous information systems for library use. The free of charge ETD system developed, called eThesys, has been used by more than 20 universities in Taiwan. Dr. Hwang received his PhD from the University of

Minnesota, Minneapolis in 1994 and has published more than 50 papers in refereed journals and conferences in workflow management, data mining, and digital libraries. He has also served as program co-chair and members of program committees of numerous international conferences.

Min-Yen Kan is an assistant professor at the National University of Singapore (NUS). His research interests include document structure acquisition, verb analysis, digital libraries and applied text summarization. Before joining NUS, he was a graduate research assistant at Columbia University, and had interned at various industry laboratories, including AT&T, IBM and Eurospider Technologies in Switzerland.

Ai-Ling Khoo is a recent graduate of the MSc (information studies) programme from Nanyang Technological University (Singapore). She received a BEng in chemical engineering from the National University of Singapore (1998). She is currently a reference librarian at the Singapore Polytechnic.

Yasushi Kiyoki received a BE, ME and PhD in electrical engineering from Keio University, Japan (1978, 1980 and 1983, respectively). He joined the Institute of Information Sciences and Electronics, University of Tsukuba as a tenured faculty member in 1984 as an assistant professor, and as an associate professor until 1996. In 1996, he joined the faculty of Keio University, where he is a tenured professor at the Department of Environmental Information. His research addresses multi-database systems, knowledge base systems, semantic associative processing, and multimedia database systems. He serves as the editor-in-chief of *Information Modelling and Knowledge Bases* published by IOS Press. He also served as the program chair for the Seventh International Conference on Database Systems for Advanced Applications.

Kar Wing Li is a PhD student with the Department of Systems Engineering and Engineering Management, The Chinese University of Hong Kong. He earned his BEng in information system engineering from Imperial College (UK) and MPhil from the Department of Systems Engineering and Engineering Management, The Chinese University of Hong Kong. His research specialization is in the areas of cross-lingual information retrieval, multimedia information retrieval, digital library, Internet information retrieval, knowledge management, machine translation, neural networks and constraint networks. His research has been published in several leading journals, and is also a reviewer for the *Journal of the American Society for Information Science and Technology.*

Chern Li Liew is a lecturer in the School of Information Management at Victoria University of Wellington, New Zealand. She holds a PhD from Nanyang Technological University, Singapore, and has worked as a multimedia resource centre manager at Telekom Malaysia in Kuala Lumpur. She has taught in the areas of bibliographic organization, information storage and retrieval, digital libraries and user-interface design. Her publications and research interests focus on the study of interaction between users and information, particularly in the electronic environments. These include design and usability of digital libraries, user-centered design, information seeking and use behavior in electronic environments, intellectual value adding of e-contents, and social informatics.

Ee-Peng Lim is an associate professor and head of Division of Information Systems with the School of Computer Engineering, Nanyang Technological University, Singapore. He received his Ph.D. from the University of Minnesota, Minneapolis (1994), and has published more than 150 refereed journal and conference articles. He is an associate editor of the *ACM Transactions on Information Systems*, and a member of the editorial review board of the *Journal of Database Management*, and guest editor of Special Issues in Web Information and Data Management for the *Data and Knowledge Journal*, and in Asian Digital Libraries for the *Journal of Digital Libraries*. Dr. Lim has been Program Co-Chair and member of program committee of numerous international conferences.

Devika P. Madalli is a lecturer at the Documentation Research and Training Institute, Bangalore, India. She holds a Ph.D. from the University of Mysore, and currently investigates problems related to multimedia applications to LIS, knowledge-based systems, and the Internet. She was the recipient of a Fulbright Professional Fellowship in Library and Information Science in the year 2002-2003. She has published over 30 papers in local and international conferences and journals.

Gary Marsden is an associate professor in the Department of Computer Science at the University of Cape Town, South Africa. He received a BSc (Honors) and a PhD in computer science from Stirling University, Scotland. He is a specialist in HCI and his interests currently lie in how ICT can be applied in a developing world situation. Besides digital libraries, he has worked on projects involving virtual reality and mobile computing

John McPherson is a graduate student with the New Zealand Digital Libraries Research Group in the Department of Computer Science at the University of

Waikato (Hamilton, New Zealand). After completing his bachelor's degree (Honors) from the University of Canterbury, he moved to Waikato in 2000 where he is currently researching the use of feedback for automatically correcting mistakes in optical sheet music recognition. He also contributes to the development of the open source Greenstone Digital Library software (*www.nzdl.org*).

Craig G. Nevill-Manning is a senior staff research scientist and director of New York Engineering at Google, Inc., USA. He is responsible for Froogle, a product search engine. Prior to his three years at Google, Dr. Nevill-Manning was an assistant professor with the Computer Science Department at Rutgers University, working on problems in information retrieval, computational biology and data compression. He holds a Ph.D. from the University of Waikato, New Zealand.

David M. Nichols is a lecturer in the Department of Computer Science at the University of Waikato, New Zealand. He received a BSc (Honors) and a PhD in computer science from Lancaster University, UK. He has taught and researched at Lancaster, at the Graduate School of Library and Information Science at the University of Illinois at Urbana-Champaign and at Waikato. His research interests include digital libraries, human computer interaction and open source software.

Natalie Lee-San Pang received a BCom from the University of Melbourne, Australia (1999), and worked as a consultant in Singapore and Malaysia as well as a teacher before completing her MSc (information science) with the Nanyang Technological University, Singapore (2003). She now works as a full-time graduate research assistant with Monash University, Malaysia, under the School of Information Technology, Information and Communication Technology Enterprise Unit, providing research, advisory, and consultancy services. Her research interests are information literacy, digital libraries, human-computer interaction, information organization, impacts of technologies on education and businesses, and electronic learning.

Dynal Patel is a PhD student at the University of Cape Town, South Africa. His research interests include digital libraries, information visualization and retrieval, mobile computing and digital electronics. More recently his research efforts have focussed on developing digital library solutions for developing countries. A large focus of this work has been on providing small screen mobile access to digital libraries and also providing tools that enable one to customize and personalize digital libraries. He is also more practically involved in the dissemination and deployment of digital library technologies in Africa. He is currently the Greenstone Digital Library Representative in Africa, a multifaceted role that involves pushing for the rapid and widespread adoption of this software suite in Africa. He received a BSc in computer engineering and a BSc (Honors) in computer science from the University of Cape Town.

Gordon W. Paynter is a researcher for the INFOMINE Project, working on the iVia Web Portal Software. His current work focuses on the problem of assigning Metadata to Web pages, with particular emphasis on using machine learning top generate library-standard Metadata. Before joining INFOMINE, Dr. Paynter worked for the New Zealand Digital Library Project on the Greenstone Digital Library Software and other projects. He holds a PhD from the University of Waikato, New Zealand.

Mila Ramos is the head librarian of the International Rice Research Institute, Library and Documentation Service, Philippines. In a span of more than 10 years of experience in a digital environment, she has regularly dealt with problems related to digital delivery, text digitization, consortia, training of librarians, etc. Her two degrees in Library Science is supplemented by an online course on cataloging of electronic resources from the University of Cincinnati and on-the-job training stints at Deakin University, Geelong, Australia, and the National Agricultural Library in Maryland. She has published papers and has served as resource person in local and foreign conferences. The author is one of the founders of PhilAgriNet, a network of agricultural librarians in the Philippines.

Edie Rasmussen is currently professor and director of the School of Library, Archival and Information Studies at the University of British Columbia, Canada. From 1988-2003, she served as professor in the School of Information Sciences, University of Pittsburgh. She has also held faculty and visiting positions at Intitut Teknoloji MARA, Kuala Lumpur; Dalhousie University, Canada; City University, London; Nanyang Technological University, Singapore; and Victoria University of Wellington, New Zealand. She teaches and conducts research on digital libraries, and has been involved in digital library projects for education and cultural heritage materials.

Nina Reeves is a graduate in mathematics and computing (York), information science (Sheffield), and has a PhD in human-computer interaction from the University of Bristol. She has been a senior lecturer at the University of Gloucestershire (UK) since 1995. Her research interests lay in the use of ethnographic methods for usability studies, the user interface design of digital libraries with a particular emphasis on the use of multimedia and the design of multimedia online HELP systems.

Hideyasu Sasaki received a BA and an LLB from the University of Tokyo (1992, 1994), an LLM from the University of Chicago Law School (Rotary Scholar) (1999), an MS and PhD with Highest Honors in media and governance (Cybernetic Knowledge Engineering) from Keio University, Japan (Koizumi Scholar) (2001 and 2003, respectively). He is an assistant professor at Department of Cybernetic Informatics, Graduate School of Media and Governance, Keio University. His research interests include content-based metadata indexing and image retrieval, digital libraries, multimedia databases, and intellectual property law and management. He has been admitted to practise law as an attorney- and –counselor-at-law in the New York State Bar of the United States since 2000.

Hussein Suleman is a senior lecturer in computer science at the University of Cape Town, Cape Town, South Africa. He holds a PhD from Virginia Tech. His research interests lie in interoperability, architecture of component-based and distributed digital library systems, and Web-based applications and application frameworks.

John Thompson has a BCMS (Honors) from the University of Waikato, New Zealand. He developed a prototype for the Greenstone Librarian Interface (GLI) as part of his degree. John joined the Greenstone team in the Department of Computer Science as a research programmer for two years where he implemented the production version of GLI. He continues to work on digital library tools, employed by DL Consulting Ltd.

Ian H. Witten is professor of computer science at the University of Waikato, New Zealand, where he directs the New Zealand Digital Library research project. His research interests include information retrieval, machine learning, text compression, and programming by demonstration. He has published widely in these areas, his most recent books being *Managing Gigabytes* (1999), *Data Mining* (2000) and *How to Build a Digital Library* (2003). He received an M.A. in mathematics from Cambridge University, U.K., a MSc in computer science from the University of Calgary, Canada, and a Ph.D. in electrical engineering from Essex University, U.K. He is a fellow of the ACM and of the Royal Society of New Zealand, and received the 2004 IFIP Namur Award, a biennial honor accorded for outstanding contribution with international impact to the awareness of social implications of information and communication technology.

Chunxiao Xing received a Ph.D. from Northwestern Polytechnical University (1999). He finished his postdoctoral fellow in the Department of Computer Science and Technology, at Tsinghua University, China, in 2001. Currently, he is professor in the Department of Computer Science and Technology at Tsinghua University. His research interests include database, machine learning, information retrieval and filtering, digital library, distributed multimedia systems, e-government, and e-commerce. He is a member of the IEEE Computer Society.

Christopher C. Yang is an associate professor in the Department of Systems Engineering and Engineering Management at the Chinese University of Hong Kong. He received a BS, MS, and PhD in electrical and computer engineering from the University of Arizona. He has published more than 100 refereed journal and conference papers. He was the chairman of the Association for Computing Machinery Hong Kong Chapter, the program co-chair of the First International Conference on Asia Digital Library, a program committee and organizing committee member for several international conferences. He has frequently served as an invited panelist in the NSF Digital Library Initiative Review Panel and the NSF Information Technology Research Review Panel in US.

Shien-chiang Yu received an MS in library and information science from Fu-Jen Catholic University and a PhD in information management from National Chiao-Tung University in 1997 and 2003 respectively. He joined the Department of Information & Communications, Shin-Hsin University (2003). His research interests include spatial database, electronic commerce, information retrieval, and metadata.

Chun Zeng completed his PhD in the Department of Computer Science and Technology, at Tsinghua University in August 2003. Currently, he works as a research member of Lucent Technologies Co. His research interests include digital library, personalization, and recommender systems.

Zhiqiang Zhang earned a PhD from the Department of Computer Science and Technology at Tsinghua University in August 2003. Currently, he works as a postdoctoral fellow in the Department of Computer Science and Technology at Tsinghua University. His research interests include digital library, ontology, Web information processing, and software testing.

Lizhu Zhou received an MS in computer science from the University of Toronto (1983). He is professor and dean of the Department of Computer Science and Technology, Tsinghua University. He and his database group has completed dozens of research projects sponsored by the Natural Science Foundation of China and the national high-tech programs in logical databases, multiple databases integration, data warehouses, massive information systems, digital library, geographical information systems etc. His major research interests include database technology, digital library, massive storage systems, data warehouses, and etcetera. He is a member of the IEEE Computer Society.

Yilu Zhou (yiluz@eller.arizona.edu) is currently a third year PhD student in management information systems at the University of Arizona (USA). She received a bachelor's degree in computer science from Shanghai Jiao Tong University, Shanghai, China. Her research interests center on the application of information retrieval and text mining techniques to knowledge management, knowledge discovery on the Web. She is an active researcher in the Artificial Intelligence Lab, where she participated in several research projects funded by NSF.

Index

Managing Psychological Factors in Information Systems Work:
An Orientation to Emotional Intelligence

Eugene Kaluzniacky, University of Winnipeg, Canada

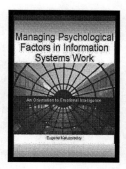

There have arisen, in various settings, unmistakable calls for involvement of psychological factors in IT work, notably in development and deployment of information systems. Managing Psychological Factors in Information Systems Work: An Orientaion to Emotional Intelligence "pulls together" areas of existing involvement, to suggest yet new areas and to present an initial, and coherent vision and framework for, essentially, extending and humanizing the sphere of IT work. It may be indeed noteworthy that, while the Industrial Revolution may have moved the human person into intellectual predominance, the IT Revolution, with its recent calls for addressing and involving the "whole person", may indeed be initiating a re-centering of the human being in his/her essential core, giving rise to new consciousness, new vision and new, empowering experiences. May this book encourage the first few steps along a new and vivifying path!

ISBN 1-59140-198-4 (h/c) • US$74.95 • ISBN 1-59140-290-5 (s/c) • US$59.95
• 250 pages • Copyright © 2004

"Although all decisions are about facts, we mediate them through our feelings. In periods of rapid change we rely much less on facts and more on our intuitions and experience. The uncertainty associated with Information Systems (IS) means that the corner-stone for success of IS professionals depends on their feelings-based abilities to work with people. With this book Eugene Kaluzniacky has filled a gap in the book-shelf of those who would wish to become successful developers of IS projects."

-Cathal Brugha, University College Dublin, Ireland